MARTIN BEHRMAN
of New Orleans

Martin Behrman, *ca.* 1916

Louisiana State Museum

MARTIN BEHRMAN
of New Orleans

Memoirs of a City Boss

Edited, with an Introduction by JOHN R. KEMP

Louisiana State University Press/Baton Rouge/London

Copyright © 1977 by Louisiana State University Press
All rights reserved

Designer: Albert Crochet
Typeface: VIP Caledonia
Typesetter: Graphic Composition, Inc.
Printer and Binder: Kingsport Press

LIBRARY OF CONGRESS CATALOGING IN PUBLICATION DATA

Behrman, Martin, 1864–1926.
  Martin Behrman of New Orleans.

  Bibliography: p.
  Includes index.
  1. Behrman, Martin, 1864–1926. 2. New Orleans—Mayors—Biography. 3. New Orleans—Politics and government. I. Kemp, John R., 1945-   II. Title.
F379.N553B443   976.3'35'060924 [B]   77-6781
ISBN 0-8071-0275-X

For Betty and Virginia

Contents

	Introduction	xi
I	Early Career in Politics, 1888–1904	1
II	Brickbats and Bouquets, 1904–1908	79
III	City and State Politics, 1906–1916	193
IV	The Reformers' Triumph, 1917–1920	289
	Epilogue	315
	Appendix: Charter of the Choctaw Club of Louisiana	343
	Index	349

Illustrations

Martin Behrman, *ca.* 1916   Frontispiece

Following page 100

    Canal Street, *ca.* 1885

    Behrman's boyhood home

    The Quay at New Orleans

    French Market

    The seventeen wards of New Orleans

    "The Lottery Octopus"

"Louisiana State Lottery Company"

    Behrman discussing deep waterway

    Behrman arrives at City Hall

    Behrman with Councilman A. J. Harmeyer

    Behrman with Alex Pujol

New Orleans City Hall

Behrman's home in Algiers

Following page 196

The Choctaw Club, 1934

Aerial view of Storyville, *ca.* 1914

Tom Anderson's Arlington Annex in Storyville

"Behrmanism Boss Rule"

"You'll Never Make It on That Steed, Martin!"

"And He Wants Another Four Years' Booking!"

"Behrmanism"

Photograph of woman in Storyville

"Bad Taste Ne'er Won Fair Maid"

"Rather Embarrassing?"

"The Maiden's Prayer!"

Governor Samuel D. McEnery

Governor Murphy J. Foster

Governor Jared Y. Sanders

Governor John M. Parker

Introduction

In his memoirs Martin Behrman, Old Regular, Choctaw chief, boss, and five-term mayor of New Orleans (1904–1920 and 1925–1926), reflected upon state political issues and politicians and upon New Orleans municipal government during the 1890s and first two decades of twentieth century. Originally, Behrman's reflections were unedited ramblings published as installments in the New Orleans *Item* between 1922 and 1923 after his defeat in the 1920 mayoralty election. The campaign had been exhausting and bitter and deeply scaring to his ego. Realizing that *ward boss*, with all its connotations, would always be associated with his name, Behrman felt it necessary to explain to his contemporaries and future generations his side of the story. His resentment toward those who constantly maligned and opposed him, especially Governor John M. Parker,[1] was the underlying theme of this work. There was no subtlety in his dislike for Parker and his "reform" followers.

---

1. John M. Parker, Behrman's perennial opponent and governor of Louisiana from 1920 to 1924, was a leading figure in such governmental reform movements as the Citizens' League (1896), the Good Government League (1912), the Louisiana Progressive Party (1916), and the Orleans Democratic Association (1919–20). Parker was also active for a time in national politics and in 1912 joined Theodore Roosevelt's Bull Moose Progressive party's campaign trail. In 1916 he was nominated by the national Progressive Party to run for vice-president on Roosevelt's ticket. The party, however, disbanded before the election. Parker returned home and ran for governor on the Louisiana Progressive party ticket but was defeated by Democrat Ruffin G. Pleasant (1916–20). During World War I, Parker was appointed food administrator for Louisiana, serving under the Federal Food Administration's director, Herbert Hoover. In 1919 the former Progressive successfully campaigned for governor as Democrat, defeating Colonel Frank B. Stubbs, Behrman's candidate. Throughout his memoirs Behrman shows his resentment towards Parker and insinuates that he and his reform allies were nothing more than political opportunists and simply "the outs wanting in." Miriam G. Reeves, *The Governors of Louisiana* (Gretna, La.: Pelican, 1972), 95–98.

Martin Behrman first entered Louisiana politics in the late 1880s during the devisive twenty-year struggle for survival and supremacy between the Democratic and Republican parties following Reconstruction and the restoration of Home Rule in 1877. The period was marked by political and social changes. Although much of it was retrogressive, the resulting political stability enabled New Orleans to begin work on sorely needed municipal services. One historian has described this era of Louisiana's history as a change from the Radical misrule of Reconstruction to Bourbon misrule.[2] As an insider, Behrman was an active witness to the rupture and bifactional struggles within the Democratic party over the Louisiana Lottery Company that climaxed in the 1892 state and municipal elections; the rise and fall of the Populist movement among the farmers in the rural parishes; the death and birth of two New Orleans political machines in 1896 and 1897; and the victory of white supremacy, then synonymous with the supremacy of the Democratic party, in the state's 1898 constitutional convention.

Behrman rose through the ranks of the Regular Democratic Organization (the Crescent Democratic Club and its successor, the Choctaw Club of Louisiana) in the classical style of most city bosses. He worked hard to bring in the vote for the machine's candidates and in return was awarded various minor

2. Louisiana Bourbons have been described as the well-to-do planters, lawyers, and businessmen of the same social and political persuasions that controlled ante bellum Louisiana. Although not exclusively, Bourbons were the planters and middle class in the cotton parishes where the black population was either greater than or equal to the white population. After Home Rule returned to the state in 1877, Bourbons strove with any and every means available to return Louisiana to the "golden age" of the pre–Civil War era; to rid the state of Republicans; and, to "make the state safe for 'true Southern ideals.'" According to William Ivy Hair, in his perceptive treatise on Louisiana politics from 1877 to 1900, the distinguishing feature between Bourbons and other conservative Democrats was the former's embracement of rabid Negrophobia. Mark T. Carleton, Perry H. Howard, and Joseph B. Parker, *Readings in Louisiana Politics* (Baton Rouge: Claitor's Publishing Division, 1975), 330–32; William Ivy Hair, *Bourbonism and Agrarian Protest; Louisiana Politics, 1877–1900* (Baton Rouge: Louisiana State University Press, 1969), 24–25.

appointed positions. After a few successes at the ballot box, particularly his election to the constitutional convention of 1898, the "young fellow from Algiers"[3] had become the recognized leader in the city's Fifteenth Ward. Such recognition entitled him to sit in the Council of Seventeen, usually referred to as the caucus, the governing body of the Choctaw Club, with the leaders of the city's other sixteen wards. By 1904, the year he was first elected mayor, Behrman had emerged as the central and dominant figure in the organization. At first he shared some of his decision-making power with several other leaders in the caucus, but by 1925, the beginning of his fifth administration and the year before his death, Martin Behrman was the undisputed boss.

The Choctaw Club, also known as the Regular Democratic Organization, the Ring, machine, Regulars, and after 1922 as the Old Regulars, represented all walks of life in the community: laborers, businessmen, attorneys, physicians, gamblers, and professional politicians. In 1936 George Reynolds, a Columbia University historian, conducted a detailed study of the New Orleans machine. Through the numerous interviews with both major and minor political figures, Reynolds' study has provided valuable insight into the structure, roles, and machinations of the New Orleans Ring. Reynolds concluded that the success of the organization was due in part to the simplicity of its structure. There were two levels, the caucus and the club. The caucus, composed of the bosses of the city's seventeen wards, was the ruling and policymaking body of the machine. Its decisions were final in all matters, and anyone not complying would find his patronage cut off.[4]

In addition to policymaking, the caucus also decided who would run for office on the Regular ticket. Before each election

3. Algiers is a suburb of New Orleans on the west bank of the Mississippi River.
4. George M. Reynolds, *Machine Politics in New Orleans, 1897–1926* (New York: Columbia University Press, 1936), 109.

Behrman and the leading members of the caucus determined the slate of nominees for the major offices as well as which nonmember candidates running for statewide offices would receive the organization's endorsement. Their decisions were later submitted to the whole caucus for approval. Often a possible candidate for governor, or other important state or national office seeker, would first check with Behrman and the council before officially announcing his candidacy. Minor positions on a ticket and all but the top political appointments were left to the individual ward leaders.[5]

The ward leader or boss was, as a member of the council, the chief political figure in his ward and usually held an elective or appointive office on the state or municipal level. As the "field commander," he was in complete charge of his ward organization. He selected his own precinct leaders and workers and gave his approval on all patronage dispersed in his ward. His primary responsibility was to see that his ward gave a majority of its votes to Ring candidates. Before election day he made sure that the voters who could be counted on to vote "the right way" were registered and their poll taxes paid. He also made necessary funds available to his precinct leaders to meet certain "election day expenses." A ward boss was only as strong as his organization, which usually ranged from nine to twenty-five precinct clubs, and his ability to build up a loyal following through "favors and patronage." Behrman attributed the success of some ward bosses to "personal traits, hard work, uneven distribution of patronage, and luck."[6]

The precinct clubs formed the nucleus of the machine's second echelon. The Ring's success was in direct proportion to the efficiency of the precinct workers. The precinct organization was built on patronage, and usually the precinct leader or cap-

5. *Ibid.*, 123–24.
6. *Ibid.*, 118–21.

tain held some minor city or parish job that gave him ample free time during political campaigns to work for the organization's candidates. The precinct leader's existence depended on his ability to carry consistently his precinct for the Ring. To do so election after election he had to have an encyclopedic knowledge of the people in his area. Their professions, problems, likes, dislikes, interests, hobbies, and aspirations all provided potential possibilities for getting their votes. His was a year-round job of nurturing prospective voters with various favors, jobs, relief in emergencies, and perhaps a friend in court when necessary. Reynolds' study revealed that a precinct leader usually had at least 100 votes he could be sure of before an election—votes that he controlled through favors and patronage. In an average precinct of 400 voters the precinct leader required only 201 votes to carry his district. Therefore, he had only to persuade 101 to vote his ticket out of the remaining 300. The opposition, without the persuasive strength of patronage, had a long and usually futile uphill fight. Several captains boasted to Reynolds that they could usually predict the outcome of an election within a few votes several days before the election.[7]

Behrman, well schooled in ward politics, realized that abuses and questionable practices existed. However, ballot box stuffing and voter intimidation, which were commonplace in New Orleans during the nineteenth century, were really not necessary for the effective and hardworking Choctaw Club. As a political realist and an organization man, Behrman denied accusations of illegal campaign methods that inevitably followed each election. When allegations were made, His Honor suggested to his opponents that charges be filed and the matter settled in court. Continued success at the polls often dictated that a back be turned or eyes closed when politically expedient or popular to do so. The machine won elections through patron-

7. *Ibid.*, 111–16.

age, favors, some legally questionable practices, and by the constant and hard work of the ward and precinct organizations during twelve months of the year. Elections were not won by the "noise and panoply of a short campaign."[8] Patronage was neither illegal nor even looked upon as morally wrong. The philosophy "You take care of me and I'll take care of you," was expounded by Behrman in his memoirs: You do not give a man a job because you want his vote but because he is already with you.

Controlling the apparatus of city government in New Orleans was not enough to ensure the Regulars of their longevity. The constitution of 1898 granted municipalities and parishes limited powers in self-government which often left them vulnerable to governors and legislators. Local issues frequently became state issues. Therefore, it was essential to the machine's survival to hold the balance of power in the State Capitol, including the New Orleans delegation in the legislature which comprised about 20 percent of that body. Moreover, it was important for the Ring to have a sympathetic governor. Usually, a gubernatorial candidate with a strong following in the country parishes made a deal with the Choctaws: their support in carrying New Orleans in return for all state patronage in the city.[9] Such was the case with Governors William Heard (1900), Newton C. Blanchard (1904), Jared Y. Sanders (1908), and Ruffin G. Pleasant (1916). Behrman discusses this in detail in these memoirs.

Running a large organization like the Regular Democratic Organization was an expensive proposition. Facilities had to be maintained and elections won. Club members paid monthly dues of one dollar and all city employees were required to belong. During election campaigns department heads col-

8. *Ibid.*, 130–35.
9. T. Harry Williams, *Huey Long* (New York: Alfred A. Knopf, 1969), 131.

lected "contributions" from all municipal employees in their sections. Aspirants for political office who sought the Choctaw nomination had to pledge 10 percent of their salaries to the organization, and in some cases, depending upon the individual and position, a higher percentage was required. Corporations, small businessmen, as well as gamblers and prostitutes were expected to "fatten the war chest." Money collected through legal sources was well accounted for, but that from questionable elements was placed in a special fund to be doled out during campaigns. When prostitution, gambling, and the sale of alcoholic beverages were illegal but tolerated by city hall, there was never any evidence to connect Behrman with campaign contributions or payoffs from the *demimonde*. Any money collected from these sources passed through the ward leaders without Behrman's official knowledge, "a practical situation dealt with in a practical way."[10]

Close cooperation with the business community was another factor contributing to the machine's longevity. Business would back any political organization that gave it special privileges, favors, low taxes, and a minimum of regulation. The Regular Democratic Organization met all these criteria. New Orleans businessmen and politicians agreed that the relationship between the two was "normal, necessary and in the interest of the city." Behrman's motto was that "nothing would be done to hurt business and business was to be judge."[11] The relationship between the Regulars and business was further enhanced by the economic growth and expansion experienced by the city between 1899 and 1920. With the exception of the national recession of 1907, the economy of the city grew sporadically; for example, in 1920 the total market value of New Orleans products trippled 1914 figures. Boosters touted New Orleans far and

10. Reynolds, *Machine Politics in New Orleans*, 133–35.
11. *Ibid.*, 138–44.

wide as "a great American city living, breathing and growing greater every hour."[12]

Behrman's relationship with business was by no means unusual. Most city bosses of the late nineteenth and early twentieth centuries had business connections of one sort or another. For example, "Colonel" Ed Butler of St. Louis, the "Honorable" William Tweed of New York, and Abraham Reuf of San Francisco were either presidents or directors of numerous corporations, and "Old Boy" George Cox of Cincinnati, Christopher Magee of Pittsburgh, and Chicago's Roger Sullivan controlled banks, street railways, and gas companies.[13]

Whenever one thinks of a city boss, one usually imagines a flashily dressed Irishman chewing on a fat cigar. A comparison of Behrman with nineteen other city bosses of the same period inevitably revealed that although bosses had much in common, they were as divergent as the members of any other profession. They were usually hardworking, loyal to friends, and from humble urban backgrounds. Of the twenty studied, most grew up in overcrowded industrial areas and had little formal education. Contrary to the stereotype, bosses did not conform to any particular physical pattern; they were not of any one ethnic group; and there were as many Democrats as Republicans. Abe

12. Bureau of Census, *Thirteenth Census of the United States, 1910: Manufacturers* (Washington, D. C.: U.S. Government Printing Office, 1912), IX, 429; *Census of Manufacturers*, 1914, I, 520, 526; *Fourteenth Census of the United States, 1920: Manufacturers* (Washington, D.C.: U. S. Government Printing Office, 1923), IX, 526–27. Market value of new orleans products: 1904—$81,410,706; 1909—$78,794,030; 1914—$69,814,081; 1920—$182,798,561; *New Orleans and the Louisiana State Museum: Facts Past and Present About the Metropolis of the South* (New Orleans: N.P.).

13. Harold Zink, *City Bosses in the United States: A Study of Twenty Municipal Bosses* (Durham, N.C.: Duke University Press, 1930), 40. The twenty bosses studied were Martin Lomasney (Boston), Tim Sullivan (Bowery, New York), William M. Tweed (New York), John Kelly (New York), Richard Croker (New York), Charles M. Murphy (New York), George W. Olvany (Brooklyn), James McManes (Philadelphia), Israel W. Durham (Philadelphia), Christopher L. Magee (Pittsburgh), William Flinn (Pittsburgh), George B. Cos (Cincinnati), Albert Ames (Minneapolis), Abraham Reuf (San Francisco), Fred Lundin (Chicago), Edward Butler (St. Louis), Roger C. Sullivan (Chicago), Hugh McLaughlin (Brooklyn), Edwin H. Vare (Philadelphia), and Martin Behrman (New Orleans).

Reuf, "Doc" Albert Ames of Minneapolis, and Tweed had a taste for flashy clothing, big cigars, and yachts. The Czar of Boston, Martin Lomasney, dressed in shabby odds and ends. Behrman and other city barons, such as New York's "Honest John" Kelly, Cox, and the Bowery's "Big Tim" Sullivan were not concerned with fashion. Of the twenty bosses, twelve either served prison terms or were indicted for specific crimes. "Curly Boss" Reuf served a fourteen-year sentence in California's San Quentin prison for bribery, and Tweed died in the Ludlow Street jail in New York. Cox was indicted for perjury and New York's Richard Coker for murder. Albert Ames and Ed Butler were both tried for bribery. Behrman's opponents often denounced him for being a machine politician and ruling the city with a heavy hand, but with one exception they always stopped short of accusing him of violating a law.[14] The exception occurred in 1905 during the power struggle for control of the New Orleans Police Department, when Dominick O'Malley, editor of the New Orleans *Item* accused Behrman of using his influence in the city council in awarding a franchise in return for stock in the company. A court trial cleared Behrman of the allegation and convicted O'Malley of criminal libel. Behrman discusses this incident in some detail in Chapter II.

The boss has had a long tradition in American urban history. By the early 1900s political rings controlled the municipal governments in Boston, Cleveland, Philadelphia, Pittsburgh, San Francisco, St. Louis, Kansas City, Chicago, San Antonio, Toledo, Minneapolis, and New Orleans. The most infamous of these organizations, the Tammany Society, founded in New York was practically as old as the country itself. One student of New York's political history wrote that machine politics existed in New York before 1765 with "bosses, campaign chests, vote-getting devices, and patronage rewards all in existence."[15]

14. *Ibid.*, 17–147.
15. Milton M. Dein, "Democracy and Politics in Colonial New York," *New York History*, XL (1959), 221–46.

In 1903 Lincoln Steffens, the muckraking journalist for *McClure's Magazine*, wrote a series of articles exposing political corruption in St. Louis, Minneapolis, Pittsburgh, Chicago, and Philadelphia. Although these cities (including New Orleans) had large immigrant populations, Steffens' studies revealed that political machines were not confined to a particular ethnic group. They were a result, concluded Steffens, of socioeconomic conditions, not culture. Immigrants arrived in cities from the American farmlands and foreign countries confused and desperately poor. They clung to anything or anyone who would give them bread and a sense of security. Bosses provided jobs, food baskets, relief in emergencies, toys at Christmas, and flowers at funerals. While reformers were shouting of the ruination of American and Western society, bosses supplied the necessities of life. Steffens pessimistically wrote that "the boss is not a political, he is an American institution, the product of a freed people who have not the spirit to be free." "But no one class," continued Steffens, "is at fault nor any one breed, nor any political interest or group of interests. The misgovernment of the American people is the misgovernment by the American people.... We break our own laws and rob our own government, the lady at the custom-house, the lyncher with his rope, and the captain of industry with his bribe and rebate. The spirit of graft and of lawlessness is the American spirit.... The people are not innocent." The boss and "practical politician," Steffens concluded, were nothing more than "political merchants" and "businessmen with a speciality."[16] Behrman simplified this concept: "The ability to get along with people and to persuade them to vote with you is not much different from the ability to sell groceries and keep your trade."

British observer James Bryce, though generally optimistic about the American system, wrote in 1888 in his astute treatise

16. Lincoln Steffens, *The Shame of the Cities* (New York: McClure, Phillips, 1904), 2–13.

on United States politics, *The American Commonwealth*, that "the government of cities is the one conspicuous failure of the United States. The deficiences of the national governments tell but little.... The faults of the state governments are insignificant compared with the extravagance, corruption, and mismanagement which has marked the administration of the great cities." "But there is not a city," Bryce observed, "with a population exceeding 200,000 where the poison germs have not sprung into vigorous life." Bryce concluded that in all large cities in the United States "constant complaints are directed against the bad paving and cleaning of the streets, the nonenforcement of the laws forbidding gambling and illicit drinking." Political machines, wrote Bryce, were a result of direct control of the legislature over local affairs and the spoils system "whereby office becomes the reward of party service, and the whole machinery of the party government made to serve, as its main objective, the getting and keeping of places."[17]

Behrman, like many city bosses, faced constant opposition from reform groups. Good government leagues sprang up in practically every city that was controlled by a machine, including New Orleans. Many of the these leagues backed the successful candidacies of such municipal crusaders as Tom L. Johnson, reform mayor of Cleveland, "Golden Rule" Samuel Jones of Toledo, and Detroit's utility fighter Hazen Pingree.

Historians continue to debate the questions of motivation and which classes or groups of people led the vanguard for political reform in the first two decades of this century. The cry for good government in New Orleans was usually for progressive democracy, that is, abstract and idealistic *versus* practical politics. Through the years, Behrman's opposition, under the banner of one reform group or another, was essentially middle class and led primarily by lawyers, businessmen, social uplifters, and

17. James Bryce, *The American Commonwealth* (2 vols., rev. ed.; New York: Macmillan, 1915), I, 640–47.

editors. It was of mixed ethnic and religious origins, with as many Catholics as Protestants, and included Jews. However, a look at a large segment of those who supported the machine revealed this same middle-class, religious, and ethnic diversity. Perhaps Behrman's analysis of his opposition as a heterogeneous conglomeration of discontented Regulars, idealists, opportunists, and "uptown silk stockings" was the most perceptive. Behrman defined the silk-stocking reformer as one "who knew all about municipal government because he read magazines and books . . . and did not know where to file his complaint if the garbage man did not come early enough to suit him." The Choctaw chief summed up his opinion of his opposition as merely "the outs wanting in."

For many years the city lacked a strong central figure around whom the reform elements could unite. In election after election they tried to depose Behrman and the machine, and each time they failed. The first organized assault on the Choctaw Club came with the Home Rulers in the 1904 municipal elections, then the Independents in 1908, and the Good Government League in 1912. It was not until 1920, under the leadership of the reform governor John M. Parker and his New Orleans-based Orleans Democratic Association (O.D.A.), that the reformers were able to grasp the reins of city government from Behrman. Behrman attributed his defeat in 1920 to the machinations of Parker and to his own failure to perceive the people's mood for change—a mood of disillusion for existing institutions and values that swept the country after World War I.

The O.D.A.'s victory was only temporary. As the postwar years wore on, the electorate grew more and more disappointed with the reform government and the constant wrangling within its ranks. It soon became evident that the only purpose of the movement was to dethrone Behrman. Once this unifying factor had been removed, the O.D.A. disintegrated into squabbling factions. After an interval of minor political sucesses in the early

1920s, Behrman was again elected mayor in 1925 for his fifth and final administration.

Behrman's political success was partially due to his affable nature, efficiency, and ability to sense public moods and needs. He was justifiably convinced that the majority of the people wanted visible and tangible signs of progress, as in improved municipal services. In this area he could count many successes, including the Public Belt Railroad, extensive street paving, a modern sewerage system, improved public health, schools, playgrounds, hospitals, and increased police and fire protection. Behrman maintained that as long as he produced, most people would remain indifferent to his type of governmental machinery. This philosophy included the belief that wage earners were practical people and not foolish idealists who thought in abstract principles of government. "Hizonner" did not understand, however, that in return the voter had to forfeit the spirit of a democratic society.

Behrman's memoirs, as they appeared in serialized form in the New Orleans *Item*, lacked continuity and were merely erratic and spontaneous discourses on various events, issues, and individuals. Therefore, it became my task to edit, collate, and organize these serializations from the newspapers for the modern reader. Many incidents and names of minor characters that may have been of some interest to a reader in 1922 and 1923 but not necessarily to today's audience were deleted. Although it was necessary to delete about 35 percent of the material, I have attempted only to refine the essence of Behrman's thoughts. To avoid an excessive use of *sic* I have silently corrected obvious typographical errors and some confusing punctuation. To assist the reader in understanding Behrman's numerous references to people and events, I have supplied annotative notes which I hope will not become burdensome.

To achieve the ultimate objective—readability—the memoirs have been divided into four chapters. They range from

Chapter I, Behrman's early life in New Orleans, through Chapter IV, his defeat in 1920 and the end of his recollections. In the first chapter the former mayor reflected upon the people, issues, and events that shaped Louisiana's politics during the last decade of the nineteenth century. He recounted his entrance into politics and the 1892 gubernatorial campaign and election between Murphy J. Foster and Samuel D. McEnery in which the Louisiana Lottery Company, a corrupt holdover from Reconstruction, was the primary devisive issue. He discussed the merits of John Fitzpatrick's controversial administration as mayor of New Orleans (1892–1896); he also describes the victory of Bourbon democracy resulting from the New Orleans and state elections of 1896 and the constitutional convention of 1898. Chapter II deals with Behrman's emergence as boss of the Choctaw Club, his philosophy on government, and several of the major incidents during his first administration. In the third chapter Behrman described important political events in New Orleans and in the state government from 1906 to 1916. More specifically, it was a discourse on the political career and influence of Governor Jared Y. Sanders and his relationship to the New Orleans machine. Behrman ended his memoirs in Chapter IV, recalling the series of events leading to his defeat by the reformers and their allied faction in the New Orleans municipal elections of 1920.

Behrman's biases and prejudices must, of course, be viewed in context. His historical accuracy in the memoirs may be accepted with caution, since his recollections were written day by day in 1922 and 1923 for daily publication and were dependent upon conversations, memories, and memorabilia. The presentation of his memoirs is not intended to be a history of the Populist and Progressive eras in New Orleans; it is intended to provide insights into one of the main characters who helped shape those eras. These insights can add to a base for future and important interpretative studies of the history of New Orleans, the state of Louisiana, and the American people.

Introduction

Twentieth-century southern history, particularly southern rural history, has provided numerous topics for writers and historians over the years, and bookshelves are lined with biographies and monographs on such political notables as Louisiana's Huey Long and Earl Long, Mississippi's James K. Vardaman, Georgia's Eugene Talmadge, South Carolina's "Pitchfork" Ben Tillman, and the Populist disciple from Georgia, Tom Watson. With few exceptions, however, little has been written about the urban South during the early decades of the 1900s. This is partly because there are relatively few metropolises in the South and also because of the dominance of state governments over local affairs. However, cities did exist, and their important histories are beginning to come into focus.

I wish to acknowledge my appreciation to the following persons for their helpful efforts and contributions to this project: Robert R. Macdonald, director of the Louisiana State Museum; Stephen J. Duplantier, New Orleans, for his photographic work; Collin B. Hamer, Jr., archivist, Louisiana Division, New Orleans Public Library; Aline H. Morris and Rose Lambert, Louisiana State Museum Library; Tamra Carboni, curator of Decorative Arts, Louisiana State Museum; Stanley Behrman, the mayor's son; and, Ray Holman, Diane Kramer, Mrs. Julia Herbert, Pat Johnson, Al Kennedy, Al Rose, and Lorraine Wegmann, all of New Orleans.

John Randolph Kemp
New Orleans

MARTIN BEHRMAN
of New Orleans

I

Early Career in Politics
1888–1904

1.

Judging by the kind of articles I have read in the public records and in magazines about famous men and big events, and realizing that such records and articles will doubtless be drawn on by future writers of history, I often wonder what will become of my own memory long after I am dead. I must confess that I am interested in that. That is one of the reasons why I am taking the trouble to set these recollections before my home people so they may know my point of view and my opinions, what the reports call my "slant" on various matters.

I would be a hypocrite if I did not frankly admit that I believe I have had an unusual career. Just a day or two ago I read that Mayor [William Hale] Thompson of Chicago is about to quit after only eight years. I was mayor for 16 years. As *The Times-Democrat* pointed out in 1908, it was a most extraordinary thing that the whole administration was returned to office. There are other matters concerning me which were not my doing, entirely, and which were out of the usual run of things. Just as Theodore Roosevelt, in my opinion, will be remembered more for the conservation policy it may happen that I will be remembered for something that I myself do not now recognize as the one outstanding feature of my life.

As my father died when I was so young that I do not remember him at all, it is natural that my earliest recollections should be entirely of my mother, who died when I was twelve years old. I do not clearly recall anything about my mother before the days when she used to take me to the bazaar section of the French Market, where she had a dry goods stand. I was too small for pants and wore a skirt as the rompers now used for little kids had not yet been discovered. Next following my mother in my memory come the Indians who sold herbs, beads and leaves of plants used to flavor food. I remember standing there and watching the Indians by the hour.

My mother, as I remember her, was a woman of energy and determination. My childhood impression was that there was nothing she could not do. A later impression that has remained always with me was her repeated advice that I should get an education. I am quite certain that if she had lived and kept good health, I would have had the best school training that New Orleans then afforded and if she had had the money she would have sent me to college.

My father was a cigar-maker. I was born in New York, October 14, 1864, and seven months later the family moved to New Orleans. I do not know where they lived at first, but the first home I remember was in a building on the uptown, lake-side corner of Bourbon and St. Peter. I would leave there with my mother early in the morning and spend the day at the French Market and get back late in the afternoon, up to the time I started to school.

The French Market and the river front there were the big world for me up to the time I was seven years old. There were no sheds over the wharves then and I used to go over to the landing with older boys and look at the sailing vessels of all kinds that brought cargoes, most of them food of one kind or another. In those days, a cargo of 4000 bunches of bananas, unloaded one by one, was a big event.

The men on the sailing ships and the schooners were all heroes to me. Among them was the late Salvatore Pizzati, who

I

Early Career in Politics
1888–1904

1.

Judging by the kind of articles I have read in the public records and in magazines about famous men and big events, and realizing that such records and articles will doubtless be drawn on by future writers of history, I often wonder what will become of my own memory long after I am dead. I must confess that I am interested in that. That is one of the reasons why I am taking the trouble to set these recollections before my home people so they may know my point of view and my opinions, what the reports call my "slant" on various matters.

I would be a hypocrite if I did not frankly admit that I believe I have had an unusual career. Just a day or two ago I read that Mayor [William Hale] Thompson of Chicago is about to quit after only eight years. I was mayor for 16 years. As *The Times-Democrat* pointed out in 1908, it was a most extraordinary thing that the whole administration was returned to office. There are other matters concerning me which were not my doing, entirely, and which were out of the usual run of things. Just as Theodore Roosevelt, in my opinion, will be remembered more for the conservation policy it may happen that I will be remembered for something that I myself do not now recognize as the one outstanding feature of my life.

As my father died when I was so young that I do not remember him at all, it is natural that my earliest recollections should be entirely of my mother, who died when I was twelve years old. I do not clearly recall anything about my mother before the days when she used to take me to the bazaar section of the French Market, where she had a dry goods stand. I was too small for pants and wore a skirt as the rompers now used for little kids had not yet been discovered. Next following my mother in my memory come the Indians who sold herbs, beads and leaves of plants used to flavor food. I remember standing there and watching the Indians by the hour.

My mother, as I remember her, was a woman of energy and determination. My childhood impression was that there was nothing she could not do. A later impression that has remained always with me was her repeated advice that I should get an education. I am quite certain that if she had lived and kept good health, I would have had the best school training that New Orleans then afforded and if she had had the money she would have sent me to college.

My father was a cigar-maker. I was born in New York, October 14, 1864, and seven months later the family moved to New Orleans. I do not know where they lived at first, but the first home I remember was in a building on the uptown, lake-side corner of Bourbon and St. Peter. I would leave there with my mother early in the morning and spend the day at the French Market and get back late in the afternoon, up to the time I started to school.

The French Market and the river front there were the big world for me up to the time I was seven years old. There were no sheds over the wharves then and I used to go over to the landing with older boys and look at the sailing vessels of all kinds that brought cargoes, most of them food of one kind or another. In those days, a cargo of 4000 bunches of bananas, unloaded one by one, was a big event.

The men on the sailing ships and the schooners were all heroes to me. Among them was the late Salvatore Pizzati, who was then captain of a schooner, the "Salvatore Pizzati".... One day Captain Pizzati beckoned me with his finger and when I got to him he gave me a big ripe banana. That was the first gift I ever received. During the half century since that event, I have been presented with every thing from a cigar to an oil portrait of myself and I have enjoyed many a delightful dinner and many formal banquets, but I have never forgotten that banana. Whenever I see a small boy eating a banana, I remember Captain Pizzati and the banana he gave me.

I was not sent to school until I was seven years old but my mother had taught me a little before then. It was in 1871 that I first went to the German-American school in Royal Street near St. Philip. I went to the drygoods stand at the French Market with my mother in the early morning and then hurried off to school at nine o'clock. Then I would go back to my mother at the market when school was over.

My mother found that I would not be admitted to the high school because of any work done at the private German-American school, so she took me from the German-American and sent me to the St. Philip school, in St. Philip street near Royal.

When I went to the St. Philip school, the pupils put in their nickels and dimes, and some of them put in quarters, to get coal to heat the rooms on the worst winter days. And in summer, we put in to get ice.

Now the children get free books as well as heated rooms and plenty of ice water. I remember my experiences in 1898 when I introduced an ordinance in the constitutional convention to provide free books; but it could not pass without an amendment requiring the child's parents to swear to an affidavit that they could not provide the books. The amendment spoiled the thing, but that has since been remedied.[1]

---

1. This was one of several bills introduced in the Louisiana constitutional convention of 1898 that will be noted later in this chapter.

St. Philip was short of teachers and the boys who had made the most progress were called on to teach Italians, Slavs, Greeks and Bohemians and a few Austrains. I was very proud to teach these newcomers, most of them older than I was. I believed I learned a great deal from that work and I can tell you it was not easy work.

I was a pupil at St. Philip when the fight against the Metropolitian police and the "carpet baggers" took place.[2] A negro policeman came running out St. Peter street, tearing off his Metropolitan buttons as he ran. He threw a Winchester rifle, with a bayonet on it, under the show case of Mr. Reboul's shoe store at St. Peter and Bourbon. I got the rifle as spoils of war and I kept it until about 1912, when I gave it to a darky down the river. The Royal hotel was the capitol then.

My mother died when I was twelve years old. I had no relatives. I was too young to undertake the management of the drygoods stand, so I went to work at Samuel's Dollar Store as assistant cashier at $15 a month. While $15 would really buy something in those days, it would not provide a handsome living even for a boy of twelve years. Samuel's store was what might be called a small department store as there was all kinds of merchandise on the counters and shelves.

I spent $2 a month of my $15 for tuition at Dolbear's night school. I studied mathematics and English. Dolbear's was in

2. Behrman is referring to the clash between Governor William Pitt Kellogg's predominantly black Metropolitan Police and the anti-Kellogg White League at the foot of Canal Street in New Orleans on September 14, 1874. All the frustrations and anxieties that festered in Louisiana during Reconstruction found a catalyst for violence in the disputed gubernatorial election of 1872. John McEnery, the fusion candidate of the Democratic and anti-President Republicans, claimed victory at the polls over Radical Republican Kellogg. The state returning board, the referee in all disputed elections, confirmed McEnery's election. Ignoring the board's decision, Kellogg with the backing of President Grant and federal troops had himself sworn in as governor. Resentment became so great that riots erupted in several areas in the state: Colfax, April, 1873 (fifty-nine blacks and two whites killed); at Coushatta in August, 1874, and in New Orleans on September 14, 1874. J. G. Randall and David Donald, *The Civil War and Reconstruction* (Lexington, Mass.: D. C. Heath, 1969), 691.

Early Career in Politics

Canal street between Rampart and Burgundy. I think it was in the building now occupied by the Economical Drug Store. Christ's Church was then at the corner of Canal and Dauphine, where the Maison Blanche is now. Between Samuel's and Dolbear's, little Behrman had about all he could do.

My next move was to leave both Samuel's and Dolbear's and go to work for Michel Gallagher in his grocery store in Algiers. I felt satisfied at the time that I had learned as much arithmetic as I could. I could read and write well enough, but I have always had the feeling that I would have been fortunate to have been able to spend more of my boyhood at school. If my mother had lived, I would have been kept at school, and I feel quite sure she would have wanted me to have a college education.

Mike Gallagher used to buy 65 proof whiskey by the barrel. He bottled it and labelled the bottles whiskey, red rum and brandy. If you ordered liquor from the bottle labelled whiskey, you paid five cents. Red rum was ten cents. Brandy was also ten cents. Afterwards, when I was with C. Doyle & Company, Gallagher ordered his barrels through me.

When I left Michel Gallagher's where I was treated very kindly, I went to work for the late James Lawton, father of Peter Lawton, at his big store, where the immigration station is now.[3] It was a big country store, with a bakery and a steamboat for deliveries on the river down to Oakville, now known as Jesuits' Bend.

Miss Julia Collins was a visitor at the Lawton home. I met her there and in 1887 we were married. Her brother, Jerry B. Collins, married Miss Catherine Lawton. Their son, Major James L. Collins, was General Pershing's aide. Their other son, Captain Joseph Collins, is an instructor at West Point.

I was married by Father Robert Moise in St. Peter and Paul's

---

3. The immigration station was built during Behrman's second term (1908–12) in Algiers, a suburb of New Orleans on the west bank of the Mississippi River opposite the city.

Catholic church in Burgundy street between Marigny and Mandeville.

When I was sitting in the parlor waiting to make arrangements for my marriage, the servant saw I was nervous. I asked her for something to read and she handed me the city directory. Being illiterate, she probably thought the biggest book in sight would be the most interesting. So I sat there and glanced over the columns of that old directory until Father Moise came in.

Just before I was married, I left the big Lawton store and went into the retail grocery business with Peter Lawton in Patterson street, Algiers.

The Algiers postoffice was at our store. Everybody called there for their mail, just as in a country town, and I made a great many acquaintances and friends.

It was not long before we gave up the retail grocery business and I went to work for Wallace & Van Horn, dealers in wholesale produce, as a salesman. This was Nathaniel D. Wallace, who later went to congress from the second district. His partner was Napoleon Bonaparte Van Horn, known as the "Potato King," because whole barges and boatloads of Irish potatoes were cosigned to him.

My next employers were F. O. Trepagnier and Edward C. Bres, wholesale dealers in butter, cheese, and eggs. Then I went to work for C. Doyle and Company, wholesale grocers, as a traveling salesman.

I had always taken an interest in politics and, as luck would have it, I usually had work that brought me in contact with many persons. During the years I worked at Mr. James Lawton's store, I made a great many friends simply by being polite and cordial to people. As I moved from one job to another, usually improving the financial situation a little with each move, I met more people and got to know them. I suppose it was my rather wide acquaintance for a young man that suggested to the active politicians that they choose me as secretary of the fifteenth ward campaign committee for Francis T. Nicholls in his campaign for governor in 1888.[4] That was my first experience in active politics and I did not go into it of my own action. I was invited and I accepted. I did the best I could and they all seemed to be satisfied with my work.

Shortly after that campaign, when I was at Opelousas [in south central Louisiana] as traveling salesman for C. Doyle and Company, Mr. Thomas Higgins, the assessor of the fifth district [Algiers], sent me a telegram offering me the position of deputy assessor. I did not reply but waited until I got home and explained the matter to my wife.

The discussion at home did not dwell much on the point of whether it would be a good thing for me to take the job and go into politics but rather on the advantages of having a job that would permit me to stay at home more. Mrs. Behrman finally decided that I should take it but in after years sometimes expressed doubt but that from the "at home" point of view I might just as well have kept the job as traveling salesman.

French I learned at the German-American school and kept up in conversation with Creoles and other French speaking friends and acquaintances got me the job as traveling salesman for C. Doyle & Company.... Their salesman for southern and southwestern Louisiana had taken sick and they selected me for that territory. A man who spoke no French would have been almost useless. I remember that on my first trip to Lake Charles I went to the courthouse to represent C. Doyle & Company in a suit and long leaf pine lands were sold in small tracts by the sheriff at

---

4. In the 1887–88 Louisiana gubernatorial contest, former Governor Francis T. Nicholls (1877–80), the Reform Democrat, defeated the incumbent, Samuel D. McEnery, of the Regular Democrats. The New Orleans vote, the deciding factor, went to Nicholls. After defeating McEnery, Nicholls had no difficulty trouncing his Republican opponent, the "Carpetbagger" former governor, Henry Clay Warmoth (1868–72), by an overwhelming vote of 136,746 to 51,993. William Ivy Hair, *Bourbonism and Agrarian Protest; Louisiana Politics, 1877–1900* (Baton Rouge: Louisiana State University Press, 1969), 136–40.

auction for $10 an acre. When I was there in 1904, during my campaign for state auditor, the same lands were selling for $100 an acre. As I have stated, I left that job to become deputy assessor at $150 a month.

A salary of even less than $150 a month does not mean poverty for any reasonable person even in these days of high prices. As I remember it, my family got along very nicely on $150 a month in those days—the late eighties and early nineties.[5] One of my children, Isabella, died when three years old. My daughter, Nellie, now Mrs. Nat Bond, was born in May of 1888 and my son Stanley in 1889. There were a great many families in those days that looked on $150 a month as an excellent income and mine was among them. We lived in a cottage across the street from the Lawton store, where the immigration station is now, and were quite content.

There was only one deputy assessor for Algiers and the assessment district was small. I did a lot of the field work and the clerical work in the office. The total assessment of the city was only $130,000,000 as late as 1900. Now [1922] it is more than $500,000,000.

The wide acquaintance I made at the big Lawton store, at the store and postoffice together with Peter Lawton and then as assessor probably included every man, woman and child in Algiers. I took the census in 1890 and that improved my knowledge of Algiers and ten years later, in 1900, I took the census of educable children, six to eighteen years for the State Board of Education. This census provided the basis for the distribution of school funds.

The streets and roads were bad in those days and unless my

---

5. Behrman was quite right. In an 1883 study the Knights of Labor estimated the cost of living for an average New Orleans working family at $480 to $624 per year. The New Orleans *Times-Democrat* reported in 1890 that the annual wage for the working class in southern cities was approximately $497. Roger W. Shugg, *Origins of Class Struggle in Louisiana* (Baton Rouge: Louisiana State University Press, 1939), 293–95.

business required such house to house work as taking the census I rode a horse. I weighed 130 pounds. It was a good thing to have a horse. The Southern Pacific [Railroad] shops, the drydocks and the boat builders provided practically all the employment. There were four dry docks in Algiers, the Vallette, the Ocean, the Marine, and the Woods.

There were four daily newspapers published in New Orleans: *The Time-Democrat, The Item, The [Daily] Picayune* and *The States. The Picayune* was generally considered the leading paper. The people seemed to have more confidence in it than in the others. I read them all very carefully every day and formed a habit that has taken a great deal of my time ever since. I read, also a great many magazines. There were comparatively few pictures in the magazines then but there were a number of weeklies that were well illustrated.

As Algiers was small, I was called on to help with the assessments in the first district, from Canal to Felicity street. That brought me in contact with a great many business men, many of whom have remained my friends during the thirty-four years since I first made their acquaintence.

I was present [on March 14, 1891] at the gathering at Henry Clay statue just before the mob went down to the old parish prison, in Orleans Street, between Treme and Marais [streets] and killed a number of Italians who had been charged with the murder of the chief of police, Dave Hennessy. John M. Parker was speaking when I stopped in the crowd, having just come over from Algiers on my way to the city hall. William S. Parkerson and John C. Wickliffe had spoken. I followed the crowd but at some distance. I saw one of the men hanging to a tree.[6]

---

6. New Orleans Police Chief, David Hennessy, was assassinated in New Orleans on October 15, 1890, after threatening to expose criminal secret societies in the city's Italian community during the Matranga-Provenzano feud. Amid shouts of jury-fixing, intimidation, and payoffs, the jury acquitted six of the defendants and ordered new trials for the other three despite overwhelming evidence, including reports of eyewitnesses. The day

Judge [Robert H.] Marr[7] presided at the trial of the Italians charged with the murder of the chief of police, David Hennessy. The Italians were lynched by a large crowd that had been addressed at Clay Statue, then on a high pedestal at Royal and Canal streets, where I saw John M. Parker, William S. Parkerson and Robert C. Wickliffe make speeches.

Judge Marr disappeared, as I remember it, on the day that John Fitzpatrick defeated Mayor Shakespeare [sic].[8] His disappearance caused a great deal of excitement and it was generally believed that he had been murdered by members of the Mafia or the Camorra. This was only a suspicion based on the assumption that members of these organizations believed his conduct of the trial had been unfair. No evidence of it was ever developed. His body was never found. He was last seen near Fischer's saw mill in Carrollton and it is possible that he was drowned in the Mississippi.

So far as I know, this was the last death of which the Mafia or the Camorra here were even suspected. I have myself never seen any real evidence that these organizations, which began as secret political societies in Italy, were actually organized here. However, everybody believes they were. When the Italians got to fighting each other years later, they were accused of having an organization known as the "Black Hand." When a native American shoots somebody, or a German, a Frenchman or a man of any other nationality shoots a man, the newspapers do

---

after the trial ended, March 14, 1891, angry mobs marched from the Henry Clay statue at St. Charles and Canal streets to the parish prison where they hanged two of the Italians and shot the rest (in all, eleven were killed). The lynchings almost caused an international incident when the Italian government withdrew its ambassador to the United States. After long negotiations the United States paid 125,000 francs to help ease the affront to that nation. Joy J. Jackson, *New Orleans in the Gilded Age; Politics and Urban Reform, 1880–1896* (Baton Rouge: Louisiana State University Press, 1969), 247–53; John Smith Kendall, *History of New Orleans* (3 Vols.; Chicago and New York: Lewis, 1922), I, 479–81.

7. Later in these memoirs Behrman corrected himself. Judge Joshua G. Baker, not Robert H. Marr, presided over the trial of the Italians charged with the murder of David Hennessy.

8. The date of the election was April 19, 1892. The correct spelling is Shakspeare.

not give us dark hints about murderous organizations. But when Italians do this, the newspapers usually manage to ring in the idea that an organization was behind it.

Every election in those days was a bitterly fought and very hot affair. Of course, the ups and downs of politics will always cool some friendships and increase some enmities, but the wildest campaigns we have nowadays are very gentlemanly affairs compared to the average of the late eighties. The voters were permitted to deposit any ticket they chose in the ballot boxes and every faction printed its own tickets. I was myself the head of a very suddenly organized faction in Algiers, that was not heard of four days before the election of delegates to a city convention, and we won. We printed our own tickets. In some parts of the city it happened that a faction would be organized the night before an election and have its tickets at the polls the next day. These elections of which I speak were the primaries held by the Democrats. They were not official, state regulated primaries controlled by statutes but simply the Democrats fighting for delegations to conventions.

The tickets all had emblems printed on their backs. Some would use a ship, others an eagle and others a heavily muscled arm wielding a hammer to represent labor. I will not attempt to describe all the emblems. There are too many of them.

Then there were the "Chinese tickets." How they got that name is beyond me. These were tickets printed with the emblem of one faction on the back and the names of the candidates of another faction on the front. They were used by timid citizens who wanted the candidates whose emblem appeared to believe they were getting the vote. They were usually printed on election morning after samples of the ballots had been obtained. It often happened that politicians would keep their emblem secret as long as possible so as to make it harder to get to the polls with a "Chinese ticket." The tickets were usually displayed at the polls on barrel heads.

Three factions in Algiers sent delegations to the convention [of 1892] that nominated John Fitzpatrick for mayor.[9] I was chairman of one of them and my delegation was seated. As chairman of the successful delegation, I was the representative of the fifteenth ward, Algiers, in the caucus held after Mayor Fitzpatrick's election.

While I was a deputy assessor under Thomas E. Higgins, Governor Nicholls dismissed Higgins and O. A. Trezevant, assessor, "for cause." We all believed that it was "because" they were both active in behalf of the [Louisiana Lottery Company] as they were both strong lottery men and the big fight against the lottery had begun.[10] As his deputy, I went to court to compel Governor Nicholls to state his reasons for discharging them but the Supreme Court decided that he did not have to do so.

I then went to President E. L. Bemiss of the Algiers Water Works & Electric Light Company and applied for a job as agent or solicitor. He knew I was an active hard worker and was well known in Algiers and as electric lights were not in general use in residence at the time I had no trouble landing a job. Bemiss was also president of the Edison [Electric Illuminating Company] on the city side of the river.

It was not so long after that that I was appointed assessor and I went to Mr. Bemiss and asked him if I could keep the job with him. I had then begun working on the city side, and the Edison company had no property in Algiers. I was assessor for Algiers. While it was true that the board of assessors formally approved all the assessments, the fact was that the assessments in each district were made by the assessor for that district.

I heard some comment on my holding both jobs and mentioned the matter to Eugene D. Saunders and Ernest Kruttschnitt [both leaders in the Democratic Central Commit-

---

9. Behrman discussed the achievements and scandals of Fitzpatrick's administration as mayor of New Orleans (1892–96) later in this chapter.

10. See footnote 11 of this chapter for the Louisiana Lottery Company and the state and New Orleans municipal elections of 1892.

Early Career in Politics

tee for Louisiana]. Neither of them saw any objection to it. There was no secret about my employment with the Edison company.

I had practically decided to stay in politics by that time and, because I thought holding jobs might eventually be used against me in politics, I quit the job with the Edison company.

It was used against me when I ran for mayor in 1904. For some reason it was not mentioned earlier that year when I was elected state auditor. I shall refer to this matter again when I come to the affairs of 1904.

2.

1891–1892 State and City Lottery Campaign[11]

I was a delegate to the convention of the [Samuel D.] McEnery, the pro-lottery faction in Pike's Hall, Baton Rouge, in the

---

11. The Louisiana Lottery Company was organized in New Orleans in 1868 during the federal occupation of Louisiana following the Civil War. Although the lottery became synonymous with the corruption of Reconstruction, the company became so wealthy that it survived numerous attempts to revoke its twenty-five-year charter after Home Rule returned to the state in 1877.

As the 1892 state and New Orleans municipal elections approached, the lottery became a central and divisive issue. On the state level, Samuel D. McEnery and Murphy J. Foster split the Democratic party between the pro and anti lottery sympathizers. In a statewide primary, Foster, the antilottery candidate defeated McEnery by 549 votes. Undaunted, McEnery bolted the party and ran for governor as an independent. The same division existed within the Republican party with the prolottery forces led by former acting governor Pinckney B. S. Pinchback, the only black man ever to hold that office in Louisiana. As a major stockholder in the Louisiana Lottery Company, Pinchback vied with Reconstruction governor Henry Clay Warmoth, leader of the antilottery Republicans, for control of the party. The result was that each Republican faction fielded its candidate for governor. With the addition of the Populist or People's party candidate, there were five contenders for the office. Everyone realized, however, that the real contest was between the two Democrats, McEnery and Foster.

The New Orleans mayoral election, held at the same time as the state contests, shared the same issue—the lottery—but with different results. The Anti-Lottery League worked for the reelection of the incumbent Joseph A. Shakspeare, while the prolottery Crescent Democratic Club (Regular Democrats) supported the former criminal sheriff and state legislator John Fitzpatrick, who had previously been a staunch opponent to the lottery company.

By election day the future existence of the lottery company was a dead issue though fall of 1891.[12] The [Murphy J.] Foster[13] [antilottery] faction met in the State House. I have some recollections of the appointment of a committee on harmony to get the two factions together, but it is not distinct, and I am told that there was no such committee. As I remember the excitement over that issue, I guess a committee on harmony would have had little chance to do anything. It would have been about as influential as Henry Ford's shipload of peacemakers that started out to harmonize the nations of Europe.

---

neither side was willing to admit it. The U.S. Supreme Court upheld a lower court's decision affirming the right of Congress to prohibit the lottery's use of the mail in its advertising. Unfortunately, factional hostilities and ambitions were too deep seated to allow a reconciliation. On April 19, 1892, Fitzpatrick defeated Shakspeare and the Anti-Lottery League by 20,547 votes to 17,289. On the state level the outcome was quite different. Foster and the antilotteryites won by a considerable margin of 79,388 votes to McEnery's 47,037.

The Louisiana Lottery Company, fatally stricken by the Supreme Court's decision in 1892, continued in Louisiana until its twenty-five-year charter expired on January 1, 1894. It moved to Honduras, but it operated illegally in Louisiana until its complete suppression in 1907. Jackson, *New Orleans in the Gilded Age*, 130–35.

12. Samuel D. McEnery (1837–1910), known as the levee governor for his conscientious work in rebuilding and improving the levee system along the Mississippi River, was elected lieutenant governor in 1879. The death of Governor Louis A. Wiltz in 1881 placed McEnery in the governor's seat. The following year McEnery was elected governor in his own right and served until his defeat by Francis T. Nicholls in 1888. Shortly after assuming office, Nicholls appointed McEnery associate justice of the Louisiana Supreme Court where he remained until his election to the U.S. Senate in 1896. McEnery made one more unsuccessful attempt for the governor's office in 1892 when defeated by Murphy J. Foster in the explosive and devisive lottery campaign. McEnery died on June 28, 1910, while serving in the U.S. Senate.

William Ivy Hair, a student of that era in Louisiana's history, wrote that the tragedy of McEnery's administration was his complete subservience to the corrupt and degenerating influences of the scandalous state treasurer, Major E. A. Burke, and the Louisiana Lottery Company. Burke and the lottery, Hair writes, were in such control of the governor that McEnery's opponents referred to him as "McLottery." John Houston, political agent of the Louisiana Lottery Company, assisted McEnery in 1890 in purchasing his New Orleans home. Houston purchased the desired property for McEnery and then sold it to him on a nine-year loan at 8 percent interest. Miriam G. Reeves, *The Governors of Louisiana* (Gretna, La.: Pelican, 1972), 83–85; Hair, *Bourbonism and Agrarian Protest*, 108–10; City of New Orleans, Records of the Registrar of Real Estate Transactions, Book 131, folio 418, Book 132, folio 454.

13. Murphy J. Foster (1849–1921) first began his political career in 1872 with his

Early Career in Politics

The Anti-Lottery League met with the Farmers' Alliance, the Louisiana organization of the Populists, and nominated [Thomas Scott] Adams. Adams [president of the Farmers' Alliance] declined the nomination. I do not remember any other Louisianian who declined a nomination for governor after it had been made. Adams took the nomination for secretary of state and won. Murphy J. Foster was then nominated for governor and Charles Parlange for lieutenant governor.[14]

---

election to the Louisiana state legislature where he served in both the house and senate for twenty years. During his final year in the state senate, Foster emerged as the leader of those opposed to the renewal of the Louisiana Lottery Company's charter. His hard line stance on the lottery issue assured his position as the antilottery Democratic candidate in the 1892 gubernatorial campaign. Reelected in 1896, Foster served two full terms as governor and then in 1900 was sent to the U.S. Senate by the state legislature. The voters returned Foster to Congress in 1906 where he remained until 1913. After a brief return to private life he was appointed collector of customs at New Orleans by President Woodrow Wilson. Reeves, *The Governors of Louisiana*, 85–88.

14. The People's or Populist party of Louisiana, like the national Populist party, was a third-party attempt by small farmers discontented with and frustrated by the old and established parties (Democrat in Louisiana's case) to exert influence in state politics. Although it had traditions dating to the 1870s, the Populist party was not formed in Louisiana until 1891. At the convention of the Louisiana Farmers' Union in Lafayette, in August, 1891, a split occurred among farmers which created the new party. The Anti-Lottery League, a faction of the Democratic party, met with the union's leaders in Lafayette and offered them the three top spots (governor, treasurer, and superintendent of education) on their faction's ticket in the 1892 state elections if they would join forces with them to gain control of the Democratic convention. Dissidents in the union protested, arguing that it was a trick intended to destroy the farmers' unity. The union's leaders agreed to support the Anti-Lottery League and the dissidents announced the formation of the Populist party of Louisiana. The Populists held their first convention in Alexandria, on October 2, 1891, and made a deliberate attempt to attract the Negro voter. The New Orleans *Daily Picayune* on October 4, branded the formation of the Populist party and its overtures to the Negro as nothing short of "revolution."

At the state Democratic convention in 1891, the Democratic party split between the pro-and antilottery factions. The former nominated Samuel D. McEnery as its candidate for governor. The Anti-Lottery League, in compliance with its agreement with the Farmer's Union, offered the nomination to Thomas S. Adams, president of the union. Under great pressure from the league and perhaps Governor Nicholls, Adams refused the nomination and chose instead to run for secretary of state. The league believed it had a much better chance to win with Murphy J. Foster leading the ticket. The Populist party also offered its gubernatorial nomination to Adams if he would leave the Democrats. Adams refused.

The Populist party of Louisiana enjoyed only minor successes during its brief political

The campaign was most bitter and the results were contested. It was agreed to submit the matter to a "returning board" composed of six factionalists, three from each side, and a seventh member as a neutral. John S. Young of Caddo [Parish] was the seventh member. E. Howard McCaleb, James C. Moise, and Frank C. Zacharie represented Foster. John Fitzpatrick, Charles Butler and A. W. Crandall represented McEnery.

Both sides produced a flood of argument and affidavits before the returning board, but a majority went for Foster. Whereupon the lottery papers lambasted the majority and howled like they had gone made. Page M. Baker [editor of the *Times-Democrat*] never quite got over the bad humor that the returning board put him in. He supported the lottery in *The Times-Democrat* with every argument he could bring out. The owners of the lottery company were interested in *The Times-Democrat* and many of the stockholders were his personal friends.

It took Page M. Baker many years to get over his bad humor. He was very much irritated with Judge [James C.] Moise whose father he had known well and with whose relatives, some cousins, he remained on good terms. But he could not stand much mention of Judge Moise for a long time, I think possibly one of the reasons for this was that Judge Moise, after the decision of the returning board had been rendered, gave the

---

history. In the 1896 state elections, the Populists, out of desperation, joined with the Regular Republicans (holdovers from Reconstruction) and the national Lily White Republican party (formed in 1894 by the state's sugar planters in opposition to President Grover Cleveland's low tariff policies) and fielded a Fusion candidate, John N. Pharr, for governor, against the incumbent Murphy Foster. Foster was reelected. The national Republicans and the Populists made another unsuccessful attempt for the governorship in 1900 when they ran the Fusion candidate Donelson Caffery, Jr., against William Heard. This was the last election in which the Louisiana Populist party entered a candidate. Hair, *Bourbonism and Agrarian Protest*, 200–79; Perry H. Howard, *Political Tendencies in Louisiana, 1812–1952* (Baton Rouge: Louisiana State University Press, 1957), 172–75.

Picayune an interview in which he pointed out that the lottery faction had overlooked some good chances to get evidence in their favor before the board. Some years later Baker and Edgar Farrar [a New Orleans attorney] had some trouble. Baker pulled a gun on Farrar. He was arrested and Judge Moise, who had been appointed to the Criminal District Court bench by Governor Foster, fined him $1000. That did nothing to improve relations between the judge and Mr. Baker.

I do not claim to have any firsthand knowledge of this phase of the incident, but I have been told that Mr. Baker specially objected to his fine because [Dominick] C. O'Malley [editor of the New Orleans *Item*] and Colonel C. Harrison Parker had been fined only $2.50 each by Judge Moise for shooting each other up in Camp street some time before Mr. Baker appeared in court.

Colonel Parker could stand all kinds of abuse and criticism without flinching and was not always very particular about what he wrote or said about his opponents, but he could not stand ridicule. *The Item* printed a cartoon, as I remember it, that ridiculed him. Perhaps it was an editorial, I am not sure. Colonel Parker greased his cannon and went around into Camp street. O'Malley came out of his office and they both yelled and started shooting. They were both good shots. I was not there and I am glad I was not there, as one of the bullets hit a newsboy in the leg, and I would prefer not to be shot in the leg or anywhere else.

Had it not been that O'Malley's first shot wounded Col. Parker in the right arm and Col. Parker's first shot nearly paralyzed O'Malley, one or the other would no doubt have been killed. As it was, both were seriously wounded. In view of the damage they did each other, they were let off with light fines. There was a rumor at the time that Judge Moise had negotiated a treaty between them in which it was agreed that they would not shoot at each other anymore. Whether that is true I do not know, but it is a fact that they did not speak to each other from that day to the time they met in Baton Rouge in 1912. I have been told that William F. Millsaps, of Monroe, one of the best lawyers in Louisiana, who went to the Capital with Governor Hall[15] as his secretary because of long friendship between them, made a suggestion to O'Malley and Col. Parker that resulted in their shaking hands and forgetting old scores.

[John S.] Young became sheriff in Caddo [Parish] shortly after Governor Foster was inaugurated. Moise was appointed to the criminal district court. I lost sight of Sheriff Young, but Judge Moise was right here in New Orleans so I saw and heard something of him. He made one of the best judges we ever had. He was continued on the bench until he died. In addition to his work as judge, he worked for a long time on a code of the criminal laws that was never adopted by the legislature.

I forgot to mention that one of the reasons for McEnery's support of the lottery was the offer of the Louisiana Lottery Company to bind itself if granted a new franchise, to maintain levees.

I forgot to state that the lottery company practically quit the fight when its business on a large scale was no longer practical. It was no longer possible, even if they had succeeded in getting their franchise amendment adopted, for them to pay the enormous sums provided for by D. Lawton and others in the terms of the amendment.

For a long time after tickets in the Honduras and the Mexican lotteries were almost openly sold in New Orleans. The daily drawings however, did not take place any more. A number of the men interested in the Louisiana Lottery Company, and others living in New York, were indicted by the grand jury at Mobile in May of 1907 for running a lottery. The case was never tried but,

---

15. Luther E. Hall was governor of Louisiana, 1912–16. Behrman discusses Hall's career as governor in more detail in Chapter III, herein.

I am told, that was the real end of the Louisiana lottery. Every now and then an arrest is made in New Orleans for violation of the anti-lottery laws, but these are small matters almost in the class of raffles.

And yet despite the law against raffles, a certain Southern city [New Orleans] is compelled by formal agreement with purchases of its bonds to conduct a raffle at legally fixed dates. The city issued what are known as "premium" bonds and the bonds are selected for payment by drawing numbers from a wheel just as the Louisiana lottery numbers were drawn under the supervision of General [P.G.T.] Beauregard and General [Jubal] Early.[16] No legal test of the premium bond lottery has even been made but I rather think the city would win out if there was a test. I do not think the anti-lottery law would hold in a case of that kind.

As I am now getting away from the days of the Louisiana lottery, I will say that I never had the luck to hold a winning ticket. I bought a fractional ticket every month. Some men with money would buy a whole ticket, but mine was always a fraction. I remember visiting the Academy of Music to see General Beauregard and General Jubal Early from the river to Rampart preside over the drawings. Despite a lot of loose talk to the contrary, the drawings of the Louisiana Lottery were above suspicion. The evil of the lottery was on the daily drawings. Persons of smaller means than mine played these daily drawings constantly. Servants would steal a few nickels from the market to play. I realized this long after the business was closed out.

One of the incidents of the lottery fight was that it brought

---

16. The monthly drawings of the Louisiana Lottery Company were conducted by former Confederate generals P. G. T. Beauregard and Jubal A. Early. Besides the theatrics of the occasion, these prominent participants added an air of respectability. The two also acted as lobbyists for the company in the state legislature. Hair, *Bourbonism and Agrarian Protest*, 26–27.

[Mayor] John Fitzpatrick and James D. Houston[17] together as friends. I remember my astonishment when I came on them in an office, both stretched full length on rattan lounges, conferring about the campaign.

It was during the years just before the lottery campaign that the growth of the city and the deaths of Patrick Mealey and Thomas Duffy shifted political power. The "Big Four" of 1888, composed of Mealey, Duffy, John Fitzpatrick and Robert C. Davey, were ward leaders and members of the caucus of seventeen. Their greater power was due to the heavy vote in their wards and the patronage they naturally controlled for this reason.

Pat Mealey was commissioner of police and public buildings when he was killed by Louis Clair.[18]

Political power tended to spread itself more evenly among the wards. Some leaders, of course, due to heavy votes in their wards or greater personal activity (and sometimes due to good luck) are always more powerful than others, but there was no more "Big Four" dominating the organization after Mealey and Duffy were gone.

One of the peculiar results of the lottery campaign was *The Times-Democrat's* loss of prestige and the fact that the ward leaders did not lose their strength through support of the lottery. This is an impression of mine, a recollection of things as they were then. It seemed to me that after the campaign there was less general confidence in *The Times-Democrat.*

While we were defeated in the state fight, we won in the city and elected John Fitzpatrick as mayor. It was during his admin-

---

17. James D. Houston was a political agent for the Louisiana Lottery Company and one of the most influential figures in the Democratic-Conservative party in New Orleans during the first two decades following Reconstruction.

18. Patrick Mealey, commissioner of Police and Public Buildings, was murdered on New Year's Day, 1888, by Louis Clare (several newspapers spelled the name as *Claire*, and the city directory for 1888 had *Clair*), a recently appointed policeman with a long record for disorderly conduct. Jackson, *New Orleans in the Gilded Age*, 236.

Early Career in Politics

istration that charges of malfeasance were made against a number of the members of the council and a few of them were convicted. A committee of 25 citizens tried to have Mayor Fitzpatrick impeached, but they did not succeed in doing so.[19]

One of the newspapers hinted that he had been guilty of wrongdoing himself and he filed suit and recovered damages.

I think this is an appropriate place to set down some of the accomplishments of the Fitzpatrick term. The public is inclined to forget and I am glad of this opportunity to remind whoever may read these recollections of mine that John Fitzpatrick was an able administrator and a progressive mayor. John Fitzpatrick was an orphan boy. He started life as a carpenter. He is the kind of man, the "silk stocking" element of those days did not consider a proper person for important public offices. I cannot review his administration in all its details without a month or more of investigation to refresh my memory, but I remember all the larger things.

The volunteer fire department was replaced by the paid department under a contract signed December 15, 1891, by Mayor Joseph Shakespeare. He was defeated for re-election and the carrying out of the contract was left to Mayor Fitzpatrick. The contract price was $700,000 for the equipment owned by the volunteers and practically all of it was paid during the

---

19. In 1894 the Citizens' Protective Association of New Orleans, while investigating cases of bribery and graft in the New Orleans city government uncovered a major scandal in the construction of the courthouse and jail on Tulane Avenue and Saratoga Street. The investigation and allegations went all the way to the city council and the office of Mayor John Fitzpatrick. Although the contract was awarded during Mayor Joseph Shakspeare's reform administration, the actual construction was begun and completed (1892-94) during Fitzpatrick's term and paid for three years ahead of time. Although no evidence of criminal misconduct was found, the citizens' group and the district attorney filed suit in civil court asking for the impeachment of Fitzpatrick on the grounds of "nonfeasance, malfeasance, favoritism, corruption, and gross misconduct." Fitzpatrick was found not guilty on all counts. In spite of the boodle scandals and the widespread labor unrest, Fitzpatrick put the city on a sound financial footing in a time when the rest of the nation was suffering severe economic recession. *Ibid.*, 136-137; Kendall, *History of New Orleans*, II, 11, 506.

Fitzpatrick administration. It was not generally expected that the money would be paid as agreed as the revenues were small, but Mayor Fitzpatrick saw the means far in advance and took advantage of the situation to the general satisfaction of all concerned.

Another big contract entered into by the Shakespeare administration and left to the "Regulars" by the "reformers" was the building and furnishing of the courthouse, parish prison and first precinct station at Tulane avenue and Saratoga street. They cost about $450,000 with the furnishings and the money was paid out during the Fitzpatrick administration.

The question of excessive wharf charges came up. The Louisiana Construction and Improvement Company had a 10-year lease that did not expire until May of 1901. Mayor Fitzpatrick helped with some missionary work among the commercial exchanges, which were already worried over the situation. The exchanges took the matter up and petitioned the [city] council to take over the wharves and have them operated by the city government. His term came to an end and the next administration, under Mayor Walter C. Flower [1896–1900] repealed the ordinance, the legislature adopted the act creating the Dock Board and putting the river front under the control of the state government.[20]

A great many streets had been improved with stone blocks and some with plank driveways before Mayor Fitzpatrick's term, but it was then gravel. Owing to the dust and the need of watering it and the fact that city traffic is harder on a roadway than country traffic, the gravel did not turn out so well as was expected, but the people were satisfied with it at the time. There was not sufficient money to use the large granite blocks that then paved Canal street in the business district, Magazine street, Poydras street and many other main thoroughfares. The financial situation made gravel the best at the time.

20. The Louisiana General Assembly created the Board of Commissioners of the Port of New Orleans, commonly referred to as the Dock Board, by Act. No. 70, in 1896.

The old gas lamps were done away with and electric lights, the present system, were installed. The small boys were deprived of the fun of annoying the gas man as he came around at sunset to light the gas lamps.

I have gone more fully into the matter in this chapter as the enemies and opponents of my old friend have done so much to obscure the good work he did and play up the fact that there was some dishonesty discovered in the council, which they always refer to as the "Fitzpatrick council" or the "boodle council." I will put it up to any responsible man like this: If John Fitzpatrick had been in any way responsible for those occurrences in the council, would he have filed suit against and recovered damages from a newspaper for an attack on his character? Could he have continued as a powerful figure in politics for another 25 years?

I had taken the position of deputy assessor [in 1888] because it appeared to be a generally better job than that of traveling salesman and Mrs. Behrman preferred to have me more at home. I got the sidelines such as taking the census simply to add a little to my income. I did not feel like I was a politician at that time. Even when I quickly organized a new faction in Algiers and beat the two older factions, I was not yet fully conscious of the fact that I had become a politician. But when I sat in the caucus with the mayor-elect, John Fitzpatrick [1892–1896] and discussed the apportionment of the patronage and found that whatever I had to say to those older and much more experienced men was listened to with real attention—well, I realized that Martin Behrman had become a politician.

I must confess that I do not remember who represented the fourteenth ward at the caucus. That was thirty years ago and the fourteenth ward was probably of not much more weight, if as much, as my ward—the fifteenth. I remember all the others.

C. Taylor Gauche, then and now assessor, who was with his brother as a firm of brokers in wholesale crockery in Natchez [street] near Magazine [street], represented the first ward.

Congressman Robert C. Davey, who was interested in F. Johnson & Sons, undertaking a livery establishment at Julia and Magazine, represented the second ward. John Fitzpatrick, who had been a carpenter but was then interested in Marion & Company, sat for the third. Victor Mauberret, an assessor, who got his main income from his printing establishment, represented the fourth.

I do not remember what private or public work Alex Pujol had just then, but he represented the fifth. John Brewster, district tax collector, was there for the sixth and Louis Knop for the seventh. Joseph Hirn, an assessor, sat for the eighth. Mr. Hirn's barber shop next to the Sazarac in Royal Street was a centre for both the local and state politicians.

Ferdinand Dudenheffer represented the ninth ward. Mr. Dudenheffer was a hard worker in every worthy cause and a sort of father to his neighborhood and his ward and he did a great deal of good in his time. It goes to show that we can never tell what will become of our personalities in the memories of the people, for only those who knew him now remember that he did anything but lead his ward and introduce the theatre-hat law at Baton Rouge. This is the law that requires ladies to remove their hats before the curtain goes up.

Peter Farrell sat for the tenth, James Malloy for the eleventh and L. B. McMurray for the twelfth ward. Mr. McMurray was a stenographer at the civil district court, as was also John T. Michel of the thirteenth ward. O. A. Trezevant was there for the sixteenth and Fred Deibel, an assessor, for the seventeenth.

I had had a conference with the men in Algiers of my faction before I went to the caucus and they agreed with me that I should go after a city hall clerkship as a fair share of the offices for Algiers. Up to that time my ward had had no offices that did not necessarily go to it under the law. I had decided on the position of clerk to the budget committee, the public order committee, and the streets and landings committee, all one job, and I had my reasons for it. There was no other place that I could get which would give me so good a chance to learn something of the city government. A great deal of business was done before discussion came to me and my ward. I told them what I wanted and got it.

Alex Pujol sat next to John Brewster in the caucus in John Fitzpatrick's home after Fitzpatrick had been elected mayor in 1892. I remember that after discussion came around to Algiers and the three clerkships to the committees of the city council, I made my position clear and Brewster said: "Well, let's give one of those clerkships to the young fellow from Algiers."

Alex leaned over and said something half-privately to Brewster. I knew he had told him the name of the young fellow from Algiers was Martin Behrman.

W. A. Brand, then an insurance man, was chairman of the budget committee. As his clerk, I assisted in drawing up the budgets of income and expenditures. No man could do that without learning a lot. Charles Noel, then of the firm of Lambou & Noel, lumber dealers, was chairman of the streets and landings committee. All applications for street paving, most of which were applications for switch track privileges and so forth came to this committee. Decision and even proposal to pave a street usually caused a near-riot.

As the city government has been in the form of a combination for ten years, there are many voters who do not remember these committees.[21] The brief references I have made to their work, however, will make it clear that their work had an excellent opportunity to learn something of municipal government. I

21. Behrman is referring to the reorganization of the New Orleans municipal government under the city charter of 1912. According to the new charter the city was to be administered by a commission form of government consisting of a mayor and four councilmen at-large. The commission replaced the city council created by the charter of 1896, which consisted of seventeen councilmen, representing each of the city's seventeen wards and two councilmen-at-large. Kendall, *History of New Orleans*, II, 523–25, 548–49.

have read many books on municipal government and hundreds of magazine articles. Most of them were written by men who did systems and details but also colored their writings with their opinions. As a result, most of them would have done better if they had actually engaged in such work as I had as a clerk of those committees.

While I was a clerk to the three most important committees of the council, budget, public order and streets and landings, I was elected to the school board. I had the pleasure of adding several schools in Algiers. While I worked for all the city in the course of my duty to the committees and the council, Algiers was always on my mind.

3.
Samuel D. McEnery

While dealing with these early years before the constitutional convention of 1898, during which Samuel Douglas McEnery, then a resident of Monroe, was an active leader in every campaign. I wish to say a few words about this remarkable man. He spent the greater part of his life in the turmoil and strife of factional politics inside the Democratic party and struggle against the Republicans and their thousands of black voters.

I heard of him for years before I ever saw him. He was one of the real leaders of the white people in the days when the alliance between some of the republicans, the carpet baggers, and the negroes was a danger to the state. Personally, he was one of the most soft-hearted kindest men I have ever known. Politically, he was a fierce and determined fighter. In later years, according to the impression that has stayed with me, McEnery was never able to put as much fire into a fight against the Republicans and the negroes. That was natural, of course.

The great work of the McEnery administration at Baton Rouge was the organization of the levee districts and levee

Early Career in Politics

boards and the beginning of the present system of protection from floods. He put his whole energy into that work and as evidence of the skill with which he organized it the fact is that there has been no substantial departure from his ideas. Time and time again efforts have been made in the legislature to change the system, and even to abolish the levee boards, but they never get more than a few votes even when they come to a vote. McEnery's idea was that those who would suffer most from a flood should have control as much as possible of the levees and it has worked out very well.

McEnery was appointed as associate justice of the state supreme court by Foster after the Foster-McEnery campaign of 1892. He looked upon himself as practically retired from politics and destined to complete his life as a judge. The crisis that took him off the bench and in 1896 sent him to the U. S. Senate in Washington for the rest of his life will be described later in these recollections. I may say now, however, that his campaign expenses when he was elected senator was the price of a telegram to Baton Rouge indicating that he would accept the toga. He borrowed $10 for his expenses to go to Baton Rouge and formally accept it.

McEnery lived such a long and interesting life that many stories are told about him. Those which concern his earlier career in the days before I knew him are not a part of my recollections, but I have often wondered why some of the newspapermen have not written the story of his life.

McEnery and Foster sat next to each other in the U. S. Senate. One day a page brought a message from a newspaperman. McEnery had become very deaf. He went out to see the newspaperman and in a few minutes returned and said to Foster:

"These reporters have got a lot of gall. That fellow called me out of the senate to ask me for a cigar."

"Did you give it to him?" Foster inquired.

"Yes. I gave it to him and turned my back on him. I did not

want him to see how mad I was. The idea of calling a senator away from his desk to ask him for a cigar."

Later in the day Foster met the newspaperman who was as much astonished as had been Senator McEnery. He had asked the deaf senator something about the tariff and received a cigar instead of a reply.

Of course, every state-wide campaign is to some extent decisive of big things. The campaign of 1882 made McEnery governor and gave us the levee system. The campaign of 1892 dealt with the death blow to the lottery campaign. But I have often thought that 1896 was the biggest year, in its ultimate effects, since the hold of the carpetbaggers on the state government had been broken. The events of that year led to the constitutional convention of 1898 in which the negroes were eliminated from political power. It put McEnery in the senate and developed the situation that put Foster there and kept him there for two terms.

The campaign made by Henry M. Pharr[22] in 1896 was the last statewide fight in which the Republicans made any real showing in Louisiana and the last general election in which the negroes cast any considerable number of votes. The Citizens' League defeated the Regular Democratic candidates in New Orleans on the same day that the state election was held. Foster had been nominated in a convention at Shreveport.[23]

---

22. John N. Pharr.
23. In the 1896 gubernatorial election, incumbent Murphy J. Foster defeated the National Republican and Populist Fusion candidate John N. Pharr by a vote of 116,216 to 90,138. The Fusionists, accusing the Democrats of voter fraud and intimidation, took their case to the state legislature hoping to get a legislative inquiry into the returns. In a special vote held on May 14, they lost their bid for the investigation by a vote of 68 to 48. The Citizens' League of New Orleans, which had formerly stood with the Populists against Foster, deserted the Fusionists during the crucial vote after receiving promises from Foster for a new city charter for New Orleans. The returns stood as reported, and Foster was reelected for a second term. This election marked the beginning of the end for the Populist party in Louisiana.

In the New Orleans mayoralty contest, held on the same day as the state elections,

That was the most bitterly fought campaign. The fight went to the legislature. The Citizens' League had elected Walter C. Flower as mayor and controlled a majority of the city delegations and the acceptance of all in regular form and properly signed, and the rejection of all others, the tabulation showed that Governor Foster had been re-elected.

There was a move to go behind the returns. Among those who voted with the majority against it were three senators elected by the Citizens' League.

There was a very intense and dangerous situation at the capitol. Captain C. Taylor Cade, sheriff of Iberia Parish, had a steamboat in the river and it was reported that he had a cannon on the boat and was ready to start a bombardment. Captain Allen Jumel, who held many state offices during his long life and died while custodian of the capitol, was one of the prominent figures on the Foster side. The leaders from New Orleans gathered with many of their men in the Jackson house a block from the state house and they had men posted all over Baton Rouge in expectation of serious trouble. The Pharr leaders had another house a block further on.

Somebody dropped a pistol on the steps going up from the ground floor of the capitol to the second floor where the senate and the house meet. It exploded. I have not since seen so many guns drawn all at one time. Everybody seemed to think that the threatened bloodshed was about to begin. But they were all cool-headed men, apparently, for nobody fired in haste and

---

Governor Foster refused to back the reform Citizens' League candidate, New Orleans businessman Walter C. Flower. Instead Foster supported the Crescent Democratic Club's (Regular) candidate, Congressman Charles F. Buck. Mayor Fitzpatrick was refused the Regular's renomination because of the boodle scandals during his administration and also because of the deep resentment Foster had for Fitzpatrick dating back to the 1892 lottery fight. The Crescent Democratic Club fell apart during the campaign, and there were mass desertions to the Citizens' League. Flower was elected mayor, receiving 23,345 votes to Buck's 17,295. Hair, *Bourbonism and Agrarian Protest*, 266–67; Jackson, *New Orleans in the Gilded Age*, 314–15.

when they saw it was an accident they all laughed and stored away their artillery again.

Walter C. Flower had been elected mayor by the Citizens' League, and that faction controlled a majority of the council. Governor Foster however, recognized the Regular Democrats and appointed them to the state jobs in New Orleans.

Governor Foster was severely roasted by one of the lottery newspapers because so many of the minor positions in the Dock Board's service were given to members of the Regular Democratic organization. I remember thinking then what nonsense it was to critize men who had the giving of such places for giving them to their political friends. How would it do to give them to your enemies? What good would it do to give them to men who took no interest in politics and would not be active in promoting the policies that had elected official(s) friendly to them? Some of the reformers, then and now, seem to think that taking an active interest in politics should disqualify a man from holding an appointive position.

[In 1896] after the Citizens' League had won but his faction had lost in the state fight, Walter Denegre[24] loomed up as a candidate for the United States senate. He was what we called a "silk stocking," a term that seems to be going out of use. It was used to designate a man of wealth and education out of touch with the average citizen and presumably unsympathetic with the great mass of the working people. Of course, none of us ever call a prominent and wealthy citizen a "silk stocking" if he happens to be with us in politics.

Newton C. Blanchard[25] was Denegre's rival in 1896 in the

---

24. Walter Denegre, a New Orleans attorney and member of the reform Young Men's Democratic Association, supported the successful candidacy of Joseph Shakspeare over the Crescent Democratic Club's Judge Robert C. Davey in the 1888 mayoralty election. In 1892 he again backed Shakspeare in his unsuccessful bid for reelection. Denegre was also a member of the Citizens' League (the Y.M.D.A.'s successor) in 1896 when its candidate, Walter C. Flower, defeated Charles F. Buck.

25. Newton C. Blanchard was governor of Louisiana, 1904–1908. See footnote 53 of this chapter for a biographical sketch.

fight for the U. S. senate. He impressed me as a very able man and but for the mention of Samuel McEnery's name I would have been very glad to see him win the election. Victor Mauberret,[26] who in later years was very close to Robert Broussard, was very close to Blanchard at the time.

It was a long, hard-fought struggle. Two members consistently voted for McEnery from the start but nobody, until practically the last minute , figured on McEnery's election. I was there through interest and watched the fight from start to finish.

Denegre was practically elected when he polled within one vote of a majority and one of the Blanchard men rose in their seat. It was plain that he intended to change his vote from Blanchard to Denegre and thus end the long fight, of which all concerned had grown heartily tired. Robert Landry was clerk. The member on his feet had the privilege of changing his vote before the result of the poll was announced. Before he could get the floor, Landry, quick as a flash, announced the vote. Then there was a motion to adjourn.

With the Blanchard vote and the two votes of the McEnery men together, either Blanchard or McEnery would have a majority over Denegre. It was impossible to get those two men over. So a telegram was sent to Samuel D. McEnery asking if he would accept the toga. I do not pretend to remember the exact words, but the answer was practically this:

"I will accept if elected but I want you to know that I am a high tariff man."

As there was plenty of free trade sentiment in those days, especially in North and Central Louisiana and in New Orleans, that was a very courageous message. McEnery was elected.

Both McEnery and Foster did all they could to get good tariff protection for Louisiana's interests. McEnery got the nickname of "Old Molasses." When the insurgents began their agitation

26. Victor Mauberret was boss of the city's Fourth Ward and one of the dominant figures in the caucuses of both the Crescent Democratic Club and its successor the Choctaw Club of Louisiana.

in Washington, with the backing of many daily papers, many weeklies and magazines, "Old Molasses" was generally held up to criticism for his high tariff votes. His only answer was that his people had twice elected him as a high tariff man and he intended to continue to be that.[27]

There was a great many intimations that McEnery had accumulated a fortune through benefits of the tariff to the sugar industry. The fact is that he was not personally interested in sugar. Just at the time he was being roasted by a magazine writer, along about 1907 or 1908, he mortgaged his home at St. Mary and Chestnut streets.

4.

Choctaw Club Formed

The theory that a thing can be done because it is a good thing to do seems to run through a great deal of what I have read about city government. That is not true. It frequently happens that a very good thing cannot be done for the simple reason that the public does not recognize it as worth the cost or the inconvenience. It frequently takes years and years of agitation and education to popularize a thing which well-informed men and women of the generation before knew to be a good thing. Then, after it has been done despite the bitter opposition of considerable numbers of citizens, complaint will be made of the way it was done. No matter what you do or do not do in municipal

---

27. Senator Samuel D. McEnery, a Democrat, fought for high protective tariffs during Republican president Theodore Roosevelt's campaign to lower tariffs on Cuban and Philippine sugar. In 1903 Roosevelt was able to get a bill through Congress giving Cuban sugar a 20 percent tariff reduction in return for a 20-to-40 percent discount on American goods entering Cuba, a decided advantage for eastern manufacturers but to the detriment of Louisiana sugarcane and western sugar beet growers. Many Democrats, their party traditionally supporting low tariffs, crossed party lines in support of Roosevelt's tariff policies. George E. Mowry, *The Era of Theodore Roosevelt and the Birth of Modern America, 1900–1912* (New York: Harper and Brothers, 1958), 129.

government, municipal politics will get you a lot of criticism. I learned this when I was a clerk of those committees.

On the other hand, it is often necessary to force a thing through despite the opposition of a majority of the people. There is no doubt in my mind that a majority of Orleanians were opposed to the cistern-screening law[28] and to the rat-proofing just as there were many opponents to vaccination all over the world for a long time.

It occurs to me to mention here the number of temporary organizations that have sprung up from time to time in opposition to the faction of which I was lately the leader.

First was the Young Men's Democratic Association of 1888. The negroes voted in those days. They [the negroes] went solidly to the Y.M.D.A., as they did in the Citizens' League campaign of 1896. The Y.M.D.A. died.

Then there came the anti-lottery organization, which had a real issue that was fought out [in 1892]. That organization won in the state fight. The "Regular" faction carried the city.

Next was the Citizens' League of 1896, which elected Walter C. Flower and defeated Charles F. Buck. It fell to pieces and most of its leaders joined the Regulars.

Following that was the "Jacksonian Democracy" of 1899. The real leaders of this movement were Walter C. Flower, running for re-election against Paul Capdevielle, Charles J. Boatner and Walter D. Denegre. Paul Capdevielle won and the Jacksonians disappeared.

Then there was the Home Rule movement in 1904, with Mr. Buck as its candidate against me. William S. Parkerson was its most conspicuous leader and the fight was brief and bitter. I will refer to it again later. However, its organization died when the returns came in.

28. The cisterns were screened in New Orleans during the 1905 yellow fever epidemic. Behrman discusses this epidemic and the city's efforts in Chapter II, herein.

Next was the Good Government League of 1912. It had an effective organization in the parishes but did not have effective organization in New Orleans. It won in the state,[29] lost in the city and disappeared.

Then the Orleans Democratic Association was organized with John M. Parker and John P. Sullivan as its leaders. It won two elections and died as soon as it suffered a defeat.[30] Another organization, however, calling itself the "New Regulars," has followed it. I must necessarily write something about these later on.

Foster's appointment of regulars to state offices in New Orleans after defeat by the Citizens' League [in 1896] was, in my opinion, the beginning of the "city organization" known as the regulars. These appointments gave him a following of about half the leaders in New Orleans. When he came to New Orleans and mixed in local politics, he did it openly. He did not send friends or agents but came himself and *The Times-Democrat* thought this was a very wicked proceeding.

There was some delay in agreeing on a name but I do not remember that any other Indian names were suggested. A souvenir of a Choctaw celebration gives a short history of the club up to that time and shows that the committee on a name considered Chicamauga, Houma, Tensas and Choctaw. Choctaw was adopted by a vote.

We followed the old fashioned way of using an Indian name for a political club. I have been told that this fashion started in New York nearly 150 years ago when a political society, known

---

29. The Good Government League helped elect Luther E. Hall governor in 1912. Behrman refers to both the city and state elections of that year in Chapter III, herein.

30. Behrman is referring to the 1920 state and New Orleans municipal elections. In the gubernatorial election in that year John M. Parker defeated Colonel Frank B. Stubbs, who had the support of Behrman and the Choctaws. The following September, in the New Orleans mayoral election, Andrew McShane, a New Orleans businessman, defeated Behrman with Governor Parker's support. Behrman discusses Parker's role in his defeat in Chapter IV, herein.

Early Career in Politics 35

around town as the "Roebucks" because they used the tail of the buck deer in their hats, went into regular, organized form and adopted the name Tammany society.[31] Tammany was an old Indian chief who was popular with the Americans in the revolution. When the British troops would shout for St. George, the Americans would shout for St. Tammany.

The purposes of the Choctaw Club were set forth in the second article of the charter as follows:

> Believing that it is the duty of every good citizen to take not only a deep interest but an active part in the political affairs of the country, and believing further that the welfare of the country and the continued prosperity of its institutions require for their preservation that the policy and character of the government shall be determined and guided by the principles of the Democratic Party, and IN ORDER TO ADD TO THE ORGANIZED STRENGTH OF THE DEMOCRATIC PARTY IN THE STATE OF LOUISIANA, the object and purposes for which this corporation is organized are declared to be:
> 1st. To uphold the advance Democratic principles.
> 2nd. To promote harmony, enjoyment and literary improvement.
> 3rd. To provide the conveniences of a club house.

It will be noticed that the club was organized [March 12, 1897], the year after the negro vote elected the Citizens' League ticket in New Orleans and came very near to electing the Republicans in the state. The convention that put the negroes out of politics came the next year, in 1898. Insofar as we are concerned, the issue of the negro in politics has come up only once during the 24 years since then. It is hard to make some people, especially some of the younger "reformers," appreciate the fact that in those days the Choctaws did not repre-

---

31. The infamous Tammany Society that dominated New York City politics for over a century was founded in New York in 1788 by William Mooney, an Irish paperhanger, upholsterer, and furniture dealer. The society claimed that it was founded "on the true and genuine principles of republicanism, and holds out as its objects the smile of charity, the chain of friendship, and the flame of liberty." Tammany Hall has become synonymous with machine politics. M. R. Werner, *Tammany Hall* (Garden City, N. Y.: Doubleday, Doran, 1928), 10.

sent a faction. They represented the Democratic party insofar as a political club could represent a party.

The Choctaws were good Democrats who organized against a Republican party in Louisiana and a combination of Republicans and "reformer" Democrats in New Orleans that had proved very strong the year before. It is to the credit of many of those "reformers" of 1896 that they realized the danger of letting the negroes stay in politics and joined with the Choctaws and the Choctaws' allies in the parishes to put an end to that danger. The taxpayers of today do not fully realize that a considerable part of their money is now going to pay interest on bonds for which they got little or nothing. The wildest statements by the "reformers" about waste of public money do not half equal the facts of the extravagances that prevailed when the Republicans governed Louisiana.

I have no doubt whatever that some of my opponents who read what I am writing will say that a great deal of it is more of a political history of my times than personal recollections of Martin Behrman. In answer to them I will say that whatever interested me and remains in my memory is part of my personal recollections. I had a hand in putting the negroes out of politics, which was the best thing done for Louisiana in my time.

Some years ago [in 1916] when John M. Parker was running for governor as a Progressive, *The Item* had it that it was not the Democrats but that it was the white people of Louisiana that did the work. That sounds good but it does not mean anything. The Democratic party represented the white people of Louisiana. Let the editor of *The Item*, look up the record and see how many Republicans sat in the convention of 1898.

It is true that a considerable number of Democrats who had combined with the Republicans to defeat the Democrats with the aid of negro votes did return to the party and help rid the state of that vote. It is not true that any Republicans did.

I am reminded of Henry Clay Warmoth[32].... I did not know him when he was active in politics as a Republican leader and governor of Louisiana, but I knew him very well in later years, and he sometimes dropped in at the mayor's parlor and told me how things should be run. When Warmoth was running for congress against Adolph Meyer, Larry O'Donnell delivered a speech for the Democratic candidates in Lafayette Square. There were a great many negroes in the audience. They tended to gather together at one side or the other of the crowd.

"The Republican party has no use for the negro except as a means of riding into office," said Larry as he turned toward the negroes. "It reminds me of the story of the white man and the negro who got to the gates of heaven at the same time.

"Do you come on foot or on horseback?" St. Peter asked.

"On foot," they replied.

"Go back and get your horses," St. Peter ordered.

They walked some distance from the gates and the white man no doubt a Republican before he died, suggested that if he got astride of the negro and announced that he was mounted, St. Peter would have the gates opened and they would both get in. So the negro consented and the white Republican rode him to the gates.

"I am mounted," he announced to St. Peter.

"Well, come in," St. Peter replied, "but leave your horse outside."

I have often thought that Larry O'Donnell's parable was about right.

After that the Republican party in Louisiana dwindled down to a few leaders and a few followers. Donelson Caffery ran for

32. Henry Clay Warmoth, Reconstruction Republican governor of Louisiana from 1868 to 1872, was impeached by the Republican majority in the state legislature in 1872 during the gubernatorial contest between Democrat John McEnery and Republican William Pitt Kellogg. John McEnery was Samuel McEnery's brother.

Governor against W. W. Heard in 1900 as a Republican or a fusion candidate.[33] The Republican party in Louisiana is now hardly more than a small group of men without hope of every casting an effective vote outside the Democratic primaries.

5.
Constitutional Convention of 1898 and the Negro Vote

Just after the Foster-Pharr and the Citizens' League campaigns of [1896], we had 1962 white and 1399 colored voters in Algiers. In the City of New Orleans there were 48,492 white and 14,174 colored. The totals in the state were 164,088 white and 130,344 colored.

In the parishes outside of New Orleans there were 115,596 whites and 116,168 colored voters.

So my ward was more than 22 per cent black and the whole state was more than 44 per cent black.

Outside New Orleans, the voters in the parishes were more than 50 per cent black.

I was defeated in 1896 by O. I. McLellan, the Citizens' League candidate in Algiers, who later was elected to the state senate from the fifteenth and second wards as the candidate of the Regular Democrats.

The Citizens' League faction was not, strictly speaking a Democratic faction. It was outside the party although most of the white men in it had been and were later members of the Regular faction.

While it was generally denied at the time, it is now generally admitted that the negro vote defeated the Regulars in 1896.

33. Donelson Caffery, Jr., a conservative Democrat and son of U.S. Senator Donelson Caffery (1892–1901), broke with the Foster administration and ran for governor in 1900. He received the support of both the People's party and the combined Populist and Republican Fusionist alliance. Caffery obtained pluralities in Cameron, Ascension, and St. James parishes. The "Regular" Republicans backed Eugene S. Reems. Hair, *Bourbonism and Agrarian Protest*, 278; Howard, *Political Tendencies in Louisiana, 1812–1952*, pp.194—95.

While denying it publicly, for purposes of reinstating political propaganda, the members of the Citizens' League did not deny it in their conduct. I do not remember one of them as an opponent of the Constitutional Convention of 1898. The main purpose of that convention was to put the negroes out of politics. The very man who had benefitted by their votes realized, as a result of the Foster-Pharr state campaign and the Flower-Buck local campaign that it was about time to change conditions.[34]

I remember seeing John Fitzpatrick's office jammed with

---

34. During the 1890s southern states one by one rewrote their constitutions with the primary objective of disfranchising the Negro voter. Each state worked into its new constitution subtle mechanisms designed to achieve this end while appearing, outwardly at least, to adhere to the Fifteenth Amendment of the U.S. Constitution. The three basic methods most employed were the literacy test, property qualifications, and the poll tax. However, certain "escape" clauses were included to allow whites, who could not meet the literacy and property qualifications, to register to vote. Mississippi added an "understanding" clause to its constitution of 1890 which provided that if a potential registrant was not able to read parts of the state constitution, he be able to give a reasonable interpretation of it when read to him. The local voter registrars administered the test. South Carolina followed Mississippi's example in 1895, and Alabama and Georgia later adopted the "good character" clause in addition to the understanding clause as a loophole for whites. Louisiana, in its 1898 constitutional convention, adopted the "grandfather clause" as an exception to the literacy and property requirements in spite of opponents' preferences, including both of Louisiana's U.S. senators, for a Mississippi-type understand clause. The grandfather clause (Article 197, section 5) read in part: "No male person who was in January 1st, 1867, or any date prior thereto, entitled to vote . . . shall be denied the right to register and vote in this state by reason of his failure to possess the educational or property qualifications . . . provided, he shall have resided in this State for five years next preceding the date at which he shall apply for registration, and shall have registered . . . prior to September 1, 1898, and no person shall be entitled to register under this section after said date." The year 1867 was significant in that it was not until the Louisiana "Black Reconstruction" constitution of 1868 that blacks in general were extended full "civil, political, and public rights." Other states copied Louisiana's grandfather clause until 1915 whenthe U.S. Supreme Court declared it unconstitutional (*Guinn and Beal v. U.S., 238 U.S. 347*; and *Myers v. Anderson, 238 U.S. 368*). These decisions did not actually affect Louisiana's constitution since the grandfather clause expired only months after its adoption. The 1921 Louisiana constitutional convention adopted the understanding clause.

Professors C. Vann Woodward and V. O. Key, Jr., asserted in their studies on the South and disfranchisement that poor whites in the hill counties and parishes of Louisiana, those who supported populism in the 1890s, were also the target of disfranchising colored preachers one day as the fight was getting hot. There was a wide variety of colored preachers there but everyone was dressed in black and most of them wore long tailed coats. Their leaders conferred with Fitzpatrick again and again but they were unable to make arrangements satisfactory to themselves and they all went to the Citizens' League.

And the methods used in those days in some of the country parishes were so fatal to colored opponents, that the convention won by 36,170 against 7,578. When the results of an election are absolutely certain, the vote is not usually very heavy.

While the rule of the carpet baggers had been done away with, there were many carpet baggers left in the Republican party in Louisiana. The days of the Ku Klux Klan were over long before my time and the hold of the carpet baggers had been broken. The negroes, however, tended to vote the Republican ticket. In some parishes, the white Democrats bought their leaders or persuaded them. This was uncertain and often expensive work, and I have heard it stated that a cheaper and equally effective method was to get possession of the ballot box and the returns and do the right thing. That kind of business was not good for anybody.

I have my reasons for believing that the negroes, particularly in New Orleans, are vastly better off than they would be if they had the vote. I shall give these reasons later. The only men who really suffered from the elimination of the negroes were some Republicans and a few silk stocking reformers who might have carried some more elections with the black vote.

The figures I have given of the registration as it was in January of 1897, shortly after the Foster-Pharr and Citizens'

---

constitutional conventions. V. O. Key, Jr., *Southern Politics in State and Nation* (New York: Alfred A. Knopf, 1949), 533–99; C. Van Woodward, *Origins of the New South, 1877–1913* (Baton Rouge: Louisiana State University Press, 1951), 321–49, Vol. IX of Wendell Holmes Stephenson and E. Merton Coulter (eds.), *A History of the South* (10 Vols.; Baton Rouge: Louisiana State University Press, 1949–).

League campaigns, indicate the situation as it was then. Between that date and January 11, 1898, the day we voted to hold the convention, the registration in the state fell to 74,133 whites and 12,902 colored voters. It had become evident that the Democrats were determined and would hesitate at nothing to put the convention across. The evidence was so strong and the determination so general.

I had opposition in Algiers when I ran for delegate to the convention but I got 647 votes out of a total of 865. Never in my life have I worked any harder in an election than I did then. I called on every white voter I could get to.

I wanted to get on the committee on suffrage and elections but there was no chance of that. I was a young man and I was not a lawyer and the business of the committee was mainly to write an article that would get around the Federal Constitution. I became a member of the committee on public education, taxation, equalization and exemptions and affairs of the city of New Orleans.[35]

35. In addition to three minor resolutions, Behrman introduced four ordinances that were adopted and added to the constitution. Ordinance 241 provided that the Board of Commissioners of the Orleans Levee District pay for land appropriated for levee purposes. At first he intended the ordinance to apply to the entire state, but fearing its defeat he amended it to apply to New Orleans only and retroactive twelve months prior to its adoption. The amended ordinance passed. Behrman added the twelve-month retroactive section so that his constituents in Algiers, whose property was confiscated after the flood of 1897, would be compensated. Ordinance 214 pertained to apportionment in the legislature, and 191 provided a coroner and assistant coroner for Algiers. The measure that he was most interested in was Ordinance 192, which would have provided children in public schools with free textbooks. He withdrew his original plan seeing its inevitable defeat in committee and later resubmitted a revised plan. The revised ordinance, which was adopted, had the proviso that parents had to swear that they could not afford to buy the books. Furthermore, the ordinance applied only to New Orleans. In later years Behrman remarked: "It turned out that I was right. Very few, if any, parents furnished the affidavit required and this article of the constitution was never much more than a 'dead letter.'"

The idea of free textbooks for Louisiana's school children had to wait another thirty years and for another man—Huey Long. In 1928 Governor Long forced a bill through the state legislature providing free textbooks to all schoolchildren, whether they attended private or public schools. Opponents of Long's bill argued that since a large

Chief Justice Francis T. Nicholls called the delegates to order. He had been badly shot up in the Civil War and he had one eye, one ear, one arm and one leg. I was told at the time that twenty years before that, when he was nominated in a convention for governor, the delegate who nominated him finished the speech as follows:

"And therefore, I nominate, for governor of Louisiana, all that remains of the Honorable Francis T. Nicholls."

John T. Michel, secretary of state, called the roll. Rev. Benjamin M. Palmer of the Presbyterian church offered the prayer. Ernest Kruttschnitt was elected president on motion of Thomas J. Kernan of Baton Rouge. Kurttschnitt made a very able speech. I will quote two or three paragraphs of it.

"In the first place, my fellow citizens," he said, "we are all aware that this convention has been called by the people of the State of Louisiana principally to deal with one question, and we know that but for the existence of that one question this assemblage would not be sitting here today. We know that this convention has been called together by the people of the state to eliminate from the electorate the mass of corrupt and illiterate voters who have degraded our politics during the last quarter of a century.

"The people of this state are not concerned as to details in this matter but they have expressed themselves upon a principle."

At the close of his speech, he said:

"May this hall, where thirty-two years ago the negro first entered upon the unequal contest for supremacy, and which

---

percentage of the schools, particularly in southern Louisiana, were Catholic schools the bill was in violation of the U.S. Constitution in the separation of church and state. Long countered this argument by stating that the books were being given to the children and not the schools. The schools were merely dispersing them (Act 100, 1928 Regular Session of the state legislature). T. Harry Williams, *Huey Long* (New York: Alfred A. Knopf, 1969), 307–308; *Official Journal of the Proceedings of the Constitutional Convention of the State of Louisiana, 1898* (New Orleans: H. J. Hearsey, Convention Printer, 1898).

has been reddened with his blood, now witness the evolution of our organic law which will establish the relations between the races upon an everlasting foundation of right and justice."

Charles J. Boatner, who had moved from Monroe to New Orleans and had been elected as a statewide delegate, offered the first piece of important business. He had been elected by 35,082 votes. He got the greatest vote given any delegate because of his long and dangerous service against the carpet bagger Republicans and negroes in North Louisiana, where the blacks were in the majority by a wide margin. Nobody had then forgotten the fact that Charles J. Boatner had had to hide out in the woods, separated for a whole year from his family and his closer friends, as the result of a clash between the two parties known as the "Colfax riot."[36]

Boatner introduced the following resolution on the second day of the convention.

"That no ordinance or proposition intended to become a part of the constitution, nor any resolution, motion or order referring to or concerning any provision in the constitution, shall be considered by this convention until the report of the committee on suffrage and elections shall have been made to and finally acted on by the convention."

When you consider Kruttschnitt's speech and Boatner's resolution the temper of the convention is easily seen. Kruttschnitt was rather a quiet man, but he got all worked up as he addressed the delegates and thought of the future. Boatner considered that the real fight was over and he was determined that the principal business of the convention should not be intefered with. So he offered what he thought was best as the "clincher."

I remember that a majority of the newspapers all over the state lambasted the convention and the delegates from begin-

---

36. For the Colfax Riot, see note 2 of this chapter.

ning to end of the sessions. The convention met February 8th and adjourned May 12th, a little over three months, and my memory is that not a day passed but that there was mention in the hall or the committee rooms or on the streets of some attack by a newspaper edition. My recollection is that most of them were not worth any attention. Anyhow, if we had tried to follow the advice of the newspaper editors, the convention would probably have broken up due to the death of the members. Most of the newspapers had predicted that the delegates to that convention had dug their political graves, which shows how much they knew about the feeling among their readers. Most of the politicians not elected to the convention said the same thing.

From the day the convention began its session to March 25th, six weeks, the matter of suffrage and the negro was the center of interest and debate. As I have said, the newspapers pounded the convention and the principal men in it every day and predicted that we were all headed for private life. I have a vague recollection that one country weekly announced that the delegate from that parish did not dare come home.

Contention over a matter that is of great interest today came up when Charles J. Boatner pressed his "understanding clause" for adoption as against the grandfather clause, educational qualifications, etc. that were finally adopted. I have no copy of the Boatner ordinance but I remember that it was a carefully prepared plan and it came very close to getting ahead of the ordinance that finally became part of the constitution. It was a legal question and not a matter of preference as to the actual working of the suffrage plan that interested the delegates. All they wanted to do was to put the negro out of politics by such means that the supreme court of the United States could not put him back again.

My recollection of the Boatner "understanding clause," as it was called, is that it was the same as the provision now in the

[1921] constitution. It was intended to get as many white men on the rolls as possible and keep out as many negroes as possible by giving the registrar of voters very great authority. They could read a short and simple section of the federal constitution to a white man and a very long and complicated one to a negro. The convention preferred the plan it adopted, with the "grandfather clause" as the chief means of reaching its end.

If Charles J. Boatner had lived, he would have had the satisfaction of reading a decision of the United States supreme court that sustained his contentions. He died in March of 1903, just before the beginning of the Blanchard-Jastremski campaign [for governor] in which I was elected state auditor.

When the supreme court finally got this matter before it so it could finally decide the issue, the decision went against the preference of the convention of 1898 and now we have the "understanding clause" in our constitution as a result of the convention of 1921. However, the work of the convention got the results the people wanted and there was no particular excitement [in 1915] when the supreme court knocked out the suffrage plan in 1898. As the negroes had no votes of any consequence and the Republicans did not have even one member of the legislature, they were powerless to prevent the adoption of the "understanding clause."

The poll tax qualification[37] caused a great deal of contention. Dr. Henry Dickson Bruns, [a delegate at large from Orleans Parish and] a member of the committee on suffrage and elections, brought in a minority report in which he objected to the omission of that provision from the ordinance as reported by the committee. This ordinance was the result of long debate in and

---

37. 1898 Constitution of Louisiana, Article 198. According to the eminent American historian C. Vann Woodward, the poll tax was another bit of machinery introduced to restrict Negro voters who were not eliminated by the grandfather clause and some of the less-desirable white voters. C. Vann Woodward, *The Strange Career of Jim Crow* (New York: Oxford University Press, 1955), 84.

out of the committee room. It was a new draft, a combination of whatever the committee liked best in the many suffrage ordinances introduced. The requirement that a voter must have paid his poll taxes for the two years prior to an election was looked upon by many as a means of putting the Choctaws and their friends in the country in the minority. I shall discuss this more in detail later on.

One of the proofs that there was no attempt to use the "steam roller" on the members who preferred another suffrage plan was that at one time I. D. Moore, later judge of the court of appeals here and [New Orleans] city attorney, made a motion that put the ordinance before the convention for debate. There was no disposition to rush it through without hearing all criticism and objections. At the end of this particular debate, the whole ordinance was withdrawn by Chairman T. F. Bell "in order to allow the committee to prepare and present a substitute ordinance which would unite all sections of the state."

There were two delegates in the convention not there as Democrats. One was John Deblieux, of Iberville [Parish] Republican, and the other B. W. Bailey, of Winn [Parish] Populist. They were both in the 28 who voted against the suffrage ordinance.

Dr. Burns explained his vote against it. He was against the grandfather clause. He pointed out that while men registered under the educational and the property clauses might be removed from the rolls by court proceedings, men registered under the grandfather clause could not be. He was against the poll tax clause as written with the addition that it would not go into effect until 1900. He wanted it to go into effect immediately. I think Dr. Burns was in favor of a straight educational qualification for the vote. That would have given the Democratic party full control because of the large number of illiterates among the negroes, but the convention worked with the idea of having as many whites and as few black voters as possible, regardless of their literacy or illiteracy. That was what the white voters wanted and that is what they got.

Both our senators at Washington were afraid that Ordinance No. 205 might be used in an attack on our representation in congress and our presidential electors. The whole South was then busy on the problem of keeping the negroes away from the polls. There was some agitation in Republican states to cut down representation by basing it on the total registration or the total vote cast rather than on population. Nothing came of it.

There were 28 delegates who voted against the suffrage ordinance. The ordinance got 95 votes. There were 134 delegates and it needed 68 to be adopted. While the exact number of votes that the suffrage ordinance would get was not known in advance, it was absolutely certain that any suffrage ordinance would be adopted. Many of us who voted for it realized that it could not claim to be absolutely perfect. However, we had to face conditions different from those of any other state.

While other states have their racial problems and immigration problems, very few of them have so widely varying populations as Louisiana. We had the Creoles[38] as a majority in the Southern and Southwestern parishes and some of the river parishes above New Orleans, the almost pure English in the central and Northern sections and the Florida parishes, with the negroes in large numbers everywhere but in the pine tree hills. I do not know of any other Southern states that had to face the conditions in Louisiana. For this reason and others it was not to be expected that any suffrage ordinance would get every vote in the convention. However, I am quite sure that every delegate present was absolutely in favor of keeping the negroes off the registration rolls.

While I have not attempted to give a complete review of the

---

38. In this context Behrman is referring to the French-speaking people in southern Louisiana. In colonial Louisiana it meant anyone who was native born, except Indians.

convention of 1898, and have no doubt forgotten for the time being many incidents I would enjoy telling about. I have told most of what I think may be of great interest at present. If other matters occur to me later I will review them at that time. I am not attempting to give everything in the order of events.

There were 108 members of the house of representatives and 30 of them were not "regular" Democrats.[39] The nine straight out Republicans included Henry Clay Warmoth Casacalvo, a negro who managed to retain a certain degree of good standing with the white people of Baton Rouge in after years.

There were no Republicans in the next legislature, elected in 1900. Some of them, of course, saw that the vast majority of the people of Louisiana were determined not to have a Republican party in the states and they became Democrats. They accepted the decision in good faith and lived up to it, at least in state and local elections.

The results are shown in the total registration of 1896 and 1900 in the following statistics:[40]

	1896	
	White	Colored
Literate	123,960	31,587
Illiterate	28,307	95,876

	1900	
	White	Colored
Under educational qualification	86,157	4,327
Under property qualification	10,793	916
Under Section	24,487	111

39. In the 1896 house of representatives of the Louisiana General Assembly there were nine Republicans, primarily from the southern sugar-growing parishes, sixteen Populists, four Independent Democrats, and two Independents.

40. Behrman's statistics were not entirely correct. In 1896 there were 153,174 white

Early Career in Politics

Section five included the grandfather clause and foreigners naturalized before 1898. This section of the constitution provided a special registration book for Section 5 to be closed August 31st, 1898, which gave a little more than three and a half months for such registration.

Look at the results. The negro vote was cut from a total of 127,463, of which three-quarters were illiterates, to 5,354 with 4,327 registered under the educational clause.

There are many other interesting things indicated by this small batch of figures. One of them is that the total white vote under the property qualification and Section 5 in 1900 was 6,973 greater than the total of white illiterates registered in 1896. The difference is doubtless due to the large number of literate white men who registered under those clauses as an example to others. Men with college educations registered under the grandfather clause so that other men, poor and illiterate, would not feel ashamed to do so.

Another means of breaking down the Republican party in Louisiana was a wide increase in the appointive power in the governor. I think this was one of the things that led to an article [in the 1898 constitution] making the governor ineligible to succeed himself.

Some of the support of that article was mere opposition to Murphy J. Foster, the governor. They wanted to put him out of politics. But he went to the [U.S.] senate in 1901 and stayed there until 1912, when Joseph E. Ransdell defeated him by a small majority.

---

and 126,822 Negro registered voters. Of the white voters, 125,860 registered as literate and the remaining 28,107 as illiterate. An examination of the Negro registration revealed that 95,577 registered as "able to make their mark" (illiterate) and 31,245 as literate. The 1900 voter registration figures indicated that there were 125,437 white voters to only 5,320 Negroes. Breaking down these figures to the various categories showed that 86,157 whites registered under the educational clause; 29,112 under section 5; and, the remainder under the property qualifications. Of the 5,320 Negro registrants, 77 qualified under section 5; 4,327 registered under the educational clause; and the remainder under registered property qualifications. *Reports of the Secretary of State to His Excellency W. W. Heard, the Governor of Louisiana, May 12, 1902.*

This reminds me that the poll tax provisions got a great deal of support from "reformers" who believed it would destroy the organization of the regulars. I do not remember now who first proposed it but I do remember that practically all the "silk stocking" element, the nice fellows who knew all about the fall of the Roman empire, the French revolution and the British House of Commons, were strong for it.

Ernest Kruttschnitt told them that the poll tax provision would help the organization for a while and not hurt it at any time. We fixed it so it did not go into effect until after 1900, to which Dr. Henry Dickson Bruns most bitterly objected.

One of the sentences of the poll tax clause was this: "Any person who shall pay the poll tax of another or advance him money for that purpose, in order to influence his vote, shall be guilty of bribery and punished accordingly."

That sounded very well but it did not mean anything. I remember John Fitzpatrick, on the stump, announcing that if any poor man in the crowd did not have a dollar to pay his poll tax, he could get it from him. One of the incidents of the campaign of 1908 was the proof that J. Y. Sanders[41] or his immediate friends had paid poll taxes in bunches. All large business establishments soon acquired the habit of paying their employees' poll taxes with one check, many of them not taking the dollars out of the envelopes on pay day. Up to about ten years ago, the poll tax provision was decided advantage to the profesional politicians and it is still of some small advantage.

This poll tax business and some of the decisions of the United States supreme court are evidence that you cannot tell much about a country by reading its constitution. According to our state constitution, most of us ought to have served terms in prison for paying other folks' poll taxes. Yet nobody has ever

---

41. Jared Y. Sanders, governor of Louisiana from 1908 to 1912. For biographical sketch see Chapter III, note 3, herein.

been charged with bribing voters by so aiding them in qualifying.

Very few of us in New Orleans have given any attention to the real effects on the negroes of keeping them out of state and local politics. There have always been a great many negroes working in Algiers and my duties as mayor have required me to come in contact with so many different phases of the city's life that perhaps I may include a few words on this subject in these recollections.

In the old days, from the time of the fight that broke the power of the carpet baggers and routed the Metropolitan police force, up to about 1904, there was always danger of serious friction between the whites and the negroes. It still existed to a great extent in 1900, when the Robert Charles riot took place.[42] I shall say something about that riot later. It was the last we had. The relations between the negroes and the whites were such that any connection between them would probably bring about bloodshed.

I grew up in those times. I saw that the fact that the negroes were able to vote was at the bottom of a great deal of trouble. While there was very little real governing done by negroes in my time, they had an influence that was resented and this resentment was like powder. All it needed was the match of some small trouble to light it and produce a considerable explosion. For instance, take the Charles riots. The only real offender was Robert Charles, and yet negroes were attacked practically all over the city.

More than 20 years have passed since we have had an outbreak in New Orleans against the negroes. The Charles riot was only three [sic] years after the convention of 1898. Now we have peace.

Naturally, white men will not get along with negroes as they

---

42. Behrman discusses the Charles Riot of 1900 later in this chapter.

will with other men. It is not to be expected. But we have a right to expect for all time that the act of one black criminal will not start a mob after innocent negroes who have done no harm to anybody. We have good reason, considering the developments of the past 20 years, to expect no racial riots in the future. Practically all the negroes of New Orleans do not try to be treated as equals by the white men and the white workers have decided, for one reason oand another, to give the negroes a great deal. They are getting that and have been getting it for a long time.

Take the river front, for instance. The unions of white and black laborers are co-operating with each other. They divide the work by agreement and they stand together when there is trouble over wages and so forth. Such an agreement could not have been made when the negroes had votes. But it works very well now and strikes on the river front are very mild affairs compared to what we had in the old days.[43] The trade of the plasterer is probably 95 percent in the control of the negroes. The bricklayers are mostly negroes. I believe the bricklayers' union is the only mixed white and black union in New Orleans. While there may be another mixed union, the fact remains that the whites and the blacks are together in the bricklayers' union and it is probably the strongest building trades union in New Orleans.

The white carpenters co-operated with the union of black carpenters for a year or two. Then there was some trouble on the

43. Behrman's statement is not completely accurate. With the exception of racial clashes following the panics of 1873 and 1893, white and Negro labor unions cooperated with each other to a great extent under a confederation of unions named the Central Trades and Labor Assembly. The bloodiest racial conflict between New Orleans laborers took place in the dock riots of 1894. Because of the general economic depression of the early 1890s tensions were very high among dock workers. Violence erupted when a British shipping firm hired Negro screwmen to work on its ships because of the lower wages paid to the Negroes. White screwmen attacked the Negroes and rioting ensued. Several people were killed and there was considerable property damage. Governor Foster eventually had to activate the state militia to suppress the disturbance. Jackson, *New Orleans in the Gilded Age*, 226–30.

Hibernia building and the white carpenters went on strike. Negroes from the colored union, mislead by their leaders, went to work in the white men's places. When the dispute was settled, the negroes were discharged and the white men got their jobs back. There was no riot. Not one negro was attacked. That would not have been true in the days when the negroes voted. A situation like this would have received the careful attention of the police and, probably, the governor would have been notified that the militia might be needed.

I remember the murder of two police officers in a negro church called the "Council of God" about 12 or 13 years ago. There was no danger of a riot. The murderers were arrested, indicted, tried and hung without the least sign of a riot. Had the two officers been deliberately murdered by negroes in my youth, anywhere from two to twenty negroes would have been killed. Perhaps more than that.

The negroes no doubt are better treated and enjoy more peace in New Orleans than in any other large city. A majority of them appreciate this. When the war was over, World War I, and some of our negroes marched in the parade, they got a rousing welcome. In Chicago on the other hand a serious riot occurred immediately after the war. The negroes vote in Chicago.

Moreover, the negroes here have accumulated some money. They live in better houses now, in spite of the high rents, than they ever did before. They have erected many churches and a good office building, the Pythian Temple at Gravier and Saratoga streets.

When the colored men from New Orleans left for the training camps in 1917, they paraded to the Union depot and several prominent citizens and I reviewed the parade at the city hall. Every man in the parade carried a fine box of luncheon that had been presented to him by white citizens. I think it was the members of the Pickwick club who gave them these boxes.

Most of our New Orleans soldiers were in the camps in December of 1917, a majority of them being at Camp Pike and

Camp Beauregard. The Choctaw Club sent Christmas packages to them and the colored men were not forgotten. Every colored sailor and soldier got his Christmas remembrance and many of the boxes were delivered personally by members of the club.

That reminds me that up to quite recently, when the women got the vote,[44] we had two kinds of male citizens: those who could vote and those whom we called "squaw men" because they had not paid their poll taxes. The "squaw voters" were something different in the earlier years of the constitution of 1898. We had also the "Papoose voter" and what *The Times-Democrat* called the "Privileged Dago Voter." That "privileged Dago voter" sounds funny now but it was taken very seriously by the reformers in 1898.

The Times-Democrat classified our voters, when we had about finished the suffrage clauses, as follows:

(1) The educated voter: that is, the voter who can read and write. He is the only one in the entire batch, except the woman voter, who is not illiterate.
(2) The property voter, illiterate, but worth $300
(3) The squaw voter (wife worth $300)
(4) The papoose voter (children worth $300)
(5) The 1868 voter.
(6) The could-have-been voter—the fellow who might have voted in 1868 but did not think it worth while.
(7) The hereditary voter.
(8) The privileged "Dago" voter.
(9) The woman property voter (on certain question only)
(10) The woman proxy voter.

The "1868 voter" was a man who had registered and voted before the federal constitution was amended and the carpet baggers and Republicans put the negroes on the books.

The "could-have-been voters" was a man who was eligible for the vote before 1868. The convention later made it 1867.

The hereditary voter was one who registered under the

---

44. Women obtained the right to vote in 1920 with the ratification of the Nineteenth Amendment.

Early Career in Politics

"father and grandfather" clause. The reports for 1900 show that 111 negroes registered under this clause on the claim that they had white ancestors. That 111 was the state total.

The "Privileged Dago Voter" was a man of foreign birth naturalized before 1898.

New Orleans and the towns of Southern Louisiana had a great many immigrants from Italy. During the years before the constitution of 1898, they were permitted to register and vote on mere declarations that they intended to stay here and become citizens. The "privileged Dago" or "foreigner" clause in the constitution, which required that they should have been naturalized before 1898 to vote other than under the educational and property clauses, shut some of them out. The editors of the paper had the idea that the Italians voted solidly with the "Regular Democrats."

The regular organization came out of the convention in fine shape. It is true that we were pretty generally condemned by the newspapers but we were not condemned by the voters. The poll tax proved a considerable benefit to us for some time after that.

After all is said and done, it must be admitted that the convention of 1898 made good with the people. We promised the people to put the negro out of politics and to keep him out. While the constitution of 1898 was not 100 per cent perfect, it contained what we had promised our voters to put in it and they were so well satisfied that they elected us time and time again.

6.

Governor Foster Builds Organization in New Orleans: Prologue to City and State Conventions of 1899–1900

State and city elections were held on the same day before 1898, when the [1898 constitutional] convention put the city election in November and the state election in April. One of the reasons given for this was that the separation would prevent trading of votes by candidates. This trading of votes was supposed to be something done only by the Regulars, and, like civil service, the Australian [secret] ballot and the primaries, the separation of the elections was looked on by some of the "outs" or "reformers" as a blow at the Regulars. It was not. The two most decisive victories of the Regulars came immediately after the convention [in 1899–1900] when Paul Capdevielle defeated Walter C. Flower for mayor [in New Orleans] and William Wright Heard defeated Eugene S. Reems, Republican, and Donelson Caffery [Jr.] People's [Populist] Party and Republican Fusion candidate [for governor]. Heard beat them both by a majority of more than 43,000 in a total vote of less than 77,000. I have no record of the Capdevielle-Flower vote but my impression is that Paul Capdevielle's majority was about 9,000.[45]

Governor Foster, who had been prevented from running for a third term by the provisions in the new [1898] constitution that no governor should succeed himself, was active in the local campaign in 1899. He had to be for two reasons, party politics and his own personal ambition to continue in office. The opposition, which was known as the Jacksonian Democracy[46] in New Orleans, had organized at several places in the state. If the

---

45. The results of the New Orleans mayoralty election of 1899: Paul Capdevielle 19,559 to Walter C. Flower's 12,988. Mayor Walter Flower provided the city with an efficient and progressive administration. Many municipal improvements were begun that would not reach fruition until well into the next century. Among his accomplishments were reduction of municipal employee salaries to the equivalent paid in private industry, establishment of a form of civil service, regained control of municipal services that had been franchised to private companies, gained important legislation to begin construction of a sewerage and water system, and reorganization of the city government under a new charter in 1896. His administration's most lasting contribution was that it made municipal reform a necessary ingredient for political success. New Orleans *Daily Picayune*, November 9, 1899; Norman Walker, "An Attempt at Municipal Reform," *Harper's Weekly*, XXXX, August 29, 1896, p. 854; New Orleans *Times-Picayune*, May 31, 1925; Kendall, *History of New Orleans*, II, 523.

46. Prior to the 1899 New Orleans municipal elections the remnants of the 1896 Citizens' League reorganized and formed the Jacksonian Democracy. The faction reluctantly nominated the incumbent mayor, Walter Flower, because of his "receptivity" to the Regular nomination. His outstanding record as mayor and reformer, however, made

regulars had lost the fight in the city, they might have lost to the opposition in the state convention and they would at least have had a hard time in the state campaign.

Foster was working to get all the Democrats together against the Republicans and the reformers long before the state and city conventions of 1899 and 1900 and he continued that work at the session of the legislature in 1900. He was working also to assure his own election as United States Senator. I think he would have preferred to be governor again as he liked the job, which is a rare liking, even with governors who have served only one term. But the [constitutional] convention of 1898 made him ineligible by providing that no governor might succeed himself.

The reformers voted for that article of the constitution because they believed it would prevent the organization of a "state machine." But the ineligible Foster, not running to succeed himself, combined the city organization and the parish politicians more completely into one faction than they have ever been since then.[47]

Foster was one of those awful lobbyists at the capitol in 1900. An "awful lobbyist" is a man who induces members of the legislature to do things you don't want them to do. An "unscrupulous lobby" is a bunch of men who go to Baton Rouge and put something over on you. I have never known a man to be the victim of patriotic citizens who disagreed with him and got what they wanted. When Foster was lobbying in 1900, one of the newspapers opposed to him called him a "pernicious meddler."

He was pernicious because he was doing all he could to promote his own candidacy for a seat in the United States Senate. One of the ways he did this was to help members draft their bills, to correct errors in their drafts, and to work against

---

him their logical choice. Kendall, *History of New Orleans*, II, 533. (Kendall mistakingly referred to the Jacksonians as "Jeffersonians.")

47. Choctaw Club of Louisiana formed in 1897.

measures his friends disapproved if he agreed with them. I do not remember the bills but I do know that Foster put in long hours on matters that benefited him personally only because the work would get him the friendship and support of those interested. Many of these bills, I was told, had no political significance whatsoever.

Foster was a hard worker, an exceptionally adroit politican and an excellent administrator of the state's business. While the *Times-Democrat* was much given to roasting him and his faction, it had to admit that he made a successful manager of the state's affairs and did this very gracefully in its editorials on his success in paying off some of the state debt.

There was no opposition to my faction in Algiers though nine of the leaders in the other wards had fights on primary day and Farrell was beaten by Ewing. I was among the delegates chosen to the city convention.

Mine was known in the newspapers as the "Mooney-Behrman" faction. Mooney had been recorder in Algiers in older years. I appointed him my deputy when I became assessor in 1896. He was president of the Crescent Democratic Club of the [Fifteenth] ward.

As soon as the [city] primary was over, one of the newspapers announced that Governor Foster would no doubt name the city ticket. As I remember it, Foster was not so much after getting any particular man on the ticket as he was to get the regulars solidly together.

I had the satisfaction of realizing in 1899, when I was 35 years old, that I had become an influential man in our city politics. I knew, of course, that a politician's life is really more beyond his control than that of most men. No matter how well you do in politics, no matter how hard you work, there are chances that things about which you know nothing until too late will put you out of office.

While I fully realize that it would be impossible for any man to spend a long life in active politics and never suffer a defeat, that prospect did not scare me. I knew also that I could make more than a living as a salesman and that I had many friends in the business world. I believe that even now, at the age of 58 years and after 32 years of almost continuous office holding, I could go into any wholesale grocery concern in New Orleans, study their business for six months and then take charge of their soliciting and business promotion and make more than a mere showing. Business methods and some of the goods are different from what they were when I was a drummer for C. Doyle & Company, but human beings are about the same.

The ability to get along with people and persuade them to vote with you is not much different from the ability to sell groceries and "keep your trade," as the saying goes.

It occurs to me that there are fewer successful men among the politicians than in any other line of activity that takes in large numbers. There are a large number of professional politicians. Most of them quit and take up pursuits in private life. Of those that remain, comparatively few rise to prominence. And my experience indicates that a great deal of the best service the public gets is from the men relatively little known to the public. Their wards know them. Their following knows them. Many businessmen know them. But because they do work that does not strike the reporters as sensational, they are not known to the general public.

My son Stanley was ten and my daughter was eleven years of age in 1899. I had a home of my own. I felt settled and confident of the future. I was the leader in Algiers.

I had not become leader by loafing and taking life easy. While I had a feeling that it would be even harder for another man to get me out of that leadership than it was for me to get it, I always kept in mind the fact that leadership requires work.

Most of the newspapers give the public the idea that what they call a "ward boss" is a lazy fellow who dresses well, drinks often, smokes big cigars and very seldom, if ever, does not work. There are many persons who believe just such foolishness as that. While there are some jobs in politics that do not require much effort, the man who holds one of them and limits himself to the job does not become a real leader.

There is nothing you can do in politics without meeting opposition. You must overcome it, and to do that it is usually necessary to see a lot of men. And often a lot of women besides. If you know them and have been of service to them either as an official or personally, your job of convincing them and getting their help is half done. If you have not been of service and do not know a great many of your fellow citizens, you are not a leader.

Mere acquaintances, which you can get by joining clubs and commercial organizations and making a big noise in political campaigns, is not enough. You must impress a wide circle of friends and acquaintances with the idea that you are practical, that you can do things and get them done and that you will not loaf on the job when they expect something from you. Then they will be disposed to help you when they can. This applies to the majority. There will always be some men who expect to break your neck in their service and will turn you down in a minute when you call on them for an effort. There are others who will take everything you have and run away from you if you come along on a rainy day without an umbrella.

Those who have an idea that a ward leader does not have to work should investigate the facts. They will find that save in exceptional circumstances, of which I do not just now call to mind, any man who had led a ward in two or three elections is a hard worker.

As to my own industry and energy, even my most bitter opponents do not charge me with any shortage of either. I shall deal with that later on as it applies to me personally.

I must admit, in all fairness, that I was full of self-confidence when the primaries took place in 1899. There have been many occasions in my life when I had the blues. These occurred mostly when I would be disappointed after months of work on some public project that did not go through. I have seldom been gloomy over pure politics.

Returning to the politics of 1899, William H. Brynes was one of the prominent men mentioned for mayor. Charles Janvier was another. Paul Capdevielle was nominated. There was a caucus of the leaders on a Sunday between the primary and the convention. The leaders whose followings totaled 40 votes in the convention left the caucus and the 56, the majority, who had attempted to "put it over on us" as Joe Hirn called it, finally gave in to the 40.

The caucus [or the Council of Seventeen] held on Sunday, September 10, 1899, two days after the primary that elected delegates to the city convention and the day before the convention, was called to allot positions on the tickets to the wards. The active politicians, big and little, and practically all the voters in the successful ward factions knew what their leaders planned to get for the wards. There was, of course, uncertainty as to what they would get.

I was very anxious to get my ward representation on the ticket and was particularly aiming to have Algiers given the place of Clerk of the Court of Appeals.... I wanted Charles H. Brownlee nominated. Joseph Hirn was fighting for the judgeship of the Second City Criminal Court for the Eighth Ward. However, we were in the minority as to the delegates, having only 40 against their 56.

The majority selected Henry B. McMurray, of the Twelfth Ward, as their spokesman. We were told very formally and coldly that McMurray would give us the "dope." While we were uncertain, we were not very nervous. We knew that we had the wards that cast heavy Democratic votes.

"In view of the fact that Mr. Behrman has been so eminently

successful in the constitution convention," said McMurray, with a smile, "and so specially successful in getting things for his ward and his people, we have decided to allow that ward no place on the ticket."

I informed my friend, McMurray, that he could go to hell and name his own ticket. I said I would support it but would have nothing to do with framing it. The crowd gave me the laugh.

"In the Eighth Ward," said McMurray, turning with a broader smile to Joseph Hirn, "we have allowed the position of judge of the Second City Criminal Court. The candidate, however, will be selected by the whole caucus."

Joe Hirn saw that would be to his finish. What he told McMurray was no more polite than what I had told him.

McMurray went down the line with us. It seemed that the minority would get the consideration we thought we deserved. That happened at the Choctaw Club, then where the Maheca Building[48] is now. We left in a bunch and went over to the Cosmopolitan Hotel, where we drank some beer and then rented two rooms upstairs.

We held a mock caucus or convention in the two rooms. Among those present and in good humor were Joseph Hirn [Eighth Ward], Alex Pujol, [Fifth Ward], Vic Mauberret [Fourth Ward], and Ferd Dudenheffer [Ninth Ward]. Vic Mauberret presided. We allotted all the ticket to our wards and planned the campaign. We sent for some cigars and won the "hot air" campaign. Then we started telling stories. By and by, Congressman Robert C. Davey called on us. He was the "harmonizer," as one of the papers called some of the leaders who got us together. However, I do not remember that the story of the mock caucus was ever printed.

"You fellows are having a hell of a good time," said Congressman Davey.

Everybody laughed and nobody answered.

---

48. It was located on Canal Street between Carondelet and Baronne streets.

"We are over there sweating blood." "Well," I told him when the noise of a loud guffaw was over, "we have no responsibilities. We can afford to have a good time."

The convention took a serious turn. We made the business short and fast and ended it with an agreement to give us all that we asked. I remember that some of the members of the mock caucus wanted to ask for more but they got over that almost immediately.

John Fitzpatrick presided over the convention in the Grand Opera House. The routine of organizing the convention are of no interest now. One detail, however, that may be mentioned is that the convention adopted a resolution favoring the amendment to the constitution to provide for a sewerage and water board and declared itself generally in favor of municipal ownership. We now have a lot of it and the people are apparently well satisfied with it.

Charles J. Theard nominated Paul Capdevielle for Mayor. An ass in the gallery yelled that he wanted no Frenchman. There was a big roar for a while. When order was restored, E. Howard McCaleb seconded the nomination.

It was while McCaleb was making his speech that the "dollar a day" cry came from the gallery. As I have stated, J. C. Denis was defeated for mayor years before, largely by the charge that he had said a dollar a day was enough for a laborer or working man.[49] It sent a chill through most of us. There were 96 delegates present and my guess is that there were ninety pairs of cold feet. The voice in the gallery kept that up until McCaleb declared there was no truth in it.

Paul Capdevielle was nearly 60 years old but a very active man when be became mayor. He was with Boone's Artillery at one time during the Civil War and was badly wounded. He was captured by the Federals and paroled and after a few days at

---

49. Behrman is referring to the 1880 New Orleans mayoral election in which Joseph A. Shakspeare defeated Jules C. Denis by a vote of 9,803 to 9,362. Jackson, *New Orleans in the Gilded Age*, 57.

home, down in the Pontalba Buildings, he made his way to Mobile and violated the parole by joining another military outfit. If he had been recaptured and recognized, he would have been shot.

I have often wondered why none of the newspaper reporters ever made a story of the details of Paul Capdevielle's service as a soldier.

At the time he was nominated, Capdevielle was a member of the Orleans Levee Board, of the City Park and Esplanade Improvement Associations, and the Prison Reform Association. He was an active member of private organizations, such as the Jesuits' Alumni. He had been a member of the school board. His brother, Armand Capdevielle, was manager of the *New Orleans Bee*. We nominated, of course, full city and parish tickets.

Charles J. Boatner and Walter D. Denegre were the leaders of the "Jacksonian Democracy," which combine or temporary faction had its start in the parishes. They backed Walter C. Flower for mayor and named a whole ticket. The "Jacksonian Democracy" did not have a chance in New Orleans and I have no doubt the leaders knew it.

The next big event in politics was the [state] Democratic Convention that nominated William Wright Heard[50] for governor in 1900.

Robert H. Snyder of Tensas Parish, known all over Louisiana as "Bob" Snyder, was generally expected to be governor after Foster. I have an old report of the Secretary of State showing that in the election of 1896, Foster had received 116,216 votes, and Bob Snyder, who was elected lieutenant governor, re-

---

50. William W. Heard (1853–1926) served in both houses of the state legislature from 1884 to 1892 and was elected auditor of public accounts on the Foster antilottery ticket in 1892. Since Heard had served as governor from 1900 to 1904 he was not eligible to succeed himself because of the one-term restriction in the 1898 constitution. Reeves, *The Governors of Louisiana*, 88.

ceived, 118,447. Snyder led the Democratic ticket. In spite of his defeat in the convention, he remained a powerful political figure and in 1904, was elected Speaker of the House of Representatives. He was a much respected and highly popular politician and a lawyer of great ability. He did a great deal to defeat Walter D. Denegre when [Samuel D.] McEnery was elected to the [U.S.] senate in [1896].

The Foster faction controlled the State Democratic Convention of 1900. While Foster had made some enemies, he was a shrewd politician and was generally popular. Foster threw his strength to William Wright Heard who had been auditor for years. Heard got the nomination.[51]

Bob Snyder's opponents sometimes claim that his advocacy of the primary system was due to his defeat in the convention. This is not true. He was the first man, so far as my memory goes, to advocate primaries. We had had all kinds of primaries but those regarded by state law and Snyder was for regulation. This regulation was meant to go with the elimination of conventions such as we had then.

Snyder claimed and perhaps with good reason that if there had been a statewide Democratic primary in 1899 he would have won the nomination. He was much liked and respected in New Orleans and had a tremendous hold on the people in north and central Louisiana, and, I think, in the Florida parishes.[52] As a result to a great extent of Snyder's agitation of the subject, a

51. Heard was the compromise Democratic nominee after the convention resulted in deadlock between John Fitzpatrick, former mayor of New Orleans, Lieutenant Governor Robert H. Snyder, and state senator S. McC. Lawrason. In the general election Heard defeated his Regular Republican opponent Eugene S. Reems and the Populist-Republican Fusionist candidate Donelson Caffery, Jr., receiving 78 percent of the votes. This was the last election in Louisiana in which the Louisiana People's party would field candidates. Howard, *Political Tendencies in Louisiana*, 194; Hair, *Bourbonism and Agrarian Protest*, 278.

52. The Florida Parishes are those in southeastern Louisiana north of Lake Pontchartrain and east of the Mississippi River. At the time of the Louisiana Purchase in 1803 this area was a part of Spanish West Florida.

committee was appointed in 1904 to draw up a law that finally got on the books in 1906.[53]

Governor Heard has all his life been a thorough, painstaking, hardworking official. His duties as auditor gave him a first hand knowledge of state finances. His term does not stand out in the memories of many who voted for him because he was not a governor of the excitable kind, he had no radical programme to carry out, and he seldom got in a fight with anybody. He was the governor, however. He had the power and he used it effectively but he did not explode every now and then. Moreover, he did not meet the kind of opposition that keeps a governor always in the public eye.

I know it had been stated that while Heard occupied the office, Foster was the governor. This report, doubtless intended to belittle Heard, was based on two things. First, that Foster's support was necessary to make Heard governor. Second, that Heard did not care whether they said it or not. He had been auditor during the eight years that Foster had been governor. I have no inside knowledge of what passed between them but I know their character and my guess is that Auditor Heard had the same influence with Governor Foster that Senator Foster had with Governor Heard. If there is any mistake about this, I will be glad to have W. W. Heard correct it.

One of the results in the city and state elections of 1899 and 1900 was that Murphy J. Foster went to the Senate [U.S.] and stayed there for two terms.

Paul Capdevielle gave the ward leaders a dinner at his resi-

---

53. Traditionally candidates for political office in Louisiana were chosen at the party nominating conventions. Voters in the general elections merely "rubber stamped" the conventions' nominees. In 1900 reformers were able to get a watered-down primary election bill through the legislature. However, it did not make primaries mandatory (Act. No. 133). The legislature passed a stronger bill in 1906 making it obligatory that nominees of all political parties be chosen by direct primaries (Act No. 49). George M. Reynolds, *Machine Politics in New Orleans, 1897–1926* (New York: Columbia University Press, 1936), 82–83.

dence on Esplanade Street a few days after his victory over Walter C. Flower and the Jacksonian Democracy. Shortly after his inauguration [in 1900], Mayor Capdevielle's home became a place of almost continual semi-official, semi-social events, and before long, he had a permanent electric light system constructed over his lawn and garden so that he might give outdoor parties on short notice without inconvenience of the usual Japanese lanterns.

Ward leaders, of course, usually come from the mass of people and not all of us acquire what might be called the best manners. While I remember nothing at the dinner which would have required an apology either from or to such a polished gentleman as Paul Capdevielle, I clearly remember that he was a little astonished at the remarks made by some of those present. We enjoyed that dinner and conversation in all its details. The mayor-elect, however, did not agree with us in our references to our opponents.

One of the episodes [during Capdevielle's administration] in which I was called for unofficial services was during the Charles Riots. Citizens were called on to act as special police and were sent out armed. I was the commissary general who had charge of seeing that they got their meals. William Mehle, as acting mayor, issued the first call for emergency police. Mayor Capdevielle soon got back to the city and took charge.

Robert Charles was then what we called a "race" negro. That is, he was always worked up over the alleged grievances of the colored people. He and another negro were waiting and loitering around a house occupied by Virginia Banks, a negress, in Dryades Street, between Washington and Sixth. This happened in July of 1900, more than 22 years ago.

The conduct of the two negroes caused the neighbors to send for the police. Charles shot Officer August T. Mora in the hip and got away to a house somewhere in Fourth Street not far from where the trouble started. He loaded a Winchester rifle and killed Captain John T. Day and Patrolman Peter T. Lamb. They died in the alley. The other officers then got into another room in the same house. Patrolman Trenchard was accused of cowardice for this, as I remember it, and was dismissed from the force. I did not follow the trial in the sense of being present to hear the testimony, but I could not see that there was necessarily any cowardice in getting out of a dark alley in which a negro might easily shoot with a Winchester without exposing more than his hands and forearms. Charles escaped from that place made his way to another house in Saratoga street, two or three blocks to the uptown side of the Union depot. A riot began the day after Charles killed the two policemen at the house on Fourth street. Three or four negroes were killed and seven or eight were injured. Captain Allen Jumel, then adjutant general, came to New Orleans and the militia was called out. The proclamation was issued for emergency police, and I was called on to act as commissary general.

One of the things the mob did was to break into the pawn shops in Rampart Street and steal weapons and other things of value, but not of enough value to go into the safes. The pawnbrokers presented the claims against the city later on and these claims were enormous. I do not remember how they were settled but I do remember that their earnest attention was called to the wide difference between the value of their stocks of unredeemed pledges as stated to the assessors and as stated in their claims.

The police and *The Times-Democrat* got anonymous messages that Charles was hiding in the Saratoga street house. Nothing was expected to come of it when Sargeant Gabriel Porteous and other officers were assigned to search the house. They had searched all but a little closet under the stairs which they had not noticed, when Sargeant Porteous saw a bucket of water and a dipper near the door of the closet. He crossed the room and leaned over to pick up the dipper. Charles was in the

Early Career in Politics

closet. He shot and killed Porteous and got out of the closet and ran upstairs before the other police officers could kill him.

If Sargeant Porteous had not been thirsty, Charles would probably have escaped.

A call for help was sent out. Police and citizens came from all directions. The rear building, two stories, where Charles was with his Winchester, was soon surrounded by policemen, and citizens who poured bullets into the windows at the least sign of movement. Charles broke a hole in the walls so as to shoot from windows on all four sides.

A New Orleans newspaper reporter who prefers that I do not mention his name, got his first newspaper experience in "police work" at the killing of Charles. He took a position on the shed at the rear of the building. He tells me that Andrew Van Kuren, standing in the doorway of a residence that was rear to rear with the building Charles occupied, was waving his hat and shouting encouragments to the men on the sheds and roofs all around. This reporter, who had come off the shed to reload his pistol, told Van Kuren that as he had no weapon he should go inside.

"I will stand here," Van Kuren cried, "and curse that blankety-blank coon until they get him."

Then the negro got Van Kuren with a slug in the chest. He died a few minutes later. On the following Sunday almost the whole staff of *The Times-Democrat* visited the place and the young reporter, who believes he shot Charles in the face after Van Kuren fell, put himself in the position Charles must have been in to kill Van Kuren. He was astonished to find that it would have been easier for the negro to have killed him and he had chosen to kill the man Van Kuren rather than the boy himself.

It was Page M. Baker, [editor of *The Times-Democrat*], I believe who suggested that the house from which Charles was shooting should be set afire. The mob in the streets had just killed two more negroes as the place was set afire. That drove Charles out.

Just as Charles was coming down one stairway, old man King, a fireman was going up the other. I understand King was armed with two bricks. The story told me is that he explained he was an expert with bricks and not with firearms and that if he could get into the room with the negro, he would certainly kill him with the bricks.

The trouble started at Virginia Banks' house uptown, five days before Charles was killed. The rioting lasted four days. My impression is that about 10 negroes were killed and that many were injured and not reported to the police. The mob shot into the house uptown and killed a negro and mortally wounded an old black woman who was in her bed. She died in the hospital.

There was some argument as to whether a sargeant of militia, Anderson, or Dr. Charles A. Noiret, got the finishing bullet into Charles as he came down the stairs. I do not remember just how they decided that. Rewards were offered for Charles and one of these two got the rewards.

What difference did it make? Both of them, as I remember it, claimed the killing of Charles and declared they would give the money to charity if they got it. They were both there and both putting their lives in danger to put an end to Charles.

Other men stood openly on sheds, climbed chimneys, and straddled rooftops to swap shots with the negro and many of them were hurt. Trenchard, accused of cowardice, stood openly on a shed and sent buck shot at the negro. Charles was reeling when he finally came downstairs to avoid smothering in smoke, no doubt having been hit often by the flocks of bullets that went at him, and whoever killed him showed no more nerve or skill than many others.

I do not mean by this to take any credit from Noiret or Anderson. If they had been short of nerve or grit, they would not have been where they were. They knew that the smoke would soon drive Charles to them and that he would probably see them first and that he could certainly handle that rifle skillfully. On the other hand, as told to me by the boy who did his first reporting later that evening, every man who showed as much as his face where Charles could see was in danger.

That was the last occurrence of the kind in New Orleans and all of us are glad of it. Twenty-two years without a race riot is a good record in view of what has happened in other cities. As I stated in detail earlier in these recollections, the relations between the whites and the blacks are such here today that I do not think it possible for our white people to form mobs and kill negroes who have committed no offense beyond simply being negroes.

7.

Gubernational Campaign of 1903–1904: Behrman Becomes Auditor

It was some time in the early months [of 1903] that Col. C. C. Bird of Baton Rouge, suggested that I become a candidate for [state] auditor. He spoke to me about it again in New Orleans. After some inquiry among my friends, I decided to make the race.

My opponents were LeDoux E. Smith, then state treasurer, and again state treasurer in 1912–1916, and W. S. Frazee, then auditor. This was the campaign in which Newton C. Blanchard was elected [governor] over General Leon Jastremski.[54]

---

54. Newton C. Blanchard (1849–1922) had a long successful career in Louisiana politics. He first gained recognition in the Louisiana Democratic party during Reconstruction when he was charged but acquitted by federal authorities of intimidating Negro voters. His allegiance and dedication to the party was rewarded with positions on the staff of Governors Louis A. Wiltz and Samuel McEnery. Blanchard served five terms in the U.S. House of Representatives and in 1893 was appointed by Governor Foster to

The campaign opened [in early 1903] when General Jastremski, then secretary to Gov. Heard and one of the really powerful politicians, wrote a letter to Blanchard, J. T. Watkins of Webster [Parish], W. H. Price of Lafourche [Parish], and John T. Michel, asking them to join him in a petition to the Democratic state central committee to call a primary election to select candidates for the state offices. This unusual request might have been ignored if made by a politician of less power, influence and personal prestige.

One of the irrelevant but interesting coincidences of General Jastremski's movements at that time was that he announced his candidacy twice and the second announcement made at Baton Rouge, came just as the great reunion of Confederate Veterans in New Orleans was at its end on Saturday, May 23, 1903. I remember the reunion very well. It was the last big event of its kind in New Orleans. General Jastremski was himself a distinguished veteran.

Blanchard replied to the general's letter with a statement of which the chief points were that the election was nine months off and it was too early to ask the committee to meet and call a primary. He said he was busy with his work as a justice of the Supreme Court and he thought the committee should meet in about three months.

Price was opposed to the primary. Later on, after the primary was called, he decided not to run. His name had been brought forward after a conference at Alexandria. Had he decided to

---

the U.S. Senate to complete the unexpired term of Edward Douglass White who had been appointed to the U.S. Supreme Court by President Grover Cleveland. In the Senate, Blanchard worked to gain favorable tariff legislation for Louisiana's agricultural industries. In 1897, Blanchard resigned his seat in the senate and accepted an appointment as an associate justice to the Louisiana Supreme Court where he served until his election as governor in 1904. During his gubernatorial administration, Blanchard significantly increased state aid to education and reduced the appointive power of the governor's office by making numerous state offices elective rather than appointed positions. Reeves, *The Governors of Louisiana*, 89–91. General Leon Jastremski was mayor of Baton Rouge, from 1876 to 1882 and U.S. consul to Callao, Peru, from 1893 to 1897.

run, there is no telling what might have resulted. For many years, Price had been recognized as a leader in the third [congressional] district. He was a personal friend of Robert Broussard's and helped him in all his campaigns just as he helped the present [U.S.] senator, Edwin Broussard, in his campaign. He was and is well liked all over his district and was on very friendly terms with the leaders in New Orleans. Had he stayed in the race, it would have become a very tangled affair and there is no telling who would have been elected.

Ernest Kruttschnitt, chairman of the Democratic state central committee, was also against calling a direct state primary. He said they would make the campaigns long and expensive, that there would be a great many costly second primaries, and that primaries had been tried in 1882 and had not given satisfactory results. He declared that among other things, they "left a legacy of hatred."

For the benefit of the younger voters, I must explain that the direct primary then proposed was to substitute an election of candidates by voters in the party rather than the election of delegates to a convention to choose the candidates. The primaries held before 1906 were for delegates to conventions.

I was against the primary for the same reasons that prompted Kruttschnitt's opposition. Kruttsschnitt, however, was of the opinion that this method of choosing candidates would break up the regular organization, which had become a real organization only four years before. I did not agree with him. I said that the regulars would vote solidly for whomever they decided on and that the silk stocking reformers and others in the opposition would split up and divide their votes among two or more candidates. I was right on my main contention, that the regulars would not be hurt by the primary system, and I was, to some extent, wrong on the idea that opposition would divide. It is true that it did divide sometimes but not often enough to fulfill my expectations.

Blanchard announced his candidacy later in a letter to W. H.

Wise, of Shreveport. Wise had presided at a mass meeting at Shreveport in March of 1903. Resolutions had been adopted asking Blanchard to become a chairman. When he came out with the announcement, he included a statement in favor of a direct state primary.

The agitation of the subject by Bob Snyder and its support by General Jastremski convinced the public that the primary would be a good thing. The committee decided to bow to what was apparently the popular will, although it did not consider that the advocacy of the *The* [New Orleans] *Times-Democrat* was a clear cut reflection of the popular will. That paper, as I remember it, supported the state primary idea on the ground that it would put the regulars out of business. Like the poll tax provision, the change of dates of the elections so that the city fight came after instead of on the same day as the state election and other devices welcomed by *The Times-Democrat* as fatal to the regulars, the primary did not come up to that newspaper's expectations. Before the Blanchard-Jastremski campaign, however, there had been another change.

Instead of holding the city fight first and then the state fight, the state campaign in which Blanchard and Jastremski fought it out came first and the Behrman-Buck or "Home Rule" campaign came later in the summer [of 1904]. This was effected by an amendment to the city charter that extended Capdevielle's term to December of 1904 and at the same time, provided for four more councilmen to be elected from districts, bringing the council from 17 to 21 members.[55]

The struggle for the governorship soon narrowed down to Blanchard and Jastremski and was a most strenuously fought and bitter campaign. I was running for auditor and visited practically every parish in the state, many of them with Blan-

---

55. Act 216, *Acts Passed by the General Assembly of the State of Louisiana at the Regular Session, 1902.*

Early Career in Politics

chard. The campaign opened at Morgan City [in south central Louisiana].

The committee of citizens at Morgan City had provided low rate excursions on the Atchafalaya River and Bayou Teche and on the railroads and also a big barbeque and one of the biggest crowds I have ever seen outside of a big city gathered there.

There I made the first political speech of my career to a crowd larger than a ward meeting. It was after all the big men had spoken that I was introduced. I thought I saw a million people before me. My feet would not stay put and I did not know what to do with my hands. I think I probably stammered a little at first. Then I blurted out that I was a candidate for state auditor which they already knew. But it gave me some satisfaction to say it. Once that was said, I felt alright. I have never since then had as much trouble in starting a speech, though not even sixteen years as a mayor made an orator of me.

I told that audience that if I thought that the office of auditor required an orator I would not be a candidate for the place because I did not have that qualification. That is all I said. It seemed to me that it suited them better than if I had made a long speech. I had a very large campaign committee in New Orleans. I have searched my home and rummaged in newspaper files to get this list and cannot find it.

A joint debate was arranged between Blanchard and Jastremski at Pontchatoula [across Lake Ponchartrain from New Orleans]. I was on that platform. Either Blanchard or Jastremski said that the other one was a liar and Blanchard struck Jastremski. There was a grand row and a large number of revolvers were pulled. I spent most of about two minutes changing positions so that if Chairman Davidson decided to pull the trigger, the bullet would not hit me. That was the last joint debates in Louisiana campaigns. When Ruffin Pleasant was challenged to a joint debate by John Parker in 1916, I believe one of the reasons given for his refusal was that Blanchard and Jastremski had not finished their debate without disorder in Pontchatoula 12 years before.

[W. S.] Frazee, one of my opponents, was a good stump speaker. I was not and I knew it. So I made it my business to get in touch with the local committees wherever we were to speak from the same platform and arrange the program so that Frazee would speak first. Then I would speak briefly and point out that the work of an auditor did not require much oratory.

We were together at Winnsboro, Franklin Parish, on Thanksgiving Day. Frazee spoke for quite a while and at the close of his talk, argued that he was entitled to re-election as for many years the state auditors had been elected to two terms. He claimed that Heard had improved the office and its methods during his two terms and that Heard's predecessor had doubtless improved on the work of his predecessor.

When I got up I said that it seemed that improvements in the work of that office took place under the administrations of new auditors and that I would like very much to be auditor. I told them I was making no sacrifices to get the place and that they would make no sacrifices if they elected me.

The fact that the regulars in New Orleans were supporting him [Blanchard] was stated in the form of a charge against Blanchard. He replied that he had our support and that he was glad of it and that any man running for governor should be glad to have the support of an organization that could get him a majority in the biggest city in the state.

While General Jastremski was a strong contender and he kept Blanchard working hard all through the campaign. Blanchard himself had every quality that goes to make a good candidate. He was a man of great mind and much learning and he had the manners that usually attract attention without displeasing anybody. He had been a justice of the [Louisiana] Supreme Court, a member of congress, and a senator and the newspaper reports indicated that even in his few years at Washington he got the respectful consideration of the biggest men there.

One little thing not a part of my recollections but which has come as evidence of Blanchard's prestige is that Senator Isaac Stephenson, who wrote his memoirs six or seven years ago, mentions Blanchard as one of the men with whom he often had luncheon because he profited by his conversation. Stephenson did not consider it necessary to identify the Louisiana senator other than simply as "Blanchard," just as he would have referred to Cleveland, Roosevelt, McKinley, or Wilson. I have been told, also, that Blanchard wrote the conservation bills that embodied the Roosevelt policy.

It occurs to me then, that Blanchard did a most important part of the work of the most lasting features of the [Theodore] Roosevelt administration. When you come right down to the facts, the conservation policy established by Roosevelt with the help of [Gifford] Pinchot,[56] who is now about to become governor of Pennsylvania, was the only real policy that Roosevelt "nailed in" so it would stay put.

Blanchard was elected governor,[57] J. Y. Sanders, lieutenant

56. Gifford Pinchot, chief of the U.S. Forest Service during the administrations of Presidents Theodore Roosevent (1901–1908) and William Howard Taft (1908–12), was fired by Taft in 1910 as a result of the "Ballinger-Pinchot" controversy. Pinchot accused Secretary of Interior Richard A. Ballinger of sacrificing public lands and conservation to the interests of private corporations. The name-calling battle that ensued further antagonized the factional split in the Republican party between President Taft and the "Insurgent Republicans."

57. In the Democratic primary held on January 19, 1904, Blanchard received 42,113 votes to Jastremski's 29,957. In the general election, April 19, 1904, Blanchard polled 48,345 votes compared to his Republican opponent's W. J. Behan's 5,877. The 54,222 votes cast in the election were approximately 20,000 less than the total vote in 1900. One explanation for Behan's low vote, about 10 percent, was that many of the Republicans in the sugar-growing parishes and the Populists of north central Louisiana had returned to the Democratic party by 1904. The 1904 general election reflected the triumph of one party dominance in Louisiana. Elections in the future would be internal and factional struggles within the Democratic party. *Report of the Secretary of State to the Honorable Newton C. Blanchard, Governor of Louisiana, January 1, 1905*; Howard, *Political Tendencies in Louisiana*, 197.

governor, O. B. Steele, treasurer, John T. Michel, secretary of state, and myself auditor.

I went to Baton Rouge in great good spirits. I got a great deal of satisfaction out of the campaign which had brought me into contact with men all over the state and had, in a way, improved my education. I had made it my business to talk something else besides my candidacy to those I met and I learned a great deal of the country people's attitude toward various things. I had largely gotten over the "stage fright" that so often hampers a man when he is addressing an audience in which he cannot find a familiar face.

I was not entirely ignorant of the work of auditor, as I have stated. I looked forward to four years in that office with pleasant work that appealed to me as interesting and important.

The auditors in those days had not only their duties in seeing that no money was paid out other than as directed by the legislature but also a vote in selecting the board of appraisers, which fixed the assessments of the public service corporations and a vote as members of the board of liquidation of the state debt. I forgot to mention in connection with my campaign for auditor that I did not get a majority of votes in the first primary. I came within about 600 votes of doing this. I got ready for the second primary called by the Democratic state central committee and organized a campaign committee in New Orleans with about 1000 members. I announced that the names of my state committee would be published the following week. But no one entered against me, so I was declared the nominee.

II

Brickbats and Bouquets
1904–1908

1.

An organization styled the "Democratic Primary League" petitioned the Orleans Parish Democratic Committee in August of 1904 that a direct primary election be held to nominate the city ticket. A committee of 17 citizens prepared this long petition in which they detailed the terms and conditions of the primary they advocated.

The only member of the parish committee who favored a municipal primary was George W. Flynn of the third ward who was then at outs with John Fitzpatrick and the [Regular] organization. The parish committee got up a set of rules for the election of delegates to a convention to be held September 19th [1904] and the convention on September 21st.

It was on August 24, 1904, that I announced my candidacy for mayor.

The first I heard of myself as a possible candidate for mayor was at a meeting in *The Picayune* office. I was called from Baton Rouge to attend the meeting. Among those present were Robert Ewing, Murphy J. Foster, Charles Janvier, Samuel L. Gilmore, T. H. Thorpe, and T. G. Rapier. I went home late in the evening after the meeting and told Mrs. Behrman what was up. "Oh, Papa," she said, "don't let them make you do it."

I was in complete agreement with Mrs. Behrman. I did not want to be mayor. I was satisfied with my work as auditor. The salary and extras from the levee board as auditor totaled about $6,000, which was the mayor's salary then. I had just been through a state fight and I was not looking for another campaign.

I was in favor of Charles Janvier for mayor.[1] I did all I could to get him the support of the leaders. For business reasons he declined to become a candidate.

I called on my friend, Arthur D. Parker, and asked him to run. I had left the conference in *The Picayune* office fully determined that I would not run for mayor. Alex Pujol [leader of the Fifth Ward], I think, went to see Arthur Parker for me. Several days later he let us know that he would not run. We had told him we were almost sure we could get him the unanimous support of the seventeen leaders and that this assured his election. Had he accepted our support, he would have been elected mayor in 1904.

I returned to Baton Rouge the next morning and on my return to New Orleans a few days later, I met a great many leaders and numbers of their lieutenants. They pressed me to give up my position [as auditor] in Baton Rouge. They argued that I was the one man who could get all the leaders to work together and that I owed it to the party and the organization and my friends to accept the nomination. I finally gave in.

I appreciated the great honor of a nomination for mayor and the greater honor of being mayor of such a city as New Orleans. I was not after the place for any reason of purely personal ambition. If it had been that, I would have accepted the support of the men in the conference at the *Picayune* office as soon as it had been tendered. I knew that I was swapping four years of pleasant work in congenial surroundings and among friends and that as auditor I would not always be in a fight and a

---

1. Charles Janvier was founder and president of the Citizens' League of 1896.

struggle. I knew also what a mayor had to do. While I felt the compliment that had been paid me, and was influenced by the appeals of my friends and political allies, I was fully aware of the fact that brickbats come to mayors as often as bouquets.

Anyhow, I decided to run and announced on August 24, 1904.

The *Times-Democrat* somewhat viciously opposed my nomination the following day.[2] On the day after, the *Times-Democrat* published an interview with me. The interview was as follows:

> "The Algiers leader returned to New Orleans from Baton Rouge last night and expressed himself as to his course in case his candidacy should be approved by the people.
>
> "I know", he said, "that the time is past in New Orleans for what some people call a ward boss administration. I am going to give the city, if elected, a clean business administration if I have the health and strength to do it. The electric car has knocked out the horse car and messenger boys have given way to the telephone and just as surely politics is not what it used to be.
>
> I know that a man who is mayor of New Orleans during the next four years will stand or fall for all his career by what he does during that time. I know that a man who would fail would be politically dead for all of his life and I do not want to die politically or otherwise."[3]

The first sentence of that interview was not exactly what I said or how I expressed whatever I said, but I stood by it. I think the words "ward boss administration" were used to put me in the position of taking a slap at the ward leaders or of hinting to

---

2. The New Orleans *Times-Democrat*'s reaction to Behrman's candidacy: "A man of pleasant personality and popularity . . . Mr. Behrman does not rise to the standards but represents the very elements that would assure misgovernment ot the city and seriously hinder and check its prosperity. . . . When New Orleans falls into the hands of the ring, when the arch masters of the politicians, the bosses, get possession of its government and administer it in the interest of the ward workers, hangers on and all of the others of the great army of janissaries who make up the machine, it suffers in every department, in every branch of government and in its business as well." New Orleans *Times-Democrat*, August 25, 1904.

3. *Ibid.*

them that I would not stand with them politically after I was elected.

I did the best I could during all my sixteen years to comply with the promise in the second sentence to give the city a business administration. Some things went wrong. Is there any large business in which nothing went wrong from 1904 to 1920? I must necessarily deal with the larger details of the business side of the city government in later articles. Now I shall content myself with pointing out that the administration side of the city government during my sixteen years was not attacked, so far as I can remember, during the campaigns of 1912 and 1920.

Some attacks were made at various times. Most of them, as I see it, were not entirely justified though not wholly without some justice. Everybody in this country has a legal and moral right to attack public officials at any time and for any reason they see fit. While I have been unjustly attacked on purely business management, I have also been quite justly criticized. I do not claim that I was 100 per cent perfect. I would have been a conceited ass to have believed that I would be. I would be a fool to claim I was.

But I do claim that I gave my time and energies and the best years of my life to hard work for the city of New Orleans and that all in all, I did my work successfully. I am willing to compare my record with any other public official in Louisiana. Also, with that of the presidents of any corporations that employ as many or more men. I had a tougher job than many men who got from two to ten times the salary I received and who did not have to account to anybody but his board of directors and who could conceal many of his mistakes.

I am glad I took the nomination in 1904. It was the beginning of a real career. While there are some things I would like to forget, there are so many that I remember with pleasure that I prefer my own career to that of any other citizen of Louisiana. I am getting old now and I am quite happy although I would rather not have been defeated in 1920. My sympathy for the good friends who went down with me is about the only thing which causes me any great regret.

That sentence about the change from mule cars to electric cars and from messenger boys to telephones was right to the point. Now that I am 18 years older and better able to express my ideas, I wish to say that I am proud of it.

Most people are always figuring on getting things fixed to suit them and then having them stay fixed. There is no such thing as staying fixed in this life. Everything changes and moves. I realized that at the time. The people complain about the number of laws that are passed and the number amended at each session of the legislature. They blame it on the incompetence of the legislature. That may be sometimes but it is not true most of the time.

Things change. The people's ideas change from time to time. What they approved of in 1920 may be very unpopular in 1924. Once upon a time you could easily condemn anything by saying it was "Socialistic." When it was decided in 1910 to build the public cotton warehouse, *The Times-Democrat* said it was "Socialistic." Nobody paid the least attention to that.

A politician has to keep up with public opinion. I do not mean that he has to change his course to suit every preference of the public as indicated by what the newspapers say the public thinks. I mean he has to know what the public really wants. Once or twice I have felt justified in "bucking the public."

I was right in saying that what I did and left undone as mayor in 1904 would make or ruin me. I was re-elected without opposition. That is most of the answer to any question regarding the quality of my work.

It is extremely probable that I would have been elected [in 1904] without opposition, at least without serious opposition, but for an issue that grew out of the preference of [Governor Newton C.] Blanchard for Porter Parker as [Orleans Parish] district attorney. He was against Chandler C. Luzenberg, who was a candidate to succeed himself. I was in favor of Luzenberg.

Luzenberg had been an excellent district attorney. As governor, however, Blanchard was a strong influence. In addition to the power of his patronage, which he had not lessened by making his appointments and therefore had all his aspirants to state jobs among his followers, he had great influence with some of the leaders.

It was rumored that Blanchard was in favor of Lionel Adams as Chandler Luzenberg's successor. I know that he did not urge him very strongly. Adams was then practicing law and writing editorials for *The Item*, which was controlled by Dominick C. O'Malley.

A majority of the leaders were in favor of Luzenberg. I was one of this majority.

Blanchard discussed the matter with me at length. He had been friendly to me and I finally agreed to support Porter Parker.

Blanchard went to the St. Louis exposition [in the summer of 1904]. It was rumored that Samuel A. Montgomery, himself mentioned as a candidate for district attorney, went to Bay St. Louis and got on the train on which Blanchard was returning to New Orleans and told him he would have to do some hard work if he wanted to defeat Luzenberg and get Porter Parker nominated.

Blanchard sent for the leaders when he reached New Orleans. He found that Robert Ewing, James Henriques, and Samuel Gilmore were against Porter Parker.

In the convention, Henriques nominated Luzenberg and Colonel E. M. Hudson of the tenth ward seconded the nomination. Col. Hudson called Blanchard "Cataline." I found out that this Cataline had led a revolt in Rome about 2000 years before and got the much worst of it and lost his life. I could not understand then and I do not understand now why Col. Hudson rang in Cataline. I knew from a little book I read that Napoleon Bonaparte used to go all over Europe and tell them who was to get the principal jobs as kings, prime ministers and so forth. It seems to me that it would have been more to the point to call Blanchard a Napoleon instead of a Cataline. However, I do not think Blanchard cared a rap what anybody called him. I have myself been called worse things than either Cataline or Napoleon.

Porter Parker was nominated.

Among those present was John M. Parker. I am told he was there because "blood is thicker than water," Porter being his brother. I have never understood that expression about blood and water but I can understand how John M. felt. He wanted Porter to get the job. I do not blame him. If I had a brother in politics and that brother had been mentioned for district attorney, I would probably have supported him all I could.

But I would not have supported his nomination by a political organization of which I did not approve.

I do not remember that John M. Parker took any active part in the hot campaign of 1904 when I was elected mayor.

The city Democratic convention of 1904, which nominated me, was held in the old Athenaeum,[4] the scene of many an event that has influenced this community and concerned me as a citizen, personally and officially. That great hall was crowded. It seemed to me there was political electricity in the air although I had no opposition and I had no reason to expect serious opposition in the campaign.

I was nominated by Peter Clement of Algiers, who was afterwards Judge Clement.

"As an humble citizen from the Fifteenth ward," he said, "I desire to place in nomination for the mayoralty of this great city of ours one of our beloved citizens, one who is known by every

---

4. The Athenaeum was located at 1205 St. Charles Avenue.

man, woman, and child in the district in which he lives, one who bears an enviable reputation and whose character had never been assailed either in private or public life.

"I do not desire at the present time, knowing the man as I do, to eulogize his good qualities but simply to place his name before the convention and I do now nominate for mayor Honorable Martin Behrman."

Seconding speeches were made by James O'Connor, now congressman,[5] then chief lieutenant of Alex Pujol in the Fifth Ward, and A. P. Marmouget of the Ninth ward, a friend of Ferd Dudenheffer's. A motion was then made that the nomination be closed and that I be nominated by a rising vote. The delegates all stood up and the chairman of the convention, James C. Henriques, declared me nominated.

The Times-Democrat had had an editorial almost every day protesting against my nomination. I had learned that while newspapers have the power that comes from the opportunity to give or shut off publicity, and even to misrepresent a candidate or a situation, it was not easy to do at that time in New Orleans. That paper carried a lot of interviews or supposed interviews with un-named leaders who predicted I would not be nominated.

As I stood on the platform, facing that enormous crowd, I glanced at the galleries. I did not see Page M. Baker [editor of the *Times-Democrat*] there. While I was not so quiet as I have often been in my rocking chair in the evening, I was not much excited. The excitement, I thought, was all over. I was wrong on that but I felt satisfied and victorious and I would have liked very much to have seen Page M. Baker and to give him a pleasant smile.

There is no doubt that Martin Behrman was in a very good

---

5. James O'Connor, U.S. Representative from the First Congressional District (New Orleans), 1919–31.

humor when he stood on that platform to accept the nomination. I remember thinking the day after the nomination, just as I thought recently, that the world moves fast. In all countries, I understand, men rise from the ranks of the very poorest people to high places of trust, of honor, and of power. But that happens more often in our country. I was not yet 40 years old when I was nominated. Perhaps some will think I should have been more modest and give luck and fate the credit for my rise in politics.

I am not trying to be modest. I am trying to tell just how I felt and what I thought about various things of importance and perhaps of interest because they are important, or seem important, to a four times mayor. I was quite proud of myself when I was nominated. And I am a great way from being ashamed of myself now.

I was ready to make that speech. My pronunciation was probably not equal to that of many men among my hearers but my speech was exactly what I wanted to say.

"I assure you," I told the delegates, "that I cannot find words of my own to express my gratification at this unanimous selection to head the Democratic forces in the coming fight for the high and honorable position of this great city."

> As you all know who know me well, I am not a public speaker. I have been as you all know, a worker in the ranks, and with this nomination today, which I know means an election, I promise you to work as I have always worked for the next four years.
>
> In accepting this nomination, I do it with full knowledge of the responsibility. I know that a great deal more will be expected, in certain directions, than would be from a man who is in the higher walks of life, but I know also that you will believe me when I tell you that I will bend every energy to reflect credit on your choice today.
>
> It seems to me that in a great city like this, a city with its great and promising future, that a candidate for the office of mayor can properly come from the people. To the working men of this city, if you want to know who Martin Behrman is ask the men in the shops

on the other side of the river. Ask the men in the shipyards who have been my associates all my life. If you want to know my business abilities, ask the men on Poydras street with whom I have worked for several years.

If you want to know my capacity as a public officer, ask anybody who had business relations with the various offices I have filled during the 16 years of my political life. Ask the professional man, the business man who had dealings with the Board of Assessors over which I had the honor to preside for several years. I will leave the verdict with them.

I want to say that our streets today are not in the condition they ought to be and I shall actively cooperate with the Commissioner of Public Works in bringing about a better state of affairs in that respect.

And I want to say to you, and I will tell it to you here frankly, that if there are any sinecures in any part of the city government they will be wiped out and that none will be created during my administration of the public affairs of this great city. I do not want to keep you any longer. The weather is warm and you have a great deal of business to transact, but I do want to thank you again from the bottom of my heart for the high honor you have conferred on me today. I thank you very much.

When I said that a great deal more would be expected from me "in certain directions" than would be expected from a man in "the higher walks of life," I meant that I would be subjected to criticism by *The Times-Democrat*, the silk stockings, and the reformers on matters that would probably be overlooked if a more prominent citizen and not a professional politician had been nominated. Somehow or other, the old silk stocking crowd seemed to think that one of their own kind could do things not permitted to such men as myself. If one of them got dead drunk at a prominent club, that was all right. He was only having a good time. But I suppose if I got drunk at the Cosmopolitan or the Choctaw Club, that would be all wrong. This idea applies also to official conduct.

No matter what may have been their school and college

education, the refinement of their manners and the quality of their clothes, the silk stockings in politics were not so superior morally and mentally as they thought themselves. They know this now themselves and there is no such thing as the old type of silk stocking politician left among us. At least, I do not know of any. The people have completely done away with them in politics. There was just a mere taste of it last summer when one of the candidates did a little bragging about his distinguished grandfather. He soon quit it.

The Times-Democrat, however, had the silk stocking point of view in that campaign. It seriously charged that I was "uncouth" and therefore should not be mayor. As I stated early in these recollections, while discussing Page M. Baker and his ideas, I was opposed then with the argument that I was "uncouth." Sixteen years later, when I had the benefit of contact with all kinds of people as mayor, one of the arguments brought against me was that I was too far from uncouth to have any sympathy with the masses of the people. Yet all that time, I lived in the same house, associated almost entirely with the same people, and I did not change my habits and preferences except as ordered by the doctor. It seems that because my job as mayor forced me to attend a lot of functions and deal with important citizens whom I would not have known as assessor or in private life, I had become what we used to call a "silk stocking." That is the way the newspapers handled it.

It was on August 28th, 1904, a little less than a month before the convention of September 21st, that Henry L. Garland, Jr. [New Orleans attorney] suggested in a letter to *The Times-Democrat* that an organization to be styled "The Crescent City Democracy" be formed to prevent my election.

The opposition, I soon learned, was bitter and determined. Most of the leaders in it were opposed to Luzenberg because he had been appointed after the assassination of District Attorney J. Ward Gurley by a lunatic [July, 1903] through our influence.

Their natural tendency would have been to support Porter Parker. They did not have a real issue. Then one developed for them.

As I remember it, *The States* first suggested a mass meeting at the Liberty statue in protest against Blanchard's success in keeping Luzenberg off the ticket and putting Porter Parker on for district attorney. Anyhow, a meeting was held.

I was told at the time that James E. Edmonds, then a reporter on *The Times-Democrat* called on [Governor] Blanchard and expressed some of Page M. Baker's tremendous indignation over the developments. Blanchard, the story goes, turned to Edmonds and said:

"What are you going to do about it?"

Whether it was Edmonds or not that got it, that sentence became a campaign slogan in what was known as the "Home Rule" movement. They printed it almost daily in *The Times-Democrat* as Blanchard's defiance of the people of the city who, they inferred, wanted Luzenberg and none other for district attorney. They printed it on dodgers in English, French, German, and Italian. They printed it across their campaign letter head with the Liberty monument[6] in the center above it.

With the exception of William S. Parkerson,[7] I got on friendly terms with practically all the leading "Home Rulers" before the end of my first term as Mayor.

It was Parkerson who charged me with "grafting" on the Edison Electric Light company and with having obtained a pass for a woman to take a trip on a railroad.

As I stated in an earlier chapter of these recollections, I had

---

6. The liberty monument was erected at the foot of Canal Street in 1891 in memory of the victory of the White Citizens' League over Republican Governor Kellogg's Metropolitan Police during Reconstruction on September 14, 1874.

7. William S. Parkerson, New Orleans businessman and perennial opponent of the Ring, was a prominent member of such political reform movements as the Young Men's Democratic Association (1888), Anti-Lottery League (1892), Citizens' League (1896), Jacksonian Democracy (1900), and the Home Rulers (1904).

no real control over the assessment of the electric light property on this side of the river at that time. I was assessor for Algiers. But I had worked for the company for a time. Its assessment was reduced. I do not remember the reasons for the reduction. In fact, I knew very little about it. But the connection between my salary as a solicitor for a short time and the reduction was furnished by William S. Parkerson, who obtained affidavits from two employees of the company that they considered it "graft."

This matter had not been raised against me in the state campaign [for auditor]. When Parkerson announced that he intended to ask me some questions, I was not sure what he was driving at. If it were not that my temporary employment by the company, which I had quit because I believed it would be used against me in politics, was publicly known, as I have explained in detail, that might have occurred to me.

Parkerson announced on the stump for about three weeks that he had his questions to ask. As I have stated, I was not sure what he intended to ask and did not see that my employment with the electric light company would come into the city fight as it had not come into the fight for auditor. I was advised, however, to get ready for that. I did so by getting an affidavit from E. L. Bemiss, who had employed me for the company. As I stated earlier in these recollections, I got the job as solicitor after I was forced out of the position of deputy assessor by the dismissal of Thomas Higgins, the assessor, by Governor Nicholls. I kept it for a short while after I was appointed assessor, working then for the company on the New Orleans side. I consulted ... Kruttschnitt [chairman of the Democratic Central Committee] and others and they saw nothing wrong in my keeping it. I soon after quit the job because my employment might be used against me in politics.

John T. Michel [Louisiana secretary of state] and James C. Henriques delivered William S. Parkerson a written demand from me that he hurry up and ask his questions. He did not give any real answer but just kept telling his audiences that he would ask the questions and demand answers. I was over in Algiers when he finally asked them. I crossed the river and went to Earnest Kruttschnitt's office to talk to somebody or other, I have forgotten, who was connected with the Home Rule headquarters at Royal and Canal.

In making his charges that my employment and a reduction in the assessments of one of the electric light companies were cause and result, Parkerson made the mistake of getting his figures wrong. That struck me as something of a real "faux pas."

I remember that when I spoke in the fourteenth ward, then looked upon as the stronghold of the silk stockings, I made three campaign pledges. I told them that I would be elected and that, while mayor, I would never dance a german, never join the Boston Club, and never join the Pickwick Club. I defy anybody to produce evidence that I broke these promises.

While Robert Ewing and *The States* and Dominick C. O'Malley and *The Item* were supporting me, they took cracks at each other right in the middle of the campaign. O'Malley printed some "charges" against Ewing that were possibly a little embarassing but had nothing whatever to do with the campaign. They were about as serious, as I saw it then, as if Ewing had been charged with riding a bicycle on the sidewalk.

One of the amusing "inside facts" of the fight was a sort of inspiration meeting of the Home Rulers on the Sunday before the election. They had their factional leaders from the wards gathered together and Parkerson made them some talks. Then each ward leader would rise and estimate the majority he would get for Charles F. Buck in his ward. They had me beat down to about 4000 votes as I got the story. Two young men from Algiers were more conservative then the others. They claimed they would "break even with them," meaning the Regulars. They got Mr. Buck 187 votes against my 785.

If every man able to qualify as a voter had paid his poll taxes for 1902 and 1903 and registered, I would probably have been defeated in 1904. I say probably to be conservative. I believe I would have been defeated. But it happened that the regulars, who were to be destroyed by the poll tax provision, had paid theirs and had seen that their friends did the same. I got a larger majority than I expected to get.[8]

While Governor Blanchard's successful work in preventing the nomination of Chandler C. Luzenberg for district attorney and inducing the leaders to support Porter Parker furnished the battle cry of the Home Rule faction, and the charges William Parkerson made against me considerably increased the political temperature, back behind it was a sort of main idea of the opposition. That idea was that a ward leader, which is what we call what they call a "ward boss," was not fit to be mayor. The impression they conveyed was that a professional politician was unfit for an office of honor because he was a professional politician.

Judging by the plain fact that a majority of the citizens on the streets appeared to be against me, I had the idea that I might lose the votes of a great many, who would have supported me, if that issue had not been raised. I mean, if it had not been directly and indirectly "played up" so strongly. Before the campaign was over, I was of the opinion that those who would vote against me for this reason were practically all opposed to my faction anyhow and that few, if any, would desert the Regular faction for that reason. It was not until the last week of the campaign that I knew, from the reports made by members of the organization, that the Home Rule faction had more followers than voters. As I have said, the poll tax provision, welcomed by some as a means of destroying our organization, had a great deal to do with cutting down the possible total for my distinguished and able opponent, Charles F. Buck.

8. Behrman received 13,962 votes to Buck's 10,047.

However, I had just come out of a campaign[9] in which my ward leadership in New Orleans was in some sections a decided disadvantage. I reasoned that, since the country voters were not so much against a "ward boss" as their newspapers and politicians often indicated, New Orleans would not be so much against me on that score.

I shall never forget a meeting at Homer, in Claiborne Parish. I had a good friend there, Senator [J. C.] Madden, on whom I knew I could depend to get me all the votes he could in that race for auditor. He spoke plainly to me. He told me there was a great prejudice in that section against the "ward bosses" and he thought it might not be discreet on his part to take me around but advised me that there would be a meeting in Haynesville in the same parish, near the Arkansas line, and that I should go there and see how I took with the people. I took his advice and went as suggested.

I did not attempt to misrepresent myself. I told them that I was the Regular leader in Algiers and talked for about an hour to a little group of men on city politics. Some of them seemed to have the idea that city politics consisted mostly of hanging around saloons and treating to drinks and cigars. I told them of life in Algiers and my acquaintances with many small farmers down the river and so forth. I made a short speech at the meeting.

I must have done well, for the next day at the meeting in Homer, over which Senator Madden presided, he seemed to take great pleasure in introducing me to the crowd. I remember practically what he said.

"I want to present to you," he announced, "my friend, Martin Behrman. He is one of those so-called 'New Orleans ward

---

9. Behrman is referring to his 1903–1904 campaign for state auditor. He did not resign that position until after being elected mayor in 1904.

bosses.' I know him. He is a good man. You notice he does not wear horns. The only horns he wears are on his coat."

Senator Madden referred to an Elk button.

There was an agricultural fair in progress. I suggested to the audience that I thought they were probably more interested in the exhibits than in political speeches and that the meeting adjourn and we would visit the booths and stalls. I did and we did. I believe I was quite as much of an attraction as the animals.

I could hear them saying in half-whispers, "That's him," and "There is the ward boss." I am not quite sure but that some of the little children might have been frightened by the sight of a ward boss.

Old man Goodwin,[10] who published the *Colfax Chronicle,* which circulated all over Grant parish and that vicinity, wrote a humorous article about my visit to Colfax. He said it had served a very useful purpose as the children had been told by their parents that if they did not behave the New Orleans ward boss would get them.

Having just come out of a campaign in which the "ward boss" business had been raised about me, and having won, I was not so much upset by the same issue in New Orleans.

The Times-Democrat took a somewhat inconsistent attitude during the campaign. Inconsistency in *The Times-Democrat,* I may say, is not confined to what I did back in 1904. That paper, and many of the speakers for the alleged "cause of the Home Rulers," had done everything possible to get Blanchard to insist that I be put to one side and that another man more satisfactory to them be given the nomination. While I did not seek the nomination and had done everything I could to get another man for it, once my candidacy was publically known, I was deter-

---

10. Howard G. Goodwyn.

mined to get the nomination. I could not afford to have done otherwise.

This was the same *Times-Democrat* that denounced Blanchard for working to keep Luzenberg off the ticket and to put Porter Parker on it.

There were some who defended Blanchard's attitude by the claim that the office of district attorney is really a state office since he has to do with the enforcement of state laws, and that the office of mayor is a local and municipal office and has nothing to do with state business. So far as I am concerned, that argument has little force. As I saw it then, Blanchard was doing exactly what every other governor had done. None of them did it more skillfully and completely than [Murphy J.] Foster. All of them took a hand in our city politics when they thought they could do so. In after years, I became of the opinion that Louisiana's governors should not take any hand in our city politics but I do not know how it is possible to bring this about.

The influence of governors in the local politics of cities and counties is exercised all over the United States. I do not know of any way of preventing this and I will not say that no good ever comes of it. While I believe in the "local option" idea on Principle, I believe it is not practical. If the governors are to keep out of local politics in the cities, they should do so in the parishes and counties. If they keep out of all local politics, they will soon find themselves out of all politics.

There are, of course, serious abuses as a result of the activities of some governors in local politics. But so long as the local politicians have any interest in the state government and its boards and officers, just so long will the governors have an interest in local politics.

I rather expected to see John M. Parker's name among about 150 prominent citizens who signed the call for the mass meeting that started the open fight against me in 1904. I expected it, possibly, because he was a member of the Cotton Exchange and

I did not have as many as five votes in that crowd. It was not there.

One of the laughs [during the 1904 campaign] I had was when *The Times-Democrat* described a visit by [local labor union leaders] Robert E. Lee and Tom Harrison, to John Fitzpatrick, our campaign manager, as a "faux pas." It happened that these leaders simply called and advised Captain Fitzpatrick that I had been endorsed by their unions and would probably get a large majority of the votes of the union men. *The Times-Democrat* called that an attempt to "deliver the union vote" and described it as a "faux pas." I knew enough French to know that "faux pas" was what most of us now call a "bad break." I wondered whether it would have been a "faux pas" to "delivery the labor vote" to Charles F. Buck.

The Regular headquarters were at the Choctaw Club, then next to the Grand Opear House [on Canal Street], but I had three rooms at the Cosmopolitan Hotel as my personal headquarters. Joseph Voegtle was running the Cosmopolitan and these rooms were part of his personal contribution to my campaign.

There was a great deal of betting done on that election. I had a small share in a big pool and we won a lot of money. I did a little two to one betting. O'Malley went around in Varieties Alley, back of the Cotton Exchange, and offered to make some large bets. The members of the exchange were game and extravagant. They accepted the bets, knowing their failure to do so would show a lack of confidence in the Home Rule movement.

During that campaign of 1904, in which Frank A. Daniels and William S. Parkerson were the formal leaders of the "Home Rule" movement and Page M. Baker and the *Times-Democrat* were the real leaders, it was rumored around that I had accumulated a fortune in politics. This was one of those persistently circulated "rumors" that appeared in almost every campaign.

Somebody or other reported to the *Times-Democrat* that I

had built a handsome mansion in Algiers. It was talked around on the streets that I had spent $30,000 on my palace and that it was filled with fancy furniture and large sideboards loaded down with cut glass decanters full of the finest wines. I believe they raised it to $40,000 uptown. Then they added several grand pianos, rugs and carpets from Europe and Asia, oil paintings from the best collections in foreign countries and all the kind of things that Pierpont Morgan used to put in the Sunday supplements after he formed the United States Steel Corporation. A house that cost $30,000 in those days would cost somewhere between $60,000 and $70,000 at present. This will give the younger generation a clue to what their rumors meant in 1904.

The Times-Democrat sent a photographer over to Algiers to get a photograph of the Behrman mansion. He got it. But it was not satisfactory. I suppose the house did not come up to advance notices and being a very small and modest little home, it was not suitable for their campaign purposes. In fact, if the photograph had been printed it would have helped my candidacy as mine was and is the kind of home that probably suits the average man.

The only thing about my home that has ever caused me any displeasure is the telephone. I had to have a telephone, of course, and therefore I had to accept the inconvenience and disturbance of it with the benefits. It has saved me many a trip across the river and has cost me many an hour of sleep and it has interruped my breakfast and dinners frequently. Men who have finished their work when they leave their offices do not know what luck they have. My telephone always made it impossible for me to forget municipal business and politics. That telephone has also saved many a newspaper reporter's time. I have sometimes been amused by reading a reporter's description of my manner and the expression on my face, as I told him something over the telephone.

Most of my readers, not being familiar with the inside situations in the newspaper offices back in 1904, probably see some inconsistency in the fact that I was first asked to run for mayor at a meeting in the *Picayune* office and that paper did not support me in the campaign. On the surface, this looks wrong. As a matter of fact, it was alright.

There were a number of stockholders and older officers and employees at *The Picayune* who each had his say in deciding what would be the policy of the paper on any important matter. When they sent for me to attend that meeting, nothing was said that I remember on the point of whether *The Picayune* would support me. It inferred [implied] that it would but as I knew the system in that office I was not right in doing so. I felt no resentment whatsoever against *The Picayune* when it came out for the Home Rulers and Charles F. Buck. The support of the paper had been in no way committed to me.

The conduct of *The Picayune* during the campaign was admirable. It printed everything sent it by James E. Edmonds and Fred Waltz, the young reporters who had the titles of "assistant secretaries" in the Home Rule headquarters. Edmonds was a *Times-Democrat* and Waltz a *Picayune* man. Neither of them hesitated at anything for lack of nerve and audacity.

As I remember it, *The Times-Democrat* and *The Picayune* both printed substantially the same things against me and *The Times-Democrat* did not follow the *Picayune's* good example of giving me a square deal on the publicity. *The Picayune* kept the Home Rule stuff on page one. Most of the time, the political news and propaganda, of both sides, appeared side by side on page one of the *Picayune*.

That appealed to me as fair dealing. I appreciated it at the time and have never forgotten it. I do not care what the papers say about me in their editorial columns short of criminal libel but I do care what they do with their news columns. The one sided slant given everything in politics by some of the newspapers is practically a confession that their editorial columns have no influence. In writing this criticism, which is just and fair, I do not want to put myself in the position of claiming any superior virtue. It is entirely possible that I might subject myself to the same criticism if I were running a newspaper. However, I would not try to deserve it.

During the many years I was mayor I have often heard it said that I always had the political support of the brewers. This was not true in 1904, when I made that first campaign. The only brewery support I had was in Algiers. All the brewers on the city side supported Charles F. Buck, who was attorney for many of them and who as I remember it, was one of the attorneys of the New Orleans Brewing Association in former years. The influence of the brewers was probably greater then than it was later as up to that time there had been no fight on the saloons.

One of the speakers in my behalf was Col. John P. Sullivan, Captain John Fitzpatrick's son-in-law.[11] I heard a number of Sullivan's speeches and they were good. I am not saying this merely because he supported me. I think that the newspaper files will show that he made serious speeches and stuck to the subject, though some of his expressions were a little extravagant. One sentence of his stands out in my memory and always brings a smile when I think of it.

Sullivan was telling his audience all the different ugly and undesirable things he would rather be than be William S. Parkerson. Finally he got to this:

"I would rather be a maggot in the suppurating carcass of an insane mule than that man Parkerson."

Within less than a month after I was inaugurated as mayor,

---

11. Colonel John Sullivan, a long-time member of the Regular Democratic Organization and son-in-law of John Fitzpatrick, broke with the Regulars in 1919, formed a splinter group called the Orleans Democratic Association, and backed the successful gubernatorial candidacy of John M. Parker in 1920. That same year Sullivan and the O.D.A. supported Andrew McShane for mayor. Shortly after McShane's victory, Sullivan organized the New Regulars hoping to give himself an organizational base to fill the political vacuum in New Orleans with Behrman's defeat.

George François Mugnier photograph, Louisiana State Museum
Canal Street, *ca.* 1885

Louisiana State Museum
Behrman's childhood home on Bourbon Street, *ca.* 1939

George François Mugnier, Louisiana State Museum
The Quay at New Orleans, *ca.* 1900

George François Mugnier photograph, Louisiana State Museum
The French Market where Behrman worked and played as a boy, *ca.* 1895

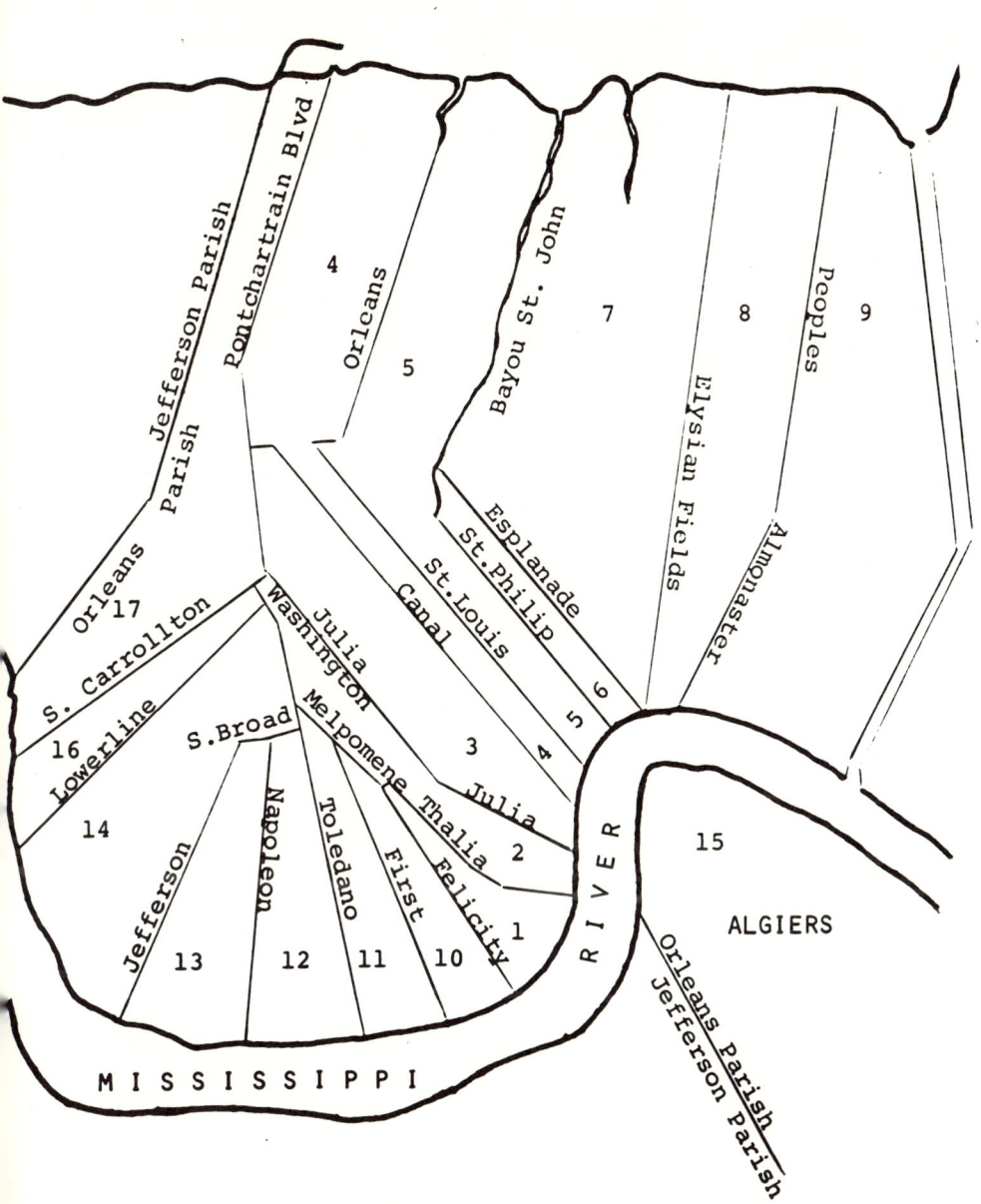

The seventeen wards of New Orleans

"The Lottery Octopus," ca. 1890

J. Denechaud Papers, Louisiana State Museum

"Louisiana State Lottery Company"

"9:15 A.M., Discussing Deep Waterway with a Friend on the Ferry"

"9:30 A.M., Mayor Reaches City Hall and Opens His Mail"

"11:40 A.M., Councilman [A. J.] Harmeyer of the 16th Ward Calls"

"11:45 A.M., Mr. [Alex] Pujol Calls"

From a series of photographs of a typical day in the life of Mayor Behrman, by J. H. Coquille, New Orleans Times-Democrat, ca. 1910. New Orleans Public Library

George François Mugnier photograph, New Orleans Public Library
New Orleans City Hall (Gallier Hall), *ca.* 1900

Behrman's home in Algiers, 1976

Sullivan was appointed an assistant city attorney. He kept that place about five or six years and resigned it either late in 1909 or early in 1910.

I cannot say that I was the best speaker on my side. Mr. Buck, however, was undoubtedly the best speaker on his side. Having already described him as a speaker, it is not necessary to do so now. Professor Alcee Fortier was among the speakers for Charles F. Buck.

One of the unconscious jokes of the campaign was *The Times-Democrat*'s analysis of the probable vote on October 21, 1904, eighteen days before the election. It gave the Home Rulers and Charles Buck a minimum majority of about 5,200 which was greater than the majority I got.

RING—Original ring certain vote 9,000 less 2,000 lost by Lee-Fitzpatrick-Harrison faux pas	7,000
Negroes, mainly in the Third and Fourth Ward, including Storyville Contingent	300
Voters marked "doubtful" who have been won over by promises of positions in City Hall, especially assistant city attorneys and counsels for various boards	1,000
Doubtful voters who may have been tricked into believing the ring will win (they may change before elections)	1,000
TOTAL	9,300
HOME RULE—Original independent vote always opposing ring	9,000
Labor vote insulted by Lee-Fitzpatrick-Harrison	2,000
Doubtful voters who have come over during the week, convinced by argument or believing Home Rule will win	3,000
Republicans who want good city government	500
TOTAL	14,500
Hesitating voters who have made up their minds but want to make sure which side will win and Republican vote	3,200

The foregoing was seriously presented as an analysis of the preferences of the voters eighteen days before the election.

"These figures are, of course, subject to change between now and election day," *The Times-Democrat* proceeded, "but if the tide sweeps on as strong as it did last week nearly all the hesitating or doubtful voters will find their way under the banner of Home Rule and assure the usual big majority against the ring whenever the patriotism and civic spirit of the voters are aroused."

On Monday, the day before the election, *The Times-Democrat* assured its readers that there was no way to defeat Home Rule and that city was assured by a majority of 3,500.

I got 13,962 votes and Mr. Buck got 10,047. My majority was 3,915.[12]

The Republican candidate, John A. Wogan, got 496 votes. The Socialist candidate, W. Covington Hall, got 179.

Covington Hall was a poet and writer and "militant socialist." I was then told that the only business in which he engaged was selling insurance as it was the only business that appealed to him as absolutely fair and on the level.

I do not mean by this that he considered that a majority of us are crooks. He was against all our institutions. He was against what they call "the hell hounds of the capitalistic system," the form of government, the system of doing business, the "crooked press," and everything else that goes to make his life what it it. I have not seen Covington Hall for many years but I am told he has not changed his ideas of how things should be but has practically given up hope of reforming the whole world.

12. The final returns showed Behrman with 13,962 votes to Buck's 10,047. Buck remarked after the election that Behrman's victory was a turning point in New Orleans history: "By the election of the ring ticket to power, the progress and development of the city has been retarded." The New Orleans *Daily Picayune*, which supported Buck and the Home Rulers, admonished the approximately nine thousand voters who failed to vote as indirectly sanctioning government by "boss rule, jobbery, and graft." New Orleans *Daily Picayune*, November 10, 1904.

I have often felt a great deal of sympathy for consistent men who sacrifice their lives in devotion to their ideas. While Covington Hall was an extreme radical, as radicals went in those days, from my point of view he was and is in some ways in the same class as many impractical men who are considered quite conservative and who do not realize that you cannot drive people into making big changes all of a sudden.[13] It takes many

13. William Covington Hall (1871–1952), son of a Woodville, Mississippi, Presbyterian minister, was active in the Louisiana socialist party for over fifty years. In his numerous poems and essays, Hall urged the workers and farmers to rise and unite against capitalism. In the preface of his book, *Battle Hymns of Toil* (Oklahoma, ca. 1946), Hall is quoted as saying that he was "born in the midst of tumults and riots and, if I live a few years or months longer, I expect to die in the midst of tumults and riots." "I have," continued the quotation, "seen the collapse and downfall of two great social systems, Southern Feudalism and, now, of Capitalism; and I see no hope for a free and Democratic Republic and world other than in Cooperative Democracy, a Confederation of the world based on the Jeffersonian principle of 'Equal rights and opportunities to all and special privileges to none.'" Paradoxically, Hall was Adjutant of Camp Beauregard, United Sons of the Confederate Veterans in 1903.

In an undated manuscript, entitled "Labor Struggles in the Deep South," Hall wrote a disjointed history of labor struggles in Louisiana, particularly in New Orleans, from the pre–Civil War years to the second decade of the twentieth century. Other works by Hall were *Rhymes of a Rebel* (New Orleans, 1931) and *Songs of Rebellion* (New Orleans, 1915). Between January, 1915, and June, 1914, Hall published an unsuccessful pamphlet, entitled *The Lodestar* (later changed to *Rebellion*), which consisted of poems and essays espousing the cause of revolution. According to the preface in the first issue, the pamphlet was "of the Rebels, for the Rebels, and for the Rebel Workers of the World. . . . a magazine of Rebel thought, a journal where in we can say what we damn please, 'regardless of affiliation.'" In an autobiographic poem published in *Songs of Rebellion*, Hall put into verse the reasons he became a "Rebel." Three stanzas from the poem, "Why I am a Revolutionist," read:

> I have heard the child-slaves weeping when the world was fair and bright,
> Heard them begging, begging for the playgrounds and the light!
> I have seen the statesmen holding all save truth, a vested right. (stanza 1)
> In these wild and frightful moments, I have felt my reason reel,
> Felt an impulse like the Tiger's over all my being steal;
> Felt it would not be a murder if my hand the blow could deal,
> That would brand upon your temple the death Angel's mark and seal. (stanza 7)
> Then I heard a voice crying, "Workers of the World Unite!"

years to develop conditions that make it possible to overthrow even such a detail as the election of United States senators by popular vote instead of by legislature.

Public ownership of such facilities as our grain elevators, cotton warehouses, coal tipple and public belt, was condemned as "Socialistic" and "radical" ideas when I was young. Now public ownership of such facilities is quite conservative and hard boiled bankers and business men all over the United States are strong for it. These, however, are mere minor details in the large programmes of the radicals.

They are fighting human nature when they try to upset what they called the "capitalistic system." No matter what things may go wrong under the "capitalistic system," the vast majority of people are for it. That is due to the fact that so many of us are satisfied with things as they are and so many of us, no matter how poor, look forward to the day when we or our children will be "Hell hounds of the capitalistic system" even though only on a small scale.

It sounds very nice when you say it fast, to have a system under which every man will work and get the same share of clothes, food, house, and so forth. But you will have a hard time convincing the average laborer on the riverfront that he should help support one of those painters who produces pictures of the Pontalba buildings, the St. Louis Cathedral and Jackson Square. And that average laborer on the river front has a vote and plenty of it.

> And the vanguard of Marxians broke upon my hopeless sight,
> Serried ranks of Rebels marching 'neath the Crimson flag
>   of right,
>   To call our class to action, to arouse it to its might.
>   (stanza 8)

Hall's published and unpublished works are located at the Special Collections Division, Howard-Tilton Memorial Library, Tulane University, New Orleans. For additional reading on Louisiana socialism see Grady McWhiney, "Louisiana Socialists in the Early Twentieth Century: A Study of Rustic Radicalism," *Journal of Southern History*, XX (1954).

The votes for the candidates showed that very few of the voters cared to split their tickets. Our slogan was "Stamp the Rooster"![14] A majority did it. The Regulars, The Home Rulers, and the Republicans all had full tickets.

All the votes were being counted, a number of citizens, mostly Home Rulers, were sworn in by Mayor Capdevielle as special police to prevent disorder at the polls.

The fact that the country parishes took such an intense interest as they did in the city fight may have been due in part to my having been elected a state auditor. A number of telegrams came to my headquarters at the Cosmopolitan. One of them from Shreveport read: "Is it true you have been beaten? They are betting four to one against you." I replied: "Election over, votes being counted, and I have been elected." The Regulars knew that night before the totals were reached, that we had won.[15]

I have been through a lot of campaigns and political struggles since 1904 but that fight stands out in my memory with the state fight of 1912, when John T. Michel was defeated [in the gubernatorial election]. Had I been defeated in 1904, it is possible that I would have retired from politics.

2.

Behrman's Philosophy on Government: Politicians versus Silk Stockings

I have heard a great many orators in my time and a large number of good ones. But not in my 32 years of public work and political campaigns, attendance at lectures and visits all over the United States, have I heard a better speaker than Charles F. Buck. If I was the only one who thought he was the best speaker in my

---

14. The rooster was the symbol of the Democratic party in Louisiana and of the Regular Democratic Organization in New Orleans.
15. The Regulars lost three seats in the city council: the 12, 14, and 16 "silk stocking" wards.

time in politics, I would think that was because he appealed to my personal taste, but any man of the older generation in New Orleans will tell you this opinion is justified.

Buck was the candidate of the Regulars against Walter C. Flower in 1896, when the negroes went solid to the Citizen's League ticket and elected Flower. He was again a candidate for mayor in 1904, against me. Eighteen years are passed since then. There is not a speaker here today who can give one the treat that we got when we listened to Mr. Buck. I did not, of course, hear his speeches and lectures, talks on Shakespeare and other literary objects, and as the chief speaker at formal banquets. There are many still with us who remember him well.

With the possible exception of Page M. Baker, editor of *The Times-Democrat*, Mr. Buck had read more than any man I ever met. He was a student of Shakespeare and I believe he and Ashton Phelps, who managed the commercial page and wrote editorials for *The Times-Democrat*, knew every line that Shakespeare ever wrote. In these days it was not unusual for long letters about what somebody said in one of Shakespeare's plays to be printed in the "Letters from the People" departments of the newspapers.

Without any preparation whatever and often with only a few minutes' notice, Mr. Buck could deliver a speech that sounded as if he had spent weeks preparing it. It was not a string of jokes or just a lot of words that we got from him. He usually had something to say on any subject of public interest and what he had to say was worth hearing. He had the knack of quoting Shakespeare, and many authors that I never heard of before and have not heard of since, and quoting them so that everybody got the point. He was never simply an entertainer on the stump. No matter whether you agreed with him or not, you had to admit that he had a real opinion and that it was based on the facts.

I did not know Page M. Baker, editor of *The Times-Democrat*, in any personal way until after I had been elected mayor in 1904. But for a long time before that, being a careful reader of all the newspapers, I knew him pretty well as an editor. The first time I ever saw him, so far as memory goes, was at a meeting of the public order committee in the council chamber. The committee met in connection with the bids for the public printing. I was working as its clerk.

Page M. Baker and one or two others from *The Times-Democrat* were there. Dominick C. O'Malley was there for *The Item*. Peter Kiernan represented *The News*, Robert Ewing, Joseph C. Aby and Walker Ross appeared for *The States*. The meeting had just begun when the gentlemen of the press began quarreling with each other. It was hard to keep any kind of order. Then a general row started and everybody was talking at once and somebody called another gentlemen a damned liar.

I think it was Aby that pulled the gun. I was seated with my back to the wall and no way to get out. The gun looked like a howitzer to me. The others made for the doors and windows, but I stayed there, not from choice, but because I was wedged in, and fumbled with my papers and hoped the artillery would not open fire. As luck would have it, nothing serious happened but the committee meeting had been informally adjourned by the gun and did not resume business that day. The grand jury investigated the affair but nothing came of the investigation.

My reading of the political articles and editorials in *The Times-Democrat* of Page M. Baker's days made it evident to me that he did not think plain citizens such as myself should aspire to large public offices. As I understood his position and read between the lines of his many editorials, as he was always opposed to the organization, his idea was that professional politicians should not have political power and that the public places that have power should go to gentlemen of literary learning, students of history and prominent citizens in charge of large establishments, such as banks, railroads and so forth. He was for what we called the "silk stocking element in politics."

There was a great deal of talk in my early days about preserving the people's liberty by "rotation in office." All of it did not come from Page M. Baker and men of his turn of mind, but a great deal of it did. It seemed to me he wanted the offices to rotate to his silk stocking friends. His main idea was that plain men from the less fortunate families living on side streets in small houses, men who spent their whole lives actively in politics, should never be promoted to positions of power in government.

In those days the words "silk stocking" were used to point out a type of citizen who knew all about municipal government because he read magazines and books and the Life of Jefferson and did not know where to file his complaint if the garbage man did not come around early enough to suit him. The high class silk stocking always knew what led to the fall of the Roman empire, but he did not seem to know that the bulk of the voters were more interested in schools, police, firemen, the charity hospital, the parks and squares and labor troubles than the Roman empire. In those days the political opinions and preferences of the average voter were based more on what he met every day on his job and in the streets than on what happened to the Roman empire. Yet the silk stockings used to do it uptown a great deal.

I am glad to notice that we have no more of that "silk stocking" idea in New Orleans. There is no longer a "silk stocking" ward in New Orleans. The people have come to realize that book learning and a wise look are not so important as the old time "silk stocking" seemed to think, and the time passed a long time ago when a newspaper editor would oppose a candidate for mayor on the ground that he was "uncouth."

One of the reasons given by the *The Times-Democrat* for opposing me in 1904 was that I was uncouth. When I first say that word "uncouth," I did not know exactly what it meant. I looked it up. It meant that I was ignorant and awkward and clumsy and did not have good manners. Before discussing this, I must call attention to the fact that 16 years later it was argued against me that I had become associated with men of education and high position, directors of large corporations, professional men, members of clubs and so forth. When I was young I was no good because I was uncouth. When I was older and more experienced, I was no good because I was not uncouth. You cannot please all the people all the time. No matter what you are, your opponents point it out as a reason why you will not do.

Mr. Baker's "uncouth" shows his attitude very well. Some time has passed since then and I believe I am now in a position to discuss it better than I could in 1904.

Mr. Baker meant that I was ignorant. Was I so ignorant? I had had 16 years of real experience once as deputy assessor, assessor, clerk of the three most important committees of the city council, member of the school board, and member of the constitutional convention of 1898. I was a member of the convention's committees on education, taxation and affairs of the City of New Orleans. I had just been elected state auditor. Mr. Baker knew this. He knew also that I was a charter member of the Progressive Union and that I had associated a great deal with business men and interested myself in commercial affairs of the city.

It is true that I could not quote Shakespeare and tell about the fall of the Roman empire and what was going on in the British House of Commons and the Reichstag. I had not developed a liking for the opera. But I did know the city finances, the organization of the police and fire departments and all the machinery of city government, and I knew what improvements were most needed. I knew far more about the actual workings of the city government than Mr. Baker, who was busy on other matters.

As to my manners and whether I was awkward and clumsy, it seems to me that my manners must have been enough. I was practically always treated with politeness and consideration. I will admit that in my younger days, and even after I was elected mayor, I did feel a little nervous sometimes when I had to meet admirals, generals and presidents in a formal way.

My political influence has often been attributed by my opponents to intrigue, machinations, plots, "sinister combines," the "ring" and all that kind of thing. Without having definitely and clearly said so, stump speakers among the "reformers" and their newspapers have suggested and hinted that some moral short comings in me have largely formed the basis of my influence. The answer is that if these things were true many of my opponents would have vast political power instead of none.

If you want to be a precinct captain, you have to work. If you want to be a ward leader, you have to work much more. If you want to be a real political chief, you must be "on the job" day and night. And if you want to be Mayor and at the same time leader of a big city organization, and stay in office sixteen years, you have to do so much more work that by the time you are fifty eight years, which I am now, the doctors will be telling you what you cannot eat and to avoid all strenuous excitement. That's what they have told me.

Mr. Baker was opposed to the professional politicians, what he called the "job hunter." I was not and am not opposed to such men.

All other things being equal, the voters should support the professional politicians. Nine times out of ten, perhaps, oftener than that, he makes a better official. He is not concerning himself only with the job he has at the time, but looking forward to re-election or another job and that gives him a good reason to do the best he can. The amateur or "now and then" politican, who usually comes out for office when he thinks there is a wave on against the professionals, seldom expects more than one term. He seldom gets more than one.

My observation and experience leads me to believe that the

"here and now and absent tomorrow" politician does not make a good official. He is not looking forward to promotion, or even to keeping his job, so he is inclined either to neglect his work or to use his place to get another job in private life. He has neither experience nor a determination to stick.

The people should vote for active politicians unless there are good reasons to turn them down. It is bound to happen now and then that a real politician gets a job that is too much for him and he does not give satisfaction; and it also happens that men without any experience in politics, if advised and supported by politicians, make excellent records.

When I write "professional politician" I mean not only men who make their living by holding public jobs but also men who spend a great deal of time either in politics or on public jobs. It very seldom happens that an inexperienced man, no matter how successful in business, makes a good public official.

All our governors have been politicians. Some have been brilliant successes and none of them has been a 100 per cent failure. Most of the solid work in the municipal government of New Orleans, has been done by professional politicians. Some of the biggest and best ideas have come from men with no steady interest in politics but they had to be worked out and put in effect by politicians. The man who takes no active interest in the grind and routine of politics, which is government, frequently makes a first-class member of a board. But even then he usually gets the benefit of the advice and assistance of the professionals.

Without setting myself up as a professor of history, I wish to say that I do not know of any kind of government that can do without a large number of professional politicians. I mean regular, constant job holders, always interested in public affairs, public jobs and public improvements. The professionals get to know each other and naturally flock together, just as do lawyers, doctors, and merchants. They usually organize and have their meeting places, such as the old Crescent Democratic Club and the Choctaw Club. They welcome citizens of all walks of life to these clubs. They keep in touch with all details of public affairs.

Suppose Mr. Baker's ideas were adopted. Then when a man who liked politics found that he had some ability to handle large jobs, he would probably quit politics because he could not be elected to a big position. We would be always electing a new lot of inexperienced men. The greater number of office holders would be either men never heard of in politics or the impractical citizen who likes the excitement of campaigns and keeps away from a public job until offered a chance to get one of the big positions. Sometimes they get them. Most of them who do get them are sorry before their terms are over. They are usually not half so sorry as the voters that put them in.

The professional politician, who looks forward to continuance in an important elective office or promotion to another, knows that the voters can and will hold him responsible for results. If he has any sense at all, he knows also that he will be constantly under attack and that he cannot please everybody. He will do the best he can to give satisfaction to the majority. There will be times when he will feel justified in ignoring the popular demand, trusting to the future to justify his course. That is what I did when Warren Easton died and it was necessary to chose his successor as superintendent of the public schools. As a general rule, the election of active politicians to the important places makes for responsible government.

On the other hand, as a general rule, when you fill the government with newcomers in politics you usually get what is known as "invisible government." This means that the man or the men who adopt policies and decide on their details of operation are not the men in office. The worst government in the big cities of the United States have been such as these, the governments controlled by men out of office.

When a man out of office and not to be held directly responsible for what is done gathers the real power into his hands, he is in a position to put things across that he would not stand for if he had to sign his name to the papers. Then, after resentment has been directed at the men in office, he gets him another lot of candidates and they go before the people as "'fresh meat."

So far as I am concerned, I have never tried to dodge responsibility for anything that was done by the city government while I was mayor. I am willing to be judged by the total of the results. Some things did not turn out well. What can you expect in sixteen years, the last of which were years of disturbance and distress due to the high prices that affected everybody and everything?

As to the honesty of the professional politicians, I wish to say that it is not below that of any class of workers that includes large numbers. The newspapers, usually the opposition newspapers, make a great row whenever dishonesty is discovered in the government. It is right that they should do this but it is wrong that they should constantly suggest that there is any less honesty among the politicians than among bankers, railroad men, merchants, etc.

A cash shortage of $2,000 in public funds is naturally of more public interest than a cash shortage of $2,000 in a newspaper office. The first gets big headlines and the second usually gets very little attention. When a bank cashier gets away with some money, the public is not given to understand that the president and the board of directors were in cahoots with him. When a clerk on a public job does the same thing, the public is given to understand that the whole administration was directly responsible.

The books at the city hall, from Lafayette to Carondelet street, are open to every citizen. As I remember it, during my sixteen years as mayor there was one shortage in the city's money and another in the funds of the Sewerage and Water Board. I would like to ask the auditors of the railroads entering this city if their books show so good a record. I ask them the same thing of the managers of the newspapers. Have the bank presidents of 1904 to 1920 noticed no dishonesty in their institutions? Is there any large business institution employing so many men as were employed under the direction of the municipal officers during those 16 years that can show a better record?

There was a scandal in the council during the Fitzpatrick administration.[16] But none the less that administration gave New Orleans a splendid administration. What I want to point out now is that John Fitzpatrick was both a professional politician and a good manager of the city's business. He had foresight and he had had the experience of fighting his own way. He spent his early boyhood in St. Mary's Asylum for Catholic Orphan Boys. He went into politics when he was a carpenter. He made a living in politics and accumulated some money through fortunate investments. He was the kind of politician that Page M. Baker opposed simply because he was a professional politician.

I wonder how many college educated silk stockings, who knew all about the Roman empire, and did not know the details of their tax bills would have followed John Fitzpatrick's example when he burdened himself with debt to make good a moral obligation to the State of Louisiana.

C. Harrison Parker had a clerk in the state tax office who seemed to know its business very well. John Fitzpatrick kept this man because he seemed to be a reliable worker. When the fellow robbed the state of a large sum, John Fitzpatrick felt that he was responsible for it. Since he had kept that clerk all those years, he felt that he was in duty bound to make good the loss. His lawyers said he, John Fitzpatrick was responsible only to the amount of the bond he had given the state. But he went out and mortgaged everything he had and the state did not lose one

---

16. Behrman was referring to the boodle scandal in the city council during Mayor Fitzpatrick's administration (1892–96). See note 19, Chapter 1 herein.

cent. He did not stand on the fine points of the law but on his own ideas of the justice and honesty of the matter.[17]

How many of John Fitzpatrick's silk stocking critics would have done the same thing? So far as I am concerned, I think there are on the average just as many good citizens among the "silk stockings" as any other element, but I must admit that they include some of the most irritating persons I have ever met. I can tolerate ignorance except when ignorance goes with an assumption of superior knowledge or superior viture. The trouble with the unpopular men among the "silk stockings" was that they thought they knew it all when they really knew very little about their fellow citizens and so seldom had a practical program in mind.

I wish to say here that the average reformer always considers himself to be the real progressive because he is, usually, opposed to the party or faction in power. The word "reformers" originally meant men or a faction that planned to lift municipal government from their alleged wickedness and make them pure and holy, according to their ideas of what was purity and holiness.

From my point of view, the reformers contained many elements. Among them were men of high character and patriotism who had impractical ideas, for the most part, but who consistently fought for those ideas both against the Regulars and against the fake reformers in their faction. Such men as these usually got tired and quit in disgust.

17. Although John Fitzpatrick's administration as mayor of New Orleans ended in April, 1896, he continued to be active in state and city politics until his death on April 8, 1919. During the administration of Governor William Heard (1900–1904), Fitzpatrick was appointed tax collector for the first district (New Orleans). While holding this office, one of his deputies embezzled approximately $116,000 in state funds. Fitzpatrick, apparently feeling a sense of responsibility for the actions of his deputies, repaid the entire sum above the $30,000 liability bond from his own pocket. John S. Kendall, *History of New Orleans* (3 Vols.; Chicago and New York: The Lewis Publishing Company, 1922) II, 516.

Then there were the men who advanced good ideas and made them popular and got something done. There were a lot of such men, for instance, and a great many women, in the movement for a juvenile court.

But the majority of the "reformers" were always simply the "outs." They were fake reformers trying out this and that as an issue to defeat the Regulers and get political power into their own hands for their own benefit.

It seems to me that there are some political fakers among the patriots who have it that Martin Behrman is dumb whenever anybody says "progress."

Who, after all, are the real reformers? I hate to apply the word "reformer" to the men I have in mind and will not do so because that word has become rediculous.

When it became necessary to reorganize and "reform" the organization for protecting Louisiana from floods, no silk stocking did it. Samuel D. McEnery did it.

When the lottery was killed, practical politicians did the work under the leadership of Murphy J. Foster. There were a lot of silk stockings on both sides of that issue but it was the practical politicians that did the real work.

It was the practical politicians and not the reformers that put the negroes out of politics in 1898. They had had the benefit of the negro vote and they joined in the movement to eliminate the negroes when they saw it had to be done and would be done.

As I recall the work done by men in their private business and their connection with public affairs, it reminds me that the public often forgets and more often does not know the real relation of their lives to the progress of the city. The politicians, however, which is another and a shorter way of saying "the men who run the government," do know to what a great extent men whose names seldom, if ever, appear in politics render service to the public in advising public officials. Some of the men I have named never appeared in politics. From deputy assessor to ex-mayor, I have always recognized the value of their advice and friendship even when I did not agree with them and went ahead with programs of which they strongly disapproved. It is a great satisfaction to a public official to be able to consult with disinterested men who will tell him what they think and have no immediate personal interest in the results.

When the Progressive Union, which was succeeded by the Association of Commerce (in 1913), was organized [in 1902], I had not yet become even a "prominent politician" as the term goes. But I had always cultivated the friendship and companionship of businessmen and I was much complimented but not much surprised when I was made a member of the first board of directors.

My opponents in politics have more than once declared or charged, whichever they wish to call it, that I got friendly with the Progressive Union when it became a strong organization.

Politicians frequently pass up such things as this because they have not the time to answer every inaccurate statement that is made about them. The fact is that my friends and acquaintances among the merchants and other business men of New Orleans were a little unorganized progressive union long before that organization was thought of. I did my share in getting up the organization and worked hard on its committees for many years.

I now come to a rather exciting episode in my first administration, the dismissal of John Journee as chief of police, the election of Edward Stanley Whittaker [sic] and the elimination of Dominick C. O'Malley as an influence in police affairs.[18]

18. Edward S. Whitaker, judge, member of the state legislature, city attorney, and police inspector, had a stormy career in Louisiana politics. During the 1890s, while serving as judge of the recorder's court, Whitaker was indicted for embezzlement. But after three mistrials, the charge was dropped. From 1905 to 1908 he served as police inspector for New Orleans but was forced to resign after attempting to murder Joseph M. Leveque, editor of the *Morning World*. Whitaker died on January 5, 1912, while serving

3.
Big Police Fight of 1905

Dominick C. O'Malley came to New Orleans from Cleveland, Ohio, and after a few months here went to Mobile. He returned here and engaged in work as a private detective, his first case being the defense in a divorce suit. He settled in New Orleans and was employed as a detective by a committee of citizens who were fighting the councilmen of 1893–1896. I understand that during or immediately following that affair he bought *The Item*, which was in debt, for $3000 cash and the assumption of the debts.

It appears that Judge [R. H.] Marr did not preside at the trials of the men charged with the killing of David Hennessy, chief of police, but did preside at the trials of the Provenzanos for the killing of the Matrangas [on May 6, 1890] as an outgrowth of competition in unloading cargoes of bananas. O'Malley was employed by the Matranga family or faction. Convictions were obtained and while an appeal to the Supreme Court was pending David Hennessy was assassinated. It is reported that he was warned not to interfere in the feud. It was Judge [Joshua G.] Baker who presided at the trials of the men charged with the killing of David Hennessy.

O'Malley worked for the men charged with the killing of Hennessy. He is said to have received an enormous fee. I have heard it put at $60,000. He had to go into hiding at the time of the lynching but soon after re-appeared and proceeded as usual.

When O'Malley first appeared in our politics he was very friendly with Edward Stanley Whittaker and he either loaned

---

a ten-year prison sentence for committing sex crimes with little girls. John Wilds, *Afternoon Story: A Century of the New Orleans States-Item* (Baton Rouge: Louisiana State University Press, 1976), 165, 174–75; New Orleans *Daily Picayune*, January 6, 1912.

Whittaker the money or gave him the money for his campaign fund. Then they fell out . . . over one of the lotteries in which O'Malley was interested and Whittaker had it broken up.

Soon after that Whittaker was suspended as recorder on a charge that the fines collected in his court had not all been turned into the city treasury. As I get it, this charge and others to the same effect, were promoted by O'Malley. Whittaker was tried and found not guilty. Whittaker claimed that if anything had gone wrong his clerks were responsible and the circumstances were such that this was accepted by the courts and the public.

From that time on, Whittaker and O'Malley were bitter enemies. I do not know what started the row they had in St. Charles street near Commercial Alley, but Whittaker pulled a gun and shot O'Malley and ran him through the alley. Later when Whittaker was elected Inspector of Police, O'Malley announced in *The Item* that the next time Whittaker came after him he would be armed. That was telegraphed all over the country as a challenge from a newspaper publisher to the inspector of police to settle their differences with revolvers.

I had seen practically nothing of O'Malley up to the time I ran for Mayor. He and *The Item* supported me in that campaign. It was not long after my election when I heard that he had stated he could handle me. "I will handle that little Dutchman," he was reported to have said.

The new police act required that the board of three members fill the office of inspector of police at its first meeting in January of 1905. It provided for an inspector of police at $3000 a year and gave the board the authority to abolish the position of superintendent of police which paid $3,000 a year, whenever a vacancy occurred.[19]

---

19. Act 32, *Acts Passed by the General Assembly of the State of Louisiana at the Regular Session, 1904.*

Col. John P. Sullivan was a candidate for inspector of police. *The Times-Picayune* opposed him on political grounds. That paper said that making Sullivan inspector of police would turn the force over to his father-in-law, Captain John Fitzpatrick and make him a political dictator and me a figurehead. Sullivan was not elected because he was just six months under the age limit fixed in the law.

E. A. O'Sullivan, city attorney in the Fitzpatrick administration and one of the speakers in my behalf in the campaign of 1904; Sidney Story, the steamship agent, who had been in the council of the Flower administration; and, Captain William Barrett, a police Captain, were the others mentioned. O'Sullivan was one of O'Malley's lawyers in the civil courts.

The police board was composed of Joseph A. Hincks, secretary of the Board of Administrators of of the Tulane Fund, Samuel Diamond, a boss drayman, and myself. I was ex-officio, a member as mayor. The board elected John Journee as inspector and abolished the office of superintendent. I did not vote for Journee. A few days later Sam Diamond resigned.

"It is impossible for me to serve on the board," Diamond said in his letter of resignation, "as no matter what is done you cannot please the public try as you will. I done my duty as I thought best but it seems that I made a mistake."

I said that the election of Journee was a mistake and that they should not have elected him because that choice would not be satisfactory.

The Times-Democrat came out with a recommendation that Whittaker be appointed, or elected, inspector. When the old charges, to which I have referred, were revived by O'Malley in *The Item*, the *Times-Democrat* defended Whittaker. Whittaker's grandfather, G. K. Whittaker, was an editor of *The Times* long before it combined with *The Democrat*.

Whittaker studied law with his uncle, Judge R. Whittaker, and represented the second ward in the legislature in 1884. He was elected recorder in 1892. He raised a company of volunteers for the Spanish-American war and was commissioned captain by President McKinley. He was at Santiago for six months and General Leonard Wood made him Judge advocate. He was interested in hunting big game and took several trips to the far west for this purpose.

I had a conference with Page M. Baker of *The Times-Democrat*, Thomas G. Rapier of *The Picayune* and Robert Ewing of *The States*. While I had thought of Whittaker as a good man to destroy O'Malley's influence over the police force, I was not sure that it would be a good appointment and had by no means decided definitely to propose it when I went into that conference. That is my present recollection of my frame of mind at that time.

The newspaper men argued, naturally, that the main work at hand was to get rid of O'Malley's influence with the police and that in the circumstances Whittaker would be a good man for that purpose. They agreed that they would endorse his selection, which they did.

Journee was at a convention of police chiefs in Washington when the grand jury brought in a report that exposed the conditions in the police force. Among other things, the grand jury said Inspector Journee was incompetent, that there was corruption on a large scale in the police department, that the police and the detectives were so jealous of each other that they did not cooperate as they should and that there were a number of unfaithful officers on the force.

I knew that Journee was not the man for the job and had said so. The three newspaper publishers of what was then referred to as "The United Democratic Press" agreed with us that Journee was honest and that he should be provided for. They and I wanted him to resign and accept a new place, which would have been fixed for him, at $3500 a year. He would not resign.

When Journee got news of the grand jury's report, he hastened back from Washington and William P. Ball, my secretary, met him early in the morning and they came together to my home. I had a talk with him and when he left I thought he would resign. He did not do so. I suspended him on a charge of incompetency and put Captain John P. Boyle in charge as senior captain.

Then beginning on the basis of the grand jury's report, and with the help of information volunteered by citizens, Col. John P. Sullivan and I worked out the details of the charges of incompetence against Journee. We saw in more detail what we already knew, that Journee had no real control over the force. Sullivan and I interviewed a great many witnesses and I was astonished to find as much rottenness as we uncovered.

Men who make their living by sharing the earnings of women in the district had a club or association and the dues of the members, it was reliably reported, were turned over to some of the police. Lotteries were run freely. The police force had certainly become rotten. Not all of them, but enough to warrant my saying that the force was rotten.

Journee was tried by the board and dismissed and Whittaker was immediately elected inspector of police.

Absolutely nothing connecting Dominick C. O'Malley with the evil conditions, other than gambling was developed by any private investigation or at any public hearing. He was interested in gambling houses and he was interested in lotteries. There was no doubt of the identity of the officers on whom he had a hold, however, and they were dismissed by Whittaker.

I remember that in former years, when O'Malley was attacking certain dance halls, he was referred to as "Dirty Convict" O'Malley. This was based on a report that he was an ex-convict, having served a term in Ohio for stealing a watch. This story was not true.

The facts were that O'Malley was the oldest of a gang of boys at Cleveland and these boys had either built a boat or come legitimately into possession of a boat. The boat needed ballast and the boys went onto a foundry and took some brass to use for ballast. They were taking it for the weight and not for the value and iron would have done as well if iron had been handy. The owner of the foundry had them arrested. The judge got the facts of the case, discharged all the boys but O'Malley, the oldest, and gave him a few days in the lock-up as an example. This came out in some trial or other at which O'Malley was either a litigant or a witness.

Inspector Whittaker's chief work was to get rid of all O'Malley's friends and connections on the police force. I think a few resigned but most of them were tried and dismissed. I rather got the idea that they were much astonished that a friend of O'Malley's could be dismissed from the force.

There is no doubt in my mind that fully half the town thought it was certain that O'Malley would be killed. They expected him to be killed by Inspector Whittaker personally or to be "bumped off while resisting arrest," as one man put it. I dare say there were many who thought I wanted him killed.

If O'Malley had been killed, it would have had a very bad effect on my political career. The fact that the newspapers, except O'Malley's *Item*, were vigorously supporting me would not have helped me much. I felt that O'Malley might be killed, as he was considerable of a gunman himself, but I certainly did not want that to happen.

If he had been killed, I would have been held responsible for it. The public would have theorized that Martin Behrman had either encouraged or instigated the killing to get solid with O'Malley's enemies. I would never have been able to get away from that charge.

Moreover, O'Malley had a lot of friends. There were many of them who were perfectly willing that his political power be destroyed. But they would not have been favorably impressed by an assassination.

I believed it would ruin me politically if that happened. I knew it would ruin me politically if he were permitted to continue running a large part of the police force. I was much relieved when the crisis passed without any killings at all.

The crisis, insofar as the possibility of an assassination was concerned, came when it was reported that O'Malley and his editorial writer, Walter C. Smalley, were plotting to assassinate Whittaker. They were arrested and charged with conspiracy to murder.

It is unnecessary to recite the circumstances of all the arrests of D. C. O'Malley at that time. He was arrested frequently and thoroughly. Everything he did, as I remember it, that could furnish the basis of a charge of violation of the law resulted in an arrest. The purpose of this was to convince all and everybody that O'Malley's influence was gone, since being unable to avoid arrest himself he was obviously unable to keep any other person from being arrested. In the meantime, his friends on the force were being tried and fired right along. It was not difficult to get the evidence against them.

It is entirely possible that O'Malley would not have been jailed but that he grossly libelled me.

This is what he printed in *The Item* [June 16, 1905]: "When the public learns that this man Behrman has been saved by my instrumentality from indictment, prosecution and a possible penitentiary sentence, I rather fancy that the public will appreciate some of the circumstances governing the incident of this morning."

The "incident of this morning" was his arrest on the charge of conspiring to murder Whittaker.

I filed charges of criminal libel against him. The grand jury later indicted him for criminal libel on my account and also on account of something or other he wrote about Whittaker. He was not indicted on the charge of conspiring to murder Whittaker and that matter was dropped.

While all this was going on, with O'Malley denouncing "The

United Democratic Press," and Whittaker dismissing police officers and raiding gambling places and worse resorts, [New Orleans District Attorney] Chandler C. Luzenberg lost a suit for $30,000 damages against O'Malley and *The Item* in Judge Sommerville's division of the Civil District Court. Luzenberg appealed to the Supreme Court and the decision of the jury was reversed, some months later, and O'Malley paid $10,000 and costs for his libel of Luzenberg.

That was a political matter. O'Malley had charged that there was crookedness in the office of district attorney and he had so stated it that the inference was plain that he meant Luzenberg was dishonest. The point of the case, as I remember it, was whether the charge included Luzenberg. The jury decided it did not. The Supreme Court decided it did.

It doubtless gave O'Malley considerable satisfaction to win something even in a lower court, for the whole matter was spread on page one of *The Item* with a large picture of his attorney, E. A. O'Sullivan.

Whatever else may be said about him, Dominick O'Malley had the nerve. He knew that the end of his power was close at hand and that there was no chance whatever for him to survive as an influence. Yet, he fought through *The Item* with every weapon he could get. When he libelled me, he was desperate. But he was as cool as he was desperate.

One morning, just to make a good newspaper story, he went direct from his home to the first precinct station.

"I want to surrender to you," he said to the clerk. "I suppose the detectives are making a search for me again. They are probably waiting for me at *The Item* Office."

"But there are no charges against you," said the clerk. "If there are I don't know anything about them."

O'Malley then welked over to Judge Edward K. Skinner's court and was advised there also that there was no charge against him that morning.

"I came here and surrendered this morning," he told Judge

Skinner, "because I thought there were some charges against me. I was convinced that there were some more charges when I saw four officers loitering around my place."

He waited around the Criminal Courts building until 2 o'clock in the afternoon for some more charges, but none were filed.

I have tried to locate a bit of poetry that appeared in *The Item* about the middle of the row. My clipping of it has become torn and faded, but I remember the sense of the thing. It had me as nurse to Robert Ewing and rocking him to sleep in a cradle with a song to the effect that we would soon have O'Malley out of business. One verse of it, referring to Colonel Ewing, was as follows:

> "Sweet visions of power! What comfort to feel
> That Baker and Rapier are right at your heel;
> And who would not smile in the consciousness dim,
> That the chief of police was working for him?

O'Malley then filed suit against Whittaker for alleged "persecution" in the rapid-fire arrests.

I won the libel trial against O'Malley. He produced a letter, with the head of it torn off, which I had written him in connection with a proposed investigation of something or other in the city treasurer's office. This he presented as a letter written him, as I remember it, while I was assessor. I took from my pocket a letter on the stationary of the office of the state auditor and showed the court that it was the same paper.

"Your client is somewhat clumsy," I told O'Malley's lawyer. O'Malley, it seems, jumped to the erroneous conclusion that I had had something to do with what was known as the "Badger gas ordinance" of 1901. As I have said, he was desperate and he probably knew he was taking a chance of going to jail for that attack. He took the chance and he paid a $500 fine and served five months of the six months sentence.

I do not claim to remember all the details of the story of the Badger gas ordinance. My somewhat remote connection with the matter was due to my friendship with August Schabel, councilman for Algiers.

I heard some rumors that an offer had been made to give stock and bonds in the proposed gas company in return for votes in the council or for the influences that might get votes. I told August Schabel of this and I warned him to be careful of what he did. Had he voted for the ordinance and had there been any truth in the rumors, he would have been under suspicion.

Schabel was a member of the committee. I think it was called the "fire and lighting committee," that passed on the ordinance and he forced the adoption of an amendment to strike out the words "Badger & Company" and insert the words "the highest bidder" so that there might be competition for the proposed grant of a franchise.

I was a member of the board of assessors at the time and officially had nothing to do with this business. However, if I had always confined myself to doing things that were officially my business, I would not have been mayor for sixteen years and this city would not have some of the good things it now enjoys. At least, it would not have obtained them as soon as it did.

Both being from Algiers, Schabel and I disucssed city business very often. We were particularly drawn together as we were in a group that did not have the sympathy and the approval of the majority. Some memoranda recently made of the newspaper stories of the trial of O'Malley brought out the fact that some time before that one of the newspapers, probably the *States*, had reported that:

"Schabel could not get a drink of water from the council if he asked for it."

I think it was probably Schabel's amendment that resulted in the defeat of the ordinance before the committee, which gave it an unfavorable report, and its withdrawal from the council.

Shortly after that I had several of my friends at my home for breakfast and the subject of the ordinance came up. I repeated the rumors I had heard. They had become general and the grand jury decided to investigate them. August Schabel was called and refused to tell who had talked with him about the rumors that stocks and bonds were to be given in return for work or votes in behalf of the ordinance. Schabel's reason was that he thought it might injure me but later, after consultation with me and others, he appeared before the grand jury a third time and told them that Martin Behrman was the man. He informed the grand jury that he had opposed the ordinance on my advice to do so.

Henry L. Lazarus, the lawyer, advised Schabel that in withholding my name he was creating a situation that might later do me an injury. *The Times-Democrat* had already mentioned me in connection with the matter but almost immediately corrected its error in an editorial. O'Malley came into Lazarus' office shortly after Schabel had signed a letter to the grand jury and, as Lazarus testified at the trial for libel, he said to me: "I've got it on you, Martin."

I told him where he could go, that I did not like that kind of talk and if he had anything on me to go ahead and use it. This was one of the two or three times I met O'Malley before the campaign of 1904.

So far as I remember nothing more was heard of the "Badger gas ordinance" from that time to the day it came into the testimony at O'Malley's trial. Mayor Capdevielle was much outraged over the current reports and I believe he had the grand jury investigate them.

O'Malley tried two defenses. One was that he was not responsible for the article in *The Item* to the effect that he had saved me from the penitentiary. That was soon knocked out by the testimony of one of his own reporters. The other was in the use of the letters to which I referred in the section of recollections preceding this one. The letter, or letters, I have forgotten whether there was one or two, were written on the paper I used while I was state auditor. The letter heads and the dates were torn off. They were presented as letters written in 1901, when I was assessor. As I remember it, my communications to O'Malley concerned something or other in the treasurer's office. When they handed them to me, I identified the handwriting as mine and admitted that I had written them. Then I produced complete letter heads from the auditor's office and showed Judge Joshua Baker, who presided at the trial, that the letters produced in evidence were on the same paper.

O'Malley was found guilty. He did not bat an eye. He did not appear to be much disturbed. He said something or other angrily but I do not remember it. I suppose he knew he had put his foot in it long before the testimony closed and all the excitement was over.

My experience has been that there is always somebody or other who has "got the goods on Martin Behrman." I suppose O'Malley figured that there were necessarily "goods to be got" on me and that I would pass up his charge and not go into court against him.

O'Malley was sentenced to $500 fine and six months in the parish prison. When he finally went to the parish prison, I am told, he had his own bed, a "talking machine" as we then spoke of phonographs, and a lot of fancy poodle dogs and spaniels for company. He was there five months when he was released on the certification of a physician that he was in danger of dying. He lived about 16 years after his release. O'Malley then settled down to a comparatively quiet life as a dealer in fish and oysters. He lived mostly what the French call "La Ravanche."[20] I am reliably informed that he was much pleased when I was finally defeated for office in 1920. O'Malley always got into the good

20. Perhaps Behrman was referring to *La Revenge*, meaning revenge.

graces of whomever might be opposing me at the time. He became friendly with [Governor Newton C.] Blanchard. He did a lot of quiet work for the Good Government League that elected [Luther E.] Hall [governor] in 1912, just as he did the same thing in Theodore Wilkinson's behalf [in the 1908 gubernatorial campaign]. He visited John M. Parker at least once in 1916, I am told.

O'Malley closed out the American Fish, Game and Oyster Company and some time later interested himself in *The Morning American.* He was with that paper only a short time.

J. M. Leveque, better known as "Joe Leveque," was running *Harlequin,* a semi-political weekly, at the time Whittaker was made inspector of police. He denounced Whittaker's selection and declared it would make trouble. Shortly after that Leveque and his associates started the *Morning World* and that paper severely criticized Whittaker. I never could understand why a man capable of restraining himself in the face of O'Malley's attacks lost his head because of Leveque's comparatively mild criticisms.

Whittaker and some of the detectives went into the *World* office and Whittaker attempted to kill Leveque. The police board met immediately and dismissed him. The detectives were relieved of responsibility because they accompanied Whittaker under orders as the head of their force. Whittaker served a term in the parish prison for the attempt to shoot Leveque.[21]

Whittaker's election as inspector of police, as I have indicated, served its purpose. While O'Malley busied himself with all devices and schemes he could think up to injure me and the publishers of the "United Democratic Press," he was no longer

21. On January 17, 1908, Whitaker and several of his detectives went to the *Morning World* and shot Leveque. The detectives, unaware of Whitaker's intentions, were exonerated. Whitaker, however, was found guilty and sentenced to serve a brief term in the Orleans parish prison. New Orleans *Daily Picayune,* February 20, 1908.

in a position to do any harm to the community as a whole through improper influence with the police.

4.

1905 *Yellow Fever Epidemic*

One of the astonishing things that attracted my attention when the yellow fever broke out in July of 1905 was the large number of citizens who found something in it to laugh about. I was myself more than nervous over the situation but the people I would meet on the ferry included many who joked about the fever just as they joked about the war and other really serious things in which I could see nothing funny.

I was on the ferry one morning early and I was tired from the work of the day before, which ran almost to midnight, and I was not feeling very well either as mayor or as the head of a family that might get the fever. A man whom I did not know and have never seen since came up to me. He was smiling.

"Buck up, Mr. Mayor," he said, "Show 'em a grin. If you let them see you in the dumps, some of these galoots will think things are worse than they really are."

"Thank you," I said, realizing that he had given me some good advice. "I think we have seen the worst of it."

"Maybe so, but I've got a bet of ten dollars next week will be higher than last week. I made the bet just to scare the fellows at Bertucci's saloon."

I asked the man his name and got it but I have now forgotten who he was. However, there were lots just like him. They seemed to think yellow fever was close to a sporting event. What he told me and what he had done were not consistent and he knew it and laughed over it.

However, it was no laughing matter for the city as a whole. That was the last epidemic of yellow fever, more than 17 years ago, and the thousands who worked to keep it down and kill it out will agree with me that there was nothing humorous in the situation.[22]

As I remember it, the first cases suspected of being yellow fever were at the Hotel Dieu.[23] Dr. Edmond Souchon was president of the Louisiana State Board of Health. There had been instances in past years when attempts were made to conceal the fact that there was some yellow fever in New Orleans but that practice had been dropped and as soon as Dr. Souchon decided these cases probably were yellow fever he immediately notified presidents of the state boards of health all over the country.

A bunch of health officers arrived from the capitals of the Southern states within the next two days. They inspected the situation. They made up their minds to leave and go home and declare quarantine against us.

I pleaded with these men to stay with us a while and watch the developments. The patients were very sick and I begged the visiting doctors to wait until they died so that examination of the bodies could make it sure whether they had yellow fever. But they all left and as soon as they got home they declared their quarantines.

This system of state quarantines against us did the Port of New Orleans a great injury. Our commercial rivals had in former years established quarantines on the slightest excuse. At the close of my recollections of the fever of 1905 I will tell how we stopped them by getting the federal government to take charge.

22. The epidemic of 1905 was the last yellow fever epidemic to hit New Orleans. From its founding the city had been plagued by the almost yearly visitation of the yellow death. During the nineteenth century there were several major epidemics; for example in the 1850s approximately 25,000 people died as a result of the fever with slightly over 8,000 in 1853 alone. In the epidemic of 1878 almost 4,000 deaths were recorded. The city had epidemics again in 1879, 1880, 1883, 1897, and 1899. Robert C. Reinders, *End of an Era; New Orleans, 1850–1860* (Gretna, La.: Pelican, 1964), 95–105; Edwin Adam Davis, *Louisiana: A Narrative History* (Baton Rouge: Claitor's, 1965), 324.

23. Hotel Dieu is a private hospital in New Orleans administered by the order of St. Vincent de Paul.

Even when no quarantines were established in former years, we would be threatened with quarantines. Many of us believed this was done merely to advertize the fact that New Orleans might have yellow fever. Once when I was assessor and the fever broke out here, the health officials of Alabama refused to admit a carload of carbolic acid from New Orleans. At another time, either Alabama or another state notified us that a shipment of sulphur would be turned back. It is hard to make me believe that these officials were afraid of yellow fever germs in carbolic acid and sulphur.

While a considerable number of our citizens sent their families to Covington, Hammond and other places in the pine tree country [north of Lake Pontchartrain], and a few ran away from town as though they were sure to die if they stayed, the people of New Orleans did not lose their nerve. In fact, I have never known this city to become so panic stricken as to interfere with the work of putting down disease. The idea then was that there was something about the climate of the pine tree hills that prevented yellow fever. We know now that it was lack of breeding places for the fever mosquito, the "stegomyia." It thrives only in clear water, such as cistern water. Our cisterns were the breeding places and by oiling the cisterns immediately and screening them as fast as possible we kept the fever far within the record it would otherwise have made. The people in the pine tree country did not have many cisterns and so did not have much chance of a real epidemic of fever.

I do not know who discovered that the stegomyia mosquito transmitted the yellow fever.[24] A number of physicians and scientists have been given credit for that discovery. A brilliant young man, Dr. Richardson of New Orleans, lost his life in experimenting with the stegomyia. But it was Major General Gorgas, a relative of George and Walter Denegre, who applied

24. Dr. Walter Reed and his associates, while conducting experiments in Cuba in 1899 and 1900, conclusively proved that the *stegomyia fosciata* mosquito was the carrier of yellow fever.

the mosquito theory at Havana and proved it to be correct.[25]

While Dr. Gorgas did not take charge here, and this matter has nothing to do with the yellow fever of 1905, I may be pardoned for stating that a little incident at Camp Beauregard late in 1917 shows the spirit in which the federal medical officers acted in 1905 and have acted ever since. That is why we wanted them to take charge of all quarantines, thus removing from the state authorities the power to quarantine us without sufficient reasons. There was spinal meningitis and other trouble at the camp. Major General Gorgas and his subordinate officers, Dr. Isadore Dyer of New Orleans and Dr. Oscar Dowling, president of our state board of health, spent a day inspecting the camp.

At the end of the day, Major General Gorgas met an *Item* reporter at the depot. This had been arranged either by Dr. Dyer or Dr. Dowling. The reporter told the Major General that from what he had been told by Colonel Schauffler, the division sanitary officer, and from what he had heard in Alexandria and New Orleans, the rumors and reports of the conditions at the camp were so much worse than the facts that it would be a good thing for him to make a statement. *The Item* got a scoop on a very important piece of news and many a distressed family was put more or less at ease by that authoritative declaration of the actual conditions.

It is hard to maintain a statement that any one man or group of men did either the most or the best work here in 1905. Every-

---

25. William C. Gorgas (1854–1920), a native of Alabama, received his medical education at Bellevue Hospital Medical College in New York where he graduated in 1879. In 1880 he was appointed to the U.S. Army Medical Corps. After Walter Reed established in 1900 that the *stegomyia* mosquito was the carrier of yellow fever, Dr. Gorgas gained international fame for ridding Havana, Cuba, and the Panama Canal Zone of this infectious insect's breeding grounds. In 1914 he was promoted to the rank of brigadier general and in 1916 sent on "yellow fever missions" by the International Health Board to Central and South America. During World War I, Gorgas headed the Army Medical Service. Richard B. Morris and Henry Steele Commager (eds.), *400 Notable Americans* (New York: Harper and Row, 1953), 111–12.

body called on for any service did their full duty. I would have to dig into all the officials records and the newspaper files to make up a list of those who most deserve compliments on their conduct during the epidemic; and all of them would not be white men. While most of the negroes, like some of the whites, looked on the mosquito theory as "bughouse stuff," which was a familiar expression at that time, they carried out their orders to oil all standing water and to have their cisterns screened. Their leaders spread the doctrine of the mosquito theory and sometimes had fun poked at them.

But only two years before that, when some propaganda in favor of the mosquito theory was sent out from the city board of health, some of our councilmen poked fun at it. It is hard to blame the blacks for doing what the whites had done.

I was many years later at fault myself in the same way. Dr. Dowling was treating us rather roughly in some controversy, probably about the markets, and I either issued or approved a reply that included some jokes about the germ theory. I should not have done that and I now apologize to Doc Dowling and all others in his line of business for having done it.[26] As there are still some persons who do not believe in what practically all of us know to be true about germs, it was very bad judgement on the part of the mayor to encourage them in their ignorance by making fun of the Louisiana germ demon and the germs.

While a little off the subject of yellow fever, I may stay off it another paragraph or so to say that the germ theory is not old. The elder physicians of New Orleans were practicing when Dr. Paul Emile Archinard left New Orleans to go to Paris and look into Dr. Pasteur's reports of his discoveries. Dr. Archinard, I am told, was the first physician in New Orleans to commit himself absolutely and without reservation to the germ theory.

It was late in 1905 that Dr. Archinard was busy in his labora-

26. Under pressure from Dr. Dowling to screen the public markets, Behrman reportedly commented that a simpler solution would be to require the flies to bathe.

tory on yellow fever work. He was trying to segregate the germ as Noguchi, the Jap, did later in New York.[27] The reporters worried him. Finally one of them came rushing in and said:

"Hey, Doc! Did you catch that germ yet?"

It was only by some very fast stepping that the reporter got away without getting hurt.

Without any disrespect to the distinguished Japanese microscope man, I wish to say that I would much rather that he had failed and one of our local scientists had succeeded in that work. So many doctors here spent years on that job that it does not seem fair that a Jap should get the honors. Dr. Noguchi, of course, had the benefit of the work done by Dr. Pothier, Dr. Archinard and many others. But, as a general rule, the public gives the credit to the man who finished the job and forgets those who made it possible for him to finish it.

Without the least desire to dim the fame of the many who did more than their mere duty in 1905, or did their duty so well as to deserve all the praise the two outstanding names are those of Dr. Beverly Warner of Trinity [Episcopal] church and Dr. Quitman Kohnke, city health officer.

I do not remember the exact name of the committee that Dr. Warner headed, but it was a citizens' committee that directed the work of oiling all surfaces of standing water and getting the cisterns screened. This organization had for the most of its working force those men whom the silk stockings and reformers call "ward heelers" and "ward strikers" and all that sort of thing; and similar words to the general effect that they were not men of sense. The only comment I have to make on that is that Dr. Warner was a little uncertain of them at first but he soon found, despite a little friction here and there, that they were a real working force and he really enjoyed the job. Some of the boys

27. Hideyo Noguchi (1876–1928), Japanese physician and bacteriologist. In 1918 Noguchi isolated the yellow fever microorganism and later developed a serum that eventually led to a cure for the dreaded disease. Noguchi died in 1928 of the same disease that he fought to eliminate while in Africa conducting comparative studies between the African and American varieties of yellow fever.

were as much surprised by Dr. Warner as he was by them.

Dr. Warner was the rector of what many of my followers in politics considered to be a very aristocratic church, Trinity. Its congregation was made up mostly of prominent citizens of the Garden District. Many of the boys expected "that preacher" to take a lofty, dictatorial and "I am much better than you" attitude toward them. It was not long before one of them told me:

"That guy is good."

"What guy?" I inquired.

"Dr. Warner, I say he's a good man. We ought to get him into the organization."

I told my friend not to refer to Dr. Warner as a "guy" and that he could consider himself a committee of one to get him into the organization. That committee never reported back to me. I think the committee probably made a failure of the negotiations.

Some time in the next winter, several of the magazines had articles about Dr. Warner's work with the ward lieutenants. They seemed to think there was something unexpected and extrordinary that a rather literary and somewhat aristocratic minister should get along with the ward workers.

That is because most people do not know a real aristocrat when they see one. Most of the alleged aristocrats are imitations, men and women who seem to think that being an aristocrat consists of having money, spending it on pleasure and turning up their noses at their fellow citizens.

He was, as I remember him, a real aristocrat. He was the kind of an aristocrat that could get into such work as he took in 1905 and never do or say anything in a personal way that justified the least resentment or irritation. He was the real thing, not the annoying imitation.

Dr. Quitman Kohnke was the Doc Dowling of 1905.[28] The main difference between the two is that Dr. Kohnke busied

28. Dr. Quitman Kohnke was chairman of New Orleans' first city board of health from 1898 until his death in 1906.

himself with one germ at one time and the people he worked on, whether convinced or not, had to do what he wanted and do it fast. Dr. Dowling concerns himself with all germs and sometimes meets trouble with people who buck him.

Long before the fever of 1905, Dr. Kohnke preached death to the stegomyia. He spoke all over the city during the epidemic and explained the matter so clearly that only the worst "dumb bells" did not get it. He lectured with the aid of a screen on which the images of mosquitoes in water were seen rising to the top to get air. Then he would show them the same mosquitoes rising to an oiled surface, and, not getting any air, struggling for a while and then dying. He had an elaborate lot of latern slides showing mosquitoes much magnified and educated many a citizen to the point of being able to tell a stegomyia from any other mosquito.

[During the 1905 epidemic] Ward and neighborhood clubs to fight the stegomyia, some subordinate to the organization headed by Dr. Warner and some a part of it, were organized all over the city. The women were organized. It was not necessary to organize the Italians as practically all of them were already members of their racial societies.

Arthuro Dell Orto, Anthony Patorno, Charles Papini, the consul for Italy, and Father P. Scotti got the presidents of the Italian societies together and they in turn worked through the societies. The results were almost immediate. In some instances Italians who spoke no English, and who possibly had not heard of the germ theory or the stegomyia before were at work themselves oiling and screening their cisterns.

I have no other knowledge of the incident but the story told me, but I heard that one of the Italian leaders had told some of his friends that inspectors were authorized to destroy their household goods and put them in jail if their cisterns were not oiled and screened by a certain day.

I do not intend to attempt to enter into a scientific discussion

Brickbats and Bouquets

of climates and the process of "acclimating" human beings and the reasons why Italians in New Orleans seem to suffer first and most from epidemic diseases.[29]

The plain fact is that all newcomers in New Orleans are more subject to malaria and, when we had it, yellow fever. There can be nothing whatever in theory that the Italians are more subject to sickness because they live, to such a great extent, in the old city, the *Vieux Carre*, as malaria, yellow fever, and bubonic plague are not propagated any faster or easier in the *Vieux Carre* than in Carrollton or over in Algiers. Mosquitoes will fly just as readily to a cottage in Carrollton as an old brick building in the *Vieux Carre* and the rats that carry the fleas that transmit the bubonic plague are not particular where they go.

Personally, I have a hunch that the liability of our Italian fellow citizens has been due to their change of climate. I do not thing anything else can explain it. They are a hardy, healthy and intelligent section of the community. They eat well and dress comfortably. Yet they suffered more than the rest of us when malaria was common in New Orleans, when the yellow fever visited us 17 years ago and when the bubonic plague got in eight years ago.

My impression is that the record will bear me out in stating that the sons and daughters of Italian immigrants suffer no more than the oldest Creole families and those whom the Creoles called "Americans" when I was a boy.

For some reason or other, an Italian was considered a dangerous citizen in 1905. Dr. Charles McVea and Henry L. Fuqua, now president of the board of control of the state penitentiary,[30]

---

29. The epidemic took its greatest toll from among the Italian immigrants crowded in tenements in the lower half of the French Quarter near the markets. It was in this area that the first cases of the fever were reported. At the height of the epidemic, however, cases were appearing all over the city and in the suburbs. Of the 3,403 estimated cases, approximately 437 deaths were certified as resulting from yellow fever. *Biennial Reports of the Board of Health of the City of New Orleans, 1904–1905.*

30. Henry L. Fuqua, Governor of Louisiana, 1924–26.

were members of the board health at Baton Rouge that passed quarantine regulations against us and specially requested that the ticket agents on the railroads refuse to sell tickets to Italians to come to Baton Rouge. Men of their intelligence would not have done this but for the conviction that an Italian was much more liable to bring some yellow fever with him that any other citizen.

I will mention some details of the regulations at Baton Rouge, which impressed me as probably the most reasonable of the many quarantine rules made by parishes and towns in our own state of Louisiana. They put guards on all the trains and on the ferries across the Mississippi. They took the home addresses and the addresses in Baton Rouge of every visitor and they required the visitors to report daily for five days so they could be examined to make sure they did not have the fever. They instructed their guards on the trains and ferries to see that no Italians got into their city. I was told that a Creole, who was heard speaking in Italian to a son of "Sunny Italy," got by the guards by getting the conductor to identify him as a descendant of French and Spanish ancestors who had lived in New Orleans for four or five generations.

I do not remember that any other quarantine was as reasonable as that established at Baton Rouge. Some of our Louisiana towns simply shut out all persons from New Orleans. I do not remember that distant cities did this but it was general all over the South. Some quarantined against passengers and baggage only. Others would receive no shipments of goods from us. This was the very extreme of foolishness as engine and train crews were changed at the division points on the railroads and there was no chance that the stegomyia mosquito would take a long journey and live in a box car.

It was different with ships and boats. You cannot change crews while on the way. After a conference in the mayor's parlor, the fumigation of all vessels was decided on. That was to protect us against new cases from the tropics. Mobile and Galveston, as I remember it, would not permit ships from New Orleans to call at their docks.

Texas insisted on fumigating Pullman cars at the state line. The state health officer of Texas, however, traveled from New Orleans to Galveston without stopping to be fumigated. Galveston, where there was no fever, was more scared in 1905 than New Orleans. That state health officer got a good roasting from the Texas newspapers.

Never has New Orleans seen such a "drive" as was made on the stegomyia mosquito that year. Liberty loan drives, Red Cross drives, suffering American drives and all the tag days we ever had did not get the active support of as many of us as got into that campaign of education on the subject of that stegomyia. Everybody competent to make a speech was called on and, so far as I know, no man declined.

I think we were slow in adopting the screening and oiling. It should have been done before. But we made up for lost time as best we could and when wire netting gave out we used cheese cloth for screens. We were four years behind the times as it had been four years since Havana had proved the mosquito theory to be correct and had stamped out yellow fever. Havana, however, had suffered from it every summer and we had it only occasionally.

It was something of a joke on us that Havana, after more than a hundred years of almost constant yellow fever in the summer months, established a quarantine against New Orleans. I can call it a joke now. But I could not see anything funny in it then.

My recollection is that there were so many cisterns to be screened that the price of the work in some neighborhoods was put down to $1 each. That was pretty low, even for those days. The department stores and dry goods stores did not take advantage of the suddenly increased demand for mosquito bars. On the contrary, I remember that there was some kind of conference among the managers and individual merchants and mosquito bars were sold for less than the prices asked in May and June. It was absolutely necessary to provide plenty of bars and our merchants came across handsomely.

It takes trouble to bring the people of New Orleans together. They are always scrapping with each other when there is no trouble cloud on the horizon or overhead. "Let's get together" was for a long time my favorite slogan. Lots of people thought I meant "Let's all vote for Behrman and his friends." Sometimes, of course, I meant that; but not even most of the time. I do not remember ever saying it during a campaign. I usually rang it in when I was promoting some public business. I did not need it during the epidemic of 1905. We just got together.

Most of what I did during the epidemic, excepting the speeches I made, was on the advice of Doctors White and Blue, the federal health officers. I issued proclamations advising the people what to do to prevent catching the fever and what to do if they got sick at all. The main point was to get under a mosquito bar and stay there until the doctor arrived.

Charles Janvier, one of the chiefs of the general citizens' committee, designed a button that was worn by citizens whose premises had been cleaned and whose cisterns were oiled and screened.

Another significant thing done by our merchants on Canal Street was to order their fall goods just as if nothing had happened here.

"What the hell's the difference?" one of them said to me. "If we're going to bust, let's bust right."

I think it was Mr. [W. J.] Gilbert of the D. H. Holmes company who made the remark. The others were absolutely with him. There were no drummers here to take the orders and no buyers went out. They sent the orders East by mail and wire.

A report of the city board of health shows that 3,403 cases were reported and that 437 persons were buried on certificates

Brickbats and Bouquets 143

that they had died of yellow fever. It is added that 15 to 20 of these 437 probably did not have the fever. There is no telling what would have happened but for the great work done in the oiling and screening.

It was in the first week in August [1905] that we called on President Theodore Roosevelt to put the federal government in charge. We were then getting from 30 to 50 reports of new cases each day. The maximum came later, on August 12, with 105 new cases reported in a single day.[31]

There is no way of finding out what the epidemic of 1905 really cost us but when Surgeon General [Walter] Wyman put Surgeon [J. H.] White in charge, the banks and wealthier citizens guaranteed a fund of $250,000. The state government borrowed $100,000. Ward and precinct donations were so many and so large that I doubt that anybody ever knew the total.

When our citizens committee had been informed that the Federal officers would have to be guaranteed a fund of $250,000 when they took charge of the fever prevention work, Charles Janvier rang me up at my home and the next day, Sunday, he and William Adler, president of the State National Bank, were among the citizens who gathered in the mayor's parlor. I told them I could not guarantee the $250,000 in the name of the city unless I had more time to make arrangements, see the members of the council and so forth. Janvier, then president of the Canal-Louisiana Bank, and Adler speaking for themselves and the other bankers of New Orleans, declared they would underwrite the $250,000.

The city government as I remember it, gave $50,000, the state government $100,000 and the donations ran close to $150,000,

---

31. On August 4, 1905, New Orleans invited the U.S. Public Health Service to direct the yellow fever prevention work in the city. Federal authorities agreed to do so only with the guarantee that the city and state would pay $250,000 to help finance the campaign and that they be given full control over operations. Kendall, *History of New Orleans*, II, 769.

including the proceeds from the "Diamond Festival" and a large number of smaller benefits for the fever fund.

Looking at it from another point of view, that was a small part of the damage as our business was badly hurt. Taking another view, we got good value for every cent spent and possibly for ever life that ended in that epidemic as the principal results were complete prevention of another epidemic, federal quarantine and the final abandonment of cisterns.

The Elks organized and conducted what we called th the "Diamond Festival." It occurred September 16, 1905. The "Diamond Festival" was humourously referred to in several eastern newspapers as "New Orleans Celebrates Yellow Fever." That was a headline in one of them.

The Festival was on the surface a means of raising money for the yellow fever fund. We had collected about $133,000 from individuals, banks, private business houses and so forth and we needed about $15,000 more. But that was not the main purpose. The idea was to hold some kind of celebration as an indication that we were not downhearted. It succeeded.

The festival was a big parade through the business district and out to Athletic park, where the ball park is now. There were a number of special features, such as the "ugly men's contest," the baseball game between the Glycozones and the Parker-Blakes and the working girl's contest.

The novel feature of the parade was about seven hundred Elks, of whom I was one, dressed in suits of cheese cloth and wearing hats made in good imitations of screened cisterns.

President Roosevelt opened the festival by telegraph and, as mayor, I replied. His telegram was copied on an enormous board provided by T. P. Cummings of the Western Union at the Park. When he was with us October 26, he inquired about the festival and among other things I told him about the hat. He asked me to send him one of the hats. I intended to keep mine but could not get another, so I suppose it went out of the White House with the Roosevelt administration.

Brickbats and Bouquets

The female stegomyia, not the male, was the carrier of the yellow fever germs. As a result of this, some of the paraders would shout ever now and then that line: "And the female of the species is more deadly than the male." It got a laugh everywhere.

One of the Elks' banners read:
AND IT HAD TO BE A FEMALE!

I am setting down these details of that festival of 17 years ago to indicate the spirit of the people of New Orleans at a time when most communities would suffer from the "glooms." We all knew that we were in trouble. We were confident, most of us, that we would get out of it. We knew that the eyes of the whole country were on us. Work on the sewerage and drainage system was in progress. The public belt [railroad] was actually started during the epidemic. All of us felt that a show of good cheer would do New Orleans great credit. That was the main idea of the festival.

An hour or so with an old file of *The Times-Democrat* recalls to my mind that only three days later I sat as head of the police board and approved the dismissal of a police captain, that we had a strike of the painters and another strike of the teamsters in the very middle of the epidemic and that the decision to put up the Canal-Louisiana office building at Camp and Gravier Streets was announced Saturday, September 10, 1905, when the Marine Hospital Service reported 41 new cases of fever. The file shows that the yacht races proceeded as usual, that the Denechauds went ahead with their plans for what is now the Hotel DeSoto [on Baronne and Poydras streets] and that preparation for the opening of the opera season went along as if there was no fever. We could not afford to show how bad some of us felt.

It was in this epidemic that some doctor arrived from a far off place and advised us to take arsenic to prevent fever. His theory, as I remember it, was that the fever germs occupied spaces in the blood that would not be there if they were filled with arsenic. I know, as a matter of fact, that many citizens of New Orleans took arsenic for a while. The doctors of New Orleans announced that the arsenic man was "off his base," as one of them expressed it to me, and that arsenic gave no immunity.

Probably the worst "bust" during the epidemic, was the publication by *The Times-Democrat* of a "Peruna" announcement. This newspaper was bitterly attacked some time later for that by a writer in *Collier's Weekly*, then campaigning against all "household preparations" and "patent medicines." The campaign was successful.

As practically all of us were very busy convincing the rest of us that the mosquito theory was correct, I was much astonished to read the Peruna ad, which was in the form of an interview with Dr. Hartman. I have a copy of it. This Dr. Hartman was handing us some advice.

"The infection from yellow fever," he said, "enters the system by way of the air that is breathed into the lungs, by the water which we drink or the food which we eat."

After several paragraphs of his bunk, Dr. Hartman said that most of us have defects and little holes in the "mucuous membranes" through which "the infectious poison can enter the system."

"In all such cases," the Doc went on, "it is advisable for the person to take Peruna. No one should neglect this important detail."

The Doc finished his advice as follows:

"The belief that mosquitoes are in some way responsible for the spread of yellow fever makes it prudent at least for everyone to protect themselves from their bites by having the houses perfectly screened from those pests."

"In order to be on the safe side, however, Peruna should be used during the whole course of the epidemic."

"I feel sure that any person following this advice is in no danger of taking yellow fever."

Surgeon White of the U. S. Marine hospital, Dr. Beverly

Warner and the physicians did not know whether to laugh or to cry when they read that Peruna ad. While I did not declare prohibition on myself during the epidemic, we all knew or believed that alcohol was bad for the kidneys and that it takes sound kidneys to pull a man through an attack of yellow fever.

Peruna had alcohol in it. I never took a drink of it myself but I have heard stories to the effect that when we of the U.S.A. were dry in spots there was a great demand for Peruna at the dry spots.

Whatever else Peruna had in it, I do not know, but I do know that Peruna people changed the makeup of their goods when the federal government passed the drug act about 15 years ago.[32] They printed the new list of contents on big bill boards all over the country and I did not recognize the name of anything I knew about in that list. At first I thought it was a practical joke.

Anyhow, *The Times-Democrat* made a fearful "bust" and was duly lambasted and roasted for it. Doc Hartman's advice did not reappear but other Peruna advertisements were run.

The natural conclusion is that Doc Hartman's advice was sent to the business office with orders to run it in so much space on a certain day. It would be silly to suppose that Page M. Baker . . . would have permitted it to run if any one of them had read it before it went into the paper.

While New Orleans, as I remember it, was the only place in Louisiana that had an epidemic, there was considerable yellow fever in the smaller towns of the state. I remember that a case appeared at Lake Providence [in northeastern Louisiana] and the local board of health there promptly quarantined all the Italians and the local health office took their temperatures three or four times a day. The scare was so great that some one or two of the parishes of Louisiana considered preventing the running through of through trains from New Orleans to their destina-

---

32. Pure Food and Drug Act of June 30, 1906.

tions, regardless of the fact that they would not stop in those parishes.

Detention camps were common in Louisiana and Mississippi. They were used to hold visitors, even visitors with health certificates from the federal authorities here, for five days to make sure they would not develop the disease.

Sulphur fumes were the most convenient way to kill such mosquitoes as might be in a home or an office or warehouse and large quantities of sulphur were consumed in New Orleans that summer. Many business men had their offices sealed up with pasted paper on Saturday afternoon, when the iron pots of sulphur would be lighted, and left them closed until Monday morning. This was the most popular method of fumigation. A special powder that killed all insects was also used.

The epidemic was by no means ended but the yellow fever was on the down grade, with fewer cases reported each day, when President Theodore Roosevelt visited New Orleans [in October, 1905]. The disease was stamped out before the first cold weather, which satisfied even most of the disagreeing minority that the mosquito theory was correct.

Roosevelt had arranged a tour that included New Orleans. He was reported to be about to change the schedule and leave out New Orleans, Congressman Adolph Meyer and Robert Davey got our whole Louisiana delegation together and appealed to Roosevelt not to leave us out. He saw that leaving us out would injure the city, so he declared he would keep New Orleans in the schedule.

"I'm glad you won't be here long," I told Roosevelt as we rode through the cheering crowds. "I'd rather this city would stay Democratic."

Some years later Roosevelt and I were conversing in Washington and he recalled my remark and said:

"If the people there would vote like they shout, New Orleans would be the best Republican city in the U.S.A."

We all appreciated Roosevelt's visit. Our delegates did us a

Brickbats and Bouquets

great service in getting him to come here and he did us a great service in coming. Hundreds of citizens wrote him letters of thanks. The newspapers all over the United States recognized the fact that even at its worst yellow fever was not so bad as they once thought it. The oiling and screening got results and Roosevelt's visit advertised the results.

On the day that we got the news that President Roosevelt had returned New Orleans to the schedule for his trip, there were 19 new cases of fever and three deaths from fever. The newspapers of New Orleans printed the facts day by day and every evening the correspondents of newspapers in the other cities sent out the figures. One of the results was that Roosevelt was advised not to come to New Orleans. In fact, considerable pressure was brought to keep him from doing so. Had he remained away from New Orleans, that would have done us a great deal of harm. The fact that he came did us a great deal of good.

Roosevelt reached here over the Illinois Central October 26, 1905, and got off the train at the Stuyvesant Docks because we wanted him to see the port in the forenoon and have a big parade in the afternoon. Surgeon J. H. White, the federal doctor in charge of the fever situation, Governor Blanchard and myself were the chiefs of the reception committee. Senators McEnery and Foster, who had met the president at Hammond, [Louisiana] were with the big party that went "sight seeing" on the *Comus*, a southern Pacific vessel.

While he was on the *Comus*, Roosevelt asked for a newspaper. He glanced over the first page, full of pictures of himself, and then rapidly reviewed the inside pages. Then he turned back to the first page and spent about a minute on the "Gist of the News." I recently looked at a copy of this paper, *The Times-Democrat*, for that day. If Roosevelt noticed that we had nine new cases of fever and two deaths the day before, he did not show it. Philip Werlein smiled with appreciation of the President's apparent tact in not mentioning the fever record reported that morning.

The parade started at 11:30 AM and Roosevelt reached the City Hall at about one o'clock. He had received the greatest ovation ever given a visitor in New Orleans in my time. William McKinley's visit [in 1901] was a funeral march compared to it. All the Mardi Gras rolled into one would be dull to the enthusiasm that greeted Roosevelt.

Yellow fever, the quarantine, the good work done by Surgeon White and similar matters came into the conversation later. Charles Janvier, Dr. Beverly Warner and myself conferred with the president in the afternoon and as I remember it, we started the movement for federal control of quarantines.

Roosevelt mentioned in his speech that he had seen the school children of New Orleans gathered at the statue of Robert E. Lee and then noticed a big picture of Lincoln on the route of the parade. He talked about the fever, the levees, the Panama Canal. In fact, he seemed to have an instinctive knowledge of just what would interest us.

In closing my brief address of welcome I said:

"Among the most cherished of New Orleans' memories will be preserved that of the day when Theodore Roosevelt, President of the United States of America, broke bread with her at her board."

This may have sounded to some as flowery language from a mayor to a president, but I meant it. I have no reason to qualify it now. That was a long time ago and we have had no such trouble since the yellow fever of 1905, but it would probably have taken years of "press agent" work to get the results we got through Roosevelt's visit.

The president left New Orleans on a lighthouse tender, the *Magnolia*, which was to take him out into the Gulf where the battleship *West Virginia* was waiting to take him back to Washington. The *Magnolia* and one of the United Fruit company's ships, the *Esparta*, collided and the lighthouse tender was beached. Another lighthouse tender, the *Ivy*, was sent for and when she arrived the president had to be awakened. The party boarded the *Ivy* and got to the *West Virginia* on schedule time.

Governor Blanchard and I both sent the president wireless messages. Mine was as follows:

"Theodore Roosevelt, President, Aboard Cruiser *West Virginia*.

"People regret accident of last night. Rejoice it had no serious consequences. Trust your voyage to Washington will be pleasant and devoid of further mishap.

MARTIN BEHRMAN"

Several years later I went to Washington for a session of the Rivers and Harbors Congress and after the adjournment of the congress, as was the custom, the delegates visited the White House to present the resolutions they had adopted. Congressmen and senators accompanied their constituents to introduce them to the president.

Senator [Joseph E.] Ransdell was about to introduce me when Roosevelt waived his hand and said:

"Senator, you don't have to introduce me to my friend, the Mayor of New Orleans. How are you, Mr. Behrman," the President continued as he grasped my hand. "I have not seen you since I received the wireless."

I think this is an evidence of Roosevelt's extraordinary memory. I was one of a number of mayors whom he had met on that trip, with a large lot of governors, heads of organizations and so forth mixed with the mayors. I have never been a very imposing figure and I do not think I would be easy for a man to pick out in a crowd if he had seen me only on one day. I attribute his recollection of me to the association with what he admitted was the most enthusiastic and joyous welcome he had ever received.

Some time after the epidemic there was a conference, attended by Governor Blanchard and a party of New Orleans business men, at Chattanooga [Tennessee].

The conferees were there for a discussion of quarantine,

which was a sore subject with most of the Southern states and particularly with us of New Orleans and Louisiana. They declared in favor of control of all maritime quarantine by the Federal government, which was to prevent state governments from stopping ships from one of our ports to another.

Not long after that I was one of a big party of Orleaneans who went to Washington to get the United States government to take over the control of all quarantines, land and sea. John M. Parker was with us. We had learned that nothing we could do would prevent unnecessary quarantines against us by state governments for commercial purposes.

No matter who might be on our state and local boards of health, no matter how fair and honest they might be in their announcements and statements of the conditions, other state governments and cities would shut our business out. They always said or insinuated that they could not depend on us to make the whole truth public and that we delayed announcements of the existence of the fever and then reported only some of the cases when we had to make the announcements.

Surgeon General [Walter] Wyman was strongly in favor of Federal and no state quarantines. He agreed with us that the Public Health Service would not be accused of suppressing any facts or of favoring any locality and that it was just that we should have Federal control of the quarantines.

Leslie M. Shaw was Secretary of the Treasury. He and Doc Wyman were not on very good terms. We had to have a bill by Congress to give the Public Health Service control of quarantines and whoever wrote the bill included a raise in salary for Doc Wyman. That did not help much with Leslie Shaw. But when we went into details about the situation, Leslie Shaw came across like a real man and we got what we wanted and Doc Wyman got his raise.

"Behrman, do you know that one of those quarantine stations cost $300,000 last year and treated only one case?" Shaw asked me.

"Was it a case of yellow fever?" I asked, hoping it was so I could argue that the quarantine of that case had prevented an epidemic.

"How in hell do I know?" he came back. "Do you expect to have the Secretary of the Treasury snooping all the hospitals. The man might have had Riggs' disease for all I know".

I remember that there was a lot of talk about "state rights" at Washington and elsewhere when we were after Federal quarantine. It seemed to me that we had enough of the rights of states to kill our business and nobody in an official position in Louisiana or at Washington paid any attention to the great dangers of over-riding such state rights.

One of the amusing incidents of the epidemic of 1905 was the near-war between Louisiana and Mississippi. Mississippi had guards somewhere on or near the boundary line, or in that immediate vicinity, and a dispute arose as to the exact location of the Mississippi-Louisiana boundary line. The Governor of Mississippi[33] ordered out his militia. Governor Blanchard did the same, though I do not remember that any Louisiana soldiers were actually sent into the field, or into Lake Borgne. There was considerable of a row and all over the United States newspaper readers got the information that a civil war was about to break out between Louisiana and Mississippi.

Dr. J. H. White, the Federal Officer in charge of the fever situation here, was caught across the line by the Mississippi militia and put into their detention camp. He had some trouble getting out. He had been made a Colonel on the [Louisiana] Governor's staff.

"If they wouldn't let you leave as a Federal officer, why didn't you tell them you are a Colonel?" I asked Dr. White.

"Because they would have jailed me for that," he replied. "They would have thought I was spying on their troops."

While the last case of yellow fever was reported as late as

---

33. James K. Vardaman, governor of Mississippi, 1904–1908; U.S. senator, 1913–19.

November 24, the quarantines against us began falling in the middle of October. The epidemic had been conquered by scientific knowledge and hard work.

Before they left New Orleans, however, one of the federal health officers recommended that we build up into the air rather than spread the city all over the map. That was the only thing any of them said that I now remember and with which I did not and do not agree. Anybody who has visited northern cities knows that the more you build up in the air the less air you get. It seems that the higher they build them the closer they put them together.

Now that cisterns are no more and so many of our homes are screened, nobody but the patients would be bothered by as many as 25 or 30 cases of yellow fever in New Orleans.

5.
Prohibition, Saloons, and "Orleanians Obey the Law"

Beer, Wines and Whiskey were subjects of great interest when I first became mayor of New Orleans. Before the end of my first year, the successful campaign to increase the license taxes on them attracted considerable attention. A greater increase came later but it is not necessary to deal with that as it was of minor interest. Now that the federal government has legislated against liquors, except as drugs, interest in the subject is, naturally, merely a sort of interest in history.[34]

There are, of course, a few who still take a drink now and then, but only after a physician has diagnosed their sickness or troubles and prescribed for them. The red stuff, I understand, is is still used for colds, for indigestion and sometimes expected

---

34. The Volstead Act or National Prohibition Enforcement Act was passed by Congress over President Wilson's veto on October 27, 1919. The act was an attempt to aid enforcement of the Eighteenth Amendment (January, 1919). That act also defined the alcoholic content specifications for intoxicating beverages as containing more than .5 percent alcohol.

indigestion, for attacks of the "blues" and the "glooms," and as a means of overcoming a desire for alcoholic drinks. This is considered by some to be a great improvement over the conditions prevailing when a man would go get a drink for the sole reason that he liked it.

I can remember the time when there were nearly 2000 saloons in New Orleans but in many of them you could get only beer. There were famous places for their drinks, such as Ginn Fizz, Sazarac Coctail, Absinthe, imported beer and so forth. These 2000 saloons did not get as much space in the newspapers then as rumors and reports do now. We were promised that everything would be much more quiet and gentlemanly when those places were closed.

Yet, with a grand total of nearly 2000 and with all the special drinks easily obtainable within easy walking distance of anywhere downtown, we probably had less disturbance that we do now. I do not remember that the delegates to any convention in those days threw the hotel furniture into the street. Yet recently, when there was not a drop to be had, that happened and the delegates to the convention had to organize their own special military police to assist the regular force in trying to keep the peace.

I have talked to the effect that in the big cities up in the East, where the people are so much less law abiding than we of New Orleans, the United States government is having a lot of trouble in enforcing the law. Having visited those cities often, I realize that some of us were right when we maintained that prohibition would not completely prohibit. New Orleans, where the people have such great respect for the law (even the Volstead law), is an exception to the rule. I knew that we would go bone-dry as soon as we were officially advised to do so.

My advice on the subject was not based on any lack of confidence in the voters who so often and so thoroughly voted for me.

But, knowing the conditions in other cities, I maintained that absolute prohibition would not be a good thing. I was not able to put my own opinions into law. I am not able to do so now. If I had that power, beer would be sold under a reasonable license tax in almost every grocery store, in bottles and ready to drink. The lighter wines would be sold in bottles at the groceries and in all the restaurants. Both would be sold in some places. The whole thing would be regulated so that the evils from which we suffered, and about which many of us howled, would be reduced to a minimum. The governments, national, state and local, would draw an enormous revenue from the "Liquor traffic."

Only a few days ago, Sir Basil Thompson, the head of Scotland Yard (which means in effect the foremost police official in England), when asked whether prohibition would be adopted there, replied that the British are very slow to enact laws that cannot be enforced.

He said that immediately after his arrival here, so his statement goes, that the law is not enforced does not apply to New Orleans.

I wish our Congress had felt the same way about it.

Public opinion in this country would undoubtedly support the closest and most detailed regulation of the liquor business. It would most probably support the taxing of the liquor business to such an extent as to reduce the number of merchants selling liquor to somewhere between a third and a half of the total number of saloons in the days before the war.

One of the main reasons why the liberal element has not been able to make much of an impression at Washington is that it is so hard to talk in favor of a modification of the Volstead law without putting yourself in the position of defending the worst features of the old conditions. I am confident that this will not continue to be the case very much longer and that we will get some beer.

Then, if all goes well, we may get some light wines.

But I do not think this will come about soon unless the

present law has been rigidly enforced for a year or more in such cities as Chicago, Detroit, New York, Philadelphia, Boston, Baltimore, Savannah, Tampa, Pensacola, Key West, Mobile, Gulfport, Galveston, Los Angeles, San Francisco, Portland and Seattle and the cities and towns and rural areas having railroad connections with them.

If the government succeeds in enforcing the law in the territory indicated, there will be something like an uprising of the people and Congress will arrange to relieve the pressure and lower the price. As public opinion does not seem to be very encouraging for the dry agents, except in spots, it does not seem probable that the law will be throughly enforced in the near future.

On the other hand, if the present conditions in the cities and rural areas to the north, east, south and west of New Orleans continue very long, the people may become disgusted and demand a change. I have been more or less disgusted myself ever since Thanksgiving Day but my demands for a change have had no effect whatever. Perhaps they will when the majority openly comes out in agreement with my way of thinking and makes that majority opinion effective by going into politics with it.

We of New Orleans have not received the recognition that is due us for our fidelity to the government. We are a patriotic and nationally a law abiding people. But there are a lot of scandalous rumors going around about us.

I trust no serious minded person will pay any attention to these rumors. I have not seen a saloon in New Orleans for years. A friend of mine says they are there, whether I can see them or not. I am too busy to go snooping around investigating such foolishness. There are none. There is no illegal liquor sold in New Orleans. Whatever supplies may be on hand were purchased legally, long before the law passed. We are nationally a law abiding people.

The conditions at a distance from us are plain and ample

proof of what I have always said: That you cannot enforce a really unpopular law.

Take the Sunday Law.[35]

I have no first hand information about this subject as I have always been very busy on Sundays, or out of town or at home with my family. I have learned since I retired from the City Hall and went into private life, that this law was not strictly enforced in New Orleans. I have a vague recollection of an argument about it with Commissioner Harold Newman. I will refresh my memory on this argument later and tell my readers about it.

However, after I retired to private life, I learned that the police, having been advised that the people of New Orleans did not want the Sunday law enforced, adopted a policy described by a local newspaper as "unobtrusive nonobservance of the law." I have discovered, after long research and talks with elder statesmen, that this policy prevailed for many years before I became mayor and that the people were well satisfied with it. My information is so reliable that I will state as a fact that this policy gave general satisfaction.

I was too busy while I was mayor to keep up with public opinion on all subjects but my investigations since then prove that the police had the correct interpretation of public opinion on the Sunday law. The way the voters voted certainly showed this to be true. While there were always some citizens raising Cain about the Sunday law, I have been told, a majority of the people delighted in the "unobtrusive non-observance."

I shall later refresh my memory on this subject and tell something about various objections to that non-observance. If it was going on, the people were well satisfied with it.

---

35. The "Sunday law" required all stores, shops, groceries, saloons, and all places of public business to be closed on Sundays. Exempted were certain categories of establishments, such as hotels, restaurants, boarding houses, etc. They could not, however, sell alcoholic beverages other than table wines on Sundays. Act 18, *Acts Passed by the General Assembly of the State of Louisiana at the Regular Session, 1886.*

It would be hard for me to pay myself a greater compliment than to point out that, without the least knowledge of what I was doing, I did just what the vast majority of my fellow citizens wanted me to do. It is extremely difficult to know exactly what the people want and to do what the people want when you are wide awake and fully informed. Think how much brighter, or luckier, I was to do what they wanted without ever knowing that I was doing it.

I have been told that the brewers were much pleased with that non-observance policy of the police. Their interest in the people was very great and they loved to think that they were serving the people and making them happy on Sundays. I would interpret, from what I have heard, that the brewers were particularly interested, much more so than the red liquor folks. It seems, according to the reports that have reached me, that there was no very great excess of consumption of red liquor on Sundays as over Saturdays but there was a vastly greater consumption of beer.

Red liquor was consumed in greatest quantities on Saturday nights. Beer, on the other hand, was an all day drink on Sundays.

Some day I will investigate to discover how these relative quantities of consumption applied at the private saloons, such as the Boston, Pickwick, Chess & Checkers, Louisiana [clubs], etc.[36]

I was told that the Boston [Club] once intended to buy the late Frank T. Howard's house next door to the city hall but backed out when it discovered that this house was too close to a church to get a permit to sell alcoholic drink in its private saloon.

No matter what my friends may tell me about the public saloons I feel quite sure that the Sunday law was strictly observed at the Boston, the Pickwick, the Chess & Checkers, the Louisiana, etc.

36. "Silk Stocking" organizations.

As none of these clubs have been in any financial difficulties since prohibition, and none of them have raised their dues, it is clear to me that they got no considerable revenue from selling liquor and beer.

These are my present recollections and impressions on the subjects. Later, when my memory has been refreshed, I may remember more.

I do remember that there was some agitation for a higher liquor license when I was an assessor. A bartender an exceptionally intelligent bartender at the Cosmopolitan in New Orleans told me as early as the winter of 1903 that he thought the people were coming to the conclusion that the saloons were not paying enough taxes. He mentioned some cities in which they paid more taxes than they paid here.

The movement gained considerable force about the time I became mayor. I think it was probably due to yellow fever, the rumpus stirred up by the campaign against Dominick C. O'Malley . . . that kept public attention off the high license affair for a while. But only for a while.

I found that the city, particularly the schools, needed more money. I soon came to the conclusion that an increase in the saloon license taxes was the best way to get it.

I told my friends that before long there would be such a public demand for higher license on the saloons that it could not be resisted. Not that I cared to resist anything within reason, although I was against the proposal that the minimum be $1000 and knocked it all I could, but that I wished to get as little political damage as possible out of whatever happened.

No matter what "run ins" I had with the brewers and the saloon people, at that time they were with me politically. On the other hand, I certainly did not intend to let the city suffer for funds while the saloons paid less than they could reasonably afford to pay.

The "high license" group as they were sometimes referred to, were asking for much more than they expected to get. They practically got what they wanted. I was much gratified to find that I lost nothing and gained a great deal. The city got the money, the schools certainly needed it. It was not very long before everybody was apparently satisfied. Had there been any genuine dissatisfaction with the license taxes levied, I would not have been re-elected so easily in 1908. This license fight came in 1906.

There were very serious evils in the saloon system of selling drinks. A general effort was evident, even on the part of some of the brewers toward the last, to separate beer from whiskey. It was the intemperate use of whiskey that led to the present situation of prohibition. As the constitution stands now, Congress can declare beer and some of the wines non-intoxicating and keep the whiskey on the forbidden list. This, in brief, is what I believe and hope will be done.

I attended a lecture once at the "Catholic Winter School," at which school was a weekly lecture on some subject of importance. A Professor Walsh, as I remember his name, called attention to the fact that there was no race of men on the face of the earth but that they had some way of making alcoholic drinks of one kind or another and that they made them. His point was that it would not do to try to cut off all alcholic drinks. It has been more than 25 years since I heard this statement and I believed then and I know now that it was right.

The high license crowd in New Orleans started their real fight, after many months of propaganda in *The Times-Democrat*, before the yellow fever epidemic of 1905 and finished it with the passage of a high license ordinance in December of 1906.

As it would not interest my readers to get into all the minor details of this great historic episode, I will state now that we politicians were not organized against it. Political friends and political opponents of the regulars and members of our "Council of Seventeen" were on both sides of the issue.

I was not in the least surprised when Alex Pujol [of the Fifth Ward] came out publicly in favor of high license as he had told me long before that he favored it. I knew that Robert Ewing [Tenth Ward] favored it long before Ewing's paper *The States* declared for it. I knew also, that a majority of the management of *The Picayune* were for high license. Anybody who knows anything whatever of politics need only read the names I mention in this article to see that high license was not a factional issue, although *The Times-Democrat* did at times declare or intimate that the regulars were dead set against it.

As I remember it, everybody had a kind word for beer. No matter what their position might be on the exact figure of a proper license, they all said nice things about beer. Those were the days when it was dangerous to speak disrespectfully of beer. Beer had a host of friends. I do not think it has lost any since then, but beer fell in with bad company for a while and a lot of people blamed it for things it did not do.

It seems that somebody or other must have been thinking about saloons in the convention of 1898 for that convention gave the local governments the right to levy heavier license taxes than the state license tax applied only to saloons. Some of our leading booze merchants were much astonished when they found this out and they had the nerve to claim that the convention had done something unconstitutional.

I mean that one friend of mine who had invested one hundred percent of his capital in a saloon told me that it was not constitutional to make an exception of the saloons and let the city council "soak 'em." I replied that I thought anything done by a constitutional convention within the bounds of the United States constitution and the law calling the convention was undoubtedly constitutional.

This good but mistaken man came back with the reply that not even a constitutional convention could put across anything so unfair as that and he left me and went around to see his lawyer. I did not hear from him on that subject again.

Another operator told me that he intended to fight the high license in the federal courts and take the case right on up to the United States Supreme Court. Those were the times when things were being discovered in the United States Constitution that nobody ever knew were there.

That reminds me of what William Jennings Bryan said about a barrel of beer when he spoke at the Athenaeum in New Orleans some years later. Bryan said that once upon a time the railroads were full of constitutional law. No matter what you wanted to do, some railroad lawyer would pull out a list of decisions and prove it could not be done on account of the constitution of the United States.

"But now," said Bryan, as I remember it . . . "all those things have been done and if you want to get a really fine flow of constitutional law you have got to tap a barrel of beer. My friends, there is more constitution in a small barrel of beer than there ever was in all the railroad systems of the United States. The very foam of it throws up fine points of constitutional laws."

The brewers claimed that a tax of even $100 would hamper the sale of beer in the outlying sections of the city where the working men "rushed the growler." They presented the council with a carefully drawn up memorial in which they expressed great sympathy for the working people. They did not wish to see the mechanics and laborers deprived of their beer.

I learned then that beer, which I had always looked upon as a good drink, was also absolutely necessary as food.

Frank B. Thomas, who represented the Security Brewing Company, argued that beer was liquid bread. That was at a meeting of the council's committee.

Councilman Peter Graham got excited when he heard this

claim. He was for but he did not want to put it in the class with bread.

"Why don't the bakers sell it," he demanded of Thomas, who got by somehow or other and turned to the argument that beer was not intoxicating. He put one of the brew masters on the stand, a great big man.

"How many glasses of beer do you drink a day?" Thomas asked him.

"Sometimes ninety, sometimes a hundred glasses a day."

Councilman Graham, who was strong for beer and strong against all "bunk" and pretense, stood up.

"Do you mean to tell this committee that a man cannot get drunk on beer?" he asked.

"Well, yes, he can," the brew masters replied, "if he wants to make a hog of himself."

"I have seen people drunk from getting full of that kind of bread," Graham commented after the hearing was over.

[One beer proponent] estimated that we spent $3,000,000 a year for beer. I figure that this meant about 200 glasses of beer per year for each resident of New Orleans, estimating our population then at 300,000. I am of the opinion that he underestimated our expenditures for beer. He probably meant that we spent that much for beer produced in New Orleans, and exclusive of Anheuser-Busch's Budweiser, Schlitz, Moerlein and Joe Voegtle's justly celebrated importations from Munich.

Robert Mogel [a New Orleans grocer] appeared for the retail grocers. Mogel declared that the license proposed would so cut down the number of filling stations that some poor workingmen would have to walk as much as 30 blocks to get a glass of beer. Mogel also attacked the railroad ordinances granted during the previous administration and made the point that the railroads and not the saloons should be made to put up the money for schools, policemen, firemen and so forth.

Brickbats and Bouquets

Both sides quoted distinguished professors to support their contentions.

One set of professors and doctors with odd lots of the alphabet behind their names, had it that beer dissolved the liver and wrecked the kidneys and would in time ruin all of us. I was astonished that nobody attributed the fall of the Roman Empire to beer. There were a lot of those present who knew about that Roman Empire.

Another set of professors had the proof that the nation could not get along without beer. One of the speakers had a professor for authority that all the really civilized nations used large quantities of beer. He did not tell them what the savages drank.

Gus Lemle appeared for the brewers. He had something by the professor to the effect that beer was a liquid food.

At one of the meetings in the City Hall, Ernest Kruttschnitt answered that "distance for a beer" argument by pointing out that there were only 148 precincts in New Orleans and therefore only 148 places to vote and that there were nearly 2000 saloons. This 2000 includes the groceries that sold a little beer, it sounded for a few minutes as if Kruttschnitt wanted to cut the 2000 down to about 148. That was very disturbing.

Thomas Harrison, who ran with me on the city ticket in 1920, was there to protect the laborers on the river front from any reduction in their favorite places. It was generally believed that the higher license would force a large number of them out of business.

Tom Harrison, speaking for the Cotton Screwmen's Association, claimed that the high license would close up many of the river front places where the screwmen usually got their midday meals and sometimes all three meals. This high license would force them to eat cold lunch or walk long distances to get hot lunch. It would be very interesting to find out what they are doing now.

On the other hand, one of the ladies attacked the free lunch system maintained by the saloons. Tom Harrison was against cold lunch and this lady was against free lunch. She said the free lunch was unfair competition with boarding houses and that many men learned to drink too much because they went to the saloons for beer and free lunch.

I think that free lunch was great. Some saloons had a real free lunch and everybody who did not over-do the things could get a snack without even asking. I remember once, when I was in a hurry, I dropped into Ramos' place at Gravier and Carondelet and stood at the free lunch counter for fully ten minutes eating up sausages, pickles, cold ham, bread and crackers and then drank a glass of beer.

The Crescent Hall had one of the best lunches in town. You got a drink and a heavy, substantial meal for fifteen cents. Most of the boys took claret with their lunch there. The old time Sazerac lunch was great stuff.

This free lunch business developed several very nice restaurants. The merchants in the rice row on North Peters street and at the Sugar Exchange had their favorite place in that neighborhood and the Board of Trade crowd had and still has Martin's place as a successor to Ned Praphit's [Ed Prophit's]. It is not necessary for me to depress my readers by recalling more details of those happy, happy days.

I shall now recall the scene in the city council chamber when the high license ordinance was passed in December of 1906.

There was a great crowd in the council and the corridors of the city hall when the high license ordinance, introduced by Councilman E. P. Brandao by request came up for a final vote on December 4th, 1906. I have a cold-blooded copy of the official proceedings of the city council for that day and it contains nothing whatever to indicate the warmth of the occasion.

Ed Brandao moved that the ordinance come up early as the

crowd was dense, all members of the council were present and everybody knew that it would pass. That did not keep [Councilman] Charles O'Connor from making a last minute fight. He introduced, in the form of an amendment, an entire new ordinance that made the minimum license $100. The decisive vote came on that amendment and it was defeated. The vote was 11 to 10.

As he explained to some others several days before the meeting of the council, Councilman Graham had had a conversation with His Grace, The Most Reverend James Blenk, the Archbishop of the Diocese of New Orleans. Councilman Graham had been against the ordinance but he was doubtful after he had his conversation with Archbishop Blenk. On the afternoon of the day of the council meet, Councilman Graham and the archbishop conversed over the telephone and as a result of that conversation Councilman Graham voted for the high license.

It will be remembered that the main argument in favor of the high license, aside from the appeal that a promised reduction in the number of saloons made to some people, was that this would greatly increase the revenue for the schools. These were the public schools. As we all know, no tax money goes to the parochial schools. One of the reasons given by the Archbishop for his activity in working with Councilman Graham and other councilmen and city officials was that the public schools needed the money. I am pointing out this feature for the consideration of some citizens of New Orleans who believe that the Catholics think there should be no schools but the parochial schools.

Many catholics send their children to the parochial schools. Many send them to the public schools. The fact that I am a Catholic did not keep me from doing everything I could to promote the public schools nor does it keep me now from pointing with pride to the fact that the parochial [Catholic] schools have made such tremendous advances during the past ten years. My son went to the public schools.[37]

I do not see why there should be any objection to the parochial schools by anybody. Looking at it from a purely public point of view, I will say as I have always said that any citizen who pays taxes to support the public schools and then sends his children to the private schools is paying twice. Let him do it if he wants to. The parochial schools are private schools.

I have heard uninformed men say now and then that the state should not subsidize the parochial schools by keeping them free of taxes. They forget that no educational institutions and no churches pay taxes in Louisiana. The state subsidizes all religion and all education to that extent.

I know that while Archbishop Blenk was strongly in favor of Catholic schools and colleges he was also strongly in favor of the public schools and wanted to see them get all the support possible. He was not a Puritan and he did not believe that the moral level of the human race could be raised by the simple device of depriving men of a chance to get a drink. On the other hand, he was a very effective advocate of temperance.

After the vote of 11 to 10 showing that high license would pass, it did pass by 14 to seven. [Councilman Charles] Hauer could not stand the strain of staying there and voting again.

Had the ordinance not passed that evening, it would have passed in the near future. If not that, then another ordinance carrying a higher minimum than $250 license would have been passed.

Even though this ordinance did pass and the license went up again to a minimum of $500 in 1909, as a result of a general raise my political opponents never ceased declaring that my administration was controlled by the saloons. The number of saloons,

---

37. Catholic parochial schools accounted for about 20 percent of the elementary and secondary school population.

principally through the perfectly legitimate promotion by the brewers, increased considerably later on as the city grew and spread out.

6.

Fight with Banks and Stand on Taxation

Before getting to the somewhat more lively incidents of 1907 and 1908, I was to recall the more important and interesting facts of the successful fight I made to compel the payment of interest on public money by the banks. It was calculated some time ago that the total of this interest, obtained principally through my efforts, was greater during my time as mayor than my $10,000 salary, of which there was so much criticism. I notice there is no rush on just now to reduce the lambasted salary, though reductions are coming in other directions.

I made a motion as a member of the Board of Liquidation[38] at a meeting on June 6, 1906, that the board advertise for bids for sealed proposals for the custody of the funds from the one percent debt tax and that the deposits be given to the bank or banks offering the highest interest. President [Robert] M. Walmsley[39] of the board declared he did not believe the board had a legal right to accept the interest.

A motion was then made to proceed with the selection of a fiscal agent and the New Orleans National Bank was then selected as the fiscal agent or bank of deposit for the funds. I told the board that neither I nor the city treasurer nor the

---

38. The Board of Liquidation was created by Act 133 during the regular session of the Louisiana General Assembly on April 10, 1880. The purpose of the board was to liquidate, reduce, and consolidate the New Orleans city debt. It was to have "exclusive and direction of all matters relating to the bonded debt of the City." Creation of the board was an attempt to eliminate politics in the management of the city's bonded debt. *Acts of the General Assembly of the State of Louisiana at the Regular Session, 1880*; Kendall, *History of New Orleans*, II, 591–92.

39. Robert M. Walmsley, president of the Louisiana National Bank.

comptroller, the three elected officials who were ex-officio members, approved of that as we believed all the banks should have an equal showing.

On the following day I instructed the city attorney to enter such proceedings as might be necessary to decide whether it would not be legal to deposit the money with the bank offering the highest interest and accept the interest.

I am not covering every detail of this business. These recollections would run in *The Item* for years if I did that. I am giving the main facts.

Six months later, on January 9, 1907, I introduced a resolution at a meeting of the board and read a statement which I asked be put in the minutes.

"I recall to the recollections of this board," I read from my written statement, "that on June 6, 1906, I offered a similar resolution. A substitute was offered to my resolution to the effect that the board proceed to the election of a fiscal agent. That resolution was adopted and the New Orleans National Bank was elected as the fiscal agent of the board."

> The deposit of the one percent debt tax has been made with that bank ever since without interest or security. The New Orleans National Bank is, I know, a strong and responsible bank, but I think that this fund should be additionally protected as are other public funds deposited in responsible banks and by bonded security. At that time the comptroller, the treasurer and I protested against the adoption of the substitute and I notified the board that I would as I felt it to be my duty, submit this matter to the courts. I therefore instituted a suit against the board to prevent the proposed deposit with the New Orleans National Bank, which suit is now pending.
>
> Since that action of the board and the institution of the suit, the public policy of the state has been declared to be that all boards entrusted with the funds derived from taxes paid by the people shall be made to earn interest where that is practicable under security for the safe custody and return of the funds, and has declared the vote by any member against the deposit of such funds at interest under security where the same can be obtained to be a

breach of trust, defined by the act to be a misdemeanor, punishable by a fine of not less than $1000 or imprisonment for not less than six months or more than one year or both.[40]

It is clear to my mind that the state, through its representative legislative body, in thus declaring its policy as to the keeping and administration of tax funds, has spoken as plainly to this board as to any other board in the state. It has become the unquestionable duty of this board to take this action which is in obedience to the behest of the state in this regard.

The resolution provoked a very heated discussion. Mr. H. Generes Dufour, attorney for the board, stated that the act I referred to had been vetoed by the governor as unconstitutional. I replied that the fact that the governor had declared it unconstitutional did not make it so. Several members declared that in view of the pending suit they would not vote for my resolution. The resolution was voted on and lost. The city treasurer, the comptroller, and I voted for it and all the other members present were against it.

The suit in question was in the courts, as is plain, when the Act of 1906 was passed. Judge John St. Paul decided against my contention in this suit. It was directed, of course, against the Board of Liquidation. I immediately appealed to the Supreme Court. The Supreme Court affirmed Judge St. Paul's decision on Monday, February 18, 1907.

As the act had been passed after the suit had been filed, the Supreme Court did not express any opinion as to its legal effect on the board. It stated that the proper time to pass on the act was when some concrete case would come before the court. There were then several conferences about this business. Some of them were quite hot.

The board met again on March 12, 1907, and heard a report from Messrs. Miller, Dufour & Dufour on the decision of the

---

40. Act 128, Section 3: "Public monies must be deposited in banks paying interest thereon." *Acts Passed by the General Assembly of the State of Louisiana at the Regular Session, 1906.*

Supreme Court. The main point of it was that the board HAD A RIGHT to select its own bank or banks and if it saw fit it could require the banks to pay interest on the deposits. But the board, the Supreme Court had decided, COULD NOT BE COMPELLED to do this.

Then I called up my old resolution and stated that I thought it would be only fair to handle the funds of the one percent debt tax as other funds were handled. I mentioned several of them. I declared all the banks were in good condition and the board would not be taking any great risk in placing them with a bank that would pay for the use of them. I referred very briefly to the Act of 1906.

Mr. Ashton Phelps [of the *Times-Democrat*] then moved that the following banks be selected as the depositories and that the rate of interest to be paid would be three and one-half (3 ½) per cent: Citizens' Bank, Commercial-Germania, Hibernia, New Orleans National and the State National.

I then stated that if the board was opposed to advertising I would favor Mr. Phelps's motion as in my judgement it was the next best thing. I asked that a vote be taken on my resolution to advertise for bids and that Mr. Phelps's motion be held in abeyance.

Among many other matters of interest in connection with deposits of public money in banks, I find one worth writing about at present. It was a somewhat unusual incident, one that grew out of circumstances that will probably never be duplicated in the future.

The short way to set the matter forth is to quote a letter we wrote the liquidators of the banks that were being reorganized on November 16, 1905.

"On behalf of the City of New Orleans," I wrote them, "we here-by respectfully make formal demand for the payment to the City of New Orleans the sum of twenty-four thousand, six hundred and sixty dollars and seventy-nine cents $24,660.79, being the amount due by the Canal Bank, Louisiana National Bank, and Whitney National Bank, as fiscal agents of the City of New Orleans, for interest at the rate of six and one-third per cent per annum upon the average amount of the daily balances in said banks to the credit of the City of New Orleans from June 1, 1904, to March 10, 1905. Compliance with this demand is expected within 10 days from date hereof."

The letter was signed by myself as mayor and by Comptroller Charles R. Kennedy and City Treasurer Otto F. Briede. It had nothing to do with funds deposited by the Board of Liquidation, about which I have written somewhat at length, but concerned only deposits of the city government proper.

The banks took the position that their contracts as fiscal agents and depositories of the city had expired June 1, 1904, and that, as the city had not re-elected them as its fiscal agents, the city was in the position of an ordinary depositor. The council instructed the city attorney to proceed to collect. I have no memorandum at hand showing the date of payment or the exact amount, but my recollection is that in the end the liquidators paid up in full.

7.

Plans for Natural Gas

Harry B. Hawes,[41] of St. Louis, came to New Orleans in February of 1908 to get a gas franchise to supply the city with natural gas from the Caddo fields. The original ordinance introduced, of course, was considerably more than Hawes and his associates expected to get but they had the money and the people were so anxious to get the gas that *The States*, as I remember it, supported the ordinance practically as introduced. *The Item* attacked and many of *The Item's* criticisms were good. When the

---

41. Harry Bartow Hawes (1869–1947), lawyer, diplomat, wildlife conservationist, served in both the U.S. House of Representatives and Senate. *National Cyclopaedia of American Biography*, XLI (New York, 1956), 368.

details of the ordinance were finally settled on, *The States* showed considerable courage and character in an editorial in which it admitted that it had been mistaken in most of its contentions. It is not usual for a newspaper to admit that it has not been absolutely perfect.

Hawes appealed to me as a thoroughly reliable business man and an able lawyer. He had been the administrator of the Missouri state police and, I think, had been in Congress. He was defeated for governor by Joseph Folk at a time when it was practically impossible to elect a Democrat. He was Captain Hawes, of the intelligence department when I met him in Washington during the war. He is now a member of Congress.

To show that this was a serious matter and that Hawes' associates had the money to build the pipe lines, I will say that among them were Adolph Busch, president of Anheuser-Busch, reputed to be the wealthiest man west of the Mississippi, the younger Busch, President W. K. Bixby of the American Can Company of St. Louis; President H. E. Everett, of the American Bottling Works, Washington, D.C.; Lewis B. Ely, son of Frank Ely, of the firm of Ely, Walker & Company; C. H. Walker of St. Louis, and President Thomas H. West, of the St. Louis Trust Company.

I mention these names, which are a fine financial array, on account of events since then, to show that the money was there. They were financially able to carry out their work.

Hawes discussed the situation with the newspaper reporters and said his people would sell natural gas for industrial purposes at half the rate then prevailing here [for artificial gas], $1.15 per thousand cubic feet, and that the natural gas had thirty 30 percent more heat units.

I was delighted at the prospect of bringing natural gas to New Orleans, I told Hawes, however, that in view of rates for natural gas elsewhere we should put a maximum of fifty (50) cents a thousand cubic feet for households and a much lower rate for manufacturers in the ordinance. The ordinance was introduced on March 2, 1909.

On the invitation of the promoters, a party for forty-nine and nineteen councilmen visited the Caddo fields.

There was a great deal of adverse criticism of the fifty (50) year franchise but the capitalists said they could not finance the deal on the basis of a shorter period as the initial cost would be about eighteen million dollars ($18,000,000).

While the ordinance was being printed for fifteen (15) days, the legal requirement before it could be acted on, I discovered that the words "and fuel" had been omitted. Thomas Killeen, chairman of the committee on fire and lighting, stated that he had received a letter from the promoters' lawyers asking him to see that those words were written into the ordinance, when it came up in the council on March 16, 1909. When the committee got the ordinance, Chairman Killeen invited the public and all interested to discuss it. It had been considered by the Real Estate Exchange, Contractors and Dealers' Exchange, Cotton Exchange, Progressive Union, Board of Trade, Stock Exchange, Louisiana Engineering Society, Sugar and Rice Exchange, and other bodies I do not remember now.

I went before the committee and suggested that the bond for the execution of the proposed contract in the ordinance be increased from twenty thousand dollars ($20,000) to fifty thousand dollars ($50,000). This was done.

I recommended later that there be a sliding scale with 45 cents as the maximum per thousand cubic feet, that the rate go down to 40 cents when the consumption reached fifty million (50,000,000) feet and that after it reached 60,000,000 feet the rate be thirty-five (35) cents. I advised that the price of 20 cents per thousand for industrial purposes, which was fixed in the ordinance, would not insure competition with other fuels and that gas for industries should make its own price in competition with the other fuels.

The ordinance was unanimously adopted by the council and went to the franchise committee, composed of the executive heads of the departments of the city government. The franchise committee unanimously approved it. I signed it and it became a contract between New Orleans and the promoters.

One of the engineers employed by the promoters remained in Louisiana making more detailed investigation after the others had left. He reported to his people that they could not build the line as they had planned it at the cost they had figured on and supply the gas at the prices fixed in the ordinance without losing money. I was told that later other engineers approved this man's report and stated in addition that gas could be piped to various towns and cities across a different character of land and sold for even less and show a profit.

Anyhow, the Busch interests represented by Harry Hawes did not build their pipe lines. When the expiration of the time set had about arrived, it was requested that they be relieved of their bond for $50,000. This request was denied and the city got the money.

Some time in 1917 a big pocket of gas was discovered south of Houma, in Terrebonne Parish, and for a short period we all had hopes this supply could be used in New Orleans. It turned out, however, that although one of these wells was the "champion of the world" for pressure and flow, there was no certainty of a long life. I am informed that the plantations in the neighborhood that use this gas keep a large supply of coal on hand so they will not have to shut down if the wells decided to do so.

The next gas episode was, I believe, the discovery of a large field north of Monroe [in northeastern Louisiana]. Newspaper reports indicate that the time may come when New Orleans will get gas from there. Not being an expert, I will not venture an opinion, but will merely point out that it was not Martin Behrman who promised that New Orleans would get gas through some undisclosed plan for securing it. It was my distinguished critic and, as the head of a political faction in New

Orleans, my distinguished political opponent, Governor John M. Parker, who was represented by the newspapers supporting him as promising the gas. As these representatives were elaborate and were conspicuously displayed, it is but natural that I should assume that they were correct. Governor Parker did not question them—not even when they included maps showing the routes for the pipes.[42]

8.
1908 City Fight: Behrman Versus Independents

The next event worth the time it takes to tell about it was my re-election for a second term as mayor. The Democratic parish committee was called to meet July 18th, 1908, to make provision for the municipal primary and on July 11th or July 15th, I have forgotten which, a meeting was held in the office of Rolla A. Tichenor [New Orleans attorney] in the Masonic Temple to organize another faction. The meeting was executive, that is private. It was attended by twenty or more citizens and it was reported as entirely preliminary and that later on committees would be appointed.

The Democratic parish committee met at the Choctaw Club and . . . a resolution was adopted calling the municipal primary for September 1st, 1908. The Republican parish committee met that night and called a Republican Primary for the same day.

Then Rolla A. Tichenor gave out a statement that due to the fact that the people had lost confidence in primaries, owing to the Bailey-Lambremont incident in the state primary[43] more

---

42. Natural gas for New Orleans was an issue for the next two decades. In 1928 Governor Huey Long forced Mayor Arthur O'Keefe, the city council, and New Orleans Public Service (NOPSI) to provide customers with the cheap natural gas being piped to south Louisiana from the rich gas fields in the northern part of the state. T. Harry Williams, *Huey Long*, (New York: Alfred Knoph, 1969), 284–85; 299–03.

43. The Bailey-Lambremont incident that Berhman was referring to was in the 1908 Democratic party primary for lieutenant governor in which both Bailey and Lambremont vied for the nomination. This contest is discussed at some length in Chapter III herein.

than anything else, his conference had decided that it would not have candidates in the primaries but would get better results by putting an independent ticket in the field.

I got back home on July 22nd from the National Democratic Convention, four days after the Democratic and the Republican committees had met, and after winding up some matters of public business that had accumulated on my desk in the mayor's parlor, I qualified with the parish committee as a candidate for mayor.

"If I consulted my personal interest," I said in an interview published in *The Times-Democrat*, "I would not be a candidate for re-election. I am worse off financially now than when I was elected mayor. For the past three months, I have been tendered support for re-election by people in all walks of life; not only my old friends, but many who were opposed to me four years ago. I am a candidate on my record."

As will become clear to my readers, I became mayor for a second term on my record in 1908. I was re-elected again on my record in 1912. I was out for mayor again on my record in 1916 and again became mayor. I ran on my record another time in 1920 and I was defeated. I am proud of my record and I like to write about it.

When the time limit for filing papers with the Democratic committee expired on July 26, 1908, the list showed forty-three (43) unopposed candidates and I was one of the 43. None of the department heads of my administration were opposed. Some members of the council and the school board and one or two of the judges of the lower courts were opposed.

Four days later, on July 30th, 1908, a meeting was held to organize a faction to be known as the "Independent Democratic League" to put candidates out for the municipal and parish offices in the general election. This was done by some of the "Home Rulers" of 1904 and other "independents," as they called themselves, who previously met at Rolla A. Tichenor's office.

Frank A. Daniels, the formal leader of the Home Rule faction, was asked to invite his organization to the meeting with the purpose of getting the endorsement of the Home Rule organization present to form a quorum, as there were only five members present and the rules required eighteen (18) for a quorum.

The Independent Democratic League then met with Chairman Tichenor presiding. There was a disposition to postpone organization, but the chairman stated it was "now or never." So they went into permanent organization with Mr. Tichenor as Chairman. On motion of Mr. E. J. Fitzgerald of the Ninth Ward, Chairman Tichenor was authorized to appoint the executive committee of seventeen members, one from each ward.

It seems that these seventeen potential ward leaders, or "ward bosses" were not to be selected by the slow grind of years of politics, nor at any kind of an election, but were to get their honors and powers hot from Chairman Tichenor. That's what you call "Independent Democracy." It was certainly independent of most of the prevailing ideas and facts of politics.

The Times-Democrat had something to say editorially on July 31st 1908, about the ticket nominated by the Regular faction. After saying that the method of the caucus of Regulars in selecting the ticket was neither democratic nor wise, *The Times-Democrat* criticized the fact that half a dozen or so of the politicians had met "without consulting the voters," and that this was un-democratic and abhorrent. It said further that the political organization and system, which I represented, which had made me mayor and of which I was a leader, rendered it impossible for any administration chosen by it and controlled by it to accomplish what New Orleans wanted and expected.

The Times-Democrat went on to say that my knowledge of municipal affairs, my industry and my common sense had made my administration a great improvement over that of my "ring" predecessors.

"The caucus says that its slate is perfect throughout in every bureau and office," *The Times-Democrat* proceeded, "more conservative citizens will go not further than to say that the head, at least, is good, and that his excellence covers, like charity, any defects that may be found in other nominations."

Mayor Behrman is expected to carry through the weak names on the roll and is put forward as the ideal and representative of the organization. His nomination has brought him many warm compliments from men of prominence in the affairs of the city outside the ranks of politics. "An active, earnest and able public officer" and "the best Mayor New Orleans has ever had" are a few of the many commendations and endorsements he has received in the last few days.

The Times-Democrat appreciates as much as anyone in the community the official qualifications and good qualities of the Mayor. It has watched his administration carefully and dispassionately and has neglected no opportunity of complimenting him on every act of his which we believed to be in the public interest; but we disagree fundamentally with those gentlemen who believe that a ticket or any candidate selected as the ring ticket has been chosen can give New Orleans such a government as it wants and needs in its present emergencies.

Candidates chosen by the ring and from its ranks, elected by it, responsible to it first and to the people a long way afterwards, owe it their allegiance and for that reason their efficiency and public service are limited and lessened.

No one will dispute the Mayor's assiduity, the time and attention and labor he has given to the duties of his office. No mayor has worked harder or longer than he, and shown more interest in public questions, and been more willing to listen to every argument to every side of a public question. It is this quality in particular which has been his most valuable asset and which has won for him the good will of many of those who have consulted him. These are the limitations of his efficiency and fitness and they bring us face to face with the fact, true not of New Orleans alone but of every other American city, and the cause of what Mr. Bryce calls America's one political failure—its municipal government—that no mayor or other official placed in office by the "organization," "machine," "ring" or whatever name the aggregation or combination of politicians is called who control its politics, can ever free himself from the "Old Man of the Sea." Some have tried it, like Mayor [John] Weaver of Philadelphia,[44] but they have gone back sooner or later to their "False Gods" to bow before the machine, to carry out its will and to strengthen and upbuild its case.

If I had been a farmer, when I read that I would have said: "GOSH!" It was what we used to call "hot stuff."

But from the point of view of the late Page M. Baker, the editor of *The Times-Democrat*, it was absolutely fair and honest. I think Mr. Baker was trying to give me a square deal and at the same time not to sacrifice his opinions nor to let anyone get a false idea of his attitude toward "those ward bosses."

The Third Ward Independent League held a meeting August 21st, 1908, at which the speakers advised the audience to keep out of the primaries and then resolutions were adopted endorsing Hon. Joshua G. Baker for mayor and urging the committee to nominate him. A few days afterwards Rolla A. Tichenor called on Judge Baker to ask him if he would allow the committee to consider him a candidate for mayor in their "independent ticket" and the Judge expressed his appreciation of the compliment. But he said he did not desire to run.

The Independent League held another meeting on Sunday afternoon, August 23rd, 1908, and the Committee of Thirty-four, which they had organized, unanimously resolved to offer the nomination for Mayor to the late Mr. W. G. Tebault, a widely known dealer in furniture and considerable of a literary man. Mr. Tebault took an intense interest, for a time, in Joseph Leveque's *Morning World* and wrote some of that paper's warmest editorials.

---

44. John Weaver, an Independent Republican, was active in Philadelphia reform politics first as district attorney (1901–1903) and then as mayor (1903–1907).

Mr. Tebault accepted the nomination and said there would be no trouble in getting the money to finance the campaign. He predicted that the "independent" movement would enroll more than thirty-thousand (30,000) votes.

The Committee then went around to see J. Porter Parker, whose term as district attorney was about to end. Judge Parker told them he appreciated the honor but that he intended to devote himself in the future to the practice of the law and he did not care about running.

The very busy committee had an almost complete slate ready by August 28th. Only a few minor positions were not filled.

The Democratic primary election was held on September 1st, 1908, for such offices as were subjects of contention. Most of us had been nominated without opposition.

James C. Henriques, as an elector, as a member of the Democratic party, as chairman of its parish committee, and as such the representative of all the nominees of the Democratic party in New Orleans, filed an objection to the proceedings of the "Independent league" before the State Contest Board at Baton Rouge on September 8th, 1908, on the ground that their nomination papers did not contain a sufficient number of signatures and a great many of those who signed the nominating papers had voted in the [September Democratic] primary, which was in violation of the primary election law.

To which Rolla A. Tichenor, president of the "Independent League" and candidate for District Attorney, filed his objections. The board listened to both sides and then unanimously decided that with the exception of the candidate for councilman from the tenth ward, none of the "Independent" candidates had secured the necessary one hundred (100) duly qualified signers and that they were, therefore, disqualified from having their names placed on the ballot.

Six days later, on September 14th, the "Independent League" presented to [the] registrar of voters a new set of nominating papers. He refused to accept them and gave as his reasons that the time had expired for the filing of such papers and that under the law he could not certify to them. What they wanted of him was a certificate that the gentlemen who had signed their names had been enrolled as voters in New Orleans.

So on the following day the "Independent League" went into the Civil District Court to compel [the registrar of voters] to receive the nomination papers. Judge William B. Sommerville decided against the League on September 18th.

Whereupon Rolla A. Tichenor resigned as chairman of the "Independent League" and Joseph Markey of the Third ward was elected in his stead.

Clarence S. Hebert, assistant treasurer of the United States Sub-Treasury and a leader in Republican politics and an excellent lawyer, was then retained by the "Independent League" and he immediately went to Baton Rouge to appear before Judge Harvey F. Brunot and have a writ of *mandamus* issued to compel the contest board to accept the original nomination papers. But Judge Brunot was off on his vacation. Mr. Hebert filed his petition in the clerk's office.

This situation made it necessary for somebody to be appointed in Judge Brunot's place to get quick action for Mr. Hebert and the "Independent League" and the Supreme Court of the State of Louisiana immediately appointed Judge William B. Sommerville.

As Judge William B. Sommerville had given the "Independent League" a judicial but none-the-less severe wallop in another phase of the same issue, his appointment to listen to them again caused some members of the League to make remarks about the Supreme Court and the decline of our civilization. The case before Judge Sommerville developed into an application for an order to compel the Secretary of State to print the gentlemen's names on the ballot.

When Mr. W. G. Tebault, candidate for mayor, was on the stand, he was asked by the League's lawyer, Clarence Hebert, "What is the Independent League?"

"A party desirous of improving the very bad condition of New Orleans," was the answer. His Attorney explained to the court that that was not the answer he had expected.

The case of the "Independent League" of 1908 in which they sought to compel the Secretary of State to put the names of their candidates on the ballot, was decided against them by Judge Sommerville.

My recollection of Judge Sommerville's reasons, of which he gave a number, is far from clear but my impression is that one of them was that there was a "misjoiner of parties" as all the candidates were not running for the same job and they all had the same signatures on the same set of papers. If I am correct in this recollection of the legal point I mention they should have made up a set of papers for each candidate. Anyhow, Judge Sommerville decided against them and they appealed to the Supreme Court.

Incidentally, I may say without being impolite, I do not think that the general public took any great interest in these matters at the time. My impression was that most people were quite satisfied with my record as mayor and that the *Times-Democrat* and other papers had not been able to warm them up enough to stimulate a real interest in the brief career of the "Independent League."

The Supreme Court had not yet reached the case when the candidate for mayor, Mr. Tebault, gave out an interview that he would make the race no matter what the Supreme Court did. He pointed out that the election laws provided for a blank column on the ballot and that he would see to it that every voter got a ballot with a blank column. Then they could write in the names of their favorite candidates. There would be plenty pencils in the booths, Mr. Tebault said.

The Supreme Court decided on October 28, 1908, that the case presented by the "Independent League" was no good. There was no time for them to get up more nomination papers. The League was dead.

There were four parties on the ballot at the general election on November 3rd, 1908. There were the Republicans, the Democrats, the Socialists, and the Independent Party, generally known as the Hearst Party.

This was William Randolph Hearst's short lived but spectacular party.[45] I have forgotten the name of his candidate for President of the United States, but what I heard of his speech at the Athenaeum in New Orleans indicates he was a good man and a fine scrapper. Hearst had collected a lot of evidence, including photographs of letters written by [John D.] Archbold and other Standard Oil chiefs, to show that leaders in both the national parties were politically intimate with the big men in the Standard Oil and had received large campaign contributions from them. His nominee for the White House was one of the few who had given the Standard Oil a hot fight and beaten it in the oil business. Hearst figured that both parties "greased with Standard Oil," as he said at the time, the voters would flock to a man who had fought and licked Standard Oil. They did not do so.

Louisiana went Democratic again. Henry Clay Warmoth, ex-governor and a life long Republican, made a very active fight against [the Democrat] General [Albert] Estopinal in the first congressional district. That was about the only real fight at this election.

45. William Randolph Hearst (1863–1951), newspaper and magazine publisher, was quite active in New York and national politics during the early decades of the twentieth century. He was elected to the U.S. House of Representatives from New York in 1902 but was unsuccessful in 1905 in his bid for the mayoralty of New York and the governorship in the state in 1906. In the 1908 presidential election, Hearst formed the Independent party to oppose Democrat William Jennings Bryan whom he had backed in 1896 and 1900. Thomas L. Hisgen, the Independent party's candidate for president, finished fifth among eight candidates following the national prohibition party's Eugene W. Chafin.

The election returns in the city showed that I got 26,897 votes. W. G. Tebault 89 votes, and Porter, the Socialist, 270 votes. The Socialists, as usual promised better results the next time.[46]

Well, I had done my best as mayor for four years. I had been elected four years before in circumstances that would have discouraged many men with fewer faithful friends than I had. The circumstances were such that I had to run again whether I wanted to or not. But I did want to run. I was determined to run and get elected again. The small number of votes given my opponents shows there was no widespread sentiment against me. In fact, I think the total number of votes against me aside from the 270 members of the Socialist Club, was probably less than the total number of qualified voters employed by the *Times-Democrat*.

I began my second term on Monday, December 7, 1908. I received a great number of verbal and written congratulations and cordial good wishes for a successful administration. The Mayor's Parlor was filled with flowers and one of my visitors stayed only a minute because he was filled with something else. Prominent business men, bankers, lawyers, doctors, mechanics, laborers, and in fact men from all walks of life either called on me or were present in the council chamber.

All the world loves a winner. I am grateful that I have so many friends of the winning days that were as close to me after my defeat in 1920 and have stayed as close to me since then, as they were in 1904 and in 1908, in 1912 and in 1916. So far as I am personally concerned, I have gotten a great deal of satisfaction out of things that could never have happened if I had been re-elected in 1920. I do not mean by this that I did not want to be re-elected but I do mean that it is a pleasure to shake the hands

---

46. The election was held on November 3, 1908. Behrman received 26,897 votes, Tebault 89, and the Socialist candidate, Alvin Porter 270. Estopinal polled 13,185 votes to Warmoth's 1730. New Orleans *Times-Democrat,* November 7, 1908.

of some men and women to whose interests it was to quit me cold when I was defeated. However, all the world loves a winner and lots of folks told me many loving words when I was re-inaugurated in December of 1908.

Governor J. Y. Sanders sat with President James McRacken of the council and myself at my second inauguration.

Only eight members of the old council came back for the new administration. Four of them had gone to other positions.

After I had delivered my message to the old council on the day I began my second term as mayor, December 7th, 1908, a committee compiled the election returns and the new members of the council took the oath of office.

These elections over, the time had come for my first message to the new council.

"Four years ago I addressed my first message as Mayor to the Honorable City Council of New Orleans whose term of office had just come to a close," I said in opening my formal address.

> The administration selected by a majority vote of the people had just emerged from a campaign characterized chiefly by its unprecedented bitterness. From experience acquired through many years of intimate association with various administrations, I recognized that the important branch of the municipal government is the legislative department. Without its good will and co-operation, the policy of the executive department could not be put into effect and its pledges, made during the campaign, might be rendered impossible of fulfillment. Hence it was that from the very outset I brought the City Council into my closest confidence, outlining to it my views as to the course which should be pursued to insure the best result through which the administration not only would gain the respect and confidence of the community but would safeguard, advance and upbuild every interest upon which rests the development of the future greatness of New Orleans.
>
> It is a source of profound pride and gratification to me to realize that every recommendation I made in my inaugural address to your estimable predecessors four years ago was carried into effect. And let me call your attention to the fact that the course over which we

had to head during those four years was by no means one strewn with thornless flowers. You will recall that we assumed the reins of government under most inauspicious circumstances. A strong spirit of formidable discord and suspicion existed. There were many of our best and most representative citizens who apprehended honestly and sincerely, that the city administration just ushered into office neither intended nor purposed to carry its campaign pledges into effect. Had the spirit been an entirely partisan one, it might have proven less embrassing. It had existence among honest and sincere citizens but its inspiration had come from partisans.

When, therefore, there came, in the very early stages of the administration, proofs positive and irrefutable that honest efforts were being made to make good the pledges made, there was a gradual disappearance of the spirit of discontent with the resultant creation of the spirit of satisfaction and confidence, from which has been evolved a concert of action and recognition of the difficulties with which the administration is confronted in handling municipal problems. We were called upon during the very first year of our tenure to meet the pestilential visitation of the summer of 1905. The successful manner in which that trying ordeal was met and dealt with has passed into history.

Scientists from every section of the civilized world have agreed that the necessary measures and precautions to prevent yellow fever, as well as to supress the disease, were demonstrated beyond doubt in New Orleans during the summer of 1905, under the experienced and able professional leadership of Dr. J. H. White, in charge of the United States Marine Hospital Service at this port, and they with our best citizens and representative clergymen were kind enough to accord commendations and praise for the assistance rendered by the city government in the suppression of the disease and its ready response to every scientific suggestion to prevent any future incursion. Moreover, we were called to meet and cope with the unlooked for embarrassements incident to and contingent upon the ravages of storm and high waters. In the course it pursued through these afflictions, the city government won encomiums not only at home but from other communities to which assistance and relief had been extended.

Among the very proud boasts which the city administration of 1904–1908 may advance is the part it took in making possible the present successful operation of our Public Belt Railroad, an institution unique and without a peer throughout the length and breadth of our great country. It is unique in this and the realization of the strenuous and almost insuperable opposition with which it was confronted by some of the most powerful corporate interests was responsible for the grave suspicion in the minds of many of our best citizens that the city administration would not be able to make good its pledges to expedite the completion of the Public Belt Railroad and insure its being put into operation. Its inauguration and present operation, therefore, must stand as a monument to the devotion and fidelity of the city administration of 1904–1908.

Our modern systems of sewerage, drainage and water purification are rapidly drawing towards completion. We have been given every assurance which I regard to be real as well as reasonable, that our new water plant will be in readiness to assume all responsibility by the dawn of the New Year. If the test as to the potableness of the water which will be furnished by this plant shall prove as satisfactory as the demonstration we have had as to its pressure for the extinguishment of fires, the City of New Orleans will have in that institution another feature without equal or parallel throughout the country. . . .

Sooner or later, but more likely in the very early stages of your administration, your new members will come to appreciate the lessons already learned by their more experienced colleagues—that in solving the various problems which make the general welfare in a great city, such as ours is, individual and sectional claims must give away to and make room for improvements which reflect the greatest number.

Of all the difficulties and embarrassments which confront the newly made legislator, I believe the greatest to be the disappointment he must experience in his efforts to enact pet measures which he assured his constituents he would be able to put through if they would elect him to office. Hence, at the very outset of your administration, while the Personnel of your honorable body, composed as it is of members elected from the various wards and certain districts of New Orleans, would imply that the legislative assemblage is an heterogeneous one. I would appeal to you to be always mindful of the fact that all of you represent all of the people and, under the oath of office administered to you this day, you are to legislate for the general welfare of the entire community.

In this appeal, I cannot express myself with too great earnestness.

I realize fully that every one of you is interested chiefly and especially in the advancement and upbuilding of the particular ward or district he has been chosen to represent. But when it can be shown to you, that your particular purpose in any direction is at variance with the general welfare of the community, I indulge the hope that you will seek individually to cooperate in homogeneous unison for the benefit of the public at large.

You are the representatives of a most enlightened and patriotic people. You will soon come to experience that the captious criticism of the unreasonable is engulfed quickly in the stream of plaudits which always leaves the shore of honest effort and faithful endeavor.

When the hurrah and the celebration were over, I went back to work.

As I indicated in quotations from *The Times-Democrat*'s editorials, that paper admitted before I was re-elected in 1908 that my four years of experience had made me "quite valuable," as one of my friends interpreted it. On the day after I began my second term, *The Times-Democrat* complimented me on my knowledge of municipal affairs and my energy and hard work as mayor. I had then had four years of experience. Yet in 1920, when I had had almost sixteen full years of experience, *The Times-Picayune*[47] gave as one reason for its opposition that I had been there sixteen years.

"The continuance of an entire administration in office after serving four years is a novelty," said *The Times-Democrat* on the second day of my second term, "not only here but anywhere and this is the first time it has ever occurred in America. Mayors have occasionally been re-elected, although the tendency has been in the other direction."[48]

The Times-Democrat objected very strenuously to that portion of my message in which I said that "the executive department

---

47. In 1914 the New Orleans *Times-Democrat* and the New Orleans *Daily Picayune* merged to form the New Orleans *Times-Picayune*.

48. New Orleans *Times-Democrat*, December 8, 1908.

of the city government has been re-elected in its entirety by a practically unanimous vote of the people." "It is true that there was no opposition," said *The Times-Democrat* on that point, "but that fact does not mean that the candidates were the unanimous choice of the voters and that the voters would have nominated them of their own accord. But political conditions destroyed any chance for organization in opposition to the ring."

Notwithstanding the fact that *The Times-Democrat* had been urging readers since the campaign of 1904 to be prepared for the next campaign, so that the "mistake" of 1904 would not be repeated, and the further fact that the payments of poll taxes for the elections of 1908 were the largest up to that time, *The Times-Democrat* and my other opponents so managed their work against me that their total vote was eighty-nine (89) for mayor against more than twenty-six thousand (26,000) for me.

It will be universally admitted that the administration for the last four years was better than expected," *The Times-Democrat* continued.

> *The Times-Democrat* has been ever ready to praise when it thought praise was due; but while this praise has been well received, there has been a disposition to resent any criticism. The past four years have seen more done in paving and improving of the public schools than during any similar period in our history. The mayor has given more time and attention to the public business than his predecessors and, knowing a great deal of municipal conditions, has been well equipped for the questions before him. He deserves praise, too, for the investigation initiated by him to find the financial status of the various city departments.

This editorial ended with the following sentence:

"While giving due credit for what has been done in the last four years, there is much more to be done in the next four years before New Orleans will be assured of all that it is entitled to; and we will get those improvements only by pointing out the weak spots."

While there were mistakes in that editorial, when you consider that it was in a newspaper directed by the late Page M. Baker, who was always in opposition to the Regular organization, it was plainly honest and the compliments to me were undoubtedly deserved in the opinion of the editor. Far be it from me to hand myself too many bouquets, but I must say I agreed with *The Times-Democrat* in its compliments.

III

City and State Politics, 1906–1916

1.

1908 Campaign Starts at 1906 Session of Legislature

The direct primary bill was passed at the session of 1906. I told of its origin in full some time ago, so there is no use in my repeating the details touched on then. The rumblings of the coming state campaign began as soon as Robert Snyder[1] died and things began to take definite shape as soon as the politicians got together at the state capital for the session of 1906.

When the primary bill was before the senate committee, Senator T. H. Thorpe of New Orleans, in arguing against it, reviewed the political history of Louisiana, declaring that under the old regime Louisiana had its [Francis T.] Nicholls, who liberated the state from carpet bag rule; its [Samuel] McEnery, who built its levees; its [Murphy J.] Foster, who crushed the lottery; its [William] Heard, who restored its credit.

The states all around us have had primaries, Senator Thorpe declared, and "Arkansas has its Jefferson Davis, Mississippi has it [James K.] Vardaman, and we may well profit by these examples." The bill passed without much trouble.

Taxation, primary elections and curtailment of the governor's

---

1. Robert Snyder was speaker of the house in the Louisiana state legislature.

power to appoint officials and board members loomed up as the important or most prominent matters to be fought out.[2]

There was a great deal of dissatisfaction all over the state on account of the great increase in assessments. Governor Blanchard had on two occasions called the assessors from the parishes to meetings at Baton Rouge, and had urged higher assessments. That some method of revising the assessments must be provided was the cry in the country parishes as well as in New Orleans and the smaller cities and the demand that the assessors be made elective instead of continuing to be appointed by the governor was loud and determined.

While Governor Blanchard had a great deal of patronage, he did not at this time have the great prestige and popularity gained in the campaign of 1904. He did no more than his predecessors when he entered the local campaign in New Orleans in 1904, and really did much less in the way of getting into our local politics than Murphy J. Foster had done, but a change in conditions had worked out the result that this move injured him politically.

The desire for a few big changes resulted in a caucus of some members of the house in Baton Rouge a few days before the assembling of the legislature. J. M. Johnson of Madison parish was chairman and he appointed steering committees for a dis-

---

2. The 1906 regular session of the legislature was greatly concerned with the equalization of assessments, taxation, reduction of appointive power, and election reform. In the area of taxation and assessments, three significant bills were passed: Act 66, defined assessments for the purpose of taxing corporations; Act 182, created a state Board of Equalization to provide uniform property assessments throughout the state; Act 109, levied an inheritance tax for the benefit of public schools. Concerning the reduction of the appointive power of the governor, a reform long sought by former Populists, two bills were passed: Act 78, provided for the election of assessors; and Act 60, which required that members of parish school boards be elected. Also passed during this session was a primary election law (Act 49), another Populist reform, which required that all nominations by political parties for any state, parish, or municipal office "be made by a direct primary." *Acts Passed by the General Assembly of the State of Louisiana at the Regular Session, 1906.*

tinct and clear program of reform. They wanted to see that all officials should be elected by the people and that none of these then holding office could be removed by the governor before the expiration of their terms unless duly proceeded against "for malfeasance, non-feasance or mis-feasance in office."

On the second day of the session notice was given of the intention of the introduction of bills providing for the election of the heretofore appointed assessors in New Orleans and the consolidation of the seven appointed tax collectorships into one and this one also to be elected. Then they pulled off something horrible, as one of the members told me at the time. They were so enraged at the conditions that they wanted to reduce everything.

They actually threatened to introduce a bill to reduce the number of members of the governor's staff! There were then only twenty two colonels, only twenty-two lieutenant colonels and only forty three majors on the governor's staff. Somebody must have suggested that this would be going too far, as I do not remember that the bill was ever introduced. If it was, it was not passed. That put [Lieutenant Governor] J. Y. Sanders[3] in a position to have as complete a staff as he thought best. I have no statistics on the Sanders staff, but I have been told it was not a small and puny staff by any means. Some kind of a bill was

---

3. Jared Y. Sanders (1867–1944) served two terms in the state legislature and was speaker of the lower house during the administration of Governor William W. Heard (1900–1904), and one term as lieutenant governor under Governor Newton C. Blanchard (1904–1908). After being elected governor in 1908, his stand on the regulation of racetrack betting and saloons was a constant vexation to his Regular Democratic supporters. In July, 1910, Sanders was elected to the U.S. Senate by the state legislature to complete the term left vacant by the death of Senator Samuel McEnery. Sanders, however, resigned the seat before taking office to remain governor. In 1914 Sanders was elected to the U. S. Congress where he remained for two terms. As Governor McEnery has been remembered as the Levee Governor, Sanders will be known for his work to improve the state's roads and highways. Miriam G. Reeves, *The Governors of Louisiana* (Gretna, La.: Pelican, 1972), 91–93.

passed in 1912 and L. E. Hall's staff was limited. This is what caused the bear market in gold lace and uniforms in 1912, 1913, and early 1914.

Governor Blanchard had pledged himself in the state campaign of 1904, against General Jastremski, to cut down the patronage, the appointive power, of that office. He had used it for good purposes whenever and wherever he could and his intention as stated, as to leave that office reduced in that kind of power. He did not oppose the general move to do this, but pointed out that if the assessors were elected by the voters in the parishes it would be necessary to have some other check on them since this would remove the governor's control. What he meant was the Board of Equalization. As elected assessor, technically a state officer, is really a local officer as Governor Blanchard pointed out.

There are some things to which I need not refer in any detail. One is that J. Y. Sanders, well known to be a candidate for governor [in 1908] favored the bills making the officials elective as far as was practicable at the time. He also favored the creation of the tax commission of the Blanchard administration,[4] which reported in 1908 that the plan of giving the state some property and the parishes other property from which to get revenue was the best plan. This is called the "segregation plan." It was brought up again by [Governor] Hall in 1912 and was defeated as it was too novel and elaborate. When the [1906] session was over, almost everybody knew that Sanders would be in the campaign for governor or in his grave when the campaign started.

Ernest B. Kruttschnitt, chairman of the Democratic state central committee died in the summer of 1906 and the state central

---

4. Act 191 created a commission to study the system of assessment and taxation in Louisiana and in other parts of the country. The commission was to formulate and submit to the legislature a perfected system of assessments for the state. *Acts Passed by the General Assembly of the State of Louisiana at the Regular Session, 1906.*

The Choctaw Club, 1934

Charles L. Franck Collection, New Orleans

Aerial view of Storyville, *ca.* 1914

Charles L. Franck Collection, New Orleans

Tom Anderson's Arlington Annex in Storyville, *ca.* 1915

Charles L. Franck Collection, New Orleans

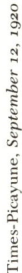

And He Wants Another Four-Years' Booking!

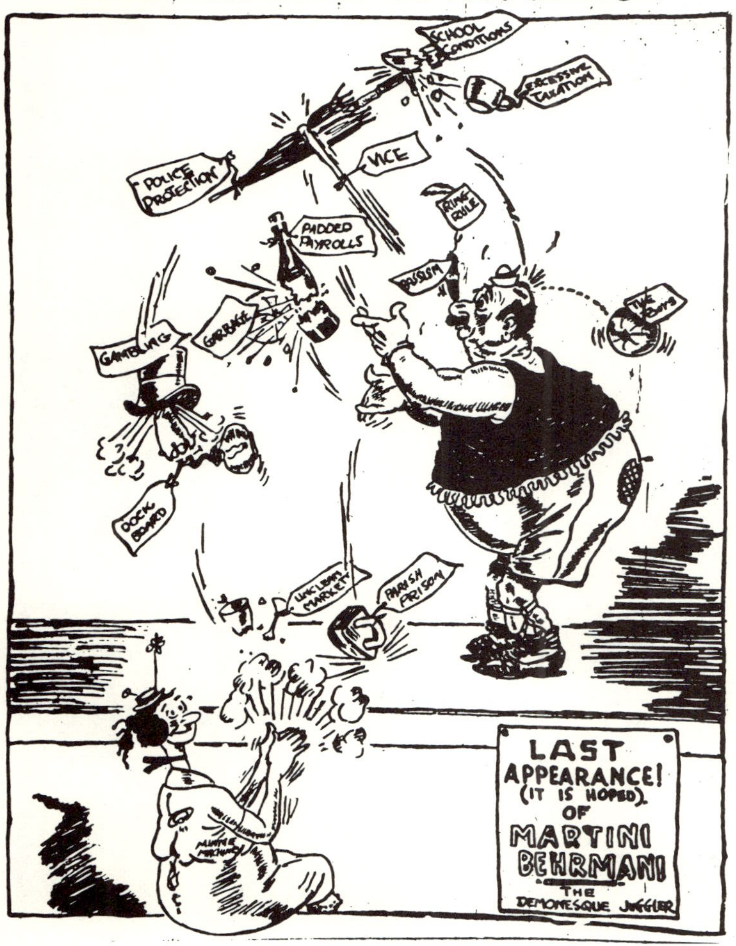

Times-Picayune, *September 11, 1920*

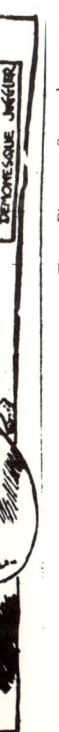

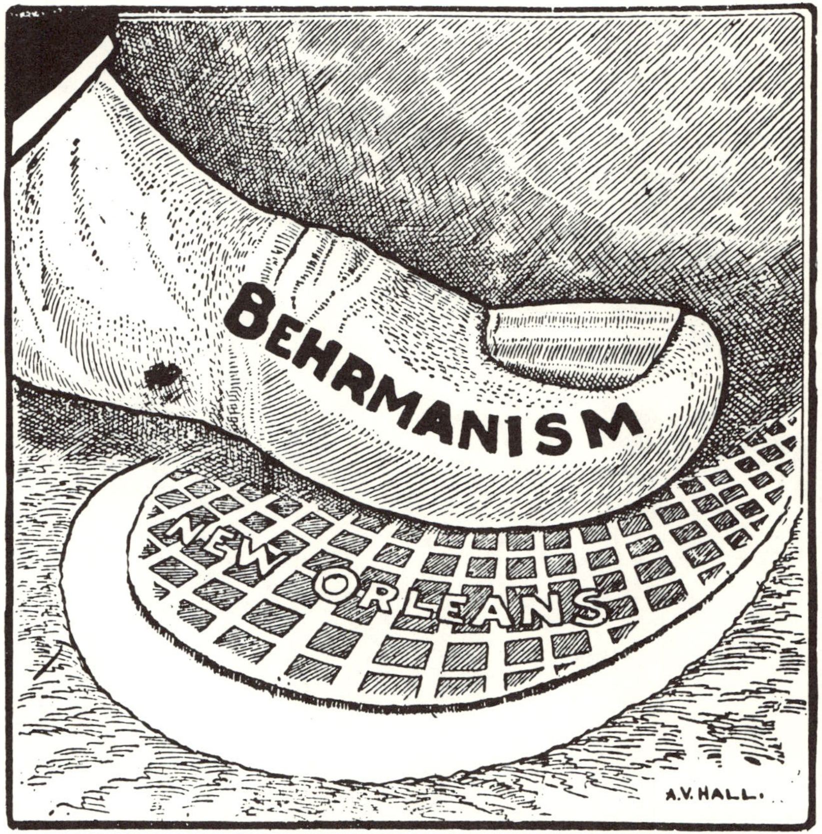

Times-Picayune, *September 12, 1920*

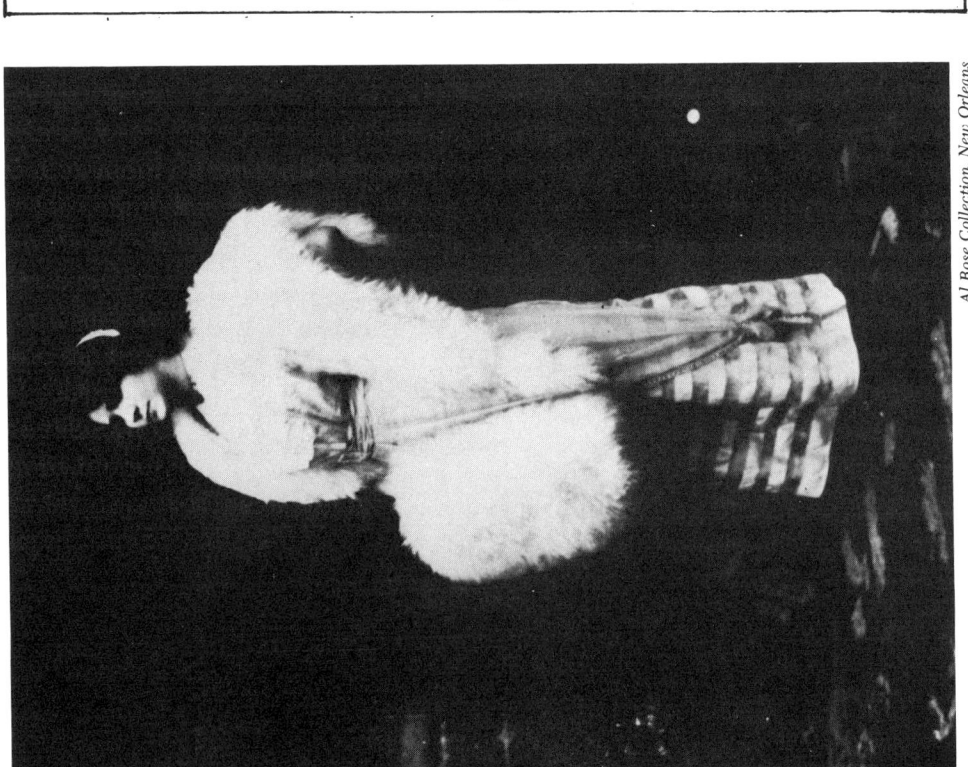

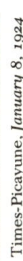

Samuel D. McEnery (1837–1910)
Governor of Louisiana, 1881–1888

Murphy J. Foster (1849–1912)
Governor of Louisiana, 1892–1900

John M. Parker (1863–1939)
Governor of Louisiana, 1920–1924

Jared Y. Sanders (1867–1944)
Governor of Louisiana, 1908–1912

committee met in New Orleans on July 28, 1906. Election of another chairman was the most conspicuous, politically, of the incidents of the meeting. I have written so much about my good friend Ernest Kruttschnitt that I need not say more now. Had he lived and retained his health, he could have had any political position he cared for. His opponents of course, would have harped on the fact that he was one of the really great corporation lawyers. But I have not yet found, in this state, that that cry ever hurt a real lawyer.

Several candidates for the chairmanship had been talked of but on the day of the meeting, only two names were mentioned. They were Charles Janvier and former Governor William Wright Heard. It was a very hotly contested election and much bitterness was displayed by both sides. Just how bitter I felt I am going to keep a dark secret as both Janvier and Heard were and are on good terms with me.

Governor Blanchard was openly accused on the floor of using the power of his office to force the election of Charles Janvier. His friends replied that Governor Blanchard was doing no more than all the governors who preceded him. That was true. Lieutenant Governor J. Y. Sanders was for [William] Heard and Senator Murphy J. Foster, of course, was with J. Y. The result was Janvier forty three and Heard thirty one, and the New Orleans [R.D.O.] delegation was badly split up. My ward, the 15th, Algiers, voted for the loser, Heard.

Ernest Kruttschnitt had been a member at large, so it was necessary to fill the vacancy. In such circumstances as these, the committee itself filled vacancies. Although I had lined up with the minority, I was unanimously elected to the committee.

When Charles Janvier took the chair he made a formal speech of acceptance in which he said that he wanted to have no part in factional fights. He said a family quarrel had just taken place, such as was likely to occur in the best regulated families. He wanted to do everything possible to soothe whatever feeling remained. He said he had forgotten that anybody had voted against him. Now that the thing is so long in the past, I can afford to say that my friend Charles Janvier showed that he could make a very fine speech and also that he had a very poor memory.

General Albert Estopinal[5] was elected vice-chairman and one of the several "fiercest meetings" of the state central committee adjourned. The aftermath of these committee elections was that a coalition between Robert F. Broussard[6] and Governor Blanchard became apparent. Broussard and his friends had supported Blanchard's candidate, Heard, and it was believed that the prestige this gained would make Broussard a strong candidate. Up to this time, however, and not for some time afterward, was there any public announcement.

A few days later, General Albert Estopinal notified Chairman Janvier that he would not accept a place of vice chairman and that he had advised the managers of Charles Janvier's campaign for the chairmanship that he would not accept if he was elected. General Estopinal declared it was impossible for him to assume the duties of that important position on account of his personal affairs. As vice chairman of the committee, he would be chairman of the executive committee and would, therefore have the bulk of the work of the committee.

Practically every move made in the legislature in 1906 and at the committee meeting described, had some bearing on the coming state campaign between J. Y. Sanders and Theodore S. Wilkinson.

Political electricity got to flashing around like heat lightning in January of 1907 when Lieutenant Governor Jared Y. Sanders

---

5. General Albert Estopinal was elected to the U.S. House of Representatives in 1908 where he served until 1919.

6. Robert F. Broussard represented Louisiana's Third Congressional District (in south central Louisiana) in the U.S. House of Representatives from 1897 to 1915 and in the U.S. Senate from 1915 until his death in 1918.

announced that he had retired from the law firm of Foster, Milling, Godchaux & Sanders and that he would continue the practice of law by himself. Nobody with any sense believed J. Y. expected to devote much time to Louisiana annuals and briefs and addresses to the courts in that year. Everybody in politics knew this meant he was about ready to announce himself as a candidate for governor. He had visited more than forty of the parishes during the year 1906 and he did not confine his conversation in them to flowers and poetry.

The only other candidate actually before the people then was General Leon Jastremski, who had been defeated by Blanchard four years before. Whereupon, those among Robert Broussard's friends who wanted him to run began urging him to announce at once. His more intimate friends, however, predicted that he would not enter the race for governor but would again be candidate for congress in the third district and would remain in Congress until 1912. Some of them freely stated that Bob Broussard would run for the Senate and for the House of Representatives in 1912. I wish I could remember just who told me this one evening in the winter of 1906–1907 as what appeared to be improbable turned out to be absolutely accurate. Broussard was elected to the Senate early in 1912 and re-elected to the house late in 1912.

General Leon Jastremski was in New Orleans on Monday, January 21st, 1907, to take part in the ceremonies incident to the hundredth anniversary of the birth of Robert E. Lee and when questioned by a reporter as to whether he was a candidate for governor he replied that he was.

"Most assuredly," he said. "I am in honor bound to make the fight. The issues today are almost identical with those of the campaign of 1903–1904 and there are other issues which I will discuss later." That last statement made some of us wonder what General Jastremski had to spring on the public. He announced his platform in the early part of March and outlined his idea, which included "fair primaries" good roads, equalization of assessments, two cents a mile for railroad passenger fares and other planks. He really did not spring a surprise. But we had all expected something unexpected.

Then Colonel Theodore S. Wilkinson,[7] as fine a man as ever drew breath, came through the mists on the political horizon and everybody who saw him emerge knew that a scrap was about to start.

It was in the early part of April that Dr. W. C. Stubbs,[8] a close personal friend of Colonel Wilkinson's stated publicly that pressure was being brought to bear from all over the state to have the Colonel announce his candidacy for governor and that he, Dr. Stubbs, had no doubt that the Colonel would do so and would shortly announce his platform. It was just after that, on April 10th, 1907, that General Albert Estopinal announced that Lieutenant Governor J. Y. Sanders would soon announce his candidacy for governor. It was then generally accepted as true that General Estopinal had refused to be vice-chairman of the Democratic state central committee so that he might manage Sanders's campaign. It was true.

While all the jockeying and strategic moves among the politicians were going on, the general public was not paying much attention. This is my impression and the record of about thirty-two years in politics justifies me in saying that my impression of what the general public is thinking, and to what it is giving its attention, are faily reliable.

The general public first sat up and paid attention when Colonel Wilkinson spoke on April 14, 1907, at a dinner given by the

---

7. Colonel Theodore S. Wilkinson, of Plaquemines Parish, was one of the prime figures in the antilottery movement in the 1880s and early 1890s. With the backing of the Anti-Lottery League and the Populists who remained loyal to the Democratic party, Wilkinson was elected president of the 1891 Democratic Nominating Convention that nominated Murphy J. Foster, as the party's antilottery gubernatorial candidate.

8. Dr. William C. Stubbs was director of the Louisiana State Agricultural Experiment Stations and a professor of agriculture at Louisiana State University.

City and State Politics 201

Ruston Progressive Union at Ruston, Lincoln Parish. He could not have started the campaign much further from home if he had tried. That speech really started the campaign.

Colonel Wilkinson touched on a very important point when he discussed the effect of the primary election law in elevating the importance of the white vote in North Louisiana. There was no public denial by his friends of the fact that the Colonel had made a hit at Ruston, and no private denial of it by his opponents.

A few days later the Colonel wrote a letter. The same letter from a man of less character and prestige would have been looked upon as an attempt to evade issues by making general statements. But everybody who knew him was aware of the fact that, although not always practical in his ideas, he always meant what he said. This letter [April, 1907] was to Dr. W. C. Stubbs, who was about to leave for the Jamestown Exposition as Commissioner for Louisiana.

"Before you leave this evening to assume your duties as Commissioner for this state at the Jamestown Exposition," Col. Wilkinson wrote, "I desire to inform you that I have definitely decided to become a candidate before the Democratic voters for their nomination for governor of this state." The colonel's letter to the doctor was immediately given to the newspapers and there were then two openly avowed candidates in the field, General Jastremski and Colonel Wilkinson. J. Y. Sanders had not irrevocably announced. In technical fact, he had not announced at all.

Three days after Colonel Wilkinson's letter, *The Time-Democrat* published one of those editorials. I read it then and I have it now.

"Believing as we do," said *The Time-Democrat* on April 26th, 1907, "that the primary is held for the purpose of allowing the voters to express their personal preferences for governor, *The Times-Democrat* proposes to take no partisan side in the contest, to advocate and urge no special candidates, but to present, in the best way it can, the utterances of all the candidates, their views and ideas, their meetings and speeches, so that the voters may know exactly what they represent and stand for."

> In a contest of this kind, it is unfair to the voters and of little benefit to the candidates themselves that the papers should select a special favorite, become his organ and sing his praises for the next eight months.
>
> If any candidate for any office is shown to be unworthy or not to be trusted, it is, of course, the duty of the press to lay all the facts bearing on the case before the voters and to warn them against him; but in the absence of such charges the papers could not perform their duty by the voters better than by furnishing them full, frank and uncolored and unpartisan news of the campaign and the political discussions that take place. Eight months of discussion and political education will enable the voters of Louisiana (a choice and selected electorate as they are) to separate the false from the true, to select the best men. It will be strange, indeed, if we do not discover their merits and demerits in a prolonged campaign and to pass upon all the political issues before them.
>
> *The Times-Democrat* believes it can do no greater service to the voters of Louisiana than by refusing to become the organ of any candidate or set of candidates and by doing equal justice to all, allowing them equal facilities to present their claims and arguments to the voters, who are the final court on this question.

In order that none of my readers may be misled, I wish to point out that this editorial was printed in 1907 and not in 1920.[9]

The late Page M. Baker was the head of *The Times-Democrat* in 1907. Mr. Baker opposed me bitterly and fought me hard most of the time, and yet I am sorry he was not the head of *The Times-Picayune* in 1920.

Daniel D. Moore was the head of *The Times-Picayune* in

---

9. Behrman is sarcastically referring to the New Orleans *Times-Picayune*'s attacks upon his candidacy for reelection in 1920.

1920. The change from Baker to Moore made quite a difference in the paper.

While Mr. Baker and I were not in sympathy on many matters, he was not the kind of a managing editor who would have given me the treatment I got from Mr. D. D. Moore in 1920. I will discuss Mr. D. D. Moore and 1920 at the close of these recollections.

J. Y. Sanders formally announced his candidacy and issued his platform on April 28th, 1907. It was a long, large platform. He and Wilkinson spoke from the same platform at Lake Providence on May 1st, Wilkinson had not issued a platform and Sanders called attention to that. James J. Bailey, candidate for lieutenant governor, also spoke there. Senator Paul M. Lambremont announced his candidacy for lieutenant governor on Friday, May 11th.

By that time things were so well started that Robert Broussard came out with a statement that the consensus of opinion among his friends was that he could serve them better at Washington than at Baton Rouge and that he would not run for governor. Broussard refused to say then just what way his influence would go. We all had good reason to believe it would go against J. Y. Sanders and hence for Col. Wilkinson, and the expectations proved to be correct.

In the latter part of August, Robert Broussard declared publicly that he was confident Colonel Wilkinson would carry the third district and stated that he would take the stump for him at a meeting to be held in New Iberia, [in south central Louisiana], and that he would speak in French as well as English. That guaranteed a crowd.

A great crowd gathered at New Iberia on Wednesday, September 25th, to hear Robert Broussard. John M. Parker also spoke at this meeting. Broussard stated he had been urged to run for governor and that this struck a responsive chord in him and met with a "willing acquiescence" as it encouraged a life-long ambition. But on his return home, he said, he had made a canvass of his congressional district and the sentiment seemed to be unanimous that he should not retire from congress. The reasons assigned, among others, that he had started many valuable public enterprises which would lag, if not [be] entirely lost, by his retirement. His people had told him there were many matters pending in congress that might turn out ruinous for their interests and that a new man in Washington might not be able to handle for their protection, no matter how wise or able he might be. A new man would lack the necessary knowledge of the situation. Broussard had become one of the best known and personally one of the most popular men in Washington.

Personal popularity is a great help to a man in what so many citizens call "hard boiled" Washington. I have not found Washington any more or less "hard boiled" than New Orleans or Baton Rouge. You will find "hard boiled" persons everywhere.

I know from personal experience that Robert Broussard, even when a member of the house, could get action out of many a "hard boiled" senator. It would have been a great mistake, from the point of view of the best interests of all Louisiana, and particularly from the point of view of the third district, for him to have become governor in 1908.

Broussard told them at New Iberia that his ambitions traveled in one direction and the interests of his people were in another and that he would stay by them. He then declared that as he had been called on to take a position in the campaign and after a careful study of the situation he was convinced he should support Colonel Wilkinson in the interests of the state. Broussard added, also, that it had been hinted J. Y. Sanders' election as governor meant his retirement from the public service. "The challenge is given and I accept it!" he declared.

It was shortly after that, October 1st, 1907, that the Democratic state central committee met and fixed January 28th, 1908, as the date of the primary.

There were a great many rumors at that time that [Choctaw leaders] Alex Pujol of the fifth, and Victor Mauberret of the fourth ward, would come out for Col. Wilkinson. I believe there were some negotiations with Alex and, it is probable, these two would have stayed together in any move they made. Alex Pujol came out flat-footed for Sanders on October 10th.

With all the candidates promising things and all of them with friends in the legislature, they were all somewhat surprised when Governor Blanchard suddenly issued a call for a special session of the legislature. This was done with the idea of helping Colonel Wilkinson, as there is no doubt that Lieutenant Governor Sanders would be held responsible for whatever happened at the special session. The shifts of politics had put him in the position of having a greater influence with the legislature than the governor.

Governor Blanchard called the session on November 11th, and gave an interval of thirty days, which would convene the legislature on December 11th [1907], and take Sanders off the stump at the hottest period of the fight. He specified the subjects of legislation as follows:

> Reducing the salaries, fees and other compensation of public officers and doing away with the fee system and putting all officers on a salary basis.
> Decreasing the cost of collecting and disbursing the revenues of the state and the abolition of unnecessary offices and the consolidation of offices where practicable.
> Amending the primary election law.
> Directing that public funds be placed on deposit in solvent banks within the state offering the highest rate of compensation under certain terms and conditions.
> Amendments to the laws to guard the better against defalcation by public officers who collected public funds.

Providing for the appointment of a special commission to investigate conditions at the Port of New Orleans with a view of ascertaining wherein lay the difference between port charges here and at other ports.

To authorize the transfer of titles to the United States to the maritime quarantine stations and plants from the state of Louisiana.

To enact the necessary legislation to carry into effect the constitutional amendments which might be proposed at the extra session.

To make an appropriation to pay the fiscal agent banks for money advanced the state since the last session of the general assembly.

To enact legislation to provide for the election of United States senators by the district vote of the people instead of by the legislatures.

To have the Senate confirm all appointments made since the regular session of the legislature of 1906.

All kinds of political motives, of course, were ascribed to the governor for calling a special session in the midst of a campaign. The governor replied that it would be much better to have legislation affecting the salaries or other incomes of officers involved in the campaign settled before the election rather than afterwards.

R. N. Sims, campaign manager for Colonel Wilkinson, announced that the colonel was completely in accord with Governor Blanchard's move. No sooner had he formally issued the call than Governor Blanchard left Louisiana to attend the Jamestown Exposition and Sanders became the acting governor. As a matter of legal fact, when the governor is absent from the state he becomes a private citizen insofar as the functions of his office in the state are concerned. The lieutenant governor is then temporarily the governor. So J. Y. Sanders went to it and added this to the call:

"Providing for the regulation and control of railroads, telephone companies and other kindred public service corporations and the kindred subject of holding them to the jurisdiction of our own courts."

When Governor Blanchard got back to Louisiana, he declared at first that what Sanders had done would not stand. As a matter of legal form, Sanders had recalled the Blanchard call and proclaimed another call that added the subject noted. Shortly after that Governor Blanchard decided to let the Sanders call stand and he declared Sanders would be held responsible for the success or the failure of the extraordinary session. He claimed or charged that Sanders had injected an element of danger in the call.

Donelson Caffery [Jr.] made his first speech in the campaign late in October. He said he and Sanders were from the same parish, St. Mary, and that it was a pleasure for him to oppose his "fellow parishoner." Don said Jared belonged to the "Tammany Hall School of Politics," and charged that Sanders, "now an exponent of white supremacy," had run on a ticket with John N. Pharr, Republican candidate for governor, and later, in 1900, with [Eugene S.] Reems, another Republican candidate for governor. It will be remembered that Foster beat Pharr in 1896 and Heard beat Reems. Caffery was also in the field on two tickets that were not Democratic. One was a Republican ticket and the other was one of those "sudden parties" that suddenly appear and suddenly disappear. As I remember it now, he was a "People's Party," meaning a Populist, candidate for governor.

Sanders, as I remember it, was running for either the legislature or some other less than state wide office on a fusion ticket.[10]

Anyhow, Caffery predicted that Sanders would not carry the parish of St. Mary. He was speaking at Donaldsonville.

Sanders replied at Jeanerette, in Iberia parish, close to the St.

10. Caffery was obviously using a campaign ploy to discredit Sanders in the eyes of Democratic voters. Sanders was and had always been a devout Democrat. He was first elected to the state legislature in 1892 on Murphy J. Foster's antilottery ticket but was defeated by a Republican in his reelection bid during the climactic 1896 state elections. Voters sent Sanders to the 1898 constitutional convention as a Democratic delegate-at-large where he served on the important Suffrage and Elections Committee. In 1900 he returned to the state legislature as a Democrat defeating his Fusionist opponent Henry N. Pharr. Mary E. Sanders, "Political Career of Jared Y. Sanders," (M.A. thesis, Louisiana State University, 1955).

Mary boundary, and complained that Caffery had read him a lesson [in] Democracy.

"Great God," said J. Y., "has it come to this? That I should be lectured on Democracy by Don Caffery! Since when he had become a Democrat?

"The last time I heard of him he was a Republican candidate for governor. Then he was recommended for judge of a federal court by a Republican state committee to a Republican president. And did Caffery demur?

"Did Caffery demur? No! And the Republicans president appointed Eugene D. Saunders, a Democrat. Did I read in the *Times-Democrat* correctly when I heard that Caffery challenged my record as a white supremacist?

"Since the adoption of the rooster as a Democrat emblem, we have always stamped the rooster on our ticket, but when did Donelson Caffery ever use the rooster?"

Sanders went ahead with a full discussion of the charges that he had run on tickets with Republican candidates for governor.

Broussard and Caffery, both campaigning for Colonel Wilkinson and both from the third congressional district, gave considerable support to the statement that Sanders would not carry it. So when Colonel William H. Price of Lafourche [Parish] announced for Sanders, he being one of the most powerful politicians in the district and always a friend of Broussard's, that created quite a sensation among politicians all over the state.

Samuel D. McEnery for United States Senator, O. B. Steele for state treasurer, James Benjamin Aswell for state superintendent of education, and Charles Shuler for commissioner of agriculture, were not opposed and so were named as the Democratic candidates when the state central committee met on Thursday, October 31st, 1907.

Caffery shortly after denounced Sanders very bitterly and demanded a retraction of some of the statements Sanders had made. Their relations became so hot that some persons expected them to shoot at each other when they met in Franklin, their home town. Some of their own townsmen expected it. But neither of them was expected by anyone who knew them well to do anything of the kind. The only danger was that their friends might start shooting.... Years later, they were both defeated for the senate by Edwin Broussard and, so far as I know, neither said anything which the other might take as personally offensive.

Governor Blanchard did everything he could to defeat J. Y. Sanders for governor. He worked on me particularly hard to get me to vote for Charles Janvier for chairman of the Democratic state central committee. He called the special session because he felt sure it would put Sanders in a jam. I am not criticizing him for this, no matter what my friends may have said about it at the time. I never deliberately knowingly criticize any man for doing what I might possibly have done myself in the same circumstances.

The Wilkinson faction opened its campaign in Washington Artillery Hall [in New Orleans] on November 16th, 1907.... The chief speakers in the Colonel's behalf were Charles J. Theard, Donelson Caffery, [Jr.] and John M. Parker.

Parker's speech was directed against "the system." In later years Parker said more than once that he had nothing against us, or me, but was so agonized and horrified by the "system" of politics of which we were supposed to be the only supporters. He was still complaining about it and denouncing it in 1920. Now that he has been governor for more than two years and he and his following have adopted that "system," with some alterations that the worst of the Old Regulars never adopted, he is not saying much these days about the "system."[11]

General Leon Jastremski was stricken with apoplexy at his

11. For padding of dock board payrolls, see Chapter IV, note 6, herein.

home in Baton Rouge. All his right side was paralyzed. He had been in bad health for some time before the campaign opened but had recovered enough to enter the race. It was thought that the strain and worries of the campaign had brought on the attack. He died on November 29th, a week after he was stricken.

Every good man in the state regretted his death. He was the kind of man that you can be at outs with and be strenuously opposed to without ever getting bitter about it. He was a man so absolutely "on the level" that I am not exaggerating it when I say that his death was generally and sincerely mourned by many who had never voted for him and never intended to do so.

His death made quite a change in the campaign and, as it turned out, made Sanders' election, or nomination, a certainty. While his campaign committee made no effort to throw his voters to one candidate or the other, Sanders managed to get the bulk of the Jastremski votes and to convince everybody that he had them. This conviction gave Sanders a lot of votes of the "high sider," those who wish to be with the winning candidate regardless of anything else.

Sanders' campaign in New Orleans opened also at the Washington Artillery Hall and *The Times-Democrat* said next day that veteran observers had declared the meeting had seldom been excelled.

There was 44,467 poll taxes paid in New Orleans and the Wilkinson campaign committee predicted that this was a sure sign of victory for Colonel Wilkinson. My rather vague recollection is that they figured they would surely carry the country parishes as a whole and that the regulars could not poll more than 20,000 votes in New Orleans. This was erroneous both ways.

The Times-Democrat once more reversed itself again. This paper had for years demanded that state and local elections be separated so that there could be no deals and dickers. They were separated by putting the city elections first. That did not prevent the politics that *The Times-Democrat* called "deals and dickers," so the city elections were put long after the state elections by prolonging the terms of the city officers.

The Times-Democrat had insisted that city and state affairs should be kept separate. They had never been. They were not. They probably never will be.

I am not discussing what would be best for us. Maybe it would be better to have a city government completely out of the hands of the state government, and in full, direct control of all that immediately concerns the people of the city. But the facts are that nothing has been done to bring this about and at no time in my life has it been practicable to do it.

But *The Times-Democrat* came out in 1907 and insisted that city affairs and city candidates and politics should be discussed in the state campaign. This should be done, it said, in order that the people should be prepared for the city campaign and not give "the bosses" the opportunity they had in the city campaign of 1904. This was one of those hints that was almost an open statement that my election in 1904 was the result of a political conspiracy hatched in wickedness during the state campaign between Blanchard and Jastremski, everybody knows I was not thought of for mayor until some time after Charles Janvier and others had refused to run. I did not think of it myself until after I had become quite comfortable in my job as state auditor.

While this campaign was on ... the late Joseph M. Leveque was issuing a daily attack on Edward Stanley Whittaker, inspector of police, in *The Morning World*. Whittaker had stood a great many attacks from others without so losing his head as to make a murderous assault on a man who certainly intended him no bodily harm and was within his rights as an editor.

Whittaker took some detectives with him and went into the editorial room of *The Morning World* [on January 17, 1908] and shot Leveque, who was not armed. Leveque got under a large table and somebody stopped Whittaker. The detectives were absolved of guilt as they had followed the inspector on his orders, and, as I remember it, believed he intended to limit himself to making an arrest. Whittaker was immediately dismissed as inspector. He was convicted in court and sentenced to a term in jail. His health was such that he was not compelled or forced to serve the term and, as I remember it, he did actually go to jail for some months after he was sentenced.

The Wilkinson campaigners, of course, dragged the Whittaker escapade into the campaign with the inference and hint, and perhaps the open charge, that the faction behind Sanders was responsible for Whittaker's murderous assault on Leveque. I interpreted this as a sign of conscious weakness. Politicians do not grab at straws like that unless they felt themselves sinking.

This was the second campaign in which some reformers of those years appeared. A newspaper man, now a friend of mine, suggested to Colonel Wilkinson and Nick Sims, his campaign manager, that they hire carriages and have speakers address impromptu meetings on the streets.

I saw [a Wilkinson supporter] speaking to fully 400 persons at Canal and Decatur from a carriage. *The States* editorially claimed that this was a confession of the "Wilkinsonians" that the people were not coming to them so they had to go to the people.

Having briefly described some of the "high spots" of the campaign of 1907–1908, I now come to the highest of them. That is, what happened on election day. I am trying to make the story clear to those who have "growed up" in the fourteen years since that campaign and the thousands of women who took no interest in politics then and take a great deal of interest in it now.

Colonel Wilkinson, I have been told, spent about $75,000 on his campaign. Knowing something of the cost of campaigns and seeing the large number of speakers his campaign managers sent from one place to another, the heavy expenses they incurred for printing, postage, bands where ever a Wilkinson man made a speech, long telegraphic reports from country meetings to their headquarters which the younger men used in their speeches and the big following that the Colonel carried with him wherever he went, I was not at all surprised to hear that it had cost him $75,000 personally. He did not have an organization behind him as Luther E. Hall had in the Good Government League in 1912. Sanders had beaten Colonel Wilkinson to the politicians and, as it turned out, the citizens in the country parishes.

Colonel Wilkinson knew two weeks before the primary that he had been beaten. He admitted it privately to his closest friends. But he was game. Not the least sign of distress or annoyance or disappointment showed in his manner or expressions during his many speeches after he realized his candidacy could not be victorious. Nor did he show any depression, so far as I know, after the returns were in. He still wore a smile and was cordial, courteous and considerate to everybody around him.

I do not mean that Colonel Wilkinson was not disappointed. What I do mean is that this man was a man all through, a gentleman in manner as well as in feeling, and that he did not wish to depress his friends by letting them see a mournful face. I am told that the only time in his life that he ever showed a sign of distress was when his financial affairs reached their lowest ebb some years ago and he wanted some money for a friend and could not get it. While this is second hand information, I feel certain it is accurate as that is the kind of man Theodore S. Wilkinson was.

No responsible person made any kind of a personal attack on Colonel Wilkinson during that hot campaign. There was none to make. He had been in politics a long time and his career was well known. So were all his alliances. As a matter of personal comparison, Sanders appealed to the voters as a younger and more energetic and progressive man and Wilkinson as what they called "one of the old school."

Sanders got 21,155 and Wilkinson 11,572 votes in New Orleans. That gave Sanders a majority of 9,583 here. Sanders got 37,827 in the country parishes and Wilkinson 33,823, a majority of 4,004 for Sanders. Sanders' total majority was 13,587.[12]

The fact that he was the "ward bosses' candidate" was raised against Sanders in every country parish and his defeat in some of the parishes has been attributed to that shout. On the other hand, the reports of a supposed or actual attempt by some of Col. Wilkinson's friends to get some of those ward bosses with the Colonel convinced others that it was not fair to condemn Sanders because of our support.

Some fireworks later developed out of the race for Lieutenant Governor, in which James J. Bailey got 38,611, Paul M. Lambremont 36,054, and S. McC. Lawrason 20,823.

Taking their votes in round figures, giving Bailey 38,000 Lambremont 36,000 and Lawrason 21,000, we find their percentages of the total vote as follows:

BAILEY 40
LAMBREMONT 33
LAWRASON 22

There was a caucus of the ward leaders (or bosses, if you wish to call them bosses) right after the primary, and it was agreed to support Paul Lambremont, Paul Capdevielle [for auditor] Walter Guion [for attorney general] and A. W. Crandall [for registrar of the Land Office.]

These are the figures in the second primary. Paul Lambre-

12. In the Democratic primary held on January 28, 1908, Sanders received 60,176 votes to Wilkinson's 46,729. In New Orleans, Sanders obtained an almost two-to-one majority over Wilkinson: 21,555 to 11,564. *Report of the Secretary of State to His Excellency, the Governor of Louisiana, March 1, 1908.*

mont carried all the wards but the fourteenth, sixteenth, and seventeenth. His total vote here was 20,336 and Bailey's was 5,205.

Paul Capdevielle carried every ward but the fourteenth, sixteenth and seventeenth. He lost the fourteenth by nine votes, the sixteenth by one hundred and six (106) and the seventeenth by six votes. Capdevielle's city vote was 20,862 and Frazee's was 4,717.

In this second primary, the candidate supported by the city organization for lieutenant governor won by a small majority. The candidates we supported for auditor and for attorney general won by large majorities. The candidate we supported for registrar of the land office, A. W. Crandall, lost by a margin that was comfortable for his successful opponent, Fred J. Grace.

It was only natural that experienced politicians expected that a cry of fraud would be raised in the Lambremont-Bailey contest, as it is usual to cry fraud whenever the majority is close. I have heard that fraud yell on occasions when the majority was plainly too big for any unprovable frauds to have affected the result, and we have yet to learn of a contested election in New Orleans in modern times being followed by proof of fraud that defeated a candidate.

But the experienced politicians were not expecting James J. Bailey and his friends to make the charges formally and press them. This they did, which is at least testimony to the effect that they were sincere in their belief that Bailey had not been fairly treated. They immediately began gathering their information and assembling testimony to put before the state central committee when it met to review the results of the second primary. And, in the meantime, some of the New Orleans newspapers convicted all of us of stuffing the ballot boxes, monkeying with the count, and falsifying the returns and practically notified us to put our affairs in order and prepare our souls for death. There is no use in my quoting the long-winded editorials. It is enough to say that we were condemned to the gallows without a formal hearing, which came later.

As soon as it became certain that James J. Bailey intended to file a formal protest and contest the nomination of Paul Lambremont before the Democratic state central committee, all the evidence the Regulars could gather in New Orleans, was got together and Paul Lambremont announced that he would file a protest against some returns from the country parishes.

Lambremont's majority of one thousand, seven hundred and eighty-six (1,786) in a total vote of seventy-eight thousand, nine hundred and ten (78,910) was really close, and there were many good citizens who had been convinced by the newspapers that something was wrong.

So there were two protests when the state central committee met on March 11th, 1908, both alleging that the other side was no good. A committee of five was appointed by the chairman and after consultation this special committee suggested and the whole committee recommended that both Bailey and Lambremont withdraw. If they had withdrawn, the state central committee would have had the authority to name the candidate for lieutenant governor.

In a long letter to the committee, Bailey refused to withdraw.

Lambremont said he was willing to withdraw if Bailey would do the same thing.

The vote on submitting this recommendation to the two candidates, however, had developed their strength and a majority of the country members stood with Lambremont. The newspapers, of course, had it that the majority stood with "those ward bosses." The vote was 55 to 21. Eliminating the "ward boss vote" from the 55 would have left 34, which would have made it 34 to 21 against Bailey. But Mr. Bailey stuck to the fight before the committee and, after some more contention, the committee proceeded to review the returns and declare the nominees:

Paul Lambremont for lieutenant governor, Walter Guion for attorney general, Paul Capdevielle for auditor and Fred J. Grace for registrar of the land office.

Mr. Bailey as was expected, appealed to the courts. He went into the civil district court the next day. He asked that the committee be compelled to show why its action declaring Paul Lambremont the nominee should not be reviewed and, as an alternative, if the court got a satisfactory reason, that the case be remanded to the committee, with instructions to hold a full, free and fair trial if the court decided that to be "more proper." As it is well remembered, Mr. Bailey lost his case in court.

Among the attacks made on his position was one that the civil district court here was without jurisdiction, as Paul Lambremont was an elector of the Parish of St. James. One of Bailey's lawyers stated that this point had been given long consideration and that, while it was not so alleged in the petition to the court, it was well known at the time that they were afraid they would not be able to get their numerous witnesses to St. James parish and, for that reason, they had decided to take a chance of getting a decision in New Orleans.

I believe it was in this case that another point was made that resulted in a radical change in the legal machinery of our politics. Whether it was in this case or not, the matter is worth writing about.

The argument was made that the Democratic state central committee, which had been provided for as it was then, when the primary system was adopted, was not responsible to the courts for its decisions. It was intended, Samuel L. Gilmore[13]

13. Samuel L. Gilmore, represented the Second Congressional District (Orleans, Jefferson, St. Charles, St. James, and St. John the Baptist parishes), in the U.S. House of Representatives from 1909 to 1911.

argued, that this committee would be politically responsible to the voters of the party and the people of Louisiana and would be free to decide all contests and that its decisions could not be legally reviewed. This situation, which I believe was confirmed by the courts in some case or other, was changed later on by providing a means of appeal to the courts. I think it was in 1912 that the courts were given unquestionable jurisdiction. This is more satisfactory as it makes it impossible for the holy reformers to cry out that a factional issue has been decided by a factional majority on a factional committee.

Mr. Bailey, of course, appealed to the supreme court. The decision of the lower court was affirmed.

Charles Janvier, chairman of the state central committee, then took Bailey's petition to the committee and a lot of other documents concerning the contest, including a large wad of newspaper clippings, to the district attorney, Porter Parker. This was done in accordance with a resolution unanimously adopted by the committee. The resolution asked that somebody should go to jail if any violations of the law were uncovered. Nobody went to jail.

I thought politics would be peaceful for a few months, anyhow. Maybe I only hoped it and mistook a hope for a thought. That's something human beings do very often.

I was soon advised by many of the Democratic leaders that the bitterness worked up by the Lambremont-Bailey contest suggested that it would not be a good thing to let the Republicans do all the campaigning. Not that there was any chance of the election of Republicans to any state-wide office, but that if they had no active opposition they might poll a big enough vote to keep them encouraged. It was decided to hold meetings of the Democrats all over the state.

At the very beginning, when the Republicans were advising the people that it was the right time for all good men to quit the

Democratic party, wagers were made that they would not poll fifteen hundred (1,500) votes in New Orleans.

One of the leading Republican leaders in New Orleans, noticing that preparations were being made for the inauguration of J. Y. Sanders, wanted to know by what right the Democrats took Sanders' election for granted. He pointed out that nobody was taking the election of the Republican candidate, Henry N. Pharr of St. Mary parish, for granted. He wanted the newspapers to discuss the matter and have the preparations delayed until after the vote was counted. If my memory serves me right, the Democrats went right ahead with their plans for the inauguration and certainly did not realize at the time that something was going to happen on inauguration day that would be more of a shock than a pleasure.

James J. Bailey, however, completely restored his political vitality in the days of his defeat when he set at rest the rumors that he would quit the Democratic party. If there had not been such persistent rumors to that effect, Bailey's announcement would have been dull and unattractive routine.

"I have never voted any other ticket in my life," Bailey told a reporter who apparently expected a different answer, "and I will never vote any but the Democratic ticket.

"From my point of view, every man who received a majority of the votes in either of the primaries is entitled in the election to the vote of every Democrat who voted in the primaries.

"I do not approve of the position taken by some of the Democrats in proposing to vote the Republican ticket. All the nominees on the Democratic ticket, save one, were honestly nominated, as far as I know, and are entitled to the support of every Democrat."

This statement from James J. Bailey was so clear and definite and so absolutely true from his point of view that it impressed the Democrats very strongly. It indicated that Bailey was a good

Democrat and that his bitter disappointments in the second primary, before the state central committee and then in the courts had not influenced his attitude toward his party. Party sentiment was stronger than it is now.

If James J. Bailey had refrained from making any statement at all, it is extremely improbable that he would ever have been elected to any state-wide office. It is improbable that he would have been elected to his office. But he came out and said what he thought and people generally approved of his attitude, regardless of whether they agreed with him that Paul Lambremont was not entitled to the nomination for lieutenant governor.

Henry N. Pharr headed the Republican ticket. Alex F. Leonhardt ran for lieutenant governor. The Socialists had J. W. Barnes of Calcasieu for governor and J. O. Steward of Calcasieu out for lieutenant governor. They were easily defeated.

Sanders got 25,253 and Pharr 2,809 in New Orleans. Barnes, the Socialist, got 161, which was probably three short of the whole roster of the Socialist club.[14] Lambremont got 24,319 and Leonhardt 3,031 for lieutenant governor; and Stewart, the Socialist, got 164, which was probably the total of said club.

2.

Governor Sanders Shocks Behrman with Saloon and Anti-Racing Laws

I have been to many an inauguration at Baton Rouge during the past thirty-six years. I think, the largest and most excited crowd I ever saw at one of these ceremonies was on May 18, 1908, when J. Y. Sanders took the oath. It was estimated that there were 5000 persons present. There was a very long parade in which the Choctaw Marching Club had a prominent part.

---

14. In the general election on April 21, 1908, Sanders polled 60,066 votes to Republican Henry N. Pharr's 7,617. Barnes, the Socialist candidate received 1,247 votes. *Report of the Secretary of State to His Excellency, the Governor of Louisiana, April 15, 1910.*

I did not laugh then, but when I think of Sanders' inaugural address now I have to laugh. Being out of office, I have fewer reasons to be unhappy and annoyed and I laugh more easily. I mean the race track recommendation as the cause of my present merriment. I was not merry then.[15]

Among the matters touched on was the regulation of saloons. The Gay-Shattuck law[16] was the direct outcome of this.

There was, of course, considerable kicking about the Gay-Shattuck law. Those of us who had given the matter some real thought knew that prohibition sentiment was becoming stronger and that there was more anti-saloon sentiment than real anti-alcohol sentiment in it. We wanted to ward off prohibition. We wanted to avoid bitterness of the savage fight that a statewide prohibition campaign would bring about.[17]

The Louisiana legislature would never have exercised its power to establish statewide prohibition by enacting a statute. It was strong for local option though that did not keep it from

15. In his inaugural address, Governor Sanders denounced gambling and vowed to rid the state of it: "The Constitution of the State denounces gambling as a vice and enjoins upon the legislature the duty of enacting laws for its suppression. . . . All forms of gambling are bad, and have no place in the economic development of the State." One can see why Behrman, mayor of a city which had two major racetracks, would oppose such a move. New Orleans *Times-Democrat*, May 19, 1908.

16. So called for the bill's authors, Edward J. Gay of Iberville Parish and S. O. Shattuck of Lake Charles, Louisiana: "An Act to regulate the business of conducting barroom, cabaret, coffee house, cafe, beer saloon, liquor exchange, drinking saloon, grog shop, beer house, beer garden or other place where alcoholic or spirituous, vinous or malt liquors or intoxicating beverages, bitters or medicinal preparations of any kind are sold, directly or indirectly, in quantities of less than five gallons, and to provide penalties for violation of this act." Act No. 176, *Acts Passed by the General Assembly of the State of Louisiana at the Regular Session, 1908*.

17. Robert W. Wiebe, in his excellent analysis of American society from 1877 to 1920, wrote that the enormous success that the national Anti-Saloon League enjoyed in its 1908 nationwide prohibition campaign was due in part to the popularity the movement gained "among America's urban-industrial leaders as a new means of mass control." Prominent citizens, including southerners, continued Wiebe, believed that with the elimination of the saloon and the "drunk" a new stabilizing discipline would emerge for both black and white laborers. This sentiment increased in popularity after 1913 resulting in the ratification of the Eighteenth Amendment to the U.S. Constitution in January, 1919. Robert H. Wiebe, *The Search for Order, 1877–1920* (New York: Hill and Wang, 1967), 290–91.

establishing prohibition by law in Bogalusa four years later when it enacted a special charter for the city of Bogalusa. But the legislature could have submitted a prohibition amendment to the constitution, which is the form legislation for all the state might have taken.

Both the prohibitionists and their opponents were at least temporarily satisfied with the Gay-Shattuck law. Superintendent A. W. Turner, of the Louisiana Anti-Saloon League, I was told, considered it a victory for his side. Colonel John P. Sullivan, apostle of the brewers to the legislature, considered that he too had achieved a substantial victory. If either of them disagree, let them fight it out between themselves. I am not deciding arguments but merely recollecting things as they were reported at the time.

This, of course, was long before the days when national prohibition was taken as a serious proposal by most of us. I think the first national prohibitionist in Louisiana was J. Y. Sanders. He declared for it in 1915 at Baton Rouge when he furnished the brains of the fight against a call for a constitutional convention.

I think it was at that time that our old friend Henry Fuqua,[18] now general manager of the Louisiana State Penitentiary, announced himself a "theoretical prohibitionist." Henry Fuqua has always been a good friend of Sanders. While some of us may be in doubt as to the attitude of the people of the United States toward our ideas, I believe Henry Fuqua is justly entitled to the satisfaction of pointing out that the vast majority of his fellow citizens are solidly with him. They are "THEORETICAL prohibitionists." They advocate the theory and they practice it whenever they have no opportunity to do otherwise.

Sanders' recommendations on the sale of liquor were good, though they were a surprise to many of those present. His

---

18. Henry L. Fuqua was governor of Louisiana, 1924–26.

declaration that he would recommend and urge the enactment of legislation prohibiting and penalizing gambling on horse races was more than a surprise. It was a shock. One of my acquaintances broke out in a sweat and left for parts unknown and did not reappear for three hours. The Locke law was the outcome of it.

I was on the platform while the governor read his inaugural address. I was mayor of New Orleans and I was pretty intimate with the governor and I hardly expected what I heard. Everybody knew and knows, how I felt. I knew that no race meetings could be successfully conducted without betting and I believed they could be regulated so as to do away with most of the incidental evils.

The trouble with some people is that if there be evils incident to anything, they want to wipe that thing off the face of the earth. I dare say that when steam boilers were first used, lots of good people wanted o abolish steam boilers because sometimes they explode. I have been told that some good folks living on Prytania Street [in New Orleans] wanted the trolley cars to keep off their street on account of the noise. They were willing to keep the mule cars. This frame of mind and general attitude toward things is responsible for a great deal of trouble in this world, and it is responsible for a great deal of rather foolish legislation in Louisiana.

After Governor Sanders had delivered his inaugural address, he took me and a few other friends to the executive mansion. This was the first opportunity I had to express myself about what he said concerning horse racing. I not only discussed the merits of the matter as it affected the whole state and the city, but I also mentioned, as I remember it, a purely "political" phase of it. I put "politics" in quotation marks here because I am now using it in the sense that is becoming most general, meaning vote getting and nothing but vote getting.

I indicated to the governor, among other things, that this

message had in effect advocated the absolute destruction of racing. While it did not say this in words, I pointed to him that it would mean that to most citizens. I added that it would not get him a single vote, would not make him a single friend.

It seems I was wrong. It did get him one vote. A newspaper friend of mine, whom I would naturally have expected to vote for Edwin Broussard in 1920,[19] voted for J. Y. Sanders. This reporter was against the races and he says his principal reason for voting for Sanders was that he, the reporter, was determined that it should not be said that J. Y. did not get even one vote as a result of the Locke Law.[20]

I told the Governor his address would receive favorable comment from a lot of prominent citizens who would never vote for him, and from some newspapers that would never support him. I told him the rank and file of our faction would be very critical.

I was right. The prominent citizens were for him then and against him when he needed their votes. The newspapers that approved his address fought him hard when he ran for the Senate in 1911–1912, did nothing whatever for him when he was twice elected to congress in the sixth district and did nothing for him, until too late, when he ran for the senate again in 1920. As I remember it, after the voters had become settled in their intentions, *The Times-Picayune* did come out with a very weak and unskillful boost of the Sanders candidacy.

The first public attack on the races in New Orleans was, so far as I remember, made by Edward J. Thilborger, my old Republican enemy, in Joe Leveque's paper, *The Morning World*. It was prominently displayed and attracted a lot of attention.

---

19. In 1920 Edwin Broussard defeated Sanders in their bids for the U.S. Senate. Broussard served in that body from 1921 to 1926.

20. Named for bill's author, Leon Locke of Lake Charles. The Locke Law read in part: "To prohibit gambling on horse races by the operation of betting books, French mutual pooling devices, auction pools, or any other device and to provide penalties for the violation of the provisions thereof." Act No. 57, *Acts Passed by the General Assembly, 1908*.

City and State Politics

A number of attempts were made to put me in the position of being more active in the fight in 1908 than I really was. Not that I was not interested, nor that I was unwilling to do all I could, but I simply did not see that I could do any good to anybody by giving all my time to the fight over the races. I did not do that.

The Times-Democrat [in support of the Locke Bill] almost daily printed the paragraphs from Governor Sanders' inaugural address that applied to the races. They were as follows:

> The Constitution of the state denounces gambling as a vice, and enjoins upon the legislature the duty of enacting laws for its suppression. Presently existing antigambling statutes are adequate enough, as far as they look to the suppression of the particular forms of gambling aimed at, but they are inadequate to reach gambling in all its phases. The manner and mode of conducting race tracks in and around New Orleans and the flagrant gambling carried on at the tracks have deservedly aroused the moral sense of the people against it.
>
> I will earnestly urge upon the general assembly the enactment of legislation prohibiting and penalizing gambling on horse racing.
>
> All forms of gambling are bad, and have no place in the economic development of the state.

The constant re-printing of those paragraphs was probably suggested by the "bunk" story that Governor Sanders was getting "cold feet." Maybe this story was started by those opposing the Locke Law. I do not remember anything that Sanders said to me that indicated he needed any wool socks. So far as I know, J. Y. Sanders has always had very warm feet.

While the Locke Bill was pending before the legislature, *The Times-Democrat* printed some vague references and hints and bits of innuendo to the effect that improper influences were being brought to bear upon the members. *The Item*, represented at Baton Rouge by Marshall Ballard, James Bennett and Jesse Webb, came out with a direct charge that $50,000 had been raised to influence the legislature against the bill.[21]

21. New Orleans *Item*, June 9, 1908.

My experience indicated that such stories as those are usually rumored about town whenever there is an important measure before the legislature, and especially when that measure affects any particular group that had its means of living under attack. The public had then, and doubtless still has, the ideal that the race track people as a whole make a great deal of money and that most of them are rich. As a matter of fact, in proportion to the numbers engaged in it, I rather think there are more peanut vendors who get rich than there are race track men who get rich.

The late Samuel Heaslip was practically the head of the lobby against the Locke Law. He was with the [New Orleans] City Park track. I do not remember having seen Barker Harrison, secretary of the [New Orleans] Fair Grounds Track Association, at Baton Rouge but once. Mr. Heaslip believed the newspaper stories hinting bribery and the intention to distribute the neat sum of $50,000 was mere propaganda to discredit the opponents of the Locke Law.

Governor Sanders took proper notice of the charge and, in a letter to Judge Harvey F. Brunot of the district court at Baton Rouge, he asked that the grand jury of the Parish of East Baton Rouge be convened and instructed to make a complete investigation.

The legislature then adopted a joint resolution[22] which called for the appointment of a committee of five from the house and four from the Senate to bring out whatever facts might have justified the publications in *The Item* and *The Times-Democrat*.

I do not remember whether the grand jury investigated the charges made by *The Item* and *The Times-Democrat* but I am quite sure that if it did no report of its findings was published. The committee, on the other hand, gave the newspaper men

---

22. House Committee Resolution passed on June 15, 1908. *Acts Passed by the General Assembly, 1908.*

concerned every opportunity to show that they had some substantial basis for their stories. They did not produce any.

Senator Robert O'Connor of Algiers is generally supposed to be the senator by whose vote the Locke Law was passed. As the bill got just enough to pass, any vote in the twenty-one (21) might be called the decisive vote. It was the fact that Senator O'Connor was expected to vote against the bill and voted for it that attracted so much attention to him at the time.

We had what we believed to be good reason to count on the vote of the Senator from my ward, Algiers, and it was very late in the fight that we were informed that Senator O'Connor was not with us. He did the informing himself. My impression is that the decisive influence in his case was that exercised by Archbishop Blenk.

I have no intention of defending myself from charges that nobody has had the audacity and impudence to make in public, but I will say that all kinds of stories were rumored to the effect that Martin Behrman was almost mad enough to send kidnapers and assassins after Senator O'Connor. There was nothing in those stories. We did what we could to get him with us and we failed. He had made up his mind what he intended to do and once he declared he would vote for the Locke Bill he never waivered for a second.

The other doubtful vote in the Senate was that of the venerable [state] Senator Martin Glynn, Sr. [of Pointe Coupee Parish]. Senator Glynn, among other things accounting for his vote, declared that he was against the operators of those days as men who had "degraded" the noble sport of horse racing.

Here is a little inside story of an interview with Senator Glynn that may have been the decisive influence in passing the Locke Law. A young newspaper reporter, who had made a careful investigation of the money spent by the race track people in New Orleans, their expenses in getting here, in maintaining their stables, *et cetera* and so forth, gathered his material together and had a talk with Senator Glynn at the St. Charles Hotel. These figures, partly obtained from Samuel Heaslip of the City Park track and Barker Harrison of the Fairgrounds Track, indicated that if the horse owners, bookmakers, track owners and all others concerned in the racing at the two tracks, were considered as a single business enterprise, they would have to collect a little less than $2,000,000 to pay their expenses for a 100 day meeting. I have never seen these figures and I think they probably contain some errors, but I am told they convinced Senator Glynn that the cost of racing was more than racing was worth.

[On June 24, 1908] *The Times-Democrat* [published an editorial] headed "A Roll of Honor," [assuring] everybody that the days of the evils were over and thereafter the legislature would be absolutely lovely. The men who wrote it did not have the spirit that would have suggested to him that the citizen who started the fight, Edward J. Thilborger, and the Governor who made it possible to win, J. Y. Sanders, were justly entitled at least to a mention.

The Item did most of the work for the Locke Bill, if the space it gave the subject is a gauge to the work done. *The Picayune*, however, struck what may have been the "knock out" blow when it prominently displayed what was represented at the time as an attempt to poison a senator [S. J. Smart] to keep him from being there to vote. He took the drug himself and upset his stomach. The railroad men were supposed to be trying to keep Senator J. S. Settoon [of Livingston Parish] from arriving in time to vote. The schedule was changed for the passenger train. Two *Item* men . . . helped Senator Settoon get to the Capital in time. He had hardly settled in his seat after voting for the bill than *The Item* of that afternoon arrived and it carried a declaration that *The Item* would "deliver" Senator Settoon at the capital. If that paper had arrived before the roll was called, Senator Settoon would have voted against the Locke Law and it would not have passed. He said so himself.

Incidentally, I may say, that story in *The Picayune* about the senator who got sick was not written by the *Picayune* reporter. The reporters have a way of doing each others' work at times and on this occasion Marshall Ballard was doing Major A. J. Newlin's work. When Ballard wrote the "red hot" story for Newlin, he either wired or telephoned the *Picayune* that the story was great stuff and they printed it with big headlines. That story influenced the public and, possibly, influenced members of the Senate.

I will now close my recollections of the "race-gamble" fight of 1908, which succeeded in putting the Locke Law on the books, with verbatim quotations of a statement I gave out a day or so before the law was passed and the editorial in which *The Times-Democrat* replied to my statement.

I predicted some things that, fortunately for all of us, did not come to pass. I predicted indiscriminate handbooking in New Orleans, I predicted that the law would not have the effect that its supporters claimed for it. Here is what I said:

> It would be well, in considering the Locke bill on final passage, to determine whether in its present shape it is not legislation calculated to emphasize rather than ameliorate what have been called the evils of the race tracks. There can be no doubt that low-grade racing, credit-betting on the tracks and indiscriminate handbooking in the city will be its inevitable consequence. These can but add to the troubles of the police, and it is for that reason that I am tempted to speak.
>
> Though I have clear views as to what should and should not be done, I have not attempted to influence the pending legislation. I have spoken to but one senator. He is the representative of my own district. The public knows the result of my request.
>
> My attention, however, has been directed to the certain effect of the Locke bill under the amendment prepared by its authors on the

eve of its introduction to pacify country opposition and prevent its defeat.

As originally drawn the bill prohibited all betting, including individual wagers. Just before it was taken to Baton Rouge, however, a phrase was inserted under which, as was announced in the press, individual betting would be allowed. It is this amendment which furnished the basis upon which pernicious conditions will be created during the next two years. The indifference of large elements of the racing population to the passage of that law can only be due to their belief that under this amendment the sport will go on without elimination of its betting features.

The Locke bill does not prohibit racing. It could not do so and hope to attract country support. What it does is to prohibit betting by means of a betting book, French mutual, auction pool, or by any other device. It is these five words which constitute the amendment under which individual betting is made permissable and which will bring about a deplorable state of affairs.

Opening the door to individual betting providing for no closed season, the Locke law will give us racing, week days and Sunday, for 365 days in the years. Unless the joker is removed we shall have the sport in its worst form, under cloak of the law, with an ingenious credit system and widespread handbooking, and the tout, the piker, the railbird, the handicapper and the dopester, will flourish as never before. I need not add that the police will be confronted with difficulties of which the public can have little conception. Instead of suppressing the evils of racing the Locke bill, which purports to have that as its legal and moral end, will encourage them and the results will be deplorable from every standpoint. Its effects will be to cut off the revenue of the big tracks and convert the half-mile tracks into perpetual gambling institutions. The net result will be a distinct loss to morality.

These facts have been pressed on my attention by gentlemen occupying high station in our citizenship who have no selfish interest to subserve, and I commend them, to the legislature and to those who are urging the passage of the Locke bill. I invite especially editorial analysis of the provisions of the bill. It will show I have not overstated the possibilities of the proposed law of suppression.[23]

23. New Orleans *Times-Democrat*, June 21, 1908.

City and State Politics

Before I issued the foregoing statement, I had given out an interview in which I condemned the Locke Law more in detail as a statute (it was then only a bill) that would not accomplish the results which its supporters claimed it would. I have no verbatim copy of that statement at hand but if I obtain one I will include it later in these recollections, provided there is anything in it not covered so far in these recollections of the matter. That foregoing statement declared simply that the bookmakers would simply adopt another system and that I requested that the legislature had not seen fit to regulate racing rather than pass the Locke Law.

The bill to regulate racing was the Cordill Bill. The supporters of the Locke Law, who had a majority, would not give it the consideration it deserved.

The following is what *The Times-Democrat* said editorially in reply to my statement:

> We published yesterday morning a statement from Mayor Behrman attacking the Locke bill. This morning we published another by the same author and of much the same tenor. His argument may be summarized thus: He fears that the passage of the Locke bill will not keep the bookmaker off the track; but will give us the racing sport, gambling included, in its worst form, 365 days of the years, Sundays included. The police, he fears will be confronted with "difficulties of which the public can have little conception." The net deplorable result, he declares, "will be a distinct loss to morality."
>
> With all due respect, *The Times-Democrat* is glad to be able to reassure the mayor. His eleventh hour fears are quite without foundation. The Locke bill has been carefully drawn. Its phraseology has been approved by competent legislators and lawyers. It has been carefully studied by intelligent and upright men in many walks of life, and of them all, it seems that the mayor alone has been able to conjure from it the horrid possibilities quoted above. If the gambling interests had the faintest hope that what the mayor has so vividly described would come to pass, not a finger of theirs would be lifted to prevent its enactment. The desperate fight they are

making to prevent its passage is in itself a guaranty that the mayor is unnecessarily alarmed.

If any additional evidence be needed, it is only necessary to cite the experience of other states which have enacted such legislation. In no case has it led to the deplorable state of affairs pictured by the mayor. In no case had it caused 365 days of racing, nor has it flourished "the tout, the dopester, the railbird," *et id omne genus.* The weight of evidence, as the lawyers would say, is all against the argument of the mayor. And the evidence is well worth considering.

The fact is that the progressive prolongation of the racing game past all reasonable limits in New Orleans has been due to the passage of laws similar to the Locke bill in other states. Instead of prospering the bookmaker and his unclean tribe, they have cast him forth in multitudes, and the multitudes have "drawn in" at the New Orleans tracks, paying the management thousands of dollars daily for the privilege of enriching themselves from the pockets of the dupes. So long as the bookmakers are sufficiently numerous to pay the track management a profit, the racing season and the gambling season is continued. When the Locke bill cuts off this source of revenue, the racing season will be shortened to reasonable limits and the sport will become legitimate and clean, as is yacht racing today. The race gambling game depends upon the licensed bookmaker who conducts his gambling operations by wholesale and divides the profits with the race managers, or upon some gambling device which affords, an equally sure "rake off" to its promoters.

Someone has apparently imposed upon the mayor's credulity or played upon his fears. The Locke bill will do precisely what it was framed to do and what the people expect it to do. No more and no less. It needs no amendment of any kind, but should be passed just as it stands. Efforts to tinker with should be defeated. The bill was framed in response to an overwhelming popular demand for suppression of the race gambling evil, after months of discussion. It has been on the legislative calendar, the subject of careful study and much debate, for weeks. Everyone is satisfied with it save the gambling interests and their friends, who will oppose any measure enforcing the constitutional edict—and the mayor. The eleventh hour alarm was to have been expected, but it should alarm no one, nor should it mislead any advocate of obedience to Louisiana's organic law, in or outside of the senate. Any motion to amend at this late day is a dilatory motion, offered for no other purpose than perpetuation of the gambling abuse.[24]

The supporters of the Locke Law declared it would eliminate the bookmakers. *The Times-Democrat* backed them in that. It did not do so and we have the bookmakers now, safe under the Supreme Courts' latest decision, and under no more regulation than in the winter season of 1907–1908.

I was wrong in my opinion that a situation would come about that would make no end of trouble for the police. I think Superintendent Maloney and District Attorney Robert H. Marr now agree with me in this opinion.

"The Locke bill will do precisely what it was framed to do," said *The Times-Democrat*, "and what the people expect it to do."

I have given detailed reasons to prove that it would not and *The Times-Democrat* said that somebody had "apparently imposed upon the mayor's credulity or played upon his fears." Imposed on MY credulity, mind you. How about the credulity of *The Times-Democrat*?

The Times-Democrat said nobody but the gamblers and Mayor Behrman was opposed to the Locke Law. That sounded plausible but it was not true. It is true that the race track people were opposed to it and so was I. The majority of those opposed were business men who like an afternoon off at the races and the hotels, restaurants, clothing stores and so forth that believed they would lose money if racing stopped. Had the bill been so written as to prohibit betting at the country fairs, it would not have passed. If the men opposed to the bill in New Orleans who bet on the races are to be classed as "the gamblers" then undoubtedly a majority of the members of the legislature believed

24. *Ibid.*, June 22, 1908.

they represented the gamblers as they would not have voted for the Locke bill without the change noted in my foregoing statement.

I do not understand, after all these years, how anybody could see consistency in a refusal to prohibit betting at parish fairs accompanying a willingness to prohibit it in New Orleans. While the supporters of the Locke Law declared themselves against any kind of a system of betting, they were informed that the country members would not stand for this and they were then warned that their altered bill would not have the effect they claimed for it.

I stand now where I stood then. I am in favor of racing and I believe it can be so regulated as to eliminate most of the incidental evils.

When serious evils developed in the country's railroad rates, nobody suggested abolishing the railroads. The Interstate Commerce Commission was established to remedy those evils so far as possible. I could mention a number of such examples as this but will content myself with one more. When it became apparent that no laws could be written that would remedy even a large number of the evils in the commercial habits of the business men of the country without doing great damage, the Federal Trade Commission was organized and it is doing its work well.

I hardly think I need say any more on this subject to make my point of view clear.

I wish, however, to call attention again to the fact that I was not so active in this matter as the newspapers indicated in later years. It was in the hottest days of the fight of 1908 that I said I had not attempted to influence the legislature further than in speaking to Senator Robert O'Connor of Algiers. Nobody questioned the absolute accuracy of that statement.

I predicted a few days before the Locke Law was passed that it would do away with the bookmaker's blackboard and his booth, but that it would not "deprive him of his cuffs, his pads or his note book, and, under the guise of the individual better, he will carry on a handbook system which no amount of ingenuity on the part of the police will be successful in blocking or destroying."

That part of what I said has turned out to be absolutely true.

The editorial from *The Times-Democrat* which I included in these memoirs was in reply to two statements from me. I will now quote what *The Item* had to say editorially in reply to the first statement and will then present, in full, what I had to say in reply to *The Item*. I would have presented all these statements in their order but that I misplaced my clippings of those fighting days.

"The policemen of New Orleans are paid to enforce the law," said *The Item*. "The Locke bill will burden them with little or no extra trouble. If it does, however, it is their duty to meet it, and his to see that they meet it."

> It is an honor and a credit to Senator Robert O'Connor that he refused the mayor's request to violate his oath of office by voting for a bill to put the solemn sanction of law on an unspeakable vice which the Constitution of Louisiana directs the legislature to suppress. Senator O'Connor has a better adviser in His Grace Archbishop James H. Blenk than he ever will find in His Honor Mayor Martin Behrman.
>
> It was necessary to satisfy the clean sportsmen of the country fairs in order to redeem New Orleans from pillage by the nation's gamblers; because, with a few honorable exceptions the city political organization is given over horse, foot and dragoons, to the gambling syndicate. A roster of the fat and easy jobs and sinecures on the race tracks last season looks like the pension list of the City Machine. We have the names and can furnish them on short notice. This is why Mayor Behrman and the bosses of several city wards have been trying for weeks in Baton Rouge to defeat the purpose of sound morality and correct economics. They have sacrificed principle to politics.
>
> It is true that the Locke bill does not prohibit racing. It does not

seek to do so. It merely puts the organized gambler and swindler under the ban of the law, by expelling the professional from the state. That will not kill the sport, if it is a sport.

Here is the testimony of John E. Madden, at Gravesend, the other day, a great turfman, beside whom the gentlemen thimble-rigging the game in New Orleans are "pikers" and "selling platers":

"The American people will not consent," he said, "to see racing killed simply because wholesale race track gambling has been abolished. I believe that the patronage here will continue to be so liberal that the racing association will be able to conduct the sport on a profitable basis. Look at these people here today for an example."

Mr. Madden probably knows what he is talking about: Mayor Behrman evidently does not.

If the Locke bill gives us racing 365 days a year, as the mayor declaims, wherein will we be the worse or our police the worse than both we and they are at present? Why has he not clamored before? What, save self-interest can cause the alarm that raises the voice of the mayor of New Orleans in so watery and specious a plea against a great reform for the city which has done him honor?

Interested patriots like the mayor declared when the Hunsicker law[25] went into effect that the police could not rid the city of pool rooms. The pool rooms are gone. The "hand book" and the "walking book" as police problems, are not so hard to reach as the picayune criminal who sells lottery policy. New Orleans was once infested with policy sellers. They are suppressed and the police have no trouble, when they wish, in keeping them down. This part of the mayor's plea is as thin and fishy as the rest of it. The difficulties exist only in a willing imagination.

The mayor clamors for the big tracks. They are the best campaign contributors. It is outrageous that the sucker should be allowed to throw his money into the maw of cheaper gamblers when the bigger stomach of the Cella and Corrigan gamblers want his money and are so good to "the boys."

The mayor, in that same paragraph, discusses the camp followers

---

25. The Hunsicker law, named for its author, Henry Hunsicker of Shreveport, provided for the suppression of poolrooms. The law carried a sentence of two to five hundred dollars fine or two to six months' imprisonment or both. Act No. 128, *Acts Passed by the General Assembly of the State of Louisiana at the Regular Session, 1904*.

of the racing swindle with a technical fluency that astonishes us. It has been only a few months since he professed utter ignorance of any horse race gambling at all in or near New Orleans. He is on record to that effect in an interview to which there were half a dozen witnesses which has never been questioned. We congratulate him, now that the gamble is assailed, upon the sudden acquisition of so much information and misinformation for its defense.

The whole composition fathered by the mayor sounds like a summary of the fallacies fed to a tired legislature for the past three weeks by Mr. Samuel F. Heaslip and Mr. George H. Terriberry. Mr. Heaslip is president of the City Park race track, a sort of shirt front of local popularity behind which the foreign gamblers who own and degrade the race tracks in New Orleans have masqueraded. His representations have not impressed the unbossed members of the legislature. We sincerely regret that the mayor of New Orleans has seen fit to lend them the dignity of an office which was bestowed upon him by all the people of the city.

More than fourteen years have passed since the foregoing was printed. I must admit that it irritated and annoyed me at the time. My reply to it then was not in tone and temper what my reply would have been had I not been riled at the style of it.

If the statement that Senator Robert O'Connor would have violated his oath of office by voting against the Locke Law [is true] then there were a large number of such violators in both houses of the legislature. As the Locke Law has not suppressed what its supporters believed it would, they all violate common sense by not taking my word for it.

The charge that my interest was in maintaining the tracks as they were because of the "fat and easy jobs and sinecures" that according to *The Item* made their pay rolls look "like the pension list of the city machine," was based on mere appearances.

I have no objection to anybody's accepting the appearances as they honestly appear to them. But I wish to point out that the same charge has been made against me in connection with every department of the municipal government with which I have ever had anything to do. I wish to point out, also, that I have reviewed my record in these recollections and will continue to review it and anybody who can uncover evidence that I ever sacrificed the public interest for political patronage should do so.

There were probably friends of mine employed in the minor positions at the tracks and I was on friendly terms with many of the larger figures, but by no means all of them.

The Item called my statement "a summary of the fallacies fed to a tired legislature" by the late Samuel Heaslip and George H. Terriberry. While I was not 100 per cent right in my predictions as to what would happen under the Locke Law, I was right in my main contention that it would not put the bookmakers out of business. It was *The Item* and its allies in support of the Locke Law who suffered from "fallacies."

No good purpose would be served by loading these recollections down with further details.

What I had to say in reply to *The Item* was as follows:

> In a statement which I furnished to the press yesterday I invited sober analysis of the pending Locke bill. I declared that instead of suppressing it would breed new forms of gambling, and that it would give us perennial racing at the half-mile tracks, with increasing degradation of the sport. If the measure was to be passed, it was my belief that it should be perfected so as to avoid creating a worse evil than it proposed to correct, the effect of which would be to add increased burdens and responsibilities upon our police department, already insufficient in numbers.
>
> What purports to be an acceptance of my invitation for such analysis appeared in *The Item* today. Instead, however, it is a mere rehash of the abuse which has characterized the attitude of that newspaper in its crusade against the tracks.
>
> My position on this matter has been consistent throughout, and I might add, no one knows this better than *The Item* itself, which sent one of its reporters to interview me on the subject some time ago, but for reasons best known to the management of the paper did not publish the interview. I declared then, have declared, and declare now that I am in favor of racing, properly regulated, but am not in favor of racing as presently conducted.

I do not believe that the Locke Law will stand the test of examination in its purpose to destroy gambling on the tracks. As first written, it would have done so undoubtedly, but when it was amended to satisfy the demands of country legislators for their country fairs so as to authorize individual betting on the tracks, it opened the doors to a system of gambling which the Police Department, if it were ten times as large, would be unable to suppress, and which indeed the courts are likely to hold that the department is incompetent to suppress, since it will find its authority in the Locke bill.

The Locke bill will not keep the bookmaker off the track. Undoubtedly it will do away with his blackboard and his booth, but it will not deprive him of his cuffs, his pads or his notebook, and, under the guise of the individual bettor, he will carry on a handbook system which no amount of ingenuity of on the part of the police will be successful in blocking or destroying.

The Item's statement that I have been in Baton Rouge working "to defeat the purpose of sound morality and correct economics" is beneath contempt. My presence there in every instance has been in the interest of public works of the highest importance to the community. Its intimation that I have a self-interest in the racing legislation is a gratuitous insult, and its charge that the Democratic organization has filled or controlled the positions at the race tracks is characteristic of that reckless statement of *The Item* so recently denounced by the General Assembly of Louisiana.

I have finished with the episode of the Locke Law in 1908 and will proceed with other matters that interest me and my interest others.

3.

The Chaotic 1910 Session of the General Assembly[26]

Before going into the episode of our attempt to hold the Panama-Pacific Exposition[27] at New Orleans, I wish to recall

26. The sessions of the state legislature concerned themselves with several problems: Louisiana's attempts to host the Panama Exposition; the deaths of two Louisiana congressmen, Senator Samuel D. McEnery and Representative Samuel L. Gilmore, and the selection of their successors and, a special session called to authorize the issuance of bonds to help finance the Panama Exposition (Act 2, 1910).

27. In 1910 New Orleans competed with San Francisco for the honor of being host to

several other matters, such as . . . an amusing incident in relation to J. Y. Sanders, and the liquor issue in Louisiana politics and the way the exposition and liquor questions were tangled together for a while at that famous [1910 session of the state legislature].

I have always been for local option, for regulation of the saloons and against prohibition. I was naturally taken a little by surprise [in 1909] when I saw that newspapers out in the country parishes were publishing stories to the effect that Governor Sanders expected to get out on a dry platform, as to the best of my knowledge he himself was for local option at that time. This was a long time before 1915, when Sanders declared, in effect, that the only real prohibition was national prohibition and he would be for it.

My inquiries on the subject got me the following information:

Jesse H. Webb, *The Item's* political reporter, dropped in at the *Item* office late one night and wrote a story to the effect that Governor Sanders was generally expected to adopt prohibition as part of his platform in the next campaign he made. This story did not quote Sanders in any way. It was entirely Webb's report of what other persons believed Sanders would do.

The Item at that time was the centre of a sort of association of Louisiana newspapers, to which it sent news. The newspaper man in charge of this work for *The Item* saw Webb's story later on in the night on the city editor's desk. He immediately made a

---

the Panama Exposition scheduled to be held in 1915 to celebrate the opening of the Panama Canal. The U.S. House of Representatives voted 188 to 159 in favor of San Francisco. Many New Orleanians credited the city's defeat to President Taft yielding under the pressure of large railraod combines to select the Bay City. Others believed Taft gave his support to California to delay anti-Japanese immigration laws threatened by the California state legislature. Taft was at that time negotiating a treaty of commerce and navigation with Japan. Both suspicions were, however, conjecture. U.S. Department of State, "Treaty of Commerce and Navigation," *Foreign Relations of the United States, 1911* (Washington, D.C.: U.S. Government Printing Office, 1918), 319. See House Debates in the *Congressional Record*, 61st Cong., 3rd Sess., February 21, to March 2, 1911, Pt. 4, p. 3211.

City and State Politics 241

number of carbon copies of it and mailed it to the country dailies. I read it either in the Lake Charles or Baton Rouge paper.

For some reason or other the story never appeared in *The Item*. As it was frankly a report of the conjectures and guesses of politicians who did not know what they were talking about, there was no important reason to run it. But it was taken very seriously by many who did read it.

This story may have served a useful purpose as I have no doubt whatever that Governor Sanders got a lot of letters from all kinds of citizens on the subject. If he did, these letters may have assisted him in getting a good idea of how the people in the country felt about state-wide prohibition.

[State] Senator Joseph Voegtle was given unanimous consent [in 1910] by the [state] Senate to introduce a joint resolution proposing an amendment to the constitution to levy a tax of three-eights of a mill for the Panama-Pacific Exposition. This tax was to pay off bonds to be issued to construct the exposition buildings, hire its working force and so forth. [State] Representative [William] Polk of Rapides [Parish] introduced a similar resolution in the House.

There was immediately a lot of talk about some liquor legislation that was to be introduced. It soon developed that both sides the wets and the dries, expected to use the exposition bill as a club over the heads of the city delegation. I naturally took an active interest in this as the representations made to me by my home people in New Orleans had committed me absolutely to do all I could for the exposition and I was already very definitely lined up on one side of the liquor issue. My purpose was to assist those who did not want the liquor issue brought forward and did not want any liquor legislation at all at that time.

The particular proposal made by the liquor interests, who were then flushed with the spirit of victory and believed that they could use the exposition situation as they pleased, was that cities with populations of more than ten thousand should be exempt from the parish unit in voting on the issue of wet or dry. They wanted these cities to be units themselves. The Parish of Caddo had recently out-voted its city, Shreveport. A bill like this would have caused a very bitter fight.

Senator Voegtle, himself by no means a minor figure among the men who opposed the prohibitionists, did not want the exposition business tangled up in such a fight. So he brought it about that a conference was arranged in Governor Sander's office between himself and [state] Senator Walter Elder [of Union Parish] and there was an understanding reached that the up-state local option people [would not be deprived] of the fruits of the victory they had won two years before.

There was a Mr. Smylie there, one of the heads of the Anti-Saloon League, who declared he had not promised there would be no attempt to have more liquor legislation passed. But, as a result of the conference between Senators Voegtle and Elder, the liquor issue was taken out of the way of the exposition and everybody but a few radical prohibitionists was satisfied.

We had been busy for a long time on the Panama-Pacific Exposition and I had been one of many delegates from New Orleans to Washington on trips which I will probably mention more in detail later on. The exposition business was a big feature of the session of 1910. The people of New Orleans were very anxious to have that celebration of the opening of the Panama Canal held here in 1915 and the country parishes were sufficiently interested to be willing to pay taxes to get the benefit that might have come to all of us.

On the very first day of the session, Senator Henry Favrot introduced a resolution with a long preamble which I will not quote. The body of the resolution was as follows:

"Resolved, by the General Assembly of the State of Louisiana, that an invitation should be extended to the Honorable Theodore Roosevelt to become the president of the Panama Exposition company and that every effort should be made and means should not be spared to secure his services to that end."

After thinking the matter over in the light of my experiences as chief executive of a small faction of the population of the United States, I have come to the conclusion that we asked a great deal when we requested the [former] chief executive of the whole population to undertake to run the exposition company for us.

I now come, in its proper order, to mention an occurrence that [also] attracted considerable attention [during the 1910 session of the legislature]. That was the death of Senator [Samuel] McEnery and the election of Governor Sanders to the senate. Honorable Samuel Douglas McEnery, senior United States Senator from Louisiana, died [on June 28, 1910] after only a few days' sickness at his [New Orleans] home at St. Mary and Chestnut streets. His death was not expected and was a shock to his host of friends. I have related so much about Senator McEnery that it is not necessary to go into many details now. His most recent work for us was his great activity in the campaign to secure the Panama Exposition for New Orleans.

Senator McEnery had gone to Washington after an open announcement that he was a high tariff man. This laid the ground work for him to make a great many friends and allies among the Republicans and his influence in the senate was such that he never had any trouble in blocking confirmation of any appointments that did not meet with his approval. In one instance, he was opposed to an appointment which President Roosevelt was very anxious to make. Whenever Roosevelt sent his friend's name to the senate, Senator McEnery rose in his seat and stated that the proposed appointee was personally objectionable to him. The senate refused to confirm the nomination and Roosevelt finally abandoned the idea that he could ever get it done.

Those interested in sugar will testify that Senator McEnery and Senator [Robert F.] Broussard were the most effective representatives sugar had at Washington. They used to call Senator McEnery "Old Molasses" in the magazines and the Eastern newspapers. I was attending a meeting of the council when I received the news of Senator McEnery's death.

"It is my sad duty to report to you," I announced to the council, "the death of a prominent citizen, a prominent statesman and a good friend. The Honorable Samuel Douglas McEnery, United States Senator from this state, died this morning at 9:40 o'clock."

The politicians were taken by surprise when Senator McEnery died and for a day or so many of them seemed to be dazed. They had little to say. But they were doing a lot of thinking.

Governor Sanders, of course, was looked upon by all as a strong candidate and by many as the logical candidate for the McEnery succession. But Senator [Murphy J.] Foster was from South Louisiana. He and Sanders came from the same town, Franklin, in St. Mary Parish.... Just as we have tacit agreements in the state senatorial districts, so had we a sort of tacit agreement of politics that the two United States Senators should not both come from the same section of the state.

Under the law, the McEnery vacancy had to be filled by the legislature, which made it almost certain that J. Y. Sanders' choice would win in that election. Senator [Henri L.] Gueydan [of Vermillion Parish] however, who was in a way a leader of the then highly developed opposition to Governor Sanders, suggested that the election be postponed and that there be a state primary, after which the legislature could meet in special session and record the will of the people. He introduced a resolution to that effect, but it was defeated and in its place a resolution was adopted fixing Tuesday, July 5, as the day on which balloting for United States Senator would take place.[28]

Governor Sanders, in the circumstances, was in control but there was considerable opposition from North Louisiana. Congressman Joseph E. Ransdell of the Fifth district, while not himself a candidate for the Senate at that time, stated that if two senators from the same town sat for Louisiana, without doubt, North Louisiana would be heard from in the elections of 1912.

When July 5th, 1910, had been fixed by the general assembly as the day for the election of a United States Senator to succeed the late Samuel D. McEnery, and Congressman Joseph E. Ransdell had thrown out the decided hint against Governor Sanders that North Louisiana would be heard from at the elections of 1912 if South Louisiana got both Louisiana's places in the Senate, some of the politicians set themselves to getting the support of Speaker H. Garland Dupre of the House for a north Louisiana candidate. Garland Dupre had a great deal of influence with the New Orleans delegation. He was personally popular with all members of the general assembly.

The proposal was made that if Dupre would swing to a north Louisiana candidate, he would get the support of the north Louisiana politicians for governor.

The Democratic State Central Committee had been called to meet and it was thought by many that the committee might take up the question of a primary election for United States Senator. But, beyond eulogizing the late Senator McEnery and the late Congressman Robert C. Davey and fixing the dates for primary elections of certain parish officers, no other business was done. Governor Sanders had been elected to the Senate by the House of Representatives before the committee met. When the joint session came [on July 6] Governor Sanders received one

28. Act No. 146 states that both houses will ballot on July 5 and compile their votes on July 6, 1910. *Acts Passed by the General Assembly of the State of Louisiana at the Regular Session, 1910.*

hundred and twenty-six (126) votes, John D. Wilkinson of Caddo twelve and Robert F. Broussard five.

The fact that Robert F. Broussard went into the contest without organized support and against Governor Sanders, at a time when Sanders was in as nearly complete dominance at Baton Rouge as it was practicable for any one man to be so, was of great help to him in the campaign of 1911–1912. It advertised him as a candidate for the Senate to the extent that no other move on his part could have advertised that candidacy.

Congressman Arsene P. Pujo,[29] who during the following two years did as much as any man at Washington to put the Republican Party "in bad" with the people, admitted in 1912 that he had not been a candidate in 1910 because he saw no use in it as Governor Sanders was sure to be elected. Broussard made considerable political capital out of this, declaring that he had always been against Sanders and that Pujo was only against him when he, Pujo, was running against him. As those were the days when Governor Sanders was not popular, the incident undoubtedly got Broussard a lot of votes.

The legislature adjourned on July 7th and on July 18th [1910] Honorable Samuel L. Gilmore, congressman for the second [Louisiana congressional] district, died at Abita Springs.

I have had a great deal to say about Sam Gilmore in other chapters of these recollections. His death was a great loss to the city. He was one of my best friends and wisest advisors and counsellors. The affair of the senator to succeed McEnery appeared to be absolutely settled when the death of Mr. Gilmore started more politics.

Most of us looked on H. Garland Dupre as the logical succes-

29. In 1912 J. Pierpont Morgan became the principal subject in Arsene Pujo's congressional committee investigation into the concentration of money and credit in the nation's banks and trust companies. The committee's findings became the foundation of President Woodrow Wilson's banking reforms. Richard B. Morris, *Encyclopedia of American History* (New York: Harper and Row, 1965), 273–74, 757.

sor, largely due to his long experience as a legislator, his work as a speaker of the house, his knowledge of parliamentary law. He had youth, vigor, the knack of making friends and a thorough knowledge of conditions in the city and the state. We believed these qualifications would make him the best representative we would get.

On the other hand, he had been urged by a great many influential men to become a candidate for governor.

We felt that with the [Panama] exposition bill pending in congress, we needed a man of Dupre's calibre to represent us there. He finally agreed to become a candidate for Congress. As the elections for Congress were to be held in November, it was thought it would not be wise to issue a call for a special election. A primary was called for September 6th, at which time candidates could be chosen both for the unexpired term of the late Congressman Gilmore and for the full term of two years.

The late Louis LeBourgeois, Sheriff of St. James Parish, had announced his candidacy for Congress before the caucus of the leaders of the Regular faction of the Democratic party resulted in their declaring for Garland Dupre. While Mr. LeBourgeois did announce, he had not qualified and he withdrew the following day. Then Victor Loisel, United States Marshal [in New Orleans] posted his deposit with the Secretary of State as the candidate of the Republican party. The campaign committees of both parties met on July 28th, 1910, ten days after the death of Congressman Gilmore. General Albert Estopinal and H. Garland Dupre were declared the Democratic and John A. Wogan and Victor Loisel the Republican candidates in the first and the second [Congressional] districts respectively.

General Estopinal and Garland Dupre, of course, were elected.

I have not given any detailed sketch of the fight for the exposition in this political story, much of which is probably of interest. I am now on the point at which it immediately affected our politics. A great deal of the Panama Exposition work, including the sending of some large delegations to Washington, took place before the session of the legislature in 1910. 1910.

The people of San Francisco had agreed to raise $7,500,000 and we were required to match that sum or else give up our plans to have the exposition at New Orleans. It was found that the amount that could be raised through sale of bonds to be paid out of the tax levy in the proposed amendment to the constitution at the November election with the large individual subscriptions, would not reach the sum of $7,500,000.

The Panama Exposition Company saw the necessity of increasing our total in some way and that this could be done only by a special session of the general assembly. So the directors prepared a request to Governor Sanders and it was endorsed by all the commercial exchanges. On Monday, August 9th, 1910, Governor Sanders issued the call for the special session.

Believing there might be some opposition to the call because of the expense to be incurred, the Exposition Company offered to pay the expense of the session. Governor Sanders, in his call, referred to this offer and said that while appreciating it he was of the opinion that it was not consistent with the dignity of the State of Louisiana to accept it. He had, therefore, included legislation to pay the per-diem and traveling expenses of the members in his proclamation.

This session was called for ten days. The legislation providing for the increased taxation was made to apply to the City of New Orleans only. The Governor included some other matters in the call which it is not necessary to relate at this time.

The General Assembly met on Monday, August 15th, 1910, and it was still in session when John T. Michel announced his candidacy for governor. He made a very short announcement. "I am a candidate for governor." he said, and that was all.

The legislature passed the exposition resolution just as it had been presented, with a practically unanimous vote as only four members were against it, and adjourned on Friday, August 19th. This was the shortest session in the history of the state, having lasted a little less than five days. It was also one of the biggest sessions, from a political point of view, as it developed a situation that affected Louisiana politics in a big way and started movements that have not yet entirely died down.

During the session it became generally understood that a great deal of "soreness" had developed on the part of Lieutenant Governor Paul M. Lambremont. He had been looked upon as a candidate for Governor. Mr. Lambremont had stated that when Governor Sanders resigned to become senator, he would call a special session of the legislature for the purpose of enacting certain election reforms and other things which I do not remember at this moment. John T. Michel's announcement undoubtedly convinced Lieutenant Governor Lambremont that he would not have the support of the Regular organization in New Orleans in a race for governor.

When I stated that John T. Michel's announcement, at the general assembly in 1910, that he would be a candidate for governor convinced Paul M. Lambremont that he, Lambremont, would not get the support of the Regular faction in New Orleans. I neglected to state that Mr. Lambremont had not received any commitments or promises of support from us.

We supported Mr. Lambremont against James J. Bailey in 1908 and on that, and his general harmony with the Regulars during the first two years of the Sanders administration, as a basis, some of the newspapers, both in New Orleans and in the parishes, charged the Regulars and their friends in the country with bad faith. In fact, as I remember it, it was stated that we had "double crossed" Lambremont.

When Jesse H. Webb, one of *The Item's* political reporters, asked me if I had "double crossed" Lambremont, he laughed when he asked it. I laughed, too, as Webb knew and I knew that nothing of that kind had happened. I told him to go to Mr. Lambremont. Webb's call on me took place some time after the special session.

Mr. Lambremont, so far as I remember, never even privately made the claim that we had "double crossed" him. He had a perfectly legitimate and honorable ambition to be governor and he had the right to seek any support that he could get.

We, on the other hand were free to support anybody that best suited us. We were strongly in favor of John T. Michel for governor. Some of our friends later wavered a little as circumstances changed the political situation and things so shaped themselves that when the campaign opened at Ruston [Louisiana] on July 4th, 1911, all but one of the political leaders in New Orleans were active for John T. Michel....

Shortly after Lieutenant Governor Lambremont let it to be known that when Sanders resigned as governor and became Senator Sanders he would call a special session and support legislation that would alter political conditions to the injury of the Regulars. Senator John D. Shaffer of Terrebonne [Parish] who was believed to have formed an alliance with Lambremont known as the "Shaffer-Lambremont Combine," announced that Lambremont would be a candidate for governor and that he would make the race unless all his friends fell away from him before the time came to qualify.

Immediately after that a conference was held in New Orleans with the purpose of organizing a movement to fight the Regulars. The Good Government League was formally organized at the Hotel Grunewald on Monday, August 23rd, 1910. The meeting was called to order by Col. C. Harrison Parker ... a platform was adopted and permanent organization was effected....[30]

30. The Good Government League, though it successfully backed the gubernatorial candidacy of Luther E. Hall in 1912, lost in the New Orleans municipal elections of that year (see note 33 of this chapter).

City and State Politics

It was less than a week after that meeting that a letter from Governor Sanders was sent to the directors of the [Panama] exposition company who had asked him to give up the senatorial toga and as he could be of more service to the exposition as Governor.

It has been said for years that Martin Behrman, as the leader of the Regular faction, was responsible for and participated in the negotiations that resulted in Sander's resignation as Senator. The fact is that while this was going on I was in St. Paul, Minn. attending a convention of the American League of Municipalities.

I recieved a telegram from Charles Janvier a prominent member of the board of directors of the Exposition company, in which he asked my authority to sign my name to the letter sent the Governor by the directors.

I was one of the directors. This telegram to me as such was the first intimation I had that anything of the kind was going on.

I still have the original telegram, which was sent by the Postal Telegraph company and was addressed as follows: "Martin Behrman, Mayor of New Orleans, St. Paul, Minn.—(Try leading hotels)."

I read the telegram carefully and considered what it might mean. I decided that in the circumstances I would join with the other directors in their position to Governor Sanders and telegraphed Mr. Janvier to sign my name with those of the other directors.

Some how or other the public gets very contrary impressions of such matters. I know that for years many sincere men have often repeated the old story about the ward leaders getting together with me at the Choctaw Club and deciding to appeal to Sanders to save them from supposedly terrible fate that would come to them with Mr. Lambremont as Governor. There was not a trace of truth in this story.

Governor Sanders wrote the directors August 27, 1910, that

he would resign as Senator and remain as Governor. He said that all his personal predictions indicated that he should accept the office of Senator, that it had long been an ambition of his to sit in that great body but that no man's ambitions and no personal predilections should govern in a matter of that kind.

Sanders went on to say that the exposition meant more to the people of Louisiana than anything else at that time and that if he could better serve the cause by remaining Governor, he was ready and willing to forego the election to the senate and would devote his energy to the movement as Governor.

It had been rumored that a plan was on foot to make him Director General at a very large salary.

"I take this opportunity of informing you and the people of Louisiana," he said, "that I am not a candidate for nor will I accept any position with the Exposition company."

After stating that he would give the exposition project all the time he could, he proceeded that while declining an office to which he had been legally and fairly elected for the term expiring March 4, 1915, and announced:

"I desire here and now to serve notice on all that I expect to be a candidate in the next Democratic primary to fill the vacancy caused by the death of the distinguished and lamented McEnery."

The legislature was not in session so the Governor had the authority to appoint the successor to Senator McEnery. It was conceded, of course, that he would not appoint a Louisianian who would be a candidate at the primary and his selection was Judge James R. Thornton at Rapides.

Judge Thornton was a distinguished citizen and beloved by all who knew him personally. I always appreciated his friendship for me. I knew him well, having served with him in the Constitutional Convention of 1898 and having met him frequently after that.

Governor Sanders' enemies, of course, attempted to make

political capital out of his resignation. They claimed he had no moral right to resign after having been elected in the circumstances and that the purposes of the resignation was political.

The board of directors of the Exposition company also came in for a lot of criticism for their part in it. It was declared that they had endangered the adoption of the constitutional amendment [for the Exposition bonds] in appealing to Sanders to remain as governor.

As Senator Thornton had not taken his seat in the [U.S.] Senate, his appointment might have lapsed if he were not confirmed or elected by the state senate at the special session [called by Sanders on November 16, 1910]. There was some debate at the time as to whether it would lapse unless the Governor failed to put the nomination before [this] special session. The Governor decided to play safe and included not the confirmation of the appointment but the election of a United States Senator in the proclamation.

As soon as this call was made public, Judge Thornton issued a statement relative to his position in the matter. He declared that he had not expected, had not sought and had not permitted anyone to solicit the appointment as Senator; but, having accepted the appointment, and having received numbers of letters of endorsement from all over the state, and as leading citizens in all the political factions had approved his going to the Senate, he felt that he had every reason to feel encouraged to offer himself as a candidate.

The Times-Democrat, of course, began to see things and to hear all kinds of rumors. As newspapers are run by human beings, it is natural that they should go wrong at times. But *The Times-Democrat* in particular seemed to be what the boys used to call "off its base," that is, on the subject of J. Y. Sanders and the Senate at this time.

The Times-Democrat had a lot of stuff about a league or

combination being formed to defeat Judge Thornton and named Congressman Robert F. Broussard as a party to it. The bad judgment in this must have been clear to every observant person as it was to me, for it was certainly not to Bob Broussard's interests to tie himself up in a combination at that time.

"A news item published in *The Times-Democrat* of Sunday, November 20, 1910," said Congressman Broussard in a public statement, "in which are mentioned Governor J. Y. Sanders, Lieutenant Governor Paul M. Lambremont, Congressman A. P. Pujo, Congressman Joseph E. Ransdell, Hon. John D. Wilkinson and myself, alleges the formation of a league.[11]

> The object of this league is said to be to defeat Judge Thornton for the Senate and to get Sanders out of this state or to block the election of a United States Senator.
>
> I am in no combination to get Sanders out of the state.
>
> I urged Governor Sanders to accept his election to the United States Senate when he was elected by the legislature. He saw his duty in a different light and he had declined the election. I have no criticism to make of his conclusion.
>
> I not only am not a party to any combination over the election of a Senator but for one I consider the position of a United States Senator too exalted in itself and too important to the people of the state to be the subject matter of combinations.
>
> The intimation that the gentlemen mentioned in that article would be parties to any agreement looking to the non-election of a Senator, at the extraordinary session of the legislature called by the Governor, is in my mind inconceivable; and, if carried out, it would be a public calamity.
>
> I have no doubt that any one of the gentlemen mentioned in the articles, as prospective candidates of this alleged league, would gladly accept the position of United States Senator should the general assembly honor him with the election and would fill the position with credit to himself and honor to the state.

The legislature met on November 28, 1910, and *The Times-Democrat* was still predicting all kinds of mishaps and accidents that were going to happen to the Thornton candidacy and even went so far as to say that Judge Thornton's chances were diminishing. To use an up-to-date expression that will give a clear idea of *The Times-Democrat's* campaign, I will put it this way: "His candidacy was no good when he announced it; and every day, in every way, it is getting worse and worse."

The legislature adopted a resolution calling on those prominently mentioned as candidates and any other Democrat who may aspire to senatorial honors are hereby invited to address the general assembly on Monday, December 5, 1910, at eight o'clock, in the hall of the House of Representatives.

Then Bob Broussard issued a statement that was a shock to some folks. "Responding to what I conceive to be the call of the people," said Congressman Broussard, "as voiced in the resolutions adopted by the legislature Wednesday, I have decided to become a candidate for the United States senate for the unexpired terms of the lamented Samuel D. McEnery."

Balloting in both houses took place on the following Tuesday, December 6. The Senate gave Judge Thornton thirty-two, Broussard five, [John] Wilkinson two, Sanders one, and [Lee] Thomas none. The House gave Judge Thornton seventy-four, Broussard twenty-three, Thomas eleven, and Wilkinson five. The two houses met together [the] next day, elected Judge Thornton, had him address them and adjourn.

4.

Salary Raise to $10,000

It was at the second session of the legislature of the Sanders administration, in [August] 1910, that the salary of the Mayor of New Orleans was raised to $10,000 despite long and loud protests from *The Times-Democrat* and, if my memory be clear on the subject, some objections from *The Item*. The city ordinance introduced some time before by Councilman Peter

Graham, without my knowledge of his intention to do so, could not become effective until the charter was amended.

I was very glad to get the raise in pay.

While my living expenses as a private citizen with two grown children who are not dependent on me for anything in the way of support, are far from the ten thousand a year, my expenses as mayor about that time were so heavy that I could hardly have gotten along without the increase when prices went up eight years ago. A mayor usually has to spend a great deal of money that he cannot charge to any expense account, especially if he feels called on to make trips all over the country in the interest of his city on affairs that are not governmental affairs.

All kinds of stories, of course, were rumored around town about that increase to $10,000. They belong in the class of the rumors about the big palace I had built in Algiers when I was an assessor. It is the same house in which I now live.

One of these stories was that I had declared to the "ring," which is what they called the Regular organization, that I would quit being mayor and go to Congress unless my pay was increased. There was nothing whatever in this. If I had wished to go to Congress, I had my chance [in 1908] when my friend the late Adolph Meyer died. I had no other idea in 1910 than to keep on being mayor.

Another story was that I had gone deep in debt and needed the money to pay off. That was not true. My friends took the position that the work of a mayor was worth $10,000. The critics were to a great extent disarmed by the fact that I had given all I could to the work. Even *The Times-Democrat*, which I have quoted on the subject, admitted that Martin Behrman had never shown any signs of laziness and that he had a big job. They pointed out that the members of the Supreme Court could expect pensions and that mayors could not.

While on this subject, I wish to say that I believe the Governor of Louisiana should be paid much more than the $7,500 he gets. It is true that with the other allowances for light and coal, the free use of the well furnished executive mansion and the household maintenance expenses that are met by the state, this position really pays much more than $7,500. But not so much more. I should say, as a guess, that the governor really gets about $12,000 a year. He should have all the allowances he now has in addition to the salary and the salary should be double what it is.

I will not make an estimate of what I think should be the mayor's salary. But I will say that it should be so much that a reasonably economical and thrifty mayor could easily set aside a quarter of it. Then he would have time to look around and arrange for another job or get back into business at the end of his term. This applies of course, to one term mayors.

I remember that either *The Item* or the editor of *The Item*, Marshall Ballard, took the position that the increase in pay I got in 1910 was not a proper proceeding that the mayoralty should be a position of honor. It is a position of honor. Moreover, so far as I am personally concerned, I have never been justly accused of overlooking a chance to get some honors or to be honored.

Yet, after more than sixteen years of honors of all kinds, ranging from the thanks of little girls for things I had done for them to resolutions of regard, re-election, having luncheon with the President of the United States at the White House, etc., etc., I wish to say from my long experience with the salary and the honors that the honors never bought shoes for the children nor paid the doctors nor did anything else that the money was good for.

I tried to deserve both the honors and the $10,000. I would have been disappointed if I had not recieved the honors. I do not know what I would have been if I had not received the $10,000. Long after I became the pestered possessor of a slary of $10,000, for that encouraged everybody to come to me for donations to everything from a lawn party for the benefit of the lost cats to funds to help the Armenians, I was cartooned as the $10,000 beauty.

Some parts of the public seem to think that unusual things should be forthcoming from a $10,000 mayor that had not been forthcoming from a mere $6,000 mayor.

Except when very much worried or excited or tired out by a hard fight, I have always been able to see the funny side of things that concerned me.

I was put in a good humor when I heard that a newspaper man who had rapped me for the $10,000 was himself making quite a noise because he could not get a raise. I suppose the big laugh I had over that shows I have a mean disposition. There was no real opposition to the $10,000 in the legislature. The city members were for it and the country members did not care one way or the other. The Senate was unanimous for it and only six members of the house voted in the negative.

There have been six regular and numerous special sessions of the legislature since I got the $10,000 in 1910 and nobody has yet formally suggested that the salary of the Mayor of New Orleans should be reduced. It is one thing to "knock" a salary when an opponent is getting it and another to cut that salary when it goes to a friend or an ally.

None of those who made political capital, or attempted to do so, on the issue of that $10,000 have ever come forward when they had a chance to reduce it. At least, I do not remember that reduction of the salary was ever advocated just before or during the session of the legislature since 1910.

Nor do I believe that the $10,000 ever lost me a vote. I do not remember that it was mentioned otherwise than in good humored way in the campaigns of 1908 and 1920, when I had real opposition I am sure it was not mentioned in 1920, for then, as a matter of fact that $10,000 would not buy much more in the way of clothes and food than the $6,000 bought in 1910.

That is all I have to say on a much discussed subject of twelve years ago. I am glad they left the salary where it was put in 1910 and I will not be found among the "knockers" if they boost it a little more and double the contingent fund.

5.
Luther E. Hall Becomes Governor in 1912[31]

I am giving my personal impressions of the late Honorable Luther E. Hall, both as a man and as a public character.

"Judge" Hall, as he was known to those closer to him, among whom I counted myself as I got to know him better after he was governor, was the only governor I have known who was elected to that office without desiring it in the least.

Word that L. E. Hall would run for governor came from Monroe in the form of a telegram signed by John M. Parker, William F. Millsaps and Charles H. Trousdale. I did not know him at the time, but I knew enough about him to realize that he would in all probability make a good campaign. I did not expect him to be elected, but I knew he would get a great many votes regardless of the support that would come to him from the Good Government League.

Judge Hall had recently been elected to the [state] Supreme Court but was not to take his seat until the next year. I had spent my life in politics and had been mayor eight years. I knew what it was to be governor. When they told me what a good judge he had been, I had a half formed opinion at once that he would

---

31. Luther E. Hall (1869–1921), governor of the state from 1912 to 1916, was elected governor in 1912 on the reform ticket of the Good Government League, a faction of the Democratic party. In the Democratic primary held on January 23, 1912, Hall received 53,407 votes to State Superintendent of Schools James B. Aswell's 23,800 and to the Regular candidate John T. Michael's 46,201 votes. Michel carried Orleans Parish with 23,694 votes to Hall's 13,986 and Aswell's 1,848 votes. Among the achievements of Hall's administration was his work to increase state revenues through a reorganization of tax assessments. In 1918 Governor Ruffin G. Pleasant appointed Hall as an assistant attorney general. In that same year Hall was defeated in a bid for the U.S. Senate. In 1921 he was once again politically unsuccessful in an attempt to secure the Democratic nomination for the Louisiana Supreme Court. *Report of the Secretary of State to His Excellency, the Governor of Louisiana, April 1, 1912*; Reeves, *The Governors of Louisiana*, 93–94.

never get any pleasure or satisfaction out of his work as governor.

"You never did like the place?" I suggested to him, half a question and half a statement, after [Governor] Col. Ruffin G. Pleasant had been inaugurated [in 1916].

"I never did," he replied. "I did not want it but I took it because, my old friends and some men in whom I then had confidence insisted that I take it. I would have been much better off if I had gone to the Supreme Court."

After the Hon. John T. Michel withdrew from the campaign, this making a second primary unnecessary, I naturally sought to get in touch with the man who was to be governor. While he was plainly not at all warm toward me at the time, still he was polite and cordial and apparently took the attitude that as leaders of two opposing factions of the same party, one dominant at the capital and the other dominant in the state's biggest city, we should maintain at least polite relations.

When the time came for the state central committee to meet and declare him the nominee, it was suggested that I get a proxy, sit as a member of the committee and move that the Governor-elect be invited to address us. I did this and, as is the custom, I was appointed chairman of the committee. We called on the Governor-elect and escorted him to the meeting and I had the pleasure of making the formal introduction.

Some of the Hall's wilder supporters immediately began to cry that their successful candidate had "gone over to the ring." There was more to that than their somewhat foolish interpretation of the appearance of the incident of my introducing him to the committee. A certain lack of sympathy had developed between Hall on one side and some of the large figures among those who supported him.

I never discussed that matter with Hall, but I was told at the time that the coolness was due to a shortage in the Good Government League's campaign fund which he, the candidate, in effect had to make good.

The story is that when John M. Parker interviewed Judge Hall at Monroe . . . Judge Hall told him that he would not be able to contribute one cent to the campaign fund. I may say now, though I did not know it when Hall first appeared as a candidate, that the support of his father and mother and his own family had kept him in debt all his life. After a term on the court of appeal, he had built a home but had it heavily mortgaged. In the middle of the campaign, after he had committed all his friends to a fight, there was no more traveling expenses coming from the treasure of the Good Government League and he put a second mortgage on his house. The house was finally sold under the mortgages.

The coolness between the Governor-elect and some of his principal supporters and the politeness he showed me, and some of the other leaders in New Orleans, was the basis of all kinds of rumors that made me laugh. I learned in later years that he too laughed at them.

The friction between the Regulars and the state faction, the [Good Government] League, did not develop into anything considerable at the first session of the legislature. What did develop, however, was acquaintance between me and Governor Hall. I soon learned that when he gave his word he could be absolutely depended on but that he was very slow about making up his mind to anything.

While Governor Hall's slow deliberation over matters put before him, an admirable quality in a judge, hampered his success in many matters, it must in fairness be added that he had to be given very strong reasons to convince him that he should change his course in any matter. Nor did he seem to be very particular about how his courses would be taken by the people at the time. I will point out one instance of this.

He decided, as an incident of the refunding of the state debt, that the holders of valid Baby Bonds (of which there are many "fakes" on the market) were entitled to payment. He was of the opinion that payment of these bonds would improve the state's credit.[32] He consulted with many lawyers and others, who had announced that he represented some holders of these bonds. Then he went after what he had decided on. He was advised that his programme was extremely unpopular. But he decided it was the best programme and he never wavered in support of it.

When he decided that the business of refining sugar should be regulated, he went after that in characteristic "Hall fashion." Nothing swerved him.

While Hall had been governor for four years, as a lawyer he was a stranger in New Orleans and I had my doubts that he could build up a good practice here in a few years in spite of his reputation as an able judge. Had there been no war [World War I] however, he would probably have succeeded at that. It was while his son and mine were both in France that we had the contest for the [U.S.] Senate that followed the death of Senator Robert Broussard [April, 1918].

I thought for a time that Hall would be elected. My friend John Overton was not succeeding very well in Southern Louisiana. Then Edward J. Gay got into the race. I had no candidate at the time and I knew Col. John P. Sullivan was

32. Behrman is referring to the bond fraud scandals of the 1880s during the administration of State Treasurer E. A. Burke. In 1888, while Burke was attending a mining conference in London, the scandal broke. A bond fraud of almost $2 million was discovered in the state treasury. These state bonds or "baby bonds," so called because of a picture of a small child imprinted on them, were allowed to circulate and collect interest after they were supposed to have been retired. When news reached Burke in London, he took up permanent residency in Honduras. Nineteen counts of embezzlement and fraud were brought against Burke and numerous attempts were made to extradite him to Louisiana. The former treasurer remained in Honduras until his death in 1928. Joy Jackson, *New Orleans in the Gilded Age*, (Baton Rouge: Louisiana State University Press, 1969) 42–43; Hair, *Bourbonism and Agrarian Protest*, 27–28.

supporting Hall. So when Ed Gay came to me at the close of a war work meeting, I told him I would support him. The fact that Col. Sullivan was supporting Hall at the time contradicts the general rumor that I too was doing so, as it can hardly be said that the Colonel and I were cooperating at anything.

I saw more of Judge Hall in a personal way after he was governor than before. My contact with him on public business will be referred to in other articles on such matters as taxation. I got to like him very much, and I saw very clearly why he was never able to get along with some of those who supported him.

While Judge Hall was by no means "conservative" or a "reactionary," he was not in sympathy with a majority of the so-called "reformers." He was a liberal man and he believed in home rule.... Even had there been no definite cause of a break between him and such men as John M. Parker and Dr. Henry Dickson Bruns, two opposite types in the ranks of the "reformers," they were sure to drift apart.

While there was obvious sincerity in Hall's campaign pledge that the leaders in New Orleans would not have much influence at Baton Rouge, and complete proof of it in his conduct, yet at the same time I believe he much preferred our style of politics to that of the more conspicuous leaders in the Good Government League, particularly John M. Parker.

Hall was a quiet, determined but good hearted man who disliked useless noise, threats, denunciations and, so far as I know, never made a speech on a subject about which he knew nothing whatever. Hall did not give his unsuccessful opponents the choice of joining him or being treated like newly arrived strangers from a port with the bubonic plague. He was against us politically. He joined with us on various programmes for the time being only. That is, he got us with him on them. But to the very end of his administration, when he supported the late Thomas C. Barret, Democratic nominee for governor [in 1916] and refrained from campaigning for his opponent, in a sense, Col. Ruffin G. Pleasant, he was against the Regulars in New Orleans.

If Judge Hall had gone to the Supreme [Court] Bench, where he would have done work he liked and would not have been subjected to the stress of politics, he would still be with us. The strain of his last fight, that of the race for the Supreme Court, was only one of many that he had to face but it was the last. He was not temperamentally fitted for that kind of a life.

It is a great pleasure to remember that, after years of opposing each other, I was able to do my friend a favor, for we had become good friends. Attorney General [Adolph V.] Coco told me that he had found reasons why it would be preferable not to appoint Judge I. D. Moore to the then vacant position of assistant attorney general.

"I would like very much to . . . have Judge Hall if he will take it," Judge Coco told me.

"I would surely like to see him take it," I replied. "He has my hearty support for it if he wants it."

"Next to sitting on the bench," Judge Hall told me with a smile that made me wonder what he was thinking of 1912 and the Supreme Court or the Godchaux-Hall contest, "I would rather be in this place than anywhere else I know."

"So you like it that much?" I replied, meaning nothing in particular but just keeping up the conversation.

"You may think I'm joking," he replied seriously, "but I would rather be here than anywhere off the bench. I guess I know my own mind."

When he said that, he was once more giving me to understand what I then knew very well, that he never cared for the position of governor and always wished he had not taken it.

Summing up Governor Hall, I will say that the queer tricks and turns of our politics placed a good, clean hard working man, mentally trained and by character a judge, in the position of an administrator. He took it because he thought it was his duty to take it; and he was always sorry he did.

6.

J. Y. Sanders Claimed Double Cross in the 1912 U.S. Senate Race

I wish to take up that old story that I "double crossed" J. Y. Sanders in 1912, when Robert Broussard beat Sanders and Arsene P. Pujo for the Senate.[33] Nothing could be more unfair than the statement that I "double crossed" Sanders, but that has not kept my enemies from using it to injure me among persons who do not know the facts. The last time this tale appeared was in the city campaign of 1920, when the faction that fought Sanders in 1908, in 1912, and again, most of them, in 1920, repeated it as one of those evidences that Martin Behrman was always all wrong.

In the first place, the fifteenth ward (Algiers) gave Sanders 705 votes as against 450 for Broussard and 365 for Pujo. Sanders percentage of the total vote in Algiers was a little more than forty-six per cent. This was a higher percentage than he got in the state as a whole, which showed thirty-four and one third percent. The highest he got in any congressional district was in the fifth, where his vote was about forty-four and three quarters percent. In the whole of New Orleans, Sanders' percentage was thirty four percent.

I will give the reasons for the temporary unpopularity of J. Y. Sanders in this article. At present, I am giving the percentage of the official returns. They show that the Algiers vote gave him

33. In the Democratic primary held on January 23, 1912, Broussard received 50,263 votes to Sanders' 40,209 and Pujo's 26,621 votes. In Orleans Parish, Broussard polled 16,672 to Sanders' 12,979 and Pujo's 8,203. Broussard's term in the Senate began in 1915 where he remained until his death in 1918. *Report of the Secretary of State to His Excellency, the Governor of Louisiana, April 1, 1912.*

the highest percentage by far in comparison with the city, the state and the congressional district. Such figures do not show that the leader of the ward, myself, was engaged in any "double cross" business.

Leaving out Algiers, and dividing New Orleans into uptown and downtown at Canal street, you find that Sanders polled thirty-five percent of the vote uptown and thirty-four percent of it downtown. The biggest vote against him uptown was in the tenth ward, where Col. Robert Ewing was the leader, and there Broussard got 1,525, Pujo 582 and Sanders 805. That has some significance as at no time that I know of was Col. Ewing very favorably inclined to Robert Broussard.

Sanders led in the third ward, where Captain John Fitzpatrick was the leader, by a small margin, Broussard getting 1456, Pujo 762 and Sanders 1684. William McCue, another friend of mine, carried his ward for Sanders, the vote in the eight being 746 for Broussard, 257 for Pujo and 1117 for Sanders.

The foregoing are most of the salient features of the situation as shown by the election returns. One or two more remain to be stated to make the situation clear.

In the third congressional district [in south central Louisiana], where the trading that goes on in every campaign reached its height, there was a more strenuous fight on Sanders than in any other, not excepting the seventh. Robert Broussard, the favorite son, was closer to the political leaders there than was Sanders at that time. Sanders had the disadvantage then, among others I will relate more in detail, of being right here in Louisiana making decisions almost every day that were bound to displease many people and always right under the guns of his enemies. Broussard, on the other hand, had the less dangerous job of representing his district in Washington which he did for years to the great satisfaction of his constituents. So, with the exception of his personal following, Sanders had the opposition of one of the shrewdest and most popular politicians Louisiana ever saw and the experienced leaders who felt bound to stand by him.

As a result of this, and the other matters I will herein review, Sanders got a little more than nineteen and one third percent, the exact figures being 19.34 of the vote there.

Arsene P. Pujo, able, clear sighted, and hard working, studious and much respected, but by no means so shrewd a politician as Robert Broussard, was and is a resident of the seventh district [in southwest Louisiana]. He had been in Congress for many years and I have no doubt that the Republican party is glad he is not there now, for he did as much as any other Democrat to put that party "on the blink" in 1912. Pujo's candidacy made it impossible for Sanders to get a majority in the seventh district, but Sanders' vote and that of Broussard were quite close. The returns there showed Broussard 3,465, Pujo 5,312, and Sanders 3,316.

I was not in the confidence of the Good Government League leaders here or in the seventh district at that time. I will not attempt to discuss the situation in the seventh district in detail. But I will say, and I have a right to say, that I think the large Broussard vote in the seventh district was due to the fact that so many of the Good Government League men were with Broussard. Pujo had come out for L. E. Hall and the other League candidates. John M. Parker was for Robert Broussard. If John M. Parker had told Arsene P. Pujo that he was for Broussard, I do not think Pujo would have been so enthusiastic in his support of the Good Government League.

Sanders was at a low mark in the third and the seventh. He did much better everywhere else. I have shown the reason why he did not do so well in these two districts. I have shown also, that so far as I am concerned there was no "double cross." I will now discuss some other features of that election.

Victor Mauberret [Choctaw leader of the Fourth Ward in New Orleans] announced long before the election that he would not ask anybody to vote for Sanders and would not do so himself. Alex Pujol [Choctaw leader of the city's Fifth Ward], who usually went along with Vic Mauberret, felt the same way. So the fourth and the fifth wards were against Sanders long before the primary. The ninth ward was just as badly against him. Leaving Pujo out, the seventh ward votes about two to one against Sanders and in favor of Broussard. This was the influence, more than anything else, of Sanders action on the Locke Law.

The only ward downtown that Sanders carried was the eighth. William McCue and his friends and followers there stood to their guns just as I did in Algiers.

The election returns, and the conditions underlying them, show that above all other things the Locke Law and the Gay-Shattuck Law defeated Sanders in New Orleans in so far as any of his own conduct contributed to that defeat. Those interested in the races and not much concerned in factional or other politics, were solid against Sanders. Many of the lesser politicians simply had to follow their friends on this issue. I never thought so very badly of the Gay-Shattuck Law but I must say that it was not popular. Nowadays it is reported that the liquor men favored it as finally enacted and claimed they "put one over on the prohibitionists."

In addition to these matters, Governor Sanders got no support whatever from those who were foremost in the fight for the Locke Law. I told him immediately after his address, in which he came out against the races, that his stand would not get him one vote. I was wrong. A friend of mine, a newspaper man, tells me he voted for Sanders in 1920 becuase of the Locke Law. I should have told Sanders he would not get two votes. Then I would have been right.

The Item and *The Times-Democrat* fought Sanders day in and day out and never gave him any credit for anything.

Now these papers support the Conservation Commission, a Sanders idea. They condemned it as a part of the "machine" then. Is it any less of a political machine now? It did good work under Sanders, under Hall, under Pleasant and under Parker, but it is practically the same organization.

It was Sanders who started out people really thinking about good roads. He fought for a statewide system of good roads as governor and again as a member of the constitutional convention of 1921. *The Item* and the *Times-Democrat*, when he first ran for the Senate, gave him no credit for initiating any good roads programs.

Nor did they say, when they were fighting Sanders, that he had an unusually hard administration. Not only was he continually rapped, roasted and grilled by *The Item* and *The Times-Democrat* but he was up against the hard choice of going to the Senate or staying with the Panama Exposition project. I have dealt with that in detail, laying particular emphasis on the proof that I had nothing to do with asking him to resign from the Senate and remain as a Governor.

The Locke Law, the Gay-Shattuck Law, some circumstances over which he had no control, and the treatment *The Item* and *The Times-Democrat* gave Sanders which was in some phases I have indicated most unfair and ungrateful defeated J. Y. in 1912. I do not know of any other man who, in the same circumstances, would have done as well at that time in the general administration of the state's affair, in the initiation of progressive ideas or in the situation put up to him by the directors of the Panama Exposition.

If Sanders had given his whole mind and heart to his own ambitions and ignored other considerations, he would not have approved the Locke Law and he would not have resigned from the Senate in 1910. They point to the vote I got later in 1912, when I was opposed by Judge Claiborne for mayor, as indicating that I could have induced our people to give Sanders the same vote. That is pure "bunk."[34]

34. The Good Government League, resolved to defeat Behrman, and the Regulars in the municipal elections on October 1, 1912, put forward Charles Claiborne, a prominent New Orleans businessman and a Leaguer. The New Orleans *Daily Picayune*, in support

The Regulars were solidly together when the local campaign began. Col. Ewing was back with us.[35] The fights in our own ranks that had made some trouble in the state primary were over. I ran on my record and my friends even went to the extent of having moving pictures made of the improvements, streets and school building and so forth, to help me. Every issue but my record had been disposed of. We won on that and nothing else; unless you want to count John M. Parker as one of the reasons for my victory.

I did not think that the absence or the presence of the Hon. John M. Parker anywhere would have affected me by as much as one hundred votes. It is the general opinion, however, that had he not deserted Hall and the [Good Government] League I would have had a harder fight on my hands. When I say he "deserted," I am using *The Item*'s term. Judge Hall used to say "Parker just quit." His reasons for the desertion or the quittance, whichever it was, do not concern this article on Sanders and 1912.[36]

Never in his life, so far as I knew, had J. Y. Sanders made a

---

of Behrman, wrote that no other candidate was better suited to lead the new commission government granted under the city charter of 1912 and that he deserved the honor. His eight years as the city's chief administrator, continued the *Picayune*, qualified Behrman for the position. The paper claimed that Behrman had done more for the city in those eight years than any other mayor in the city's history. Behrman received 23,371 votes to Claiborne's 13,917. New Orleans *Daily Picayune*, October 2, 1912.

35. Colonel Robert "Bob" Ewing, leader of the Tenth Ward and editor of the New Orleans *Daily States*, was once described as the "most insatiable patronage 'grabber' among the Choctaw leaders." Reportedly, at one time Ewing controlled one-fourth of the Choctaw patronage. In the 1912 gubernatorial campaign Ewing broke with the Regulars over their endorsement of John T. Michel. Ewing favored James B. Aswell. Later that same year the colonel joined forces with the Good Government League in their opposition to Behrman in the mayoralty contest. Ewing rejoined the Regulars but bolted again in 1920 to join Governor John M. Parker and the Orleans Democratic Association in their successful drive to oust Behrman. Behrman thought highly of Ewing's abilities and on one occasion reportedly stated that they got along better "when I was agreeing with him." Reynolds, *Machine Politics in New Orleans*, 167, 205.

36. Several months before the election, Parker, one of the main leaders in the Good Government League, left that organization to support Theodore Roosevelt's presiden-

more profound impression on an audience than he did in the speech in which he announced his withdrawal in favor of Robert Broussard. His friends from all over the state held a meeting. I was present but, I must admit, I was not in very good standing with that crowd. Captain John Fitzpatrick was also present. They were cool toward him, also, as they believed we had "knifed" their friend. In the absence of Sanders, they adopted a resolution to stand by him then and in the future. He was sent for and the resolution was read to him.

Then, Sanders addressed them. While he was talking largely about himself, his tone and manner were just as if he were speaking in behalf of a friend. He was cool, collected and seemed to have no great personal interest in the matter. That is, his manner was to that effect. Set down in type, what he said, was far from quiet. I could see he felt convinced that he had not been fairly dealt with. "You can go back home," he said after a beautifully worded appreciation of his friends' loyalty, "and tell your people in the parishes that we were not defeated. We were ambushed."

Sanders left the third [congressional] district and settled in the sixth. Owing probably more to the long continued newspaper campaign against him, he had recieved only 34.59 percent of the vote in that district when he ran for the Senate in 1912. This district elected him to congress in a close, rough fight in 1916 and then gave him a big majority in 1918.

Sanders' vote when he ran [and was defeated] for the Senate against Edwin Broussard and Don Caffery in 1920[37] show that the people were thinking more of J. Y. as he really is than of

---

tial candidacy and the insurgent Bull Moose Progressive party. Many Leaguers blamed their losses in the 1912 municipal elections on Parker and his desertion during such a critical phase of the campaign.

37. The 1920 Democratic primary for the U.S. Senate was very close with Edwin Broussard polling 49,718 votes to Sanders' 43,425. Donelson Caffery, Jr., received 15,563. *Reports of the Secretary of State to His Excellency, the Governor of Louisiana, January 1, 1920.*

what the newspapers said about him when he first ran for the Senate. He carried a majority of the parishes and most of us thought he had the hearty support of Governor John M. Parker.

Many of the Regulars voted against Sanders [in 1920] solely because they believed Parker was active in his behalf. When *The Times-Picayune* came out for Sanders, many people were convinced that Parker was active for him.

As it turned out, the appearances are that the Parker faction and the Regulars both supported Broussard. Yet, in spite of that, and with no organized support whatever, J. Y. Sanders polled an enormous vote and, as I have said, carried a majority of the parishes.

The municipal campaign, in which the Regulars were defeated and the senatorial campaign which ended with Sanders' unexpected defeat, were held at the same time [in 1920]. Sanders and I met in the state capitol, at the elevator, when we were both delegates to the constitutional convention of 1921. We looked at each other for a moment and he smiled.

"Well," I said, as I held out my hand, "we are both in the same boat now. I guess people think we are even with each other." We shook hands. Since then we have been on cordial terms.

7.
Sanders Made Ruffin G. Pleasant Governor in 1916

I dealt with J. Y. Sanders and the election of 1911–1912 and now that I have decided to write some of my impressions and recollections of the events that shaped up the campaign of 1915–1916 I find that I am back with J. Y. once more. One of my impressions is that the "Life and Battles of J. Y. Sanders" would make an excellent political history of Louisiana since he was 21 years of age.

[In 1915] J. Y. Sanders appeared once more with his fighting clothes on. There were many events intervening, of course, and

I may later say a little about one or two that are possibly not fully understood by the general public. This time he appeared at Baton Rouge and within two hours after he got busy he started the state campaign that elected Col. Ruffin G. Pleasant [governor][38] in 1916.

[By 1915] it had become evident to practically everybody in New Orleans that the only way to straighten out the judiciary and taxation situations was to hold a constitutional convention.[39] Governor Hall had tried twice to change the tax situation. The Supreme Court itself, during the fight in the legislature over the call for a convention, announced itself in favor of one; and this at a time when there was a general belief that a convention would change the terms of the members in a general re-organization of all the courts. The late Sol Wexler [New Orleans businessman] realized that the convention was a

---

38. Ruffin G. Pleasant (1871–1937) was governor from 1916 to 1920. Pleasant served as city attorney in Shreveport from 1902 to 1908 and as assistant attorney general from 1908 to 1912. In 1912 he was elected attorney general and served in that position until his election to the office of governor in 1916. During World War I, Governor Pleasant and the state received national recognition for their contributions to the war effort. In the 1916 gubernatorial campaign the Regulars supported Pleasant, and in return the governor dutifully awarded all state patronage in New Orleans to Behrman and the Regulars. Reeves, *The Governors of Louisiana*, 94–95. Behrman stated in these memoirs (Chap. III) that Governor Pleasant was the closest thing to what reformers called a tool of the Ring than any other governor.

39. The movement for a new state constitution began in 1914 when the Louisiana Supreme Court declared portions of the 1913 constitution invalid. In effect it further ruled that Louisiana was to be governed under two constitutions, the one of 1898 and the remainder of 1913. This situation brought great confusion. In 1915 the state legislature, hoping to remedy the problem, approved a call for a new constitutional convention with the provision that the call be approved by the voters of the state. After a heated campaign, the voters rejected the plan for a convention. Its defeat can be attributed to political rivalries and factionalism. Governor Luther Hall and Martin Behrman supported the call for a convention while former governor Jared Y. Sanders and gubernatorial hopeful Ruffin G. Pleasant were against it. The legislature then chose another route, attempting to cure some of the constitutional problems by adding scores of amendments to an already confused document. Luther E. Frazar, "The Constitutional Convention of 1921" (M.A. thesis, Louisiana State University, 1935), 225–26; James W. Prothro, "A Study of Constitutional Developments in the Office of Governor of Louisiana," (M.A. thesis, Louisiana State University, 1948), 89–90.

necessity. He convinced many men who possibly I could not have convinced. Then he got Col. Ewing, Governor Hall and myself together at a luncheon. The political purpose of that was to show everybody that the proposed call was not the measure of one faction.

The fact that we had gotten together was used as the basis of all kinds of nightmare charges of a political deal. If this joint action of the Mayor of Louisiana's biggest city, the Governor of the state, a political leader and newspaper publisher almost always opposed to the Governor and the one man who at that time could speak for the financial interests of the state was anything but an effort to relieve a rotten situation, then somebody held out some information on me.

The best evidence that no wickedness was planned is plain in the fact that when we got together none of us but Hall could possibly have been sure of any great political profit. He would have had the satisfaction of realizing that every one of his campaign pledges had been carried out, for a convention would have done something about the tax situation.

I wanted to be president of the convention. I think I could have been if it had been called. I could not possibly have dominated that convention as Governor John M. Parker and his immediate and most affectionate political followers, with Col. John P. Sullivan as the most prominent, did dominate the convention of 1921. I will give my reasons for that. I would have been blamed, of course, for everything the convention did that was not popular and I must confess that I had some things in mind that would probably have injured me at least temporarily. Perhaps permanently. But I would have made a fight to see to it that none of the country parishes paid less in taxes than New Orleans to the state government in proportion to real values. There is not need, however, for me to dwell on those "might have beens" of 1915.

One of the main contributions to the demand of many citizens for a convention was the fact that nobody knew what was and what was not in the constitution. The convention of 1913, called chiefly to handle the state debt, was limited by its call. The Supreme Court had decided that some things in the constitution of 1913 were null and void and others were good. Then it decided there was no such thing as the "constitution of 1913." Another matter was suffrage. The Supreme Court of the United States [in 1915] had passed on the grandfather clauses of other states and ours was in danger.

This convention of 1915 was to be held almost immediately preceding a state campaign. Whatever it did would be fresh in the minds of the people when they voted on the candidates. Governor Hall pointed this out to me as a reason for not submitting the new constitution to the people. I replied to him that it would be practically impossible to get it by the legislature. In the end this proved to be true. Before the bill was amended, Hall had been convinced that the white voters of Louisiana could be trusted to pass on the new constitution.

With a state primary [1916 Democratic gubernational primary] in the near future, and all the prominent politicians active in the convention or in connection with there was no chance whatever to play any small games of politics. Every delegate and every leader would have known that the people would soon pass on his work and then on him.

But Col. Ruffin G. Pleasant, attorney general, Speaker Lee Thomas, Representative Duncan Bute and others could see no good to come from a convention at that time. They took the position, in general, that holding a convention on the eve of a campaign (even in that campaign) was not good business. They showed no confidence in their ability to fight the leaders of the two factions, state and city, until J. Y. Sanders appeared on the scene. When I heard that J. Y. had hired the Elks Theatre at

Baton Rouge, to make a speech, I knew that we were in for a real fight. Up to that time I felt that the convention would go through with the minimum opposition.

Sanders rallied the unorganized forces against the convention. As soon as he arrived at the capital, those forces showed that they were under a leadership.

There is no need of my reviewing his speech in the Elks' Theatre in detail. It was a masterful address from a political point of view. While some of it was unfair to me personally, none of it was dull. There was "pep" and "push" in every sentence.

The bill was enacted. We elected delegates to the convention in a primary. The campaign against the convention was hot. The parishes became to a great extent convinced that "those bosses" and Governor Hall were in a fearful plot to do them up. The convention was defeated by a big majority. I have heard it reported that one of the men opposed to the convention, a prominent follower of Pleasant, said that some of the majority was due to the fact that in some parishes the leaders knew what the farmers wanted and did not trouble them to call personally at the polls. New Orleans, with both factions favoring the convention and, much to my regret, many citizens taking no interest, voted by more than 18,000 for to less than 2,000 against the convention.

I looked upon the defeat of the convention as, to a great extent, a blow to me. Nothing would have suited me better than to have been president of that convention. I am quite sure that the people would have justified the charges made by its opponents. They would have had time to think things over before they passed on the proposed new organic law. Then Martin Behrman would have been the "Big It," as I was sometimes called without such sound basis in fact. Had I been the presiding officer and appointed the committees of that convention, Louisiana would now have something far better than the constitution of 1921. At any rate, that is the way I felt then and that is the way I feel now.

The defeat of the convention, in the minds of many, left the charges against the Hall faction and the Orleans organization as proved. There was no way to disprove them. When a man charges you with intending to do something and the chance to do it is removed, you are in a sense, "up against it." You can meet him with nothing but the same denials with which you first met him.

The defeat of the convention was also the defeat of a personal ambition of mine. I was to be president as I have said. But I did not feel any bitterness against Sanders, Pleasant, Thomas or Bute. I felt a little resentful, as was natural. But they were within their rights. Whatever they had to say they said in public. While I do not think everything Pleasant put in the circulars issued was entirely fair, yet they were signed circulars and there was no "gum shoe" work as far as I know.

When the state and local campaign were over and I was once more reelected mayor, I began to make guesses to myself on the chances of calling another convention. There was, of course, no opportunity to do that in 1916. There was no session of the legislature in 1917 and there was not a chance to call a special session to submit such a proposal to the people. Moreover, while I did not confer with Governor Pleasant on the subject, I knew he would have been against a special session. But I did think we could have a call issued in 1918—until the United States declared war on Germany. Then I knew that there was no chance of a convention until the war was over.

The defeat of the convention was one defeat in which I shared and for which I have no regrets. I was on the right side. It is pleasant, of course, to be on the right side and the winning side at the same time, but if you've got to lose it is best to lose on the right side.

[Defeating the call for a convention] made J. Y. Sanders

once more a powerful leader in the state and it made Col. Pleasant governor. Many of us were more favorably inclined to [Lieutenant Governor Thomas O.] Barret than to Pleasant.

As Lieutenant Governor Thomas O. Barret of Caddo [Parish] was with the state and the city administrations in the campaign for a constitutional convention in 1915, he was more definitely lined up with the city organization than ever before. The idea that Mr. Barret was in any way an agent or even, in any way, a member of our faction in New Orleans, was prevalent though it was not justified. He had opposed measures of the state administration earlier in the Hall term. He had often voted against a majority of the Orleans delegation in the Senate during his sixteen years as a senator. There was never any doubt at any time that he would vote for the Locke Law in 1908, which he did. Yet his alignment with us in the fight for the convention in 1915 permitted his opponents to represent him as a mere creature of what they called "the Orleans ring," which was not true.

However, as I soon learned in my career as a politician, the important thing at an election, as between the facts and the opinions of a majority of the voters, is that majority opinion. The voters had made up their minds to two things that were not true. One was that the Orleans organization controlled Mr. Barret. The other was that the call for the convention was the result of a political deal for personal profit between Governor Hall and his friends and Mayor Behrman and his friends.

A new faction, as a matter of fact appeared in Louisiana politics. It was a Sanders Faction, for no matter how able and no matter how influential the other members may have been, it was Sanders who organized it at Baton Rouge when he started his fight on the convention. As that fight was successful, the new faction, which never had a name and which was soon a part of the Regulars faction obviously was in a majority in the state.

When the time came for the Regulars to make a choice between the two Democrats seeking the nomination for Governor, they followed their usual policy of going to the candidate who apparently had a majority of the votes in the parishes outside Orleans. It has sometimes turned out that the Regulars did not show accurate judgment in picking a candidate, but they have always preferred to back a man who had the country folk with him. In this instance, they decided on Ruffin G. Pleasant.

One of the reasons for this was that Pleasant was believed to be for local option. Governor Hall, true to his campaign promises, had stood always for local option and had done all he could to keep the liquor question to one side so that the struggle over it would not get in the way of other business.

Pleasant had opposed Governor Hall on many important matters, the most important of which was the refunding of the state debt. He had fought Hall, as I remember it, at every opportunity. Col. Robert Ewing did the same thing most of the time after the first session of the Hall legislature. Both his newspapers, *The States* here and *The Times* in Shreveport gave Pleasant so much publicity that this led to a general opinion that Col. Ewing had picked Pleasant for Governor.

So Governor Hall was for Lieutenant Governor Barret. While the Lieutenant Governor had, as I have said, opposed him on many measures, he was with him on many others.

Then Mr. Barret suddenly came out for statewide prohibition and we had a rather funny argument, from point of view, between the candidates. They debated the point of which of the two was the better prohibitionist. As Mr. Barret had always been for local option, his announcement was a surprise. It certainly surprised Governor Hall.

The only question left in doubt after that announcement was the size of Pleasant's majority. There are thousands of voters who are devoted to prohibition at home so long as they may take a train to Alexandria, Eunice or New Orleans and go wet for a few hours. They are strictly local option. Their option is (or was) to be dry at home and wet when off on a visit. I knew that these would vote for Pleasant.

As attorney general, so far as I know, Pleasant was neither conspicuously able nor bad enough to deserve any unqualified condemnation.

The first big surprise he gave me was more than a mere surprise. It was considerable of a shock. That was when he came out for the national prohibition amendment [in 1919]. He had not committed himself on national prohibition. But he had been elected against Mr. Barret, a state-wider, and had gotten all the votes of the local optionists.

In fact, the vote Pleasant got in the primary was so great as to prove my accuracy in stating that, for the time being, there was a new faction in the state. The alignment of the leaders all over the state was without regard to their alignment in 1908 and 1912. The "reform" faction of these years, insofar as it still existed, was for Mr. Barret. One observer holds that both the old factions voted for Pleasant. My observation indicates that the Sanders or Sanders-Pleasant faction, born in Baton Rouge when J. Y. started his fight on the convention, was joined by the Regulars in New Orleans in the campaign; that these two factions stayed together until John M. Parker was defeated in April of 1916, and that the new faction then disappeared. More on this later.

We had elected Pleasant as a local optionist. He went dry with more than state-wide dryness. That was a surprise.

Just now, however, before going into that Bull Moose affair of 1916, I wish to say that I was most pleasantly surprised at the attitude Governor Pleasant took toward the Orleans organization and myself, in a political way, after he had become governor.

As I have indicated, he undoubtedly had a majority of the country voters with him after Sanders made him the strongest candidate in the struggle over the constitutional convention in

1915. His record, as we knew it then, gave no reason to believe he would not be a good governor. He was personally acceptable, despite some of the attitudes he took as attorney general.

Pleasant's vote [in the January, 1916, Democratic primary] outside Orleans was 54,850 and Barret's was 26,354. So Pleasant got a majority of 28,496 in the parishes. The total vote was 114,519, and Pleasant got a majority in all Louisiana of 54,850.[40]

While our support made him a sure winner and got him the votes of all the "high siders," those who want to vote with the winner no matter what the issue, the appearances were that he had a tremendous strength in the parishes. He seems to have had it, and its name was Jared Y. Sanders. I thought at the time that Sanders' influence with him would probably be considerable of an opposition for the Orleans organizaion at Baton Rouge.

In spite of the certainty of his defeat John M. Parker ran [on the Progressive party ticket]. He attracted considerable attention from *The Item*, *The Times-Picayune* was strong for him when the campaign began but seemed to get weary of it toward the close. This latter, of course, is my interpretation of its symptoms *The Times-Picayune* printed some statements that injured Mr. Parker's candidacy and which I did not believe to be true; and later, as I remember it, found were not true.

Parker had no chance to win on any issue that might possibly develop. Up to the very moment that the returns began coming in, I have been told, he thought he would win.

Platforms do not make issues. They either recognize them or take a stand on them, though it often happens that efforts are made to create issues by all kinds of "hot air" in a platform.

---

40. In the Democratic primary held on January 25, 1916, Barret obtained 30,112 votes to Pleasant's 84,407. In Orleans Parish, Pleasant received 29,557 to Barret's 3,758. In the general election on April 18, 1916, Pleasant polled an almost two-to-one majority over his opponent, John M. Parker: Pleasant's 80,801 votes to Parker's 48,068. In Orleans Parish, Pleasant received 25,827 to Parker's 14,340. *Report of the Secretary of State to His Excellency, the Governor of Louisiana, 1916.*

There were two issues in that campaign, and both of them were against John M. Parker.

In spite of the efforts of *The Item* to ridicule it, the question of whether the negroes should be given an opportunity to cast effective votes was the larger issue. If we have two parties in Louisiana, sooner or later [we] will find that a very largely purchasable, and always "foolable," negro vote will decide many elections. I dealt with that in full some time ago [in Chapter I], so there is no use in repeating details now. My opinions on that matter are too well known to make it necessary for me to repeat their history.

The other issue was whether a Democrat who has voted in a primary has a right to vote against the nominee. There are some circumstances in which, perhaps, he has the right. With practically no negroes on the rolls, this is done generally in many states. But it is not generally done here and it will not be done here until the Federal constitution has been amended so that we may limit the registration absolutely and directly to white men and women.

I do not believe that John M. Parker really favors any kind of equality between white and black men other than an equal right to make a living and common justice in the courts. But, on the other hand, many a man has killed another with a pistol he did not believe was loaded.

I thought then and I still think, and a majority of my fellow citizens in Louisiana agree with me, that the organization of a political party to oppose the Democrats in Louisiana will bring the negroes back into politics. It will not do it in one campaign but if we had another party and it made a good showing in two elections, many registrars of voters would be tempted to register negroes they believe they could control. Once that started, it would grow. Registrars in the other party would do the same thing. Little by little we would get back to the days when a colored preacher was political property with a varying price.

We would not go all the way back to the conditions of 1896.

As soon as it became evident that there were enough negroes on the rolls to turn an election one way or the other, there would be a few race riots, a lot of lynchings and mobbing of negroes. Negroes would be warned away from the polls or shot for going there.

Parker's record made him a very poor candidate as chief of a new party in 1916. The people had not forgotten 1896 and his activity in the Citizens' League. His desertion of Hall and the Hall faction in 1912 to go to Roosevelt, who had entertained Booker T. Washington at luncheon was fresh in the people's minds. Parker admitted that he had voted the straight Republican ticket in some presidential elections.

All these matters influenced voters. The biggest influence was the simple fact that until we get rid of that "race, color and previous conditions of servitude" clause in the [U.S.] constitution, we cannot have two parties and keep the negro out of politics. If that is ever done, we could pass a law giving the vote to white men only. Then we could have two parties in Louisiana. And we Choctaws and our country friends would be the only Democrats.

There are a lot of Democrats in the party who are there because they cannot influence politics from the outside. That is all well and good. It is what we intended in 1898. But plenty of them are Republicans at heart. If the negro could be put out of politics through an amendment to the Federal constitution and a state law, most of these would get into another party.

Parker polled a little less than 49,000 votes, as I remember it, that was considerably less than half the total cast in the Democratic primary. Pleasant's majority was more then 30,000. On the circumstances, this was to be expected. Which suggests the question, why did Parker run?

I have often asked myself that question and I have never yet given myself an answer that I felt sure was the right answer.

It was suggested to me that Parker ran for the advertising. It is not unusual to find a candidate in the field who is advertising himself for another campaign later on. This is, in most cases, legitimate publicity work. But I do not believe Parker then planned to run in 1920, for if he had he would have been in the Democratic primary.

It has been hinted that Theodore Roosevelt wanted him to run. There may be something in that as had a Roosevelt man been elected in Louisiana, thus breaking the "solid South," Roosevelt could have made considerable political capital out of it.

More lately it has been stated that John M. Parker was so disgusted with the Democratic party in Louisiana that he got out and ran in 1916 to set up another party and that he abandoned this effort when he saw it was useless. Perhaps so. But four years later he ran as a Democrat, was elected on the wave of discontent that followed the war and has done nothing as governor to indicate to me that this was the reason in 1916.

I have an idea that he ran simply because he likes the excitement of campaigning, the struggle and battle and all that kind of thing. He likes to be in the public eye. He likes the applause of crowds. I do not mean to insinuate that there is anything discreditable or contemptible in this. There are far worse motives sometimes, behind the conduct of candidates.

This idea of mine that Parker ran for govenor in 1916 just for the fun of it is not inconsistent with other things he had done and still does. Ever since he has been going off to distant places to make speeches. I do not know of any other governor of Louisiana who had done this.

There is not no doubt in my mind that when he got into the Good Government League organization [in 1912] and took over its leadership, apparently, he planned to build up an organization here, to beat the Regulars and then to be the most prominent politician here. It is only lately that I have felt confident that this was behind his work. This opinion is based on consideration of what has happened since then. But, of course, that could not have been his motive in running in 1916. Then he knew he had no chance.

I do not think he has ever had any determination to put across a political or governmental programme other than to seize political power and then to increase it. I base this opinion on his readiness to abandon things he favors whenever he becomes convinced they will not serve that end, and his readiness to jump to any issue that looks like it will.

He had always been against what was called the "ward boss system." He is not against it now and his candidates for local offices here were elected by an excess of abuse of the power of patronage. He was for civil service and he killed off a civil service ordinance in the [1921] constitutional convention.[41] He was for woman suffrage while running for office and appeared to be at least neutral on it when he was governor. He was for the short ballot, and then he forgot it. He was for a short constitution, and we have one [1921] that is far from short.

There is not motive or plan save one that can be attributed to John M. Parker and be sustained in the face of the facts. That one, as I see it, is simply that he enjoys politics and campaigns and speech making. I do not mean to imply that there is anything wrong in that. I enjoyed that myself to the utmost and I intend to enjoy it some more.

But it seems to me that there would be little fun in life for a man who consistently sacrifices his ideas and his preferences to anything so hollow as simply holding an important office or appearing to wield political power. If I had been always back-

---

41. Behrman gives a long discourse on Parker's actions toward civil service in Chapter IV, herein.

ing away from things I preferred or doing things I had denounced all my life, I would not look back on my years in office with any great pleasure.

The man who supports what he likes and prefers and puts across a majority of the measures he favors is the man who really enjoys a term or more as mayor or as governor. There is more real satisfaction in losing a fight for what you approve of than there is in backing down for fear of losing your power. It seems to be that Governor Parker had done considerable backing down.

The peculiarity of it, as I see it, is that he need not have backed down on many of his announced plans. I judge that he was of the opinion that insistence on his promises, direct and implied, would drive away many of the professional and semi-professional politicians who were so solidly with him up to quite recently. Some of them, of course, particularly in New Orleans, are still with him.

These impressions of our present governor [Parker], of whom I have stated so many facts in other sections of my recollections, may be finished with simple statement that he has not been seen from several points of view. We have seen him as "an agitator for a change" during many years, as a campaigner for others, as an unsuccessful candidate, as a successful candidate and, now, as governor and chief of the "ins." What he says and does now is so different from what he said and did in other parts of his career that it may be said, at the very least, that he is good at changing his mind.

This frank statement, of course, will be read as an assault on Governor Parker. I have no apologies to make if it is read that way. But my intention was more to give an estimate as briefly as possible of the man who is credited with having ended my career as mayor of New Orleans. While he has more than once said that he had nothing against me personally, his political speeches have frequently contained some very uncomplimentary estimates of me.

Which suggests what I believe to be the phase of our characters in which the governor and myself are more different than in anything else.

I do not think that anybody will lambast me for saying that I have always been what is called a "steady man." I have worked patiently and hard on both large and small matters. I must admit that as an administrator I have made mistakes but I made them with all the knowledge of the situation that I could get in the time at my disposal.

With all my work and experience in politics, I have at times made political mistakes. I do not claim that I have ever been perfect in anything. I do claim that I have "plugged along," as they call it, and have not jumped to foolish conclusions on false or partial information and denounced and made speeches and then had to back up or to reverse myself.

I do not claim that I have always been calm and dignified and generous in the face of attacks by the opposition. But the occasions on which I have been otherwise have been few.

I do not think I am handing myself a wholly undeserved compliment.

As things turned out, Governor Pleasant was fairly nice to J. Y. Sanders. He supported him for congress [in 1916], I am told, thus recognizing an obligation to Sanders much better than the present governor recognized the same obligation in 1920. But, in so far as appointments in New Orleans are concerned, I believe Governor Pleasant did more for the Orleans organization than any governor ever elected with its support.

As the leader of the Orleans organization at the time, I certainly did not expect Governor Pleasant to appoint any of our enemies to office. On the other hand, I did not expect to come so near to having one hundred per cent of our recommendations go through. I will not state that everything I wanted done was done exactly as I wanted it; but, on the other hand, the local organization had more influence with Governor Pleasant on appointments in 1916, 1917, 1918 and part of 1919 than it ever had with Governors Foster, Heard, Blanchard, and Sanders.

IV

The Reformers' Triumph, 1917–1920

1.

The campaign for state offices in 1919–1920[1] is so recent that it would be a waste of time and space for me to go into other than such larger matters as the charges made against me in connection with the tenderloin, and the reasons for the support the Orleans organization gave Col. Frank B. Stubbs of Monroe. I expect to give my recollections only on such matters as those.

A large number of politicians judged the situation in 1919 better than I did, I did not fully realize the extent or the intensity of the general dissatisfaction with things as they were. Events in the state as a whole showed a spirit of discontent that was deeper than I thought. While hindsight never serves so good a purpose as insight and foresight, I must admit that my hindsight on the events of that campaign is much better than was my foresight.

This applies to many other men who had spent a great part of their lives in politics. It applied to me then and it now applies to many of the politicians who picked the winner [John M. Parker] and backed him and are sorry they did.

---

1. In the Democratic primary held on January 20, 1920, John M. Parker defeated Frank B. Stubbs for the party's gubernatorial nomination by a vote of 77,686 to 65,685. Stubbs, however, carried Orleans Parish with 25,044 to Parker's 20,603. *Reports of the Secretary of State to His Excellency, the Governor of Louisiana, January 1, 1920.*

The first movement against the Regulars was the organization of the Liberty League. It was not able to settle on a [gubernatorial] candidate. Some close friends of Governor Pleasant tried to get the leaders of the [Regular] Orleans Organization to join him in the support of a candidate. That did not succeed. Then Governor Pleasant and all the opposition to the organization in city and country went to John M. Parker.

Col. Stubbs, member of a prominent North Louisiana family, had declared himself a candidate and was active in electioneering. He had announced his candidacy and was not fighting the Orleans organization. He had been prominently mentioned for Governor before he came back from France [after World War I] and *The Times-Picayune*, long before the two sides lined up, carried a political story to the effect that he was developing considerable strength in parishes.

So far as I remember, every other candidate had declared himself against the Orleans organization. It was a question with us of supporting Col. Stubbs or getting out another candidate and I was for Col. Stubbs. I found that the other leaders of the organization were agreeable to the Stubbs candidacy. So we declared for Col. Stubbs.

Later in the campaign, as is usual with *The Item* and *The Times-Picayune*, Col. Stubbs was represented as a mere creature of the Orleans organization, that "ring." The same charge was made against John T. Michel and against Ruffin G. Pleasant.

Governor Blanchard was in office only a few months when he proved the nonsense of that talk. Governor Sanders was in office about half an hour when he proved his independence in advocating a cause that fell short of its purpose in the enactment of the Locke Law. John T. Michel was not elected, but I have good reason to believe that he would have been far less accommodating to us, despite his years of intimate association with most of the Orleans leaders, than was Governor Pleasant. Pleasant was to the time he broke away in 1919, nearer to being what *The Item* and *The Times-Picayune* call "a mere tool of the bosses" than any other governor I have ever known.

I would have been much disappointed if Col. Stubbs, as governor, had acted as did Governor Blanchard and Governor Sanders at the beginning of their administrations or as did Governor Pleasant at the close of his. On the other hand, I would have been surprised if he had made New Orleans something wholly different from any other section of the state in the matter of appointments, as Pleasant did up to the time of the break in 1919. I think we would most probably have had a few disagreements with Col. Stubbs on legislation and appointments and would not have had our own ways all the time but that there would never have been such breaks between us as there were with Governors Blanchard and Pleasant.

As I have said, the people were wild for a change. John M. Parker had the reputation of being against everything that was and had been. That reputation was his greatest asset.

And Parker was not stingy with the promises. He promised civil service, natural gas, short ballot, economy, state enfranchisement of women, fair elections with an honest count, abolition of the political methods called by his supporters the "ward boss system," short constitution and everything else that he could think of. I have only mentioned a few of those promises as a complete catalogue would probably drive ever-thing else off this page.... All in all, John M. Parker promised to change everything with which anybody seemed to be otherwise than completely satisfied and he won the election more on that series of large promises than on anything else he did himself.

J. Y. Sanders is the man who analyzed the sentiment of the people. I do not mean to accuse Sanders of responsibility for Parker's promises. But I learned that, as soon as it became a straight fight between Parker and Col. Stubbs with no chance of a third candidate, the astute Sanders declared that no soldier could win that election. I was of the contrary opinion. I thought the Colonel of the First Louisiana would get more votes on that than would the Food Administrator for Louisiana[2] on his record in that office.

As it turned out, however, Parker's reputation as an agitator for a change gave considerable campaign value to his promises to make a series of wholesale and thorough changes, particularly in the ward boss system. A lot of politicians soon appreciated the fact that a Parker wave was on.

One of these, among the most prominent in Louisiana, visited me at my home just about the time we began to realize that we would have a harder fight than we had expected. He advised we quit the Stubb's candidacy, support Parker and thus avoid a state fight and reduce the chances of a fight in the city to a minimum. I was astonished.

"I promised Col. Stubbs that I would support him," I replied, "and I would rather cut off my right arm than break that promise."

While I realized that Parker would get a large vote, I was not one of those who was either despondent or absolutely sure that he would be the winner. On the other hand, I was unable to change candidates after I had given my word to one of them. I would not have done that if I had known exactly what was coming. The conduct of the other leaders in New Orleans who stayed with their organization then and in the city fight shows that they too believed that they should stand by their given word.

Nor need I to any of them apologize for that stand. It was personally and politically honorable; and, as a matter of what I might call "state patriotism," it was wise.

So far as I am informed, the only promise Parker made that

---

2. Behrman is referring to Parker's World War I service as food administrator for Louisiana under Federal Food Administrator Herbert Hoover.

has met any wide approval in the subsequent performance was the pledge for a larger agricultural college. Col. Stubbs made the same promise, but, I think Col. Stubbs meant the same program that Parker is pushing through. Parker deserves some credit for that, though there are many citizens who doubtless would have preferred a somewhat less ambitious plan and more immediate results through diversion of part of the construction money to the present operations of the Louisiana State University.[3]

Practically all the rest of the Parker programme has been either so handled as to disgust most of his fellow citizens or has been forgotten by Governor Parker. One of the items he has not, perhaps, wholly forgotten is the civil service measure he promised Charles Rosen he would put across in the legislature if he, Rosen, would let it go to sleep in the constitutional convention [of 1921].

None of us need regret our support of Col. Stubbs, as there is no reason whatever to believe that he would have taken a different attitude toward campaign promises than did Governor Hall.

In every state in which there is a city large enough to be a decisive factor in most elections, there is some sentiment in the country sections against whatever political organization may be dominant in the city. This sentiment in Louisiana was nursed along for years by *The Times-Democrat* and later *The Item*. The policy of building up sentiment against the Orleans organization by these papers was so thoroughly carried out that the organization was charged with the responsibility for the defeat of bills which it had heartily supported. This, also, helped the candidacy of John M. Parker.

An amusing phase of the hard work they did to represent me

---

3. During Governor Parker's administration Louisiana State University received a larger annual appropriation and was removed to its present Baton Rouge location.

and my political associates as the promoters of every evil in the city was the "New Orleans Nights" stories in *The Times-Picayune*[4] that included a lot on nights spent outside the city. I was not able to laugh at this at the time, but my recollection of that stuff now makes me smile.

As we are not now having any "New Orleans Nights," I suppose that some will theorize that the election of "the true, the beautiful and the good" has made such nights impossible. Some people might assume that the absence of "New Orleans Nights" in *The Times-Picayune* means the absence of such nights everywhere else. Maybe so. But I would prefer to look over the police reports and converse with the wicked before making any bets that this assumption is correct.

Everything that was true and everything that was not true but might temporarily be accepted as truth was used against Col. Stubbs and the New Orleans organization. Probably the best remembered of the attacks that helped to make the city organization an issue was Charles Rosen's speeches on the tenderloin and the implied charge that I was specially interested in maintaining it, which I intended to discuss later in full.

I knew the day after Stubbs was defeated that any candidate of the Orleans organization would have a hard fight. With the Parker-Sullivan control of the state patronage, the general discontent, the lack of improvements due to the war and the number of enemies I had made in the course of my work as mayor, and the absolute certainty that any organization candidate would be called a "Behrman" there was no easy time in prospect. There is no large business element in New Orleans, and no group of the people that I had not fought at times and what I heard during the weeks after Parker's election showed

---

4. Between January 11 and 15, 1920, the New Orleans *Times-Picayune* published a series of daily articles entitled, "New Orleans Nights, Little Adventures in Devilment," portraying New Orleans as a vice-ridden, wide open city of gambling and prostitution.

that some people remember what you did to them much better than what you did for them, and, in addition, I got sick.

In spite of all that happened, I believe that if the Martin Behrman of 1912 or 1916 had been present in 1920, he would have been re-elected Mayor. A sick man cannot put up the same fight as a man in good health. Moreover, the time lost while I was slowly recovering at Biloxi was valuable.

2.

Reformers and Civil Service

The city's civil service commission was established in 1896,[5] at the beginning of the Flower administration. I was opposed to it then and I am opposed to it now except as it applied to physical examination and tests. It would not be a good thing to select fireman or policemen without physical examination and tests as you need healthy men in such jobs.

The silk stocking element of the old days, known in more recent years as reformers, charged that the ward leaders had a selfish interest in their opposition to civil service. They made it a big or little issue during the many, many campaigns from 1892 down to date and John M. Parker did a great deal to make it as much of an issue as possible.

The reformers were very strong for it and pointed to it as a sure means of killing off the Regular organization just as a lot of them figured that the poll tax requirement would retire us to private life. Later in this article, I will give my reasons for

---

5. Civil service first came to New Orleans in the 1896 city charter (1896 Acts, no. 45) as an attempt to remove city employees from the political arena and to give citizens a more efficient city government. Employees were to be hired by competitive examination and could not be removed without cause. The law had strong opposition especially from the Regular Democratic Organization. In the legislature, the Regulars were able to weaken civil service with a series of bills exempting certain categories of employees from the system, such as employees of the fire department (1898), and the sewerage and water board (1899).

believing that no civil service law would have seriously affected the Regular organization, which did not manage its patronage as does the present organization of ex-regulars and political saints.

At present I wish to point out that not since 1898 and perhaps not even in that year has any faction exercised such complete control of the state and city governments and all Louisiana politics as the present combination of ex-regulars and "regular reformers" who shouted for years for civil service and plenty of it. They and their leader, John M. Parker, got control of the legislature in 1920. They took over the [New Orleans] city government. They controlled a special session of the legislature after they had had their own way in a constitutional con-

---

In 1900 opponents pushed a bill through the legislature which completely "reorganized" civil service. Under the 1900 act members of the 1896 civil service commission were removed from office, and the mayor of the city was given the power to appoint their successors. Over the next ten years most city boards came under the direct control of the mayor. Civil service became a hollow phrase as the selection of employees reverted to the age-old practice of patronage. For example, in 1909 of the 1,063 labor applicants examined, all passed. City employees were appointed for four-year periods, thereby guaranteeing loyalty to the faction in office.

Attempts to place civil service into the 1921 constitution passed in committee but failed on the floor. The convention resolved to leave the question of civil service to the legislature. The Huey Long laws of 1934 and 1935 set up a sham civil service system with a commission to watchdog employees and to follow the instructions of Governor Long.

In 1940 reform governor Sam H. Jones was able to get through the legislature a civil service bill that provided a comprehensive system for the state and municipalities of New Orleans, Shreveport, Bogalusa, Alexandria, and Baton Rouge. The act was to go into effect in 1943, but before it could do so, the Old Regulars counterattacked in 1942 with several successful bills amending the act of 1940. One change in the act was the elimination of prohibitions on political activities by classified personnel.

In 1948 Governor Earl K. Long and the legislature, after a long and drawn out conflict, repealed the 1940 civil service act. Proponents realized that the best assurance for civil service would be in the form of a constitutional amendment. After several attempts, such an amendment was ratified in 1952, creating a department of civil service for the state government and a separate department for the city of New Orleans. L. Vaughn Howard, *Civil Service Development in Louisiana*, Tulane Studies in Political Science (New Orleans: Tulane University, 1956).

vention. Then they had the recent regular session, in which they could easily have enacted any law they sincerely favored and honestly worked for.

Rival factions controlled the state and the city in 1892–96. Rival factions controlled the state in 1896–1900. There were sharp divisions and there was no definite, unquestionable control of the convention of 1898.

During 1900 to 1904, when W. W. Heard was governor and Paul Capdevielle was mayor, there was no chance to hold a constitutional convention.

While Newton C. Blanchard and I were elected governor and auditor by the same faction in 1904, there was a division immediately afterwards and Governor Blanchard did not retain the unqualified support of the city organization.

There was such turmoil and struggle over various issues during the Sanders administration that neither Sanders nor the city organization had the power they might have had if they had agreed.

Rival factions controlled the state and local administrations during the Hall administration.

The war in Europe, into which we went early in 1917, kept the state and city administrations friendly during most of that four years from such complete control of state and city affairs as the present administrations enjoy.

Then, after the war was over, the life-long "reformer" was elected governor and his faction later took complete control of the [New Orleans] municipal government. During the war they called settling in a newly won position "consolidating" the gains. By the time the constitutional convention met [in 1921], Governor John M. Parker and his faction had consolidated practically everything in sight.

I am convinced now that the ardent reformers are as much opposed to civil service as Martin Behrman. I will give my reasons for opposition and make a guess at their reasons. If they do not like the guess, they have the privilege of filing their objections.

I was a member of that convention in 1921 and the civil service matter came up. I fought it then as I had always fought it and during the debate before the committee a disagreement came up between Charles Rosen and John P. Sullivan. Rosen was for the proposal to put civil service in the constitution. At least, he was strong for it before the committee and in the corridors and hallways of the state house.

I do not know where or when or how long Rosen talked with Governor Parker about civil service.... Then it came out that a bill was being prepared in the governor's office to be introduced at the special session that followed the convention. I looked upon that as a good excuse on the part of the "reformers" to drop the subject. I was willing that they should drop it, with or without a good excuse.

That bill that was born in the governor's office died there. It was not introduced at the special session. It was not introduced at the regular session last summer.

I think civil service would injure the Parker-Sullivan faction as it has introduced a new system of handling patronage. They did not limit themselves to giving their followers the jobs but they swelled the pay rolls so greatly for the elections of 1920 that some of the most hard-boiled politicians in the city were taken by surprise. I heard it said at the time that it was hard to get the goods off and on ship because the wharves were so full of Dock Board employees.[6]

6. A long-time foe of machine politics, Parker used the same methods and tactics to defeat Behrman and the Regulars in the 1920 mayoralty campaign that he had for years denounced. After being elected governor in 1920, Parker turned his attention to Behrman and New Orleans. To subvert the Regulars, Parker denied the Choctaw Club all state patronage in the city. Instead he padded the New Orleans Dock Board payroll with anti-Behrman employees. In addition he permitted one of the oldest practices of machine politics in requiring state employees to contribute fixed sums of money to the

Another thing they do is to discharge employees for political reasons during their expected terms of office, not waiting for the end of the four years but making it plain that: "If you do not carry your precinct, you are fired."

The Regular organization had to select men who supported it and had to let them go when they did not support it. They were let out at the end of their terms. There were some jobs completely in its control that were held by men not politically in agreement with the organization. The Regulars never discharged a man right after a minor [disagreement] or "by election" because he had not carried his precinct. Nor did they ever pile up so many jobs and crowd the pay rolls as the present "reform" faction had done.

Had there been a thorough going civil service law on the books in 1920, the O.D.A. ticket would have been defeated. I will discuss some phases of this campaign later but I wish to say not that if I looked at civil service entirely as a matter of politics and getting votes and keeping the other side from getting them, I would have been in favor of a civil service law at that convention.

The idea that civil service destroys political organizations such as the Regulars is all nonsense. I think it is nonsense because it has not to my knowledge destroyed any political organization.

There is a great deal of civil service in the national government. Yet neither the Democratic nor the Republican organizations has been destroyed.

New York City has more civil service, I believe, than any other American city. The Tammany organization wins and loses just about as often as it did before civil service was introduced. The Tammany organization has been in existence almost since the days of George Washington.

---

organization during political campaigns. T. Harry Williams, *Huey Long*, 136; Reynolds, *Machine Politics in New Orleans*, 209–13.

There is considerable civil service in California and Wisconsin. The Robert M. LaFollette[7] and Hiram Johnson[8] organization in those states are the strongest I ever read about. Chicago and Illinois have a lot of it. That does not interfere with [Chicago's] Mayor [William H.] Thompson's[9] faction. From what I have heard and read, I believe there is more civil service in France and Germany than in any other countries. Yet they have their factions and parties just as we do and my impression is that the voters in France are more influenced by the desire for public positions and advancement in them than we are. I hope nobody calls on me to prove this to be true as it was long before the war that I read a magazine article on French politics that gave me this impression.

I prefer the appointive system because it gives better control of the subordinates. My opponents, of course, will come back that I prefer it because it gives control of the political activity of the job holder. But you do not appoint men, politically speaking, because you can get control of their votes but because they are already with you. Such appointments are given more often for what a man had done in a campaign and what he can do on

---

7. Robert M. LaFollette (1855–1925), governor and three-term U.S. senator from Wisconsin, was one of the leading figures in progressive politics in Wisconsin and in the national government from 1880 to 1925. He wrote the "Wisconsin Idea" (direct primaries, tax reform, railroad control, and the utilization of technical experts in government) which formed the nucleus of the progressive movement. In 1911 the senator from Wisconsin helped form the national Progressive Republican party, but the following year lost the party's nomination for President to Theodore Roosevelt. On the international scene, LaFollette was an isolationist opposing Woodrow Wilson's foreign policies and U.S. membership in the League of Nations. In 1924 as the Progressive party's candidate, he made his last and unsuccessful attempt for the presidency.

8. Hiram Johnson (1866–1945), governor and five-term U.S. senator from California, was active in cleaning up corrupt politics in San Francisco during the first decade of the twentieth century. In 1911 he was elected governor of California where he served until taking his seat in the U.S. Senate in 1917. Like LaFollette, Johnson was one of the founders of the Progressive party. In 1912 he accepted the new party's nomination to run for vice-president on Roosevelt's ticket. Johnson served in the Senate from 1917 until his death in 1945.

9. Mayor William H. Thomson of Chicago served three terms, 1915–23.

the job than for what he may do in the future. The system of the old Regulars was to keep experienced men on the jobs and to select good men from their political friends.

There was, of course, a ward division of departments and positions. And there was considerable swapping of jobs. For instance, if a certain ward controlled the patronage of the department of public works, it might happen that neither had a man who would do for the work that fell to his ward. There would be an exchange and everybody would be satisfied.

I do not see that the routine work of the city government has been any less efficient, taken as a whole, than the routine work of the many offices of the United States government under the civil service.

Deep down in their hearts, the real objection of the reformers to the appointive system is that it gives most of the jobs to active politicians. I have dealt with this phase of the subject in discussing Page M. Baker and his ideas, so there is no need of repeating them in full. But now that the combination of ardent reformers and ex-regulars have the jobs, the ardent reformers are strong for the appointive system.

If a majority of the "reformers" of 1920 had been sincerely in favor of a civil service law, we would have one now. If any one of their newspapers really favored it, it would at least have been introduced at the two sessions of the legislature since the convention.

I assumed that they killed the proposed civil service clause offered for the new constitution and did not mention it in the legislature in 1921 or 1922 because they believed it would destroy their "machine." I am not afraid of its effects on the regular organization as a political faction and I never was afraid of it. I prefer the appointive system for administrative rather than political reasons and my consistent opposition to civil service both as an "in" and as an "out" is pretty good testimony to my sincerity.

On the other hand, the conduct of my opponents as "outs" was one way and their conduct as "ins" was the other.

It made a difference who does it. It was a crime for Behrman & Company to do it. It was a statesman's noble action when the others did it.

3.

Close Storyville Says Secretary of Navy

I have now come to the restricted district [Storyville][10] and the part it played in the [city] campaign of 1920, when all of a sudden persons who were not heard from as opponents of the district when it was there became very much wrought up over a dead issue and unexpectedly made it a "live issue" by telling part of the truth and some things that were not true.

When I became mayor, I was soon aware of the fact that the district was a centre of graft. One of the reasons for the election of Edward Stanley Whittaker as chief of police was that he was a bitter enemy, personally and politically, of some men whose interests required them to let the situation in the tenderloin remain as it was. I have told the story of the clean-up that followed Whittaker's election, of the reasons for that election, of the support of it by every newspaper but one in New Orleans.

That one was D. C. O'Malley's paper, *The Item*. Nothing in what we learned of D. C. O'Malley even suggested the use of his name in connection with conditions in the district. He was connected with lotteries, with gambling and with members of

---

10. The restricted district, known as Storyville after its author, Councilman Sidney Story, was created by the New Orleans City Council on January 29, 1897. Municipal Ordinance 13,032 CS (Council Series) read in part: "From the first of October, 1897, it shall be unlawful for any public prostitute or woman notoriously abandoned to lewdness to occupy, inhabit, live or sleep in any house, room or closet situated without the following limits: Southside of Customhouse [Iberville] from Basin to Robertson Street, east side of Robertson Street from Customhouse to St. Louis Street, south side of St. Louis Street, from Robertson to Basin Street." The district was officially closed during World War I. See note 15 below.

the police force that did more than simply overlook these matters. O'Malley's influence with the police had to be broken and whatever political power he possessed had to be destroyed. He and Whittaker were bitter personal enemies. I am making this explanation in this paragraph so as not to be put in the position of charging, even by intimation, that D. C. O'Malley had anything to do with the restricted district. His reasons for fighting Whittaker were not connected with that other matter.

The restricted district known years ago as "Storyville," had been set aside by city ordinance [in 1897]. [A number of businessmen signed a] petition against the Story ordinance which gave the name "Storyville" to the district. They were men who believed their business interests would be injured by removing the scarlet women from certain stretches of Customhouse [Iberville] and Burgundy streets. Aside from that, the ordinance was generally supported.

It was about 1910 that those who did not believe the sytem of segregation or "restricted district" was the best way to handle this phase of life and vice in the big city. They used, as their main argument, that the restriction did not restrict. This, of course, had considerable basis of truth in it. Disorderly houses cropped up here and there in the city and some of them, according to my information at present, existed for years in semi-commercial neighborhoods without any protest from persons living in the immediate vicinity as there was no outward signs of their character.

The late Phillip Werlein, then President of the Progressive Union, was the first to come out with a fight against the existence of the district. I do not now clearly remember whether he ever publicly announced the abolition of the district at that time, but he was for it. As President of the Progressive Union, Mr. Werlein made a fight to eliminate Basin street as part of the district. I think the plan was to move the district back one block as the Terminal Station was immediately opposite the house facing Basin Street.

The Era Club, then led by Miss Jean Gordon and her associates, took up the fight. Miss Gordon and the members of the club protested against the existence of the restricted district and backed Mr. Werlein in his then temporarily modified demand that the Basin street front be screened.[11]

Then a number of ministers came into the fight. The Laymen's Missionary Movement took it up, declaring for the screens and "if possible, wipe out the district."

The Item was the only newspaper in New Orleans, so far as I now remember, that appeared to take any interest in the subject. But *The Item* did not make a fight for the abolition of the district, as I have heard some persons say. It said that conditions here were no worse than in other cities and it stood for the removal of part of the district so as not to be so close to the Terminal Station [on Basin and Canal streets].

The council decided that the screens were not practical unless the whole district was screened on every front and that this could not be done. In the end it was decided to let the situation, insofar as boundaries were concerned, remain as it was. The fight for the removal of part of the district, the Basin street front, and the fight for the abolition of the district had been so confused that at the end of it I issued a statement on the subject.

I pointed out in this statement that nothing had been developed to change the city's policy of setting aside a restricted district. I declared that this was the best policy and then I waited to hear something from the critics. There was no reply from any of the newspapers. The subject was dropped.

---

11. In 1910 Miss Jean Gordon, described as the Joan of Arc of New Orleans, and Philip Werlein, businessman, politician, and social reformer, organized a movement to abolish Storyville. The One Hundred for Law Enforcement, as the organization was titled, was composed of clergymen, businessmen and women activists, with the common purpose of cleaning up New Orleans. Miss Gordon decried New Orleans as a "vile and shameless market place of fallen humanity." Jean Gordon was a nationally known advocate of child labor laws and pioneer in the woman suffrage movement. New Orleans *Times-Picayune*, February 26, 1931; "Cleaning Up New Orleans," *Literary Digest*, March 24, 1917, p. 821.

Some time before the debate I have outlined, a Purity Congress was held and the members of congress handed us a few wallops. I have no record of what they said but my recollections of it is that a great deal of it was true. I have a clipping of an *Item* editorial some days after the congress adjourned. It is an editorial of November 1, 1910, which was generally complimentary to New Orleans. I wish to quote one paragraph of it that appeals to the general subject at present.

"The whole subject is a sad one," said *The Item*. "No practical preferment, personal glory or commercial gain are to be gotten from an attempt to make conditions better. Anyone who accepts service on a commission appointed to handle it is bound to come in for a great deal of unreasonable criticism, no matter what his course may be. At the same time it is a great deal better to do something than to do nothing in a matter of this sort."

I quote the foregoing as a fair statement of the truth. The nature of the subject was such that neither I nor those who opposed me in this matter could get any glory or gain out of it. Had I seen anything else to do than to let the situation remain practically as it was, I would certainly have done it, however, as I knew that my position would give my enemies an opportunity to represent me as believing in, standing for and advocating every evil in any way connected with this matter.

In another paragraph, *The Item* apparently sustained my position. Remember, though, that this was in November of 1910, many years before the campaign in which Mr. Charles Rosen became interested.

"As a matter of fact," said *The Item* on November 1st, 1910, "many of the more advanced students and experts on problems of this kind thoroughly approve of the system adopted by New Orleans and it may be said truthfully that we are ahead of the times rather than behind the times in matters of this kind."

That is, in 1910 the city administration stood just where it had stood for many years in that and other terms of office and it was ahead of the times all the time.

The fight started on the basis of moving the district on account of the Terminal Station died down. I do not remember just now that there was anything done in a way that attracted newspaper attention until 1914. With the exception of two clippings from *The Item* in 1910, I have no memoranda on the earlier history of the fight to abolish the district. If anything was done in the newspapers between 1910 and 1914, I am entirely willing to discuss it or debate it with any citizen or editor who will dig up the information and present it to me personally or in the newspapers.

In those four years, however, Solomon Wolf practically took charge of the fight against the district in the sense that he gathered information, studied it and picked out that part of it that he believed applied here. He and Miss Jean Gordon and some others who never gave up a fight until they have won kept up their agitation. I believe if Miss Gordon had been in the Confederate Army she would still be carrying a gun and debating constitutional points about secession. she has never given up even in the fights she has lost.

If there had been any newspaper advocacy of it, I would be sure on this point. But I am getting it down in these recollections so that I may not be accused of neglecting anything that I might have said in the limited space I can give to this subject.

I must say, however, that if such a bill was introduced I opposed it. That is, if I had had enough support to make a fight against it necessary, I would have made the fight. Were we not, as *The Item* said, "ahead of the times rather than behind the times" in this matter in 1910 and thereabouts?

A bill was introduced in 1914.[12] There was a hot fight in the legislature over it and the bill was killed. It received no newspaper support whatever from any newspaper in New Orleans.

---

12. In 1914 a bill was introduced into the state legislature to abolish the restricted district (Storyville). It was, however, effectively killed by the Choctaw-dominated New Orleans delegation. Reynolds, *Machine Politics in New Orleans*, 158.

This may have been due to something in the bill itself and it may have been due to the fact that this was a very "fighting" session, with taxes, politics and a strong threat of a prohibition bill that created a general tangle, much confusion and a great deal of excitement. When the fight was over, *The Item* printed a list of the members of the house of representatives who voted against the injunction and abatement bill with something to the effect that they stood for conditions as they were.

A vote against that bill of 1914 (of which I have no copy) does not mean, on the face of it, that the member so voting is in favor of dissipation, drunkenness and disease. Such a vote might very well be cast in an honest belief that the bill would not result in a law that would not gain its object and that perhaps it takes in too much ground.

As most of my readers remember, the war in Europe began less than a month after that session of the legislature adjourned. We had an unusually strenuous "off year" in politics and then the struggles of 1915 and 1916. Nothing about the tenderloin was injected into the campaigns. I rather think that strong newspaper support would have passed the bill in 1914. I know that newspaper advocacy of it would have put an anti-tenderloin plank in the Louisiana Bull Moose platform of 1916.

Shortly after we began mobilizing for the war, developments attracted considerable attention to the necessity of preventing men in the service from contracting disease. One of the phases of this is expressed in a quotation from something of Kipling's that was used in comment by a visitor at the City Hall. That was: "Single men in barracks don't grow into plaster saints." No kind of men do that. Not only in New Orleans but in every city and town that had any number of soldiers or sailors they had the same trouble. There was considerable trouble in connection with Camp Nicholls, near the City Park, that had nothing whatever to do with any restricted district.

After thinking the matter over, I called together the commanding officers of every branch of the service in New Orleans. They wanted men kept out of the district. They were right. I suggested that they should issue an order to that effect and establish a cordon of guards around the district and that these, assisted whenever necessary by the city policy, would keep all uniformed men out of the district. This was done.

Some soldiers and sailors adopted the ruse of borrowing civilian clothes and thus getting by the guards. Others did the same thing to get a drink now and then. Some of them were caught at this and were returned to their camps or stations under arrest. There is no regulation or law that cannot be "beat" by a few if hundreds try to get around it.

So far as I know, the relations between the military and the district were satisfactory to the commanding officers stationed here when a representative of the commission headed by Raymond Fosdick called on me at the Mayor's Parlor. He presented an order for me to close the district.[13]

"I think you'd better hold this up a while," I replied to him, "until you hear further from the Secretary of War [Newton D. Baker], I will communicate with him and if he gets the facts about the local situation in New Orleans he may recall this order."

Those may not have been the exact words I used, but they clearly represent a request that he consult further with the Secretary of War, whom I felt sure was not fully informed as to the situation in New Orleans. He refused to do this. Then I requested him to consult with the army, navy and marine corps commanders in New Orleans. He replied that he would not do so. Then I told him I would not accept that order and would not obey it until I had seen the Secretary of War.

---

13. During World War I, Raymond Fosdick, a member of the Navy Department, led a special federal commission, the Federal Commission on Training Camp Activities, to investigate and eliminate places of vice near military bases in the United States. "Raymond B. Fosdick," *Literary Digest*, (April–June, 1917), 1852.

That refusal was the sole basis of the charge that I refused to obey orders of the Government to close the district. In view of what had happened before that interview and what happened afterwards, it is perfectly apparent that the charge was not true. All I had asked for was that the man who had the real authority in the matter should be informed of the facts. That man was Newton D. Baker, Secretary of War.

I knew that I would be subjected to severe criticism for any results that followed anything I did in this situation. In order that there might be no misrepresentation of what I did, I called a meeting at the City Hall. Among those present were John M. Parker, Marshall Ballard of *The Item*, D. D. Moore of *The Times-Picayune* and Frank B. Hayne. As their names were later mentioned publicly in connection with this matter, I mention them now.

If the others present wish to debate what happened and the difference between it and the charges made . . . in 1919, I am willing to go into a general debate. My health has improved so much during the past two years that I have recovered my well known love of conducting an argument I know I can win.

The gist of my talk at that meeting was that I believed things should be left just as they were in the district.

No reports of this meeting at the City Hall appeared in any of the newspapers. I think that was proper as we were in the war and no good could have come from a fight in New Orleans on this question.

Yet there was no secret about what I intended to do at Washington. The fact that I had gone there specially to discuss the vice situation here with the Secretary of War was known to all persons connected with or actively interested in politics before I arrived in Washington. I repeat now what I said at the close of the campaign on January 18th, 1920, on this point: "It was then that I made the trip to Washington," I said in my speech after reciting some details already mentioned in this article, "and I told the editors of *The Item* and *The Times-Picayune* of my visit."

My political opponents, with Charles Rosen as their spokesman in chief, attacked me as "King of the Tenderloin" for doing what I thought was to the best interests of the soldiers, sailors, and marines and the city.[14] Thinking that death might possibly remove the participants in the conversation with Secretary of War Baker, I asked that a written record be made of that talk. It fits in now as the testimony of three others present as to what did happen and the attitude I expressed in Washington. One of the letters I have, dated April 20th, 1920, is from Senator Ransdell and Representative Dupre. The other was addressed to them by Newton D. Baker, the Secretary of War, April 26th, 1920.

> We are in receipt of your recent letter asking us to give you our recollection of an interview that you had with the Secretary of War in regard to the closing of the restricted district in New Orleans, and in reply beg to say:
>
> As we recall it, that interview took place some time in August 1917, and there were present the Secretary of War, yourself, the late Senator [Robert] Broussard, and the late Congressman, [Albert] Estopinal and ourselves. You stated that you had come to confer with him on a matter of importance, and that after expressing your views you would be guided entirely by his decision in the premises. You thereupon discussed with him the question of closing the restricted district in New Orleans, a request to that effect having been made to you by a representative of the Fosdick Commission.
>
> You outlined the steps that had been taken with a view to preventing soldiers, sailors and marines from entering the district both by your order to the police and by the maintenance in the district of a provost guard from the various branches of the military service, and expressed your belief that in this way the uniformed men

---

14. Behrman is reported to have once said with regard to prostitution: "You can make prostitution illegal in Louisiana, but you can't make it unpopular." Williams, *Huey Long*, 130–31.

would be better protected than if the district were closed and the women scattered throughout the city beyond police or military surveillance.

Secretary Baker, referring to his own experience as Mayor of Cleveland, took the position strongly that a restricted district was not the best way to handle this difficult situation.

The final result of the conference was that the matter would be allowed to remain in status quo, no further steps looking to the abolition of the restricted area to be taken by you until further word from the Secretary, but renewed assurance was given by you that whatever decision the War Department reached in the premises you would comply with its every request and co-operate fully.

The letter written by Secretary Baker at the request of Senator [Joseph] Ransdell and Representative [Garland] Dupre on April 26th, 1920, and addressed to them, is as follows:

With regard to your request that I endeavor to recall, as far as possible, an interview held in my office in August, 1917, at which were present the Honorable Martin Behrman, Mayor of New Orleans, Senator Broussard, Senator Ransdell, General Estopinal, Mr. Dupre and myself, I beg leave to say that Mayor Behrman's call was with reference to a request made upon him as mayor that the so-called restriced district in New Orleans be closed in the interest of the soldiers, sailors and marines in training there.

Mayor Behrman strongly urged the view that the closing of the district would scatter its inmates and make police surveillance more difficult, I urged upon him the experience I had had in Cleveland when such a district was closed without the result he feared.

I further told him, however, that my proper interest in the matter was limited to the protection of soldiers, sailors, and marines, and that if the steps taken by him and by the military and naval authorities proved adequate to prevent the danger which we were seeking to avoid, I would not feel justified in imposing an arbitrary solution of the question against his judgment as the representative of the people of New Orleans.

It was thereupon decided to allow the experiment to continue until its results could be ascertained.

Mayor Behrman, in the meantime, professed himself most desirous of aiding the Government in the protection of its uniformed men, and willing to adopt any course finally decided to be necessary by the Secretary of War.

These letters are in complete accord with what I said in January of 1920 on the subject. I had refused to obey the order of the Fosdick Commission until I saw the Secretary of War. He was sufficiently impressed by what I told him to hold up the order and watch the results here. I did not get another order from him but some time later one came from the Secretary of the Navy, [Josephus] Daniels.

I had gone as far as I thought I ought to go in impressing my opinions on one member of the cabinet and I did not care to go farther.

So when the order came from Mr. Daniels I immediately had an ordinance drafted and I introduced it myself. It passed.[15]

The next incident was the "Yarborough case" in which two policemen were convicted of an attempt to levy blackmail on a respectable woman whose husband had taken a house for his family in the area of the old district. The policemen were sent to the penitentiary. The way this matter was subsequently handled in *The Times-Picayune* was intended to suggest that I was in some way responsible for this occurrence. I wish to say, in connection with this matter, that it was the opinion of a good many informed persons that these men were not guilty.

"New Orleans Night," a special feature printed by *The Times-Picayune* with many nights outside New Orleans included, fitted in nicely with the blackmail case and the speeches [Charles] Rosen made in their attempt to hold me responsible for everything in sight.[16] Not merely responsible

---

15. New Orleans Municipal Ordinance 4656 CCS, October 10, 1917.

16. Behrman was rather candid in his memoirs in describing Charles Rosen's mercurial position in New Orleans politics:

Charles Rosen fought me when I was first elected Mayor in 1904. I do not remember just where he stood in 1908. He was for John T. Michel and then for me in 1912. He

The Reformers' Triumph 313

for them, but that I was actually guilty of promoting every evil in the city was the meaning of the *T.P.*'s [*Times-Picayune*] handling of this campaign.

The mistake I made in the state [and city] campaign[s] of 1919–1920 was in almost ignoring ... [those] speeches until the close of the campaign. I was of the opinion that the public would probably ignore these speeches as the district had been closed and I had announced that it would stay closed; and, in addition, because of the obvious hypocrisy of his attacking me on a dead issue on which he had not raised his voice when it was alive. When I saw the effect of my silence, I spoke.[17]

---

disposed of his record as an opponent of that horrible "ward boss system" in 1912, by explaining that the primary law had either done away with the wicked bosses or had cleaned them of their wickedness. Mr. Rosen remained on friendly terms with that "ward boss system" until we did not support him for the proposed constitutional convention in 1915. He, as we soon learned, was back with the true, the beautiful, and the good, the Bull Moose, the Orleans Democratic Association, that Jambalaya of politics known as the "New Regulars" and others opposed to the horrible ward bosses.

I must not neglect to say, however, that he was very good at nursing a grudge. The grudge he had against me for not getting him the support of the organization in 1915 for the convention was an honorable grudge. I must say it was an honorable grudge because I have myself at times grudges against folks who would not support me when I ran for office. But I have never called my emotions and high principles in such matters anything but a plain grudge. Rosen, on the other hand, probably believes that the proper thing for a man with a grudge is to get on a high pinacle of virtue and make a lofty speech.

17. From August 25 to September 14, 1920, the New Orleans *Times-Picayune* kept up a constant and unrelenting attack on Behrman. It carried daily front page spreads "exposing" Behrman's record, especially concerning vice, poor street conditions, and the city debt. Damaging articles and photographs appeared showing the neglect in street paving, drainage and garbage collection. In defense Behrman asked, "Why don't these damnable, slimy, unfair, newspapers print pictures of the avenues and pretty places?" The New Orleans *Times-Picayune* also charged that policemen were stationed in the city's "dives" to protect gamblers and underworld characters. In a series of articles entitled "Under the Shadow of Vultures' Wings," reporters claimed that saloons, gaming parlors, and houses of prostitution, were allowed to exist by the police and Behrman. Towards the end of the campaign, the *Picayune* made an appeal to Behrman's supporters to defect and join the opposition, the Orleans Democratic Association (O.D.A.):

> On the Road to ODA: The Plaint of the Long Suffering Regular.
> In the City Hall, while idling, thinking anxiously the while,

Miss Jean Gordon, Mr. Solomon Wolf and the others who were against the tenderloin for years before it was closed had every right to attack me all they pleased on this issue. *The Times-Picayune*, so far as I remember, had never taken any position on the subject. *The Item* had taken the position that the subject was properly one for discussion and that some kind of a local committee should look into it. No newspaper in New Orleans openly and unqualifiedly declared for the abolition of the district and made a fight for it. They had their chance in 1910 and again in 1914. In the first instance, Miss Gordon and others tried to start a fight. In the second, an "injunction and abatement" law was up in the legislature.

When I told the facts of my visit to Washington, I used the following paragraphs:

"*The Times-Picayune* and *The Item* are critical enough to ask why I went to Washington. They knew I went to Washington because I told the editors of both papers why I was going before I went. There was no secrecy about my trip to Washington.

"I ask the people to decide whether *The Times-Picayune* and *The Item* could have been prevented by me from publishing my purpose in going to Washington if they did not agree with me that I was doing the right thing."

> There's a Regular a-gazing at his fading salary pile,
> And the wind above the rafters seems to whisper, soft and low:
> "The Behrman ship is sinking; don't you think it time to go?"
> Hurdle to the ODA
> Where you'll get an even play.
> Can't you feel the ring a-slipping'
> As it totters on its way?
> On the road to ODA
> You can keep your monthly pay,
> With no Choctaw Club a-waiting' for it is just across the way.

The unceasing attacks by Governor John M. Parker, the O.D.A., and the New Orleans *Times-Picayune* were successful: Andrew McShane, a New Orleans businessman, defeated Behrman by only 1,450 votes (22,986 to 21,536). The O.D.A. also captured four of the five seats on the city council. The fifth, the only seat won by a Choctaw, went to Paul Maloney, Behrman's 1925 opponent.

Both these newspapers mentioned this as an attempt to make it appear that they joined me in what I did. I did not intend to set up any such impression. My idea was, and remains, that they were both willing to have me go ahead and do whatever I thought was best and then take the approval or the disapproval that would follow the results. I did think then and still think now that they had no right to attack me on the basis of anything but the final result, which was to close the district, when I got an order, issued by the Secretary of the Navy after he certainly had learned all the facts, to close it.

The general tone and temper of the meeting at the City Hall, which was reported at the time in the newspapers, was that they had confidence in my intentions. John M. Parker personally expressed confidence in me. Frank B. Hayne proposed that a motion of confidence be offered. Marshall Ballard offered the motion D. D. Moore seconded it.

Next in importance was the big wave of discontent that followed the war. Without ever having done anything but criticize and agitate, John M. Parker had made an impression of being against everything. It happened that the people were in the frame of mind of being against everything. They seemed to be against the war itself, in their hearts. Col. Stubbs was a soldier. That is what settled the state campaign.[18]

18. On a national level, many historians, such as Richard Hofstadter, interpreted the post–World War I mood of the nation as one of disgust and frustration with "progressive politics" and "civic participation." Woodrow Wilson's defeat in 1920, wrote Hofstadter in his Pulitzer Prize winning *The Age of Reform*, was a repudiation of the progressive spirit which had led the country into war. Perhaps Behrman was closer to the mark in saying that the people were against everything, even the war itself. The people were not so much against progress, in New Orleans at least, as they were against the vice and corruption that was being tolerated by politicians in office. One must also remember that John M. Parker had long been remembered and associated with progressive politics on the city, state, and national levels. The twenties were a continuation of an era of self-righteousness that fostered American participation in the war, antigambling laws, prohibition, religious fundamentalism, and the Ku Klux Klan. Richard Hofstadter, *The Age of Reform: From Bryan to F.D.R.* (New York: Random House, 1955), 281–82. See also George B. Tindall, *The Emergence of the New South, 1913–1945*, Baton Rouge:

Then Governor Parker used the state patronage exactly as he had criticized other governors for using it. The dock board alone controlled more votes than the number that turned the fight against me.

My defeat in 1920 was due to many causes. The very fact that I had been mayor for so long means that I had accumulated enemies. No matter what you do in public office, you still make enemies. Sixteen years of enemies is a lot of them.

Louisiana State University Press, 1967), Vol. X of Wendell Holmes Stephenson and E. Merton Coulter (eds.), *A History of the South* (10 Vols.; Baton Rouge: Louisiana State University Press, 1949–), Chap. 6.

Epilogue

The combined efforts of Governor Parker and the Orleans Democratic Association defeated Martin Behrman and the Choctaw Club in 1920. The O.D.A. was a loosely knit organization composed of old silk-stocking reformers and renegade Regular Democrats with the common goal of defeating Behrman. Once the objective had been achieved the coalition degenerated into petty factionalism, which eventually permitted the return of the Old Regulars to power.[1]

Behrman did not retire from New Orleans politics after his rejection in 1920. He stepped aside, assessed his position and planned his comeback. The old Choctaw's first step back into public life was his election to the 1921 state constitutional convention.

During the 1919 gubernatorial campaign both Parker and Stubbs called for a new convention. Parker referred to the 1913 constitution as a "patchwork" document containing more amendments than all the other forty-seven state constitutions combined. With an eye on the 1920 New Orleans municipal elections, Parker believed that it would be a mistake to convene the convention until after the city elections. "For under no circumstances," he said, "must it be a political convention."[2]

---

1. Allan Sindler, *Huey Long's Louisiana: State Politics, 1920–1952* (Baltimore: Johns Hopkins Press, 1956), 41.
2. Luther Edward Frazar, "The Constitutional Convention of 1921" (M.A. thesis, Louisiana State University, 1935), 82–83, 99.

The movement for a new constitution had begun in 1914 when the state supreme court declared provisions of the 1913 state constitution invalid. It further ruled, in effect, that Louisiana was to be governed under two constitutions, the one of 1898 and the one of 1913. This situation obviously brought great confusion. The next attempt to remedy this intolerable situation was in 1915. The state legislature approved a call for a new constitutional convention with the provision that the call be approved by the voters of the state. The voters, however, rejected it. The defeat of the 1915 call for a new constitution could be attributed to political rivalries and factionalism. Governor Luther Hall supported the measure while gubernatorial candidate Ruffin G. Pleasant and Jared Y. Sanders opposed it. After having its hopes for a new constitution defeated, the legislature chose another route to cure some of the constitutional problems. In the 1916, 1917, and 1918 session it approved scores of constitutional amendments which in the long run only added to the confusion.[3]

Probably the governmental agency to suffer most under the hodge-podge charter was the judiciary. The court structure, because of constitutional restrictions, became more and more ineffectual. Some court dockets were overcrowded causing litigation to bog down for years, while other courts were idle. The Louisiana Bar Association held a convention in Baton Rouge in May, 1919, for the sole purpose of pointing out to the people and the legislature the dire need for a new constitution.[4]

The first act of the state assembly in the 1920 session was to call for a constitutional convention to meet in 1921. One hundred and eighteen delegates were to be elected from the parishes based on the apportionment in the house, sixteen from

---

3. *Ibid.*, 225–26; James Warren Prothro, "A Study of Constitutional Developments in the Office of Governor of Louisiana" (M.A. thesis, Louisiana State University, 1948), 89–90.

4. Frazar, "Constitutional Convention," 226.

Epilogue 319

the congressional districts and twelve to be appointed by the governor. In deciding what qualifications a prospective delegate had to possess, Ruffin G. Pleasant suggested that "every citizen" of the state be eligible "whose ancestry immediately previous to the discovery of America by Christopher Columbus in the year 1492, Anno Domini, inhabited any part of the earth north of the 20° north latitude, as shown by historical and anthropolitical evidence." In other words, blacks were not permitted.[5]

The convention hit snags in the legislature even before it met. The Regulars and representatives from the hill parishes of northern Louisiana demanded that the new constitution be submitted to the voters for approval. Parker and his allies resisted, believing that the constitution would be seriously compromised if it went to the people. Parker had his way; the ring and its supporters were defeated by a vote of 59 to 35.[6]

At the convention Behrman quietly and dutifully assumed positions on such important committees as Rules and Procedures, Public Education, Affairs of the City of New Orleans, Municipal and Parochial Corporations, and Affairs, Taxation, Equalization and Exemptions. In each case he was merely a member and usually surrounded by political opponents as exemplified by the Affairs Committee for the City of New Orleans. Behrman's fellow committeemen, Esmond Phelps, Charles Claiborne, Charles Rosen, all O.D.A. members, were appointed to the convention by Parker.[7]

Behrman, seemingly satisfied in being merely a part of things, did not exhibit his old exuberance. In fact, the entire convention began on a low key. The New Orleans *Item* commented that nothing would be accomplished until "there's a big

5. *Ibid.*, 227; New Orleans *Times-Picayune*, January 31, 1920.
6. Frazar, "Constitutional Convention," 86–87.
7. *Official Journal of the Proceedings of the Constitutional Convention of the State of Louisiana, 1921* (n.p., n.d.), 90, 92, 209, 640.

sharp difference of opinion and a consequent scrap." The *Item* described the proceedings as a "stage of ordinances—ordinances to the uttermost—ordinances without stint or limit," and a "morass of parliamentary procedure." "Scarcely a week passes," observed the paper, "but what someone introduces a heavy bill such as that all red-headed and brown eyed attorneys who were born in the dark of the moon on a cloudy Thursday morning shall be exempt from paying an occupational tax." The convention was about as "interesting as an inventory clerk's requisition for additional ink erasers."[8]

The New Orleans *Item's* coverage of the convention was misleading. Behind the scenes and in the caucuses there was much debate and wrangling over a number of issues such as civil service, severance tax, state income tax, and good roads and highways. Ironically, in the case of civil service, the conflict was not between Behrman and Parker, but between Parker and a number of his New Orleans allies, led by Charles Rosen. The dispute arose during the convention between John Sullivan, the Choctaw defector to the O.D.A. in 1920, and Rosen. Rosen demanded that civil service be added to the constitution in the form of an amendment. Parker, yielding to Sullivan's pressure, fought and defeated Rosen's proposal. Parker allowed a rumor to be promulgated that he was preparing a civil service bill which he planned to introduce to the next session of the legislature after the convention. The bill, however, was never introduced and died in the governor's office. Behrman, also opposed to civil service, viewed Parker's tactic as a mere excuse to avoid the issue. During the 1920 New Orleans municipal election Parker had built a loosely knit machine on patronage and he was not about to do away with the only power he had over his shaky organization. With regard to backing Sullivan, Parker was afraid that if he did not submit to the former Choctaw ward boss,

8. New Orleans *Item*, March–April, 1921.

Sullivan would bolt the coalition and return to the Regulars. Parker's stand on civil service also cost him one of his strongest political allies in New Orleans, the *Item*. From that point on, the *Item* opposed the governor and his New Orleans group.[9]

Behrman, whose machine was based on the patronage system, was quite philosophical in his denunciation of civil service. There was civil service in the national government, he said, yet it did not destroy either the Democratic or Republican organizations. California and Wisconsin had civil service, yet Hiram Johnson and Robert LaFollette had two of the strongest organizations in the country. The old city boss preferred the appointive system because it gave him better control over his subordinates. "You do not appoint men because you can get control of their votes," he figured, "but because they are already with you." He rationalized that the city government had been no less efficient than the federal civil service.[10]

Behrman's own contributions to the constitution were slight; he offered only one ordinance and two resolutions. His ordinance, entitled, "An Ordinance Relative to the Nomination of Officials," was an attempt to set up a one-parish-one-vote primary system in the state. The measure also included a provision that if approved would treat each ward in New Orleans as a separate parish in determining a party nominee for office. One may get the impression from a cursory reading that Behrman's plan was quite democratic, at least in New Orleans, for the people in each ward would have a voice in the selection of a nominee rather than treating the city as a single unit. On the other hand, the reader must remember the structure of the Choctaw Club caucus, which was composed of the city's ward

---

9. Matthew Schott, "John M. Parker of Louisiana and the Varieties of American Progressivism" (Ph.D. dissertation, Vanderbilt University, 1969), 386; New Orleans *Item*, November 1, 1922.

10. New Orleans *Item*, November 1, 1922.

leaders. Seventeen votes instead of one would give the machine an even greater voice in state politics. However, Behrman's ordinance was killed in committee and never adopted. Although his primary proposal was defeated, his two resolutions, one pertaining to the relocation of the Marine Hospital in New Orleans and the other simply a procedural suggestion, were both accepted.[11]

Behrman supported a number of other important measures such as those calling for the inclusion of a severance tax on natural resources and for a good road and highway system. The former mayor and almost the entire convention also supported Harry Fitzpatrick's call for "unalterable allegiance to the exalted and paramount principle of maintaining purity of [the white] race, now and forever."[12] Fitzpatrick's resolution was merely a reflection of the attitudes of that era; it was never regarded with the same seriousness as the severance tax and highway system issues.

One of the primary goals of the progressives in the rural South was for an updated highway system.[13] At the Louisiana 1921 constitutional convention good-road advocates proposed that the state issue bonds to build highways and bridges. Parker's principal advisor was Jared Y. Sanders, who was opposed to the

---

11. *Proceedings of the Constitutional Convention, 1921*, pp.365, 980, Resolution 6 and 131, pp. 15, 605.

12. *Ibid.*, Resolution, 123, pp.600–601.

13. The demand for new and improved roads was one of the primary concerns to southern progressives during the first decades of the twentieth century. From 1920 to 1929 expenditures for road construction increased 157 percent. Surfaced rural roads increased from 69,797 miles in 1914 to 121,164 miles by 1921. Between 1921 and 1930 the total miles in surfaced roads in the South rose to 209,880 miles. Francis Butler Simkins wrote that "Southerners espoused highway construction with as much enthusiasm as they accorded industrial and educational progress. Good roads became the third god in the trinity of Southern progress." George B. Tindall, *The Emergence of the New South, 1913–1945* (Lousiana State University Press, 1967), Vol. X of Wendell Holmes Stephenson and E. Merton Coulter (eds.), *A History of the South* (10 Vols.; Baton Rouge: Louisiana State University Press, 1949–), 232, 256–57; Francis Butler Simkins, *A History of the South* (New York: Alfred A. Knopf, 1947), 474.

issuance of bonds and advocated a pay-as-you-go plan financed by gasoline and vehicle taxes. Under Sanders' plan automobile and truck licenses would be raised from $5.00 to $15.00 and $25.00 respectively with an additional one-cent tax on gasoline. New Orleans newspapers denounced Sanders' plan as "too cautious" and discriminatory against New Orleans for it would deny to the city money for street paving.[14]

The greatest issue during the convention was the severance tax on Louisiana's abundant natural resources. In 1919 Parker, under pressure of Commissioner of Public Service Huey Long, announced that he would support an increase in the severance tax. Under the confusion of the constitutions of 1898 and 1913, the state was not getting a fair share of the profits realized by companies exploiting its natural wealth. After Parker was inaugurated he called together the representatives of those companies most affected by an increased severance tax.[15]

The corporations, especially Standard Oil, argued that they would not pay more than 1.5 percent, but compromised with Parker at 2 percent. To quell their fears, Parker promised in a gentleman's agreement that the tax would not be raised during his administration. Even with this assurance the corporations still expressed doubts, so Parker told them, "You gentlemen can write it." The 1920 severance tax law, written by the Standard Oil Company, was passed as a license law because a severance tax law would have required a constitutional amendment. Parker wanted to save that for the 1921 constitutional convention.[16]

At the convention many of the delegates preferred a 3 percent severance tax with a percentage of it to be returned to the originating parish. Former governor Pleasant led the "three

---

14. T. Harry Williams, *Huey Long* (New York: Alfred A. Knopf, 1969), 144–45; Schott, "John M. Parker," 376–77.
15. Williams, *Huey Long*, 141; Sindler, *Long's Louisiana*, 43.
16. Schott, "John M. Parker, " 361–69; Williams, *Huey Long*, 141–42.

percenters" in denouncing the oil trusts; the rumor around the convention was that Pleasant was "getting his inspiration from Huey Long." The three percenters were gaining momentum when Parker revealed the compromise that had been made with the corporations. Those advocating 3 percent, realizing that they would not get the full amount, offered to settle for 2.5 percent. Parker, before agreeing, consulted with Standard Oil. After heated debates back and forth, the convention worked out a plan to which all parties reluctantly agreed. The severance tax clause as adopted by the convention did not set a fixed rate but maintained the current rate of 2 percent. The responsibility of rate-fixing was left to future legislatures.[17]

A study of the proceedings clearly revealed that taxation was one of the chief concerns of the delegates. Prior to the 1921 constitution the state received the bulk of its revenue from the 1920 "license tax" on industries extracting natural resources and a general property tax. During the convention however, a subcommittee traveled through northern states to study the feasibility of adopting a graduated income tax amendment until it was placed into operation. Governor Parker was very much opposed to the graduated tax on incomes which he considered "cumbersome and often misunderstood." Parker much preferred a flat rate. Under the weighty pressure of the state's financial and commercial interests, the delegates agreed to a mild and nebulous clause which permitted the legislature to levy a flat 3 percent on incomes. The provision did not actually levy the tax but merely gave the legislature the authority to do so: An income tax of 3 percent net incomes *may* be levied by the legislature.[18]

17. New Orleans *Item,* June 12, 1921; Schott, "John M. Parker," 361–69; Sindler, *Long's Louisiana,* 43; Williams, *Huey Long,* 142–44; 1921 Constitution of Louisiana, Art. X, Sec. 21.

18. Sindler, *Long's Louisiana,* 44; New Orleans *Item,* June 12, 1921; Frazar, "Constitutional Convention," 184; Leslie Moses, "The Growth of Severance Taxation in Louisiana and Its Relation to the Oil and Gas Industry," *Tuland Law Review,* XVII (1943), 610; 1921 Constitution of Louisiana, Art. X, Sec. 1.

Epilogue 325

The initial phases of the convention may have been as dull as "an inventory clerk's requisition," but after the heated debates over civil service, severance and income taxes, and good roads, tensions had reached a peak. Only two of the delegates refused to sign the new constitution, one of whom was former governor Ruffin G. Pleasant. Pleasant would not sign because he considered the severance tax to be too mild and a surrender to "certain tax paying oil interests," namely Standard Oil.

With the first signature by Mrs. Joseph Friend of New Orleans to be affixed to the constitution, pandamonium erupted. Harold Moise, another delegate from New Orleans, picked up a board on which printed ordinances had been filed and hammered it on the top of his desk. John Sullivan followed Moise's example and pounded his board on the desk with such force that it shattered. Behrman seized a huge file of printed documents and threw them at Harry Fitzpatrick. A delegate from Shreveport crumpled a piece of paper and threw it at the speaker of the house of representatives catching him under the ear. J. Y. Sanders made the motion to adjourn. Amid a "fog of paper balls and with tremendous outbursts of cheers" the convention closed.[19]

In a postconvention editorial the *Item* viewed the new constitution as a "big forward step, though safely conservative." The document was not considered to be a radical change from the former constitutions in that it dealt with the machinery of government "rather than any enunciation of new principles of fundamental law."[20]

The convention lived up to its resolution of "maintaining the purity of the white race," especially in the writing of voter qualification provisions. The grandfather clause of the 1898 constitution was replaced by a form of the Mississippi "understanding" clause. In addition to the education qualification a

19. New Orleans *Item*, June 19, 1921.
20. *Ibid.*, June 12, 1921.

"good character clause" was also added. The 1921 constitution therefore provided that a prospective voter had to understand "the duties and obligations of citizenship." If illiterate he was to "have good character . . . and give a reasonable interpretation of any article of the federal or state constitution when read to him by the registrar." A Negro could, therefore, be disqualified in several ways under the new constitution. But even if he passed the educational and good character provisions, white voter registrars possessed a great deal of latitude in determining "reasonable interpretations."[21]

With the advantages of hindsight, most Louisiana historians agree that the 1921 constitution was more a half step than a big step forward. Improvements and advances, they said, were made in state government machinery and finance, but little was done for the social welfare of the people. Matthew Schott, one of Governor Parker's biographers, took issue with their opinions. In comparison with the constitutions of 1898 and 1913, Schott concluded, the 1921 document "sharply illustrates the thrust of Louisiana progressivism." This observation was based upon such innovations as the consolidation of governmental agencies, wage and labor laws for women and children, a state department of education, concern for the conservation of natural resources, juvenile courts throughout the state, and aid to farmers in combating pests.[22]

The progressive spirit of the 1920s was directed toward good government, good schools, industry, business and great churches. Efficiency was the goal in business and government. It was the age of progress and the "Atlanta Spirit." The progressive philosophy of this period had limitations, however. Progressives were not especially concerned with the problems of

21. *Ibid.*; V. O. Key, Jr., *Southern Politics in State and Nation* (New York: Alfred A. Knopf, 1949), 535-39.
22. Sindler, *Long's Louisiana*, 35; Frazar, "Constitutional Convention," 210-11; Schott, "John M. Parker," 406-407.

Epilogue 327

the underprivileged. It was their belief that everyone's problems would be solved with economic growth and prosperity.[23] Governor Parker was a classic example of the conservative business progressive. He worked for good government based on sound and efficient business principles. Parker and the progressives of his persuasion believed that good government could only be realized through cooperation with big business. An examination of the 1921 constitution clearly demonstrates this attitude toward government and business.

Martin Behrman's attitude toward business was essentially the same as Parker's. The difference in the two men's philosophy was that Behrman was primarily a machine-orientated politician. He believed that only through the machine could society in general prosper. Business was an essential part of the scheme but was subordinate to the machine. During the constitutional convention of 1921, the former mayor was content, as mentioned earlier, to be merely a part of the proceedings, not to lead them. The most important result of the convention, for Behrman at least, was that it created for him a new aura of victory which he desperately needed after his defeat in 1920.

Behrman's comeback was temporarily halted on Wednesday, October 4, 1922, when he announced that he was retiring from politics because of poor health. The Choctaws then dubbed as their new leader Paul Maloney, commissioner of Public Utilities. Actually, Behrman's announced reasons for retiring were not quite the whole truth. Behrman resigned at the urging of the Choctaw caucus because of his defeat in 1920, failing health, and rising ambitions of younger members. The war bonnet was passed to Maloney because of the Choctaws' custom of naming as their leader the official holding the highest office. In the 1920 municipal elections, he was the only Regular

---

23. During the New South era, the Atlanta Spirit was synonymous with industrial and commercial growth. Tindall, *Emergence of the New South*, 223–33.

not to go down with Behrman. Although he faced an O.D.A. mayor and council, he served well. Reporters asked Maloney if his selection meant that he would be the 1925 Old Regular candidate for mayor. Maloney, coyly refusing to commit himself, told them that the election was too far in the future for comment.[24] Behind the mask, he did feel that he would be the natural selection for the Old Regular's endorsement, but he could not foresee Behrman's future actions and aspirations.

Maloney's life was a typical American success story. He began his career in 1892 as a fifteen-dollar-a-month office boy for the Crescent Transfer and Shipping Company. By 1917 he was the full owner. In 1914 he was elected to the state legislature after the resignation of Raoul Sere, a New Orleans businessman and Choctaw leader. The following year, 1915, he was selected as one of the delegates from New Orleans to the 1915 constitutional convention, but returned home when the convention did not convene. New Orleans had voted for a new constitution, but the northern parishes defeated the call. Maloney later described himself as "all dressed up but no place to go." In 1916 he received his first political defeat when he ran and was defeated in his bid for assessor of the Sixth District; he could have entered a second primary but stepped aside. From 1918 to 1920 he served as a member of the Orleans Levee Board and was elected president of the board over the opposition of Governor Parker. Parker appointed a special commission and sent it to New Orleans to try to oust Maloney. The commission told Maloney that his board was illegal since it had never been confirmed by the state senate, to which Maloney replied, neither was yours." The only action Parker's commission could have taken to remove Maloney was to press charges, and that

---

24. George Reynolds, *Machine Politics in New Orleans, 1897–1926* (New York: Columbia University Press, 1936), 217; New Orleans *Item*, October 5, 1922; New Orleans *States*, December 21, 1924.

would have been impossible for the only thing it had against him was that he was "anti-Parker."[25]

Though Behrman was physically ill, the excitement of a campaign, the essence of a politician's existence, and a driving ego could not keep him from actively supporting the election of two New Orleans judges in 1922, stumping for Henry L. Fuqua in the 1924 gubernatorial election, and seeking his own reelection as mayor in 1925.

The 1923-1924 gubernatorial race in Louisiana was the most controversial campaign for that office in over a quarter of a century. By the end of the summer of 1923, three main candidates and their supporters had committed themselves. They were Henry L. Fuqua, a Protestant but from southern Louisiana: Hewitt Bouanchaud, a French-Catholic from the southern parish of Pointe Coupee; and, Huey P. Long, chairman of the Louisiana Railroad Commission and a Protestant from northern Louisiana. The main issues during the campaign, in spite of efforts to avoid them, were religion and the Ku Klux Klan, which in 1924 had become an increasing state and national menace.[26]

Fuqua, the general manager of the state penitentiary at Angola, had the endorsement of former governors Sanders and Pleasant. Although Fuqua was an important member of Governor Parker's administration, he did not receive the governor's suport. Parker endorsed Hewitt Bouanchaud, his lieutenant-governor and a Catholic. Catholics, at that time at least, had

---

25. New Orleans *States*, December 21, 1924
26. Although the Klan had become a national menace by the 1920s nowhere in the country was its violence felt more than in the South. According to Professor George B. Tindall, the Klan's violence was directed less against Negroes, Catholics, and Jews than it was against the "unrighteous or unwary victims of private sadistic horseplay and grudges." The K.K.K. as a political issue reached a climax in Louisiana during the 1924 gubernatorial campaign following the Klan-instigated murders and violence in northern Louisiana. Tindall, *Emergence of the New South*, 192.

practically no chance of being elected in a statewide contest. Northern Louisiana's predominantly Protestant population coupled with Protestant voters in the southern part of the state, consistently opposed all such efforts.

Most political observers found it difficult to understand why Parker would back an almost certain loser. T. Harry Williams, one of Huey Long's biographers and a student of Louisiana history, ventured several possible reasons for Parker's commitment. First, he may have felt a sense of personal loyalty to his fellow "good government" reformer. Second, he wished to demonstrate that he could elect his own hand-picked successor over the opposition of Sanders, Pleasant, and the Old Regulars of New Orleans. Third, the reform governor, believing that both Fuqua and Long were afraid of alienating the Klan vote, felt that at least one candidate had to stand staunchly against the hooded vandals. Actually, Parker had little choice; he could hardly back Long because of the latter's attacks against his pro-Standard Oil stand during the constitutional convention of 1921. Nor could he back Fuqua who had received the enthusiastic support of Behrman.[27]

Behrman and the Old Regulars were impressed with Fuqua's strength in the country parishes. Fuqua was Protestant; he was also anti-Klan, but not as vigorously as Bouanchaud. Behrman could not support Long because he believed Long to be a "radical opponent of business." He could not join forces with Parker and back Bouanchaud; besides, he did not think the lieutenant governor had a chance to win. The Old Regulars put their entire organization to work and formed Fuqua clubs in each of the city's seventeen wards.[28] The Choctaw chief realized that a Protestant from southern Louisiana had a far

---

27. Williams, *Huey Long*, 195.
28. *Ibid.*, 196; New Orleans *Times-Picayune*, September 6, 1923.

greater chance than a Catholic. Furthermore, Fuqua's moderation toward the Klan did not alienate its members or sympathizers as did Bouanchaud's vehement attacks.

John Sullivan, because of his ties with Parker, had no choice but to back Bouanchaud with his newly formed New Regular Democratic Association. Sullivan personally did not care for Bouanchaud nor did he think Parker's man had a chance to win. Sullivan's lack of enthusiasm reflected the attitude of the New Regulars' organization. A number of its members led by the Williams brothers, Gus and Francis, who favored Huey Long, broke with Sullivan and formed the Independent Regular Democratic Association. Gus Williams accused the Pleasant, Sanders, and Parker administrations of working for business interests, and not the "business of the people," in that they extorted large sums of money from business under the guise of protecting them from "non-existent radical bugaboos."[29] Francis Williams, a fellow member with Long on the Louisiana Public Service Commission, traveled all over the state campaigning for Huey. The Independents were the only semblance of an organization that Long had in New Orleans and he told them: "Give me a handful of city votes—no more than 15,000 and I'm as good as elected."[30]

Long attacked everything and everyone. The *Item*, he said, was owned by Wall Street, and the *Times-Picayune* by New York bankers; Fuqua and Bouanchaud were both Parker's men; Behrman and Sullivan, both agents of Wall Street, were actually working together. "If Behrman took a dose of laudanum," he charged, "Sullivan would get sleepy in ten minutes."[31] But regardless of how hard he tried, Long could not evade the real issue of the campaign—the Klan.

29. New Orleans *Times-Picayune*, September 30, 1923.
30. Williams, *Huey Long*, 197.
31. *Ibid.*, 204. Laudanum formerly denoted any of a number of opium preparations.

In the beginning of the campaign each candidate expressed his position on the hooded order. Bouanchaud said that he stood for law and order and was opposed to the "Invisible Empire of the Ku Klux Klan." If elected governor, he promised, he would go to the limits of the federal and state constitutions to protect the people from the Klan. Fuqua stated that masked and secret societies bred violence and mistrust. If elected, he promised to push for an antimasking law, one that would require all secret societies to file at regular intervals with the secretary of state lists of their memberships. Long, on the other hand, attempted to evade the issue. The campaign, he said, should be free from religious agitation. He gave a long discourse on the principle of separation of church from state and hoped everyone would live by the Golden Rule. Later, when pressured for a clearer statement of his views on the Klan, the Winn Parish candidate evasively said that he was "against any unlawful practices by the Klan or anyone else." He doubted that Fuqua's plan for an antimasking law would work. He pointed out that there was already such a law in the statutes: "If it is valid," he asked, "why not enforce it?"[32]

Bouanchaud challenged his opponents to come out against the Klan "as an un-American organization that cannot exist because it is opposed to constitutional forms of government." Fuqua accused the lieutenant governor of trying to make the Invisible Empire an issue in the campaign in order to distract attention from the "real issues." The real issues for New Orleans, Long asserted, were natural gas, free text books for all school children, improved workmen's compensation laws, paving Claiborne Avenue, reduction of taxes, and elimination of governmental extravagances. Long accused Bouanchaud and Fuqua of having no issues but the Klan. The only difference between the two, he remarked, was "that Bouanchaud wanted

32. New Orleans *Times-Picayune*, September 12, 1923.

to hang them before the election and Fuqua wanted them to vote for him first then hang them."[33]

According to most predictions in New Orleans, at least among Bouanchaud supporters, Long did not have a chance. Both the *Item* and the *Times-Picayune* predicted that the lieutenant governor would win, Fuqua would finish second, and Long a miserable third. The results, however, proved them only partially correct: Bouanchaud received 82,910 votes; Fuqua 82,117 and Long a surprising 73,275. The most dramatic results were in New Orleans: Bouanchaud, the Catholic, received 23,232; Fuqua, the Protestant, 32,999; and Long, 12,303.[34] Behrman and the Old Regulars delivered fifteen out of the seventeen wards to Fuqua. In the second primary Long's supporters swung over to Fuqua giving him the final victory and the governorship.

Sullivan and the New Regulars attributed Bouanchaud's defeat in New Orleans to labor troubles that the city had been experiencing on the riverfront. Both dockworkers and shippers condemned the Parker administration for not settling the dispute. Parker's biographer saw the New Orleans debate as a result of Sullivan's unpopularity and the weakness of the "reform" city administration. Behrman and Sanders, Schott claimed, were anxious for a runoff in order to "annihilate" the New Regulars. To demonstrate further the weakness of the Parker machine in New Orleans, the *Times-Picayune* and the *Item*, previously pro-Parker, suggested that Bouanchaud should not enter a second primary but withdraw. Esmond Phelps, the *Times-Picayune* director, denounced Parker's New Orleans ally, John Sullivan, as being no better than the machine that his paper had worked for so many years to destroy. Bouanchaud did well in the second primary despite the loss of many

33. New Orleans *Times-Picayune*, December 13, 31, 1923, January 18, 1924; Sindler, *Long's Louisiana*, 48–49; Williams, *Huey Long*, 209.
34. New Orleans *Times-Picayune*, January 16, 21, 1924.

of his early supporters. Religion accounted for his success; he carried all of the French parishes in the southern part of the state except Orleans and East Baton Rouge.[35]

The ominous result of the 1924 gubernatorial campaign in New Orleans was the rise of Huey Long in the city's politics. The Public Service commissioner from Winn Parish realized that great inroads would have to be made in New Orleans if he was to have any future success in the state or national political arenas. This strategy set the pact and drew new political lines in New Orleans politics for the next two decades.[36]

The next step in Behrman's comeback was at the 1924 Democratic convention following the gubernatorial election of that year. The party met in June to select delegates for the national convention. The convention was merely a formality, for it had been the practice for many years in Louisiana for the governor to meet with other state leaders and New Orleans bosses to select the delegates. Fuqua and Behrman saw no reason why 1924 should be any different. In a secret meeting, twenty delegates were chosen, sixteen on a geographical basis and the remaining four at large. After a bit of political manipulation, Fuqua, Behrman, Sanders, and Lee E. Thomas, mayor of Shreveport, were selected as delegates at large.[37]

Huey Long denounced the secret agreements as a fraud. Sanders and Behrman, declared Long, had both been rejected by the voters in their last attempts at political office. The Winn Parish upstart vowed that he would go to the convention and help select a new slate.[38]

Actually, Long did not get a chance to change anything. From the moment the convention was called to order, Behrman and

35. Schott, "John M. Parker," 456–57, 459–60.
36. Sindler, *Long's Louisiana*, 49–50.
37. Williams, *Huey Long*, 215–16.
38. *Ibid.*; Leo Glenn Douthit, "The Governorship of Huey Long" (M.A. thesis, Tulane University, 1947), 34–36.

Sanders assumed complete control of the proceedings. Behrman was chosen permanent chairman of the convention and in turn appointed Sanders head of the resolutions committee. They ruled the meeting with as heavy a hand as any South or Central American dictator. They tabled and allowed to be shouted down all proposals with which they did not agree, such as the resolution denouncing the Klan. One delegate, advocating support for the Eighteenth Amendment, was physically thrown off the stage by Behrman. Huey Long jumped on the stand and proposed that the number of delegates-at-large be increased from four to eight. That way, he said, the "has beens," referring to Behrman and Sanders, could keep their seats while four more who reflected the will of the voters could be chosen. Huey's resolution was tabled by a voice vote. He had been beaten and New Orleans newspapers gleefully but mistakingly wrote his obituaries: "Huey Long is finished."[39]

As the 1924–1925 New Orleans mayoral election approached, Behrman, invigorated by his successes, was ready to reclaim his titles as head of the Choctaw Club and mayor of New Orleans. In a special meeting of the caucus, Behrman was selected to head the Old Regular ticket. The caucus was not unanimous, however. Paul Maloney, the only successful Choctaw candidate in the 1920 municipal elections, refused to step aside. He walked out taking many supporters with him. Behrman dubbed those Old Regulars who backed Maloney as deserters and called Maloney a champion of mediocrity.[40]

On January 4, 1925, Maloney announced his ticket and platform. The first plank was the standard homage to American democratic principles and the second promised the people freedom from one-man political autocracy. The third, fourth, and fifth assured all qualified white citizens of the right to vote

39. Williams, *Huey Long*, 218–19; New Orleans *Times-Picayune*, June 7, 1924; New Orleans *Item*, June 6, 1924.
40. New Orleans *Times-Picayune*, January 8, 1925.

and hold office. Planks six through twenty promised civic reforms. Plank twenty-one promised a "square deal for labor" and fair treatment for capital. The twenty-second plank, in line with "racial purity," recognized the principle of separate residential zones for the different races, "to keep them separate and to assure that the rights of each [are] respected."[41]

On the same day that Maloney announced his platform, Huey Long was seen meeting with the Williams brothers, John Sullivan, and Colonel Ewing, owner of the New Orleans *States*. Long was taking advantage of the unprecedented division in the Old Regular organization to gain a foothold in New Orleans politics. Shortly after their conferences the four announced that they were supporting Maloney. The *Times-Picayune* asked why, with so much against him, would Behrman run again for Mayor. Francis Williams declared that the Old Choctaw was politically sick and would be "politically dead within 30 days." He charged that Behrman, while telling labor of what a good friend he was, had his "loyalists" in the state legislature killing labor bills. Behrman, Williams said, took the working men and women of New Orleans to be a "bunch of boobs."[42]

The two main issues of the campaign were bossism and labor. On bossism, his two main opponents were Miss Jean Gordon and the *Times-Picayune.* Miss Gordon supported Maloney. "This was not the time," she said, "to take chances and be sorry afterwards." She reminded voters of Behrman's trip to Washington in 1917 to save Storyville and of his efforts to suppress enforcement of the Sunday closing law.[43]

The *Times-Picayune* said that Behrman could no more change than the "Ethiopian can change his skin." His methods, it continued, and attitudes were fixed by a life-long practice of

---

41. *Ibid.*, January 1, 1925.
42. Williams, *Huey Long*, 223–24; New Orleans *Times-Picayune*, January 4, 8, 1925; Reynolds, *Machine Politics in New Orleans*, 220.
43. New Orleans *Times-Picayune*, January 4, 1925.

autocratic leadership. He was too old and opinionated to change his views. Behrmanism, wrote the *Picayune*, was the nearest thing to despotism remaining in the United States and was the common enemy of all those who believe "in independent political thought and in public administration which serves primarily and above all else the common will of the whole community." A surprise announcement by Governor Fuqua hit Behrman hard. Fuqua stated that he was going to stay out of the New Orleans campaign and not give state patronage in the city to anyone until after the election. Fuqua warned that any promises made by either faction were without foundation.[44]

Organized labor leaders were divided between Behrman and Maloney. David Marcusy, president of the Central Trades and Labor Council, gave his full support to the incumbent, Andrew McShane. John F. Bowen, chairman of the state board of the brotherhood of Railroad Trainmen, who had made the opening speech in Behrman's 1920 campaign, backed Maloney. Bowen accused Behrman of not being loyal to the Choctaws. If he had been loyal, Bowen claimed, he would have worked to keep the organization together and not left that job to the rank-and-file. Fuqua's election in 1924, he said, was due to their efforts and not Behrman's. The Choctaws were strong again, he continued, because they had backed Fuqua, and now they could win the local election by backing the logical candidate—Maloney.[45]

Behrman, borrowing a strategem from Huey Long's 1923–1924 campaign, used the radio to broadcast his political rallies. Before a crowd at the Folly Theatre in Algiers and a radio audience, Behrman made his opening address. "Let's get together" was the keynote of the speech. He pleaded with the voters to give the "battle scarred veteran of many political

---

44. *Ibid.*, June 2, 3, 5, 1925; Reynolds, *Machine Politics in New Orleans*, 221.
45. *Ibid.*, January 4, 1925.

campaigns" the chance to move New Orleans ahead. Maloney, Behrman said, was a "gentleman of mediocre ability." He visualized for the audience a New Orleans "entering upon an era of expanding commerce and enlarged industries with new problems demanding solutions and civic enterprises requiring fulfillment." In a practical twelve-point program for civic improvement, Behrman promised: (1) construction of a seawall along the New Orleans shore of Lake Pontchartrain and the general beautification of the lakefront; (2) a comprehensive street-paving program, which was promised by the O.D.A. in 1920 but never fulfilled; (3) development of interlocking boulevards, to which World War I had put an end; (4) construction of a bridge across Lake Pontchartrain; (5) enlargement of City Park; (6) construction of a bridge across the Mississippi River; (7) more public playgrounds and bathing facilities; (8) paving Claiborne Avenue and the development of highways into Jefferson, Plaquemines, and St. Bernard parishes; (9) construction of a highway from the lakefront at New Orleans to connect with the highway to Hammond; (10) a study of the public service situation with view of extension, improvement, and reduction of rates where possible; (11) greater cooperation with the commercial interests of the city for the expansion of the convention and tourist trade; and (12) cooperation with the city and state boards of health for the regulation and improvement of public markets.

In the same broadcast, Behrman commented on the two newspapers opposing him. He said that he knew Colonel Ewing of the *States* about as well as he knew any man in the community. At times, he continued, there had been cordial relations between them, but only when "Behrmanism . . . [was] in full accord with Ewingism". But when they did not agree, Behrmanism was "as wicked a thing as the works of Satan himself." The only comment he had for the *Times-Picayune* was that it was "the prime example of consistency" in its opposition to Behrman. Behrman expressed the hope that the campaign would be conducted with more dignity than in 1920. "The reckless display of unjust and untruthful publicity," he asserted, "served [no other] purpose but to injure the standing of the city."[46]

During the campaign, a contest developed between the *Item* and the *Times-Picayune*. The *Picayune* accused the *Item* of "lending itself . . . to the baldest and oldest strategy of despots and bossdom." "For years," said the *Picayune*, "the *Item* did not have a kind word to say about Behrman and during the 1920 campaign called him King of the Tenderloin and an undesirable citizen as well as public official." But during the 1925 campaign, continued the indictment, it was Behrman's strongest supporter and defender.[47] The *Item* denounced the *Picayune* and other Maloney supporters for using smear and character assasination tactics against Behrman.

The *Picayune* said it did not have anything against Behrman personally but that he was too old and "broken under the strains of ambition". "For the safety of the city," it pleaded, "his desire to come back must be denied." His type of government, it argued, was based on patronage: "An employee has two masters, the city, who pays his salary, and the boss who gives the jobs." Loyalty to the ring superseded the welfare of the city, and it was this type of situation which had caused his downfall in 1920.[48] This was, of course, a rather strong indictment, for Behrman did not draw a dichotomy between the "ring" and the city. The ring was an integral part of the city; therefore, what was done for or by the ring was also considered good for the city.

The *Picayune* described Behrman as old and broken. It claimed that he was at his peak in 1912, for then he had "vision and drew about him alert and competent men." But as time

46. *Ibid.*, January 6, 1925.
47. *Ibid.*, January 3, 4, 1925.
48. *Ibid.*, January 7, 1925; Reynolds, *Machine Politics in New Orleans*, 222.

progressed Behrman turned to machine politics to protect his power: "Behrman the mayor talked about playgrounds and schools while Behrman the boss facilitated the marriage of the lowest strata of the 'ring' with the darkest elements of the underworld of corruption and commercial vice that poison youth and taint all society." From 1916 on, continued the denunciation, Behrman had been in a state of visible decay and had fallen victim to the strain of the high office.[49]

As the campaign neared its conclusion the *Picayune* became more vehement: "Out of the slough of degrading bossdom New Orleans clambered four years ago. Much of the mud of it, the slime of it, still clings to our governmental garments. . . . But we have climbed out." In the same edition it pleaded with voters in an editorial, entitled, "Think It Over," to consider their votes. Behrmanism and ring government, it wrote, were things of the past. Behrman, in rebuttal, said he believed the people wanted "an administration with party obligations and party responsibilities—for it is only through party government . . . that true progress has ever been made in government." The *Picayune* said what Behrman really meant was that he believed in government by faction and that faction to be completely under his control. "Papa," it continued, believed that he was the "anointed, indispensable and infallible shaper of human desires. . . . Behrman's ethics were ethics of gangdom."[50]

The voters apparently disagreed with these accusations and denunciations, for Behrman received 35,731 votes to Maloney's 33,631. Since Papa did not receive a clear majority, a second primary would have been in order. But Maloney withdrew. He accused Behrman's men of making overtures to his backers. He said that he was not surrendering but withdrawing because he had been "betrayed and sold out by men in whom [he had]

---

49. New Orleans *Times-Picayune*, January 7, 1925.
50. *Ibid.*, February 1, 2, 1925.

placed [his] trust." Maloney was referring to the defection of the Fifth and Sixth Ward leaders to Behrman. With the Fifth and Sixth wards gone, Maloney could only count on the Twelfth, Thirteenth, Fourteenth, and Sixteenth wards, and they were not enough.[51]

Behrman was reelected in 1925 over almost insurmountable odds. His opponents thought him politically dead and wondered why he had run at all. With the advantage of hindsight, his victory could be attributed to five factors: the lack of coordination among his opponents; his own popularity; voter disillusion with the "reform" administration; hard work; and, the effectiveness of the Choctaw organization. His reelection marked the climax of his political career, and he immediately began working to fulfill his campaign promises as if he knew what fate awaited him. On January 12, 1926, one year after his reelection, Martin Behrman died.

He died of *chronic myocarditis*, "which was a degeneration of the heart muscles due to overwork," said his physician. The physician also added that he had died a "martyr to the city of New Orleans." Tributes came from all quarters. Governor Fuqua wrote that Behrman "pushed himself to become mayor and it killed him. . . . He died in harness," continued Fuqua, "as he would have liked to die." Governor Alfred E. Smith of New York said that with Behrman's death he had lost a personal friend. Judge George M. Olvany, leader of New York's Tammany Hall, remarked that "Mayor Behrman was a strong organization Democrat and loyal friend. . . ." New York City Mayor Jimmie Walker, shocked at the news, gave a press conference and confided to newsmen that Behrman "was a constant source of inspiration to me. . . . His confidence of success for the regular Democratic ticket added to my own confidence

---

51. *Ibid.*, February 4, 9, 1925. In the first primary Maloney carried Wards Five, Six, Seven, Twelve, Thirteen, Fourteen, and Sixteen.

every time I talked to him. . . . The Democratic Party has lost a class A soldier in Martin Behrman." Back home in Louisiana the *Shreveport Journal*, in a special editorial praised the dead mayor for his years of public service and "usefulness." The New Orleans *Item* wrote that Behrman's monument to himself "was to make New Orleans . . . a better, more beautiful, more wholesome, and lovelier place in which to live."[52]

The *Times-Picayune*, Behrman's perennial opponent and antagonist, stated in a remarkable editorial that Behrman's death would be regretted by all. He was a politician, it wrote, who liked a good fight and had few personal enemies. His critics, continued the editorial, could never question his sincerity in wanting to do what was good for New Orleans: "His growth in vision and understanding, his broadening concepts of public service and duty, proved something better than the ordinary type of successful politician." This description was startlingly different from its condemnation of Behrman and his methods of governing just one year previous in the 1925 mayoralty campaign. The *Picayune* continued its hypocritical tribute to Behrman in describing him as "a kindly citizen, a forceful leader and a municipal servant who made the most of his opportunities for service to the city he loved."[53]

Behrman's death marked the end of a long political career. He rose from a small dry goods stand in a French Market bazaar to city boss and five-time mayor of New Orleans. His reign was long and controversial, but his energies and ambition led New Orleans out of the nineteenth century into the twentieth with many progressive civic improvements.

---

52. *Ibid.*, January 13, 1926; *Shreveport Journal*, January 13, 1926; New Orleans *Item*, January 13, 1926.
53. New Orleans *Times-Picayune*, January 13, 1926.

Appendix

CHARTER

United States of America,
State of Louisiana,
Parish of Orleans,
City of New Orleans.

Be it known that on this the 12th day of March, in the year of Our Lord One Thousand Eight Hundred and Ninety Seven, and of the Independence of the United States of America, the One Hundred and Twenty-First:

Before me Peter Stifft a Notary Public, duly commissioned, sworn and qualified, in and for the Parish of Orleans, and in the presence of the witnesses hereinafter named and undersigned,

PERSONALLY CAME AND APPEARED

The parties whose names are hereunto subscribed, who declared that availing themselves of the provisions of the laws of the State of Louisiana in such cases made and provided, they have covenanted and agreed and do by these presents covenant and agree and bind themselves, and those whom they represent, and those who may hereafter become associated with them, and their assigns, and the asignees of their assigns, to form themselves into, and form a corporation for the objects and purposes hereinafter specified, and under the stipulations, following to-wit:

ARTICLE 1.

This corporation shall be known as the Choctaw Club of Louisiana and its domicile is hereby fixed in the city of New Orleans.

ARTICLE 2.

Believing that it is the duty of every good citizen to take not only a deep interest, but also an active part in the political affairs of the Country, and believing further that the welfare of the Country, and the continual prosperity of its institutions require for their preservation that the policy and character of the Government shall be determined and guided by the principles of the Democratic Party, and in order to add to the organized strength of the Democratic Party in the State of Louisiana, the objects and purposes for which this corporation is organized, are declared to be:

1st. To uphold and advance Democratic principles.

2nd. To promote harmony, enjoyment and literary improvement.

3rd. To provide the conveniences of a Club House.

And to effect these objects and purposes, said corporation shall have, possess, enjoy and exercise all of the rights, powers and privileges of a corporate body, and shall continue and have existence for a period of ninety nine (99) years.

ARTICLE 3.

The corporate powers of this organization are hereby vested in, and shall be exercised by a Board of Governors, consisting of nine (9) members; they shall hold office for one (1) year until the succeeding second Wednesday in January of the following year, or until their successors shall have been elected.

They shall have power to fill any vacancy in their number.

They shall elect from among their number, a President and a Vice-President.

They shall have the power to appoint a Secretary who shall also be Ex-Officio Treasurer of the Club, but who shall not be a member of the Board of Governors.

All citations or other legal process shall be served upon the President, or in his absence upon the Vice-President; and in case of the absence of both, same shall be served upon the Secretary.

ARTICLE 4.

There shall be a Committee on Organization, composed of seventeen (17) members, one to be selected from each of the Wards of this City. The said members shall be elected by the members of this club from the respective wards of the city on the day preceding the annual meeting of the club, and the said election to remain subject to the ratification of a majority of the members of the club attending the annual meeting to be held on the second Wednesday of January of each year. In case of refusal to ratify, the members of the said ward, (whose representative was failed of ratification) shall proceed on the next succeeding day to a new election, and the member so elected shall be subject to ratification by the Board of Governors.

The Committee on Organization may be increased by one (1) member for each Parish of this State, whenever the members of the club from any Parish shall elect their representative on said Committee, in the manner above set forth for city members.

In the event of a vacancy from any cause in said Committee on Organization, then the Board of Governors may designate a member from such ward or Parish to serve until the members of the ward or Parish wherein said vacancy occurs, shall act in the premises, in the manner above indicated, the object being to have the Wards and Parishes represented at all times on said Committee.

The said Committee shall elect its own Chairman.

It shall be their province to act and pass upon all matters affecting the honor, preservation and integrity of the Democratic Party in this State.

They may make their own rules governing the manner of their deliberations etc., not in conflict with this Charter, or the rules or By-Laws of this Organization.

ARTICLE 5.

A general meeting of the members of this corporation shall be held annually on the second Wednesday of January of each year, for the transaction of such business as may be requisite. If no quorum be present, the presiding officer shall adjourn the meeting to any other day with the same effect as if held as above.

One (1/10) tenth of all the members of this corporation, exclusive of non-resident members, shall constitute a quorum at any general meeting of the club. Special meetings may be held as provided in the By-Laws. At all meetings, each member (in good standing) shall have one (1) vote. The decision of the majority of the quorum present shall be valid as a corporate Act.

The Board of Governors shall be elected by ballot on the second Wednesday of January, annually. The polls shall be opened in the Club rooms from such an hour as the President shall have determined, and shall be under the supervision of three (3) Commissioners to be appointed by the President; said Commissioners forthwith make returns of said election. Members of the Board so elected, shall assume their positions on the Wednesday following their election. The candidates having the largest number of votes shall be elected, and in case of a tie, a new election for said tied candidates may be proceeded with at once, or at a later date according to the wishes of the majority of the members present. The Board of Governors shall have power to collect such admission fees, dues or assessments, as shall be prescribed by the By-Laws.

The Board shall enact such By-Laws and Regulations as they may deem necessary for the management of the Club, and shall have power to alter, amend or abrogate the same.

The membership of the Club shall be divided into three (3) classes., viz:

LIFE MEMBERS.
RESIDENT MEMBERS.
NON-RESIDENT MEMBERS.

and the said Board of Directors in the By-Laws, shall regulate the admission fees, dues, and rights and privileges etc., with respect thereto. The Board of Governors may elect Honorary members, as in their judgement they deem proper.

No member shall ever be held liable or responsible for the debts, contracts or faults of this corporation, beyond the amount of any dues or assessments which he may owe for the current year.

The first Board of Governors of the Club shall be as follows:
1. W. A. Kernaghan
2. B. T. Walshe
3. P. A. Capdau
4. Peter Stifft
5. John J. Frawley
6. Frank D. Chretien
7. Jos. Frellsen
8. L. R. Garcia
9. Chas. Dickson

and they shall hold office until the second Wednesday in January 1898, or until their successors shall have been elected and qualified.

ARTICLE 6.

This corporation is authorized to lease, purchase, hold, mortgage, and convey such real estate as may be required. Should occasion arise, loan or borrow money; issue such evidence of debt or obligations as may be necessary to secure same, and generally do any act or thing authorized by law to successfully attain the objects and purposes of this organization.

ARTICLE 7.

These articles may be amended at any annual meeting of the Club, or at any special meeting called for that purpose, by a two-thirds (⅔) vote in the affirmative, a quorum being present and voting. No amendment or question of dissolution shall be acted upon unless it should have been given to the Secretary at least ten (10) days before the meeting, during which time notice of same shall be conspicuously posted in the Club room, and notice of meeting advertised for three (3) consecutive days in a City newspaper. In case of dissolution, a majority of the votes cast shall determine; provided, that at least one-half of the members in good standing have participated in person or by proxy in said meeting. Said Commissioners may adjourn the meeting from day to day until a majority in good standing shall have voted, when it shall be the duty of the Commissioners to declare forthwith the result of the vote cast.

Upon dissolution of this Club, by expiration of Charter or otherwise, its affairs shall be liquidated by three (3) Commissioners to be selected by the Board of Governors. Said Commissioners shall immediately wind up the affairs, and after payment of its liabilities, distribute the remaining funds, if any, equally among the members of the Club, in good standing.

This done and passed at my office in New Orleans, Louisiana, on the day and date first above written in the presence of William Ardill and Charles J. Colton competent witnesses, who hereunto sign their names with the said parties and me Notary.

Index

Aby, Joseph C., 107
Adams, Lionel, 84
Adams, Thomas Scott, 15–16
Algiers Water Works & Electric Light Company, 12–13
Anti-Lottery League: and 1892 New Orleans mayoral campaign, 13; and 1892 gubernatorial campaign, 15
Archinard, Emile, 135
Aswell, James B.: for state superintendent of education, 208, 259n; and 1912 gubernatorial campaign, 270n.
Athenaeum, 85

"Badger gas ordinance," 127–30
Bailey, B. W., 46
Bailey, James J.: and 1908 campaign for lieutenant governor, 203, 214–18; mentioned, 249
Baker, Joshua G., 118
Baker, Newton D., 310–12
Baker, Page M.: as editor of *Times-Democrat*, 16; and 1904 mayoral campaign, 89, 97; Behrman's criticism of, 106–12, 202–203; mentioned, 69, 121
Ballard, Marshall: 225, 229, 257, 309
Barnes, J. W., 220
Barret, Thomas O.: Regular Democratic Organization support and in 1916 gubernatorial campaign, 278–79; on prohibition, 279
Beauregard, P. G. T., 19

Behrman, Martin: defeated in 1920, xxii, 315–16; and relationship with business community, xviii, 327; compared to other city bosses, xviii–xix; success attributed to, xxiii; gives reasons for writing memoirs, 1; early life of, 1–6; first enters politics, 7; and attitude toward Mafia, 10–11; and Algiers Water Works & Electric Light Company, 12–13; and Edison Electric Illuminating Company, 12–13; joins Council of Seventeen, 23–26; attitudes toward Negroes in politics, 36–40, 51–54; and 1898 constitutional convention, 38–41; on politics and government, 59–61, 88–89, 105–17; on "silk stockings," 88–89, 105–17; elected state auditor, 71–78, 94–95; in 1904 mayoral campaign, 79–81, 87–105; and charges of grafting, 90–92; on socialism, 102–105; on prohibition, 154–60; 221–23; on Dominick C. O'Malley and police feud, 117–31; and deposit of city funds, 169–73; on natural gas, 173–77; in 1908 mayoral campaign, 177–92; 1908 inaugural address of, 187–90; on race track gambling, 229–39; and pay raise, 255–59; political ambitions of, 256; assesses Governor Hall's administration, 261; 263–65; and 1912 mayoral election figures, 269n; and Robert Ewing, 270n; 1915 calls for constitutional convention, 273–78; and

John M. Parker in 1916 gubernatorial campaign, 283–87; and Parker in 1920 gubernatorial campaign, 291–94; and civil service, 295–302; on Storyville, 302–12; comes back after 1920, pp. 315–20, 327–41; 1921 and constitutional convention, 319–22; and 1924 gubernatorial campaign, 329–31; on 1925 mayoral campaign, 335–41; death of, 341–42
Behrman, Nellie, 8
Behrman, Stanley, 8
Bennett, James, 225
Bird, C. C., 71
Bixby, W. K., 174
Blanchard, Newton C.: as 1896 candidate for U.S. Senate, 30–31; in 1904 Orleans Parish district attorney controversy, 83–85 passim; on local government, 194; biography of, 71n; and 1904 gubernatorial campaign, 71–78 passim; on patronage, 196; and 1904 tax commission, 196; mentioned, xvi, 149
Blenk, James, 167
Board of Liquidation, 169
Board of Trade, 175
Boatner, Charles J.: and "Jacksonian Democracy," 33, 64; at 1898 constitutional convention, 43
Boston Club, 159
Bouanchaud, Hewitt, 329–35
Bourbons, xii
Bowen, John F., 337
Brand, W. A., 25
Brandao, E. P., 166–67
Brewster, John, 24
Briede, Otto F., 173
Broussard, Edwin S., 73, 209
Broussard, Robert F.: 73, 262; political career of, 198n; on 1908 gubernatorial campaign, 203; and sugar tariff, 244; as candidate for U. S. Senate in 1910, p. 246; elected to U.S. Senate in 1912, pp. 265–66; mentioned, 73, 262
Brownlee, Charles H., 61
Brunot, Harvey F., 183, 226
Bruns, Henry Dickson: at 1898 constitutional convention, 45–46, 50; and Luther E. Hall, 263
Bryan, William Jennings, 163
Bryce, James, xx–xxi
Brynes, William H., 61

Buck, Charles F.: in 1896 New Orleans mayoral campaign, 29n; and 1904 mayoral campaign, 90–102; Behrman's appraisal of, 105–106
Burke, E. A., 262
Busch, Adolph, 174
Bute, Duncan, 275
Butler, Charles, 16

Cade, C. Taylor, 29
Caffery, Donelson, Jr.: in 1900 gubernatorial campaign, 16n, 37–38; in 1908 gubernatorial campaign, 207–20 passim
Capdau, P. A., 346
Capdevielle, Paul: in 1899 mayoral campaign 33, 55–56, 61–64; biography of, 63–64; as state auditor, 214–15
Casacalvo, Henry Clay, 48
Caucus. See Council of Seventeen
Central Trades and Labor Assembly, 52n, 337
Charles Riot, 51, 67–71
Charters, New Orleans city:
—1896: city council, 25; civil service, 295–96
—1912: commission council, 25n
Chess and Checkers Club, 159
Choctaw Club of Louisiana: organization of, xii–xvii; formation of, 32–38; charter of, 341–45. See also Regular Democratic Organization
Chretien, Frank D., 346
Cisterns, screening of, 33
Citizens' Bank, 172
Citizens' League: xin, and 1896 mayoral campaign, 28n, 33; and 1896 gubernatorial campaign, 30; mentioned, xin, 38, 283
Citizens' Protective Association of New Orleans, 21n
Civil service: history of in Louisiana, 295–96n; and Regular Democratic Organization, 295–302; and John M. Parker at 1921 constitutional convention, 320–21; mentioned, 285
Claiborne, Charles: and 1912 mayoral campaign, 269–70n; mentioned, 319
Clare, Louis, 20
Clement, Peter, 85
Coco, Adolph V., 264
Collins, Julia, and family, 5–6

Commercial Germania Bank, 172
Constitutions, Louisiana:
—1898: on limited local government, xvi;
  on Negro suffrage, 38–55 *passim*; on
  elections, 55–56; mentioned, 318
—1913, pp. 273n, 275, 318
—1915: pp. 273–76, 318
—1921: John M. Parker on, 274; on
  civil service 285, 297–302 *passim*,
  320–21; Behrman's comeback at, 311;
  description of, 318–24; on suffrage,
  326–26
Contractors and Dealers Exchange, 175
Cotton Exchange: opposition to Behrman,
  96–97; on natural gas, 175
Cotton Screwmen's Association, 165
Council of Seventeen, xiii–xiv, 162. *See
  also* Regular Democratic Organization;
  Choctaw Club of Louisiana
Crandall, A. W., 16, 214–15
Crescent City Democracy, 89
Crescent Democratic Club: and 1892
  mayoral campaign, 13; and 1896
  mayoral campaign, 28–29; dissolution
  of, 29n; mentioned xii
Crescent Hall, 166

Daniels, Frank A., 97, 170
Daniels, Josephus, 312
Davey, Robert C.: and Council of Seventeen, 20, 24, 62; mentioned, 148, 245
Deblieux, John (Iberville Parish), 46
Deibel, Fred, 24
Democratic party, 36–40. *See also* elections
Democratic Primary League, 79
Democratic State Central Committee, 245
Denegre, Walter D.: description of, 30;
  and 1899 mayoral campaign, 33, 64
Diamond Festival. *See* Yellow fever
  epidemic of 1905
Diamond, Samuel, 120
Dickson, Charles, 346
Disfranchisement. See Constitutions
Dock Board (Louisiana), 298
Dowling, Oscar, 134–38 *passim*
Dudenheffer, Ferdinand, 24, 62
Duffy, Thomas, 20
Dufour, H. Generes, 171
Dupre, H. Garland, 245, 311
Dyer, Isadore, 134

Early, Jubal, 19
Edison Electric Illuminating Company,
  12–13
Edmonds, James E., 90
Elder, Walter, 242
Elections:
—Louisiana: 1888 gubernatorial, 7n; 1892
  gubernatorial, 13–19; 1896 gubernatorial, 28n; 1900 gubernatorial, 56–77
  passim; 1904 gubernatorial, 71–78;
  1908 gubernatorial, 198–220; 1912
  gubernatorial, 259–61; 1916 gubernatorial, 278–88; 1920 gubernatorial, 289–
  94; 1924 gubernatorial, 329–35
—Louisiana: 1910 U.S. House of Representatives, 246–47
—Louisiana: 1910 U.S. Senate, 243–46;
  1912 U.S. Senate, 265–72; 1920 U.S. Senate, 271–72
—New Orleans: 1880 mayoral, 63n; 1896
  mayoral, 28n; 1899 mayoral, 56–77 *passim*; 1904 mayoral, 74, 79–105 *passim*;
  1908 mayoral, 177–92; 1912 mayoral,
  269–70; 1920 mayoral, 313–16; 1925
  mayoral, 335–41
Elks, 144–45
Ely, Lewis B., 174
Era Club, 304
Estopinal, Albert, 185, 198, 200, 247
Everett, H. E., 174
Ewing, Robert: 84, 107, 126; and 1904
  mayoral campaign, 92; and saloon tax,
  162; as leader of Tenth Ward, 266; description of, 270n; and 1925 mayoral
  campaign, 336
Expositions: *See* Panama-Pacific Exposition; Diamond Festival

Farmers' Alliance, 15
Farrar, Edgar, 17
Farrell, Peter, 24
Favrot, Henry, 242–43
Federal Commission on Training Camp
  Activities, 308–12
Fitzgerald, E. J., 179
Fitzpatrick, Harry, 322, 325
Fitzpatrick, John: and 1892 mayoral campaign, 13; in Big Four of 1888, p. 20;
  administration of, 21–23; and courthouse scandal, 21–23; as Third Ward
  leader, 24; in 1896 mayoral campaign,
  29n, 39–40; on poll tax, 50; in 1900

gubernatorial campaign, 65; in 1904 mayoral campaign, 97; tax collector, 114–15; mentioned xxiv, 16, 63, 271
Flower, Walter C.: in 1896 mayoral campaign, 29n; in 1899 mayoral campaign, 55–56, 64; administration of, 56n
Fortier, Alcee, 101
Fosdick, Raymond, 308–12
Fosdick Commission. *See* Fosdick, Raymond
Foster, Murphy J.: in 1892 gubernatorial campaign, 13–19; biography of, 14n; in 1896 gubernatorial campaign, 28–29; in 1896 mayoral campaign, 29n; on sugar tariff, 31, 32n; 1898 opposition to, 49; builds organization in New Orleans, 55–56; elected to U.S. Senate, 66; in local government, 96; mentioned, xxiv, 149, 194, 197, 244
Frawley, John J., 346
Frazee, W. S., 71, 76
Frellsen, Joseph, 346
Friend, Mrs. Joseph, 325
Fuqua, Henry L.: and yellow fever quarantine, 139–40; on prohibition, 222; elected governor in 1924, pp. 329–35; and 1925 mayoral campaign, 337; on Behrman's death, 341

Gambling, 224–39. *See also* Locke Law
Garcia, L. R., 346
Garland, Henry L., Jr., 89
Gauche, C. Taylor, 23
Gay, Edward J., 221n, 262–63
Gay-Shattuck Law: in regulation of saloons, 221–24; in 1912 U.S. Senate campaign, 268
Gilmore, Samuel L., 84, 217n, 217–18, 246
Glynn, Martin, Sr., 227
Good Government League: 213; in 1912 elections, 34, 259–61, 267, 269n, 270n; formation of, 250, 253–54; John M. Parker deserts in 1912, pp. 270–71; mentioned, xin, xxii, 213
Goodwyn, Howard G., 95
Gordon, Jean: and Storyville, 304, 306; and 1925 mayoral campaign, 336
Gorgas, William C., 133–34
Grace, Fred J., 215
Graham, Peter, 163–64, 255–56
Grandfather clause. *See* Constitutions, Louisiana, 1898; Negroes

Gueydan, Henri L., 244
Guion, Walter, 214
Gurley, J. Ward, 89

Hall, Luther E.: gubernatorial administration of, 259n; becomes governor in 1912, pp. 259–61, 267; Behrman's description of, 261, 263–65; calls for 1915 constitutional convention, 273–78; on prohibition, 279; mentioned, 213
Hall, William Covington, 102–103
Harrison, Barker, 226
Harrison, Tom: supports Behrman, 97, 101; fights saloon tax, 165
Hawes, Harry B., 173
Hayne, Frank B., 309
Heard, William Wright: elected governor, 56, 65n; biography of, 64n; political career of, 185; mentioned, xvi, 16n, 38, 197
Heaslip, Samuel F., 226, 237
Hebert, Clarence S., 183
Hennessy, David, 9–11
Henriques, James C., 84, 86, 91, 182
Hibernia National Bank, 172
Hincks, Joseph A., 120
Hirn, Joseph, 24, 61, 62
Hofstadter, Richard, 315
Home Rulers: and 1904 mayoral campaign, 33, 92–105; formation of, 90; mentioned, xxii
Horse racing. *See* Locke Law
Houston, James D., 20
Hudson, E. M., 84
Hunsicker, Henry, 236
Hunsicker Law. *See* Henry Hunsicker

Italians, 139. *See also* Mafia
Independent Democratic League, 179–86
Independent Regular Democratic Association, 331

Jacksonian Democracy, 33, 56, 64
Janvier, Charles: as chairman of state Democratic Central Committee, 197; mentioned, 61, 80, 142, 209, 251
Jastremski, Leon: and 1904 gubernatorial campaign, 71–78 *passim*; biography of, 72n; and 1908 gubernatorial campaign, 199–210
Johnson, Hiram, 300
Johnson, J. M., 194

Jones, Sam H., 296n
Journee, John, 117–31 *passim*
Jumel, Allen, 29

Kennedy, Charles R., 173
Kernaghan, W. A., 346
Kiernan, Peter, 107
Killeen, Thomas, 175
Knop, Louis, 24
Kohnke, Quitman, 136–38
Kruttschnitt, Ernest: on poll tax, 50; death of, 196–97; 12–13, 73, 165
Ku Klux Klan: and 1924 gubernatorial campaign, 329–35 *passim*; mentioned, 40

LaFollette, Robert M., 300
Lambremont, Paul M.: as candidate for lieutenant governor, 203, 214–20; as candidate for governor, 249–51
Lawrason, S. McC., 214
Laymen's Missionary Movement, 304
LeBourgeois, Louis, 247
Lee, Robert E., 97, 101
Legislature, Louisiana: 1906 session of, 193–96: J. Y. Sanders and 1907 special session of, 205–206; Gay-Shattuck Law of, 221–24; Locke Law of, 224–39; Hunsicker Law of, 236n; 1910 session of, 239n
Lemle, Gus, 165
Leonhardt, Alex F., 220
Leveque, Joseph M.: shot by Edward S. Whitaker, 130, 211–12; mentioned, 117n, 181
Liberty League, 290
Locke, Leon. *See* Locke Law
Locke Law: regulated racetrack gambling, 224–39, 290; in 1912 U.S. Senate campaign, 268
Loisel, Victor, 247
Long, Earl K., 296n
Long, Huey P.: and civil service, 296n; and 1924 gubernatorial campaign, 329–35; and 1925 mayoral campaign, 336; describes Behrman, 331
Lottery. *See* Louisiana Lottery Company
Louisiana Anti-Saloon League, 222
Louisiana Bar Association, 318
Louisiana Club, 159
Louisiana Engineering Society, 175
Louisiana Lottery Company: and 1892 gubernatorial campaign, 13–19; mentioned, xxiv
Louisiana Progressive party, xi*n*, 281
Louisiana State University, 293n
Luzenberg, Chandler C., 83–85

McCaleb, E. Howard, 16, 63
McClure's Magazine, xx
McCue, William, 266, 268
McEnery, Samuel D.: and 1892 gubernatorial campaign, 13–19; biography of, 14n; on sugar tariff, 31, 32n; death of, 243; mentioned, xxiv, 149
McKinley, William, 150
McMurray, Henry B., 61
McRacken, James, 187
McShane, Andrew, 314n, 337
McVea, Charles, 139–40
Mafia: and Hennessy assassination, 9–11; Behrman's attitude toward, 10–11
Malloy, James, 24
Maloney, Paul: as Choctaw leader, 327–29; in 1925 mayoral campaign, 335–41
Marcusy, David, 337
Marmouget, A. P., 86
Marr, Robert H., 118, 133
Mauberret, Victor, 24, 62, 205, 267–68
Mealey, Patrick, 20
Meyer, Adolph, 37, 148, 256
Michel, John T.: and Council of Seventeen, 24, 72, 78, 91; as 1912 gubernatorial candidate, 248–50, 260, 270n, 290
Millsaps, William F., 18, 259
Mogel, Robert, 164
Moise, Harold, 325
Moise, James C., 16, 18
Montgomery, Samuel A., 84
Moore, Daniel D., 203, 309
Moore, I. D., 46
Mora, August T., 67

National Prohibition Enforcement Act, 154n
Natural gas: Caddo fields of, 173–76; in Terrebonne Parish, 176; at Monroe, 176; for New Orleans, 177n
Negroes: and 1898 Louisiana constitution, 38–55 *passim*; Behrman's attitudes toward, 51–54; labor unions' attitudes toward, 52–53; and 1905 yellow fever epidemic, 135; and John M. Parker, 282
Newlin, A. J., 229

New Orleans Association of Commerce, 117
New Orleans *Daily Picayune*: on 1904 mayoral campaign, 99; on saloon tax, 162; on Locke Law, 228. *See also* New Orleans *Times-Picayune*
New Orleans *Daily States*: on 1904 district attorney controversy, 90; on natural gas, 173
New Orleans Fair Grounds Track Association, 226
New Orleans *Item*: on natural gas, 173; on Locke Law, 225, 228, 235–37; on Behrman's pay raise, 255–59; on 1912 U.S. Senate campaign, 268–69; on 1921 constitutional convention, 320–21, 325; on 1920 gubernatorial campaign, 290–94 *passim*; on Storyville, 305–306, 309; on Huey Long, 331; on 1925 mayoral campaign, 339; on Behrman's death, 342
New Orleans National Bank, 172
New Orleans *Times-Democrat*: on Louisiana Lottery Company, 20; on 1898 constitution, 54–55; on 1904 opposition to Behrman, 81, 86–89, 95–102, 107–108; on 1905 police row, 120; on 1908 mayoral campaign, 179–81, 190–92; on 1908 gubernatorial campaign, 201–203, 210–11; on Locke Law, 225–39 *passim*; on Good Government League, 253–54; on Behrman's pay raise, 255–59 *passim*; on 1912 U.S. Senate election, 268–69
New Orleans *Times-Picayune*: opposes Behrman in 1920, pp. 190, 313–16; on 1916 gubernatorial campaign, 281; supports Parker in 1920, pp. 290–94 *passim*, 312–13; on Storyville, 309; on Huey Long, 331; opposes Behrman in 1925, pp. 336–40; on Behrman's death, 342. *See also* New Orleans *Daily Picayune*
Nicholls, Francis T., 42
Noel, Charles, 25
Noguchi, Hideyo, 136
Noiret, Charles A., 70

O'Connor, Charles, 167
O'Connor, James, 86
O'Connor, Robert, 227, 234, 237
O'Donnell, Larry, 37

Old Regulars. *See* Regular Democratic Organization
Olvany, George M., 341
O'Malley, Dominick C.: supports Behrman in 1904, p. 92; in 1905 police row, 117–31; on saloon tax, 160; mentioned, 17, 84, 107
One Hundred for Law Enforcement, 304n
Orleans Democratic Association: and Robert Ewing, 270n; opposes Behrman in 1920, pp. 299, 313–16, 328; mentioned xi$n$, xvii, 34
Orleans Parish Democratic Committee, 79
Orto, Arthuro, 138
O'Sullivan, E. A., 120
Overton, John, 262

Panama Exposition Company, 248
Panama-Pacific Exposition: 239–43, 248–49
Parker, Arthur D., 80
Parker, C. Harrison, 17, 114
Parker, J. Porter, 83–85, 182
Parker, John M.: political career of, xi$n$; opposes Behrman in 1920, pp. xxii, 298; 313–16; on Hennessy assassination, 9; elected governor, 34, 289–94; and 1904 district attorney controversy, 85; and 1904 mayoral campaign, 96; on natural gas, 177; and 1908 gubernatorial campaign, 209; and Luther E. Hall, 259–61, 263, Good Government League, 270; and 1912 U.S. Senate election, 267; and Robert Ewing, 270n; as Progressive party candidate, 281–88; and 1920 U.S. Senate election, 272; on Negroes, 282; and 1921 constitution, 274, 319–25; on civil service, 295–302; severance tax, 323–24; and Storyville, 309; and business, 327; supports Hewitt Bouanchaud in 1924, p. 330
Parkerson, William S.: 33, 90–92, 97, 100
Parlange, Charles, 15
Patorno, Anthony, 138
Patronage. *See* Behrman, Martin S.; Civil Service
People's party. *See* Populist party
Pharr, Henry N., 207n, 219
Pharr, John N., 16, 28, 207
Phelps, Ashton, 172
Phelps, Esmond, 319, 333

Index

Pickwick Club, 159
Pinchback, P. B. S., 13
Pinchot, Gifford, 77n
Pleasant, Ruffin G.: elected governor, 272–88 *passim*; 1915 call for constitutional convention, 273–78; on prohibition, 280; and Regular Democratic Organization, 287–88; biography of, 273n; and 1920 gubernatorial campaign, 290; and 1921 constitutional convention, 319, 323–25; mentioned, xi$n$, xvi, 259–60
Police, New Orleans, 118–31
Polk, William, 241
Poll tax. *See* Taxation
Poolrooms. *See* Hunsicker, Henry
Populist Fusion, 28n
Populist party: in 1892 gubernatorial campaign, 13; history of in Louisiana, 15n; and 1900 gubernatorial election, 56
Porteous, Gabriel, 68
Porter, Alvin, 186n
Price, W. H., 72, 208
Primaries, direct, 66n, 193
Progressive Union, 117, 175, 303
Prohibition: in Louisiana, 154–60; and Sunday closing law, 158; and Gay-Shattuck Law, 221–24; and Panama-Pacific Exposition, 240–42; in 1916 gubernatorial campaign, 279; Luther E. Hall on, 279; Ruffin G. Pleasant on, 280
Prostitution. *See* Storyville
Public Health Service, 152
Pujo, Arsene P., 246, 265, 267
Pujol, Alex, 24, 62, 80, 86, 162, 205, 268

Quarantine. *See* Yellow fever

Ransdell, Joseph E., 49, 151, 245, 311
Rapier, Thomas G., 121
Reed, Walter, 133n
Reems, Eugene S., 56, 207
Reformers, xxi–xxiii. *See also* Era Club; Orleans Democratic Association; One Hundred for Law Enforcement; Citizens' League; Young Men's Democratic Association; Good Government League; Home Rulers; Liberty League; Jacksonian Democracy
Regular Democratic Organization, xii, xiii–xviii, 197, 330. *See also* Behrman, Martin

Regulars. *See* Regular Democratic Organization
Republican party, Lily White, 16n
Republican party, National, 16n
Republican Fusion, 56
Reynolds, George M., xiii–xviii
Ring. *See* Regular Democratic Organization
Roads, 322
Roosevelt, Theodore: xi$n$, 1, 143, 148–51
Rosen, Charles: and Storyville, 294, 310; on civil service, 298; Behrman's description of, 312n; mentioned, 319
Ross, Walker, 107

St. Paul, John, 171
Saloons tax, 160–69. *See also* Prohibition
Sanders, Jared Y.: on poll tax, 50; biography of, 195n; elected governor, 198–221; on prohibition, 220–24; and 1910 U.S. Senate election, 245–46, 251–52; claims Behrman double-cross, 265–73; and 1920 U.S. Senate election, 271–72; and 1915 call for constitutional convention, 273–78; supports Ruffin G. Pleasant, 272–88 *passim*; and 1921 constitutional convention, 322–23, 325; mentioned, xvi, xxiv, 77–78, 187, 196, 197, 290, 291, 330, 334
Saunders, Eugene D., 12–13, 208
Schabel, August, 127
Schott, Matthew, 326
Scotti, P., 138
Shaffer, John D., 250
Shakspeare, Joseph A., 10, 13n, 21
Shattuck, S. O.: 221n. *See also* Gay-Shattuck Law
Shaw, Leslie M., 152
Shreveport Journal, 342
Shuler, Charles, 208
"Silk stocking": and 1904 mayoral campaign, 88–89; Behrman's attitudes toward, 105–17
Sims, R. N., 206
Skinner, Edward K., 125
Smith, Alfred E., 341
Smith, LeDoux, 71
Snyder, Robert H., 193
Sommerville, William B., 183
Souchon, Edmond, 132
Standard Oil Company, 323
State National Bank, 172

Steele, O. B., 78, 208
Steffens, Lincoln, xx
Steward, J. O., 220
Stifft, Peter, 346
Stock Exchange, 175
Story, Sidney. *See* Storyville
Storyville: and 1920 gubernatorial campaign, 294; Charles Rosen on, 294, 310, 312; operation of, 302–12; 1920 mayoral campaign, 302–12; and 1925 mayoral campaign, 336. *See also* Jean Gordon; One Hundred for Law Enforcement; Philip Werlein
Stubbs, Frank B.: 1920 gubernatorial election, 289–94, 315; mentioned, xi*n*
Stubbs, W. C., 200–201
Suffrage. *See* Constitutions, Louisiana, 1898 and 1921
Sullivan, John P.: description of, 100*n*; on civil service, 298; forms Independent Regular Democratic Association, 331; 1925 mayoral campaign, 336; mentioned, 34, 120, 122, 222, 262–63, 325, 333

Tammany Society, 31
Taxation: poll tax, 45–46, 50–51; saloon tax, 160–69; 1906 legislative session, 193–96; 1904 tax commission, 196; for Panama-Pacific Exposition, 241; severance, 323–24
Tebault, W. G., 181
Tenderloin. *See* Storyville
Terriberry, George H., 237
Theard, Charles J., 63, 209
Tichenor, Rolla A., 177–85
Third Ward Independent League, 181
Thomas, Frank B., 163–64
Thomas, Lee: candidate for U.S. Senate, 255; mentioned, 275, 334
Thompson, Sir Basil, 156
Thompson, William Hale, 1, 300
Thornton, James R., 252–55
Thorpe, T. H., 193
Trezevant, O. A., 24
Trousdale, Charles H., 259
Turner, A. W., 22

Understanding clause. *See* Constitutions, Louisiana, 1898 and 1921
Unions, labor: and race relations, 52–53; and 1925 mayoral campaign, 337

Van Kuren, Andrew, 69
Voegtle, Joseph, 97, 241
Volstead Act. *See* National Prohibition Enforcement Act
Voter registration, 1896 and 1900, p. 48

Walker, C. H., 174
Walker, Jimmie, 341
Walmsley, Robert M., 169
Walshe, B. T., 346
Warmoth, Henry Clay, 13, 37, 185
Warner, Beverly, 136
Washington, Booker T., 283
Watkins, J. T., 72
Weaver, John, 181
Webb, Jesse H., 225, 240, 249–50
Werlein, Philip, 303–304
West, Thomas H., 174
Whitaker, Edward Stanley: 1905 police row, 117–31, 302; shoots Joseph M. Leveque, 211–12
White, J. H., 143, 153
Wilkinson, John D., 246, 255
Wilkinson, Theodore S., 200–20
Williams, Augustus, 331, 336
Williams, Francis, 331, 336
Williams, T. Harry, 330
Wise, W. H.: (Shreveport), 74
Wogan, John A., 102, 247
Wolf, Solomon, 306
Wyman, Walter, 143, 152

"Yarborough Case," 312
Yellow fever, epidemic of 1905: and Italian immigrants, 139; and quarantine, 140–54 *passim*; and Diamond Festival, 144–45; "Peruna" patent medicine for, 146–47; and Theodore Roosevelt's visit to New Orleans, 148–51; mentioned, 131–54
Young, John S., 16, 18
Young Men's Democratic Association, 33

Zacharie, Frank C., 16